Geoffrey Chaucer

Geoffrey Chaucer

Building the Fragments of the *Canterbury Tales*

Jerome Mandel

Rutherford • Madison • Teaneck
Fairleigh Dickinson University Press
London and Toronto: Associated University Presses

© 1992 by Associated University Presses, Inc.

All rights reserved. Authorization to photocopy items for internal or personal use, or the internal or personal use of specific clients, is granted by the copyright owner, provided that a base fee of $10.00, plus eight cents per page, per copy is paid directly to the Copyright Clearance Center, 27 Congress Street, Salem, Massachusetts 01970. [0-8386-3454-0/92 $10.00 + 8¢ pp, pc.]

Associated University Presses
440 Forsgate Drive
Cranbury, NJ 08512

Associated University Presses
25 Sicilian Avenue
London WC1A 2QH, England

Associated University Presses
P.O. Box 39, Clarkson Pstl. Stn.
Mississauga, Ontario,
L5J 3X9 Canada

The paper used in this publication meets the requirements of the American National Standard for Permanence of Paper for Printed Library Materials Z39.48-1984.

Library of Congress Cataloging-in-Publication Data

Mandel, Jerome.
  Geoffrey Chaucer : building the fragments of the Canterbury tales / Jerome Mandel
    p. cm.
  Includes bibliographical references and index.
  ISBN 0-8386-3454-0 (alk. paper)
  1. Chaucer, Geoffrey, d. 1400. Canterbury tales. 2. Chaucer, Geoffrey, d. 1400—Technique. 3. Narration (Rhetoric) 4. Rhetoric, Medieval. I. Title.
PR1874.M345 1992
821'.1—dc20   91-55041
                                                                          CIP

PRINTED IN THE UNITED STATES OF AMERICA

This book is for

Miriam

with love and thanks
for all the fun and
all the years

Contents

Preface

Introduction	13
1. Fragment IV (Group E): The Clerk's Tale and the Merchant's Tale	23
2. Fragment VI (Group C): The Physician's Tale and the Pardoner's Tale	50
3. Fragment VIII (Group G): The Second Nun's Tale and the Canon's Yeoman's Tale	71
4. Fragment V (Group F): The Squire's Tale and the Franklin's Tale	92
5. Fragment III (Group D): The Wife of Bath's Prologue and Tale, the Friar's Tale, and the Summoner's Tale	107
6. Fragment I (Group A): The General Prologue, the Knight's Tale, the Miller's Tale, the Reeve's Tale, and the Cook's Tale	128
7. Fragment VII (Group B_2): The Shipman's Tale, the Prioress' Tale, the Tale of Sir Thopas, the Tale of Melibee, the Monk's Tale, and the Nun's Priest's Tale	157
8. Conclusion	182
Appendix: Temporal References in the Squire's Tale and the Franklin's Tale	191
Notes	193
Works Cited	225
Index	245

Preface

I intended to write this book ten years ago but moved to Israel instead. In the intervening decade much has been written on Chaucer but nothing directly addressing the way Chaucer constructed the fragments of the *Canterbury Tales*. I am pleased, therefore, to offer a new book on Chaucer that I hope other students and scholars of Chaucer will find as interesting to read as I have found satisfying to write.

Perhaps if I had written this book when I originally intended to, instead of struggling with an often byzantine bureaucracy in a very busy corner of the Middle East and chairing a department for five years in a language I could neither read nor speak, I might have been able to honor my teachers before most of them died. Fortunately, their fame is secure without my contribution. Morton W. Bloomfield, Robert Mark Estrich, Francis Lee Utley, and Donald R. Howard were as warm and generous, as learned and open a group of teachers as any student could wish for. It was my good luck to be at Ohio State University when they were.

I am grateful to the friends who read the manuscript in its various forms and suggested alterations, which I have largely respected. Professor Martin Stevens, Distinguished Professor at the Graduate Center of the City University of New York, and Professor Florence Ridley of UCLA read an early draft and provided the honest critical response that every scholar appreciates. I am grateful to Professor Robert W. Frank, Jr., of Pennsylvania State University, president of the New Chaucer Society, and the editor of *The Chaucer Review*, whose infectious enthusiasm for this book and natural exuberance sustained me. I am particularly grateful to my colleague, Professor Larry Besserman of Hebrew University, who corrected the finished draft with his typically fine and critical eye. The errors that remain are mine. Doug Davison, then a graduate student at Clemson, helped gather the shoe-boxes full of note cards that we used before the MLA Bibliography became computerized. Ronald Abraham generously provided valuable support services.

GEOFFREY CHAUCER

I live with three very interesting women. I want to thank them here for providing infinite hours of comic entertainment. I have singled out one of them, the originatrix of the other two and instigatrix of most of the fun, in the dedication.

Introduction

> For everi wight that hath an hous to founde
> Ne renneth naught the werk for to bygynne
> With rakel hond, but he wol bide a stounde,
> And sende his hertes line out fro withinne
> Aldirfirst his purpos for to wynne.
> —*Troilus and Criseyde* I, 1065–69

From the moment Chaucer died, the *Canterbury Tales* was in trouble. Whatever plans Chaucer had for organizing the individual tales into a coherent work died with him, and the friends who gathered the manuscripts with the intention of preserving them were hard-pressed to arrange the various manuscripts of tales and groups of tales into a coherent order. Their problem was complicated by evidence that, at some point, Chaucer changed his mind about the organization of the tales. At one time, it seems, Chaucer intended to begin with what we now call the Man of Law's Tale, but in all the manuscripts of Fragment I the Knight's Tale followed the General Prologue. Further complications arose with what we now know are spurious tales, like the Tale of Gamelin and the Tale of Beryn, and with long prose works like the Parson's Tale and the Melibee, which may or may not have been written for the *Canterbury Tales*. Of the eleven first generation manuscripts which have been preserved, only two, Hengwrt and Ellesmere, offer some indication of Chaucer's design. But Hengwrt omits the Merchant's Prologue and the Canon's Yeoman's Prologue and Tale, and, because the order of quires was accidentally garbled in assembling the manuscript, the tales of the Monk, Nun's Priest, and Manciple are misplaced. Ellesmere, on the other hand, has been so polished and regularized and neatened that it "presents a text, not of what Chaucer wrote, but of what his editorial executors thought he should have written, or would have written if he had known as well as they did what he wished to write."[1]

As Morton Bloomfield gently put it, "we cannot always be

certain of Chaucer's intentions as to the proper position of some of his tales" (1970, 205), but the Ellesmere order, with all the problems that it entails (chiefly the Rochester/Sittingbourne inversion), still receives the approbation of most editors.[2] Scholars have proposed different organizing principles to justify the particular order in which they would like to read the tales. What used to be called the "drama of pilgrimage" (best articulated by Lumiansky 1955) has given way over the past thirty years to "thematic interlace" (Leyerle 1976, 109; Kean 1982), "concatenated binary principle" (Howard 1976, 225), and "analogy" (Allen and Moritz 1981). Among the most recent and most interesting is Helen Cooper's book on *The Structure of the Canterbury Tales*, which focuses upon the coherence of individual fragments and attempts to show "what holds the stories of the various groups together."

> We cannot appreciate the *Canterbury Tales* unless we can attempt to understand why Chaucer sets up the groups of stories in the way he does; and such an understanding casts a great deal of light not only on the work itself but on Chaucer's poetic methods—his mind and art. (1984, 108)

Chaucer's poetic methods, his mind and art, have long been a matter of critical concern. Early readers praised Chaucer's "learning" (Hoccleve, Harvey, Puttenham), his eloquence, his "ornate wrytyng" (Caxton, Dunbar), and his ability to create "various manners and humours" (Dryden) and characters (Blake). More recent readers were aware that Chaucer lacks "high seriousness" (Arnold) and registered their concern for Chaucer's language and rhetoric and reading and use of myth. Twentieth-century readers began to discover thematic patterns in the *Canterbury Tales* and to emphasize various ideas of unity.[3]

Most recently, Allen and Moritz have attempted to correct the twentieth-century bias in favor of theme by arguing for "a principle of structural rather than thematic unity" (1981, 233).[4] While all may not agree (myself among them) with their conclusions about the relation of Ovid's *Metamorphoses* to the *Canterbury Tales*, their insistence on the importance of structure is well taken. Faral (1924) reminds us that medieval *ars poetica* emphasized elegance of expression and the rhetorical patterning of individual thoughts and that they eschewed theories of narrative structure which dealt with the larger elements of text. Nonetheless, most twentieth-century critics will agree that an essential part of Chaucer's genius was a "predilection for aesthetic games"[5] most obviously revealed in parallels and balances, in echoes and ironic inversions, and, as I shall show, in the structural patterns supported by parallels of theme and character.

Chaucer's artistic achievement was accomplished "without appreciable models and with only the most jejune critical theories to guide him."[6] Like most great artists, Chaucer discovered and designed his own aesthetic principles. Among the most important of the jejune critical theories which Chaucer inherited is that of Geoffrey de Vinsauf. Although Chaucer jokes about his "deere maister soverayn" (VII, 3347) in the Nun's Priest's Tale, he quotes from the *Poetria Nova* in *Troilus and Criseyde* in a serious passage I have cited at the beginning of this Introduction. The lines Chaucer translates into the *Troilus* are these:

> Si quis habet fundare domum, non currit ad actum
> Impetuosa manus: intrinseca linea cordis
> Praemetitur opus.
>
> *Poetria Nova* 43–45

[If anyone intends to build a house, his impetuous hand does not hasten into action; his heart's inner line ("intrinsic" line, plumbline; perhaps plan) measures out the work beforehand.][7]

What Chaucer learned from Geoffrey de Vinsauf is "the basic need for taking thought, the importance of effective arrangement, and the necessity in composition for viewing a work as a whole. Such formal consideration had hitherto escaped notice by theorists and writers alike" (Preston 1952, 99). To be sure, it was a commonplace in the Middle Ages to define a work of art as the result of an idea in the artist's mind, the *intrinseca linea cordis*. It was equally commonplace to define the relationship of artist to work as that of an architect to the house that he is building (*fundare domum*).[8] To the best of my knowledge, no one has yet taken this traditional metaphor very seriously.

I take it as axiomatic that any work of art, and especiálly any work of art created in language, is created sequentially, or serially, in time. Both the nature of language (where meaning is controlled by grammar and syntax) and the nature of writing (where words are formed letter by letter) require the elements of composition (letters and then words) to be placed either before or after one another. That simple process of placing is ultimately the process of building, and one can discuss the building of grammatical structures (sentences and paragraphs) in the same way that one can discuss the building of aesthetic structures (scenes and chapters). Of course, the writer can always revise the structure: once a text is composed, the writer can easily change the order of words in a sentence or scenes in a chapter to conform more nearly to one's notions of aesthetic order; the writer can always go back to insert something which, by its insertion, changes the previous order. In the best-built narrative aesthetic structure, the "seams" or "points of episodic juncture" (Frakes 1987, 4), are smoothed over, the movement from episode to episode or scene to scene made inevitable often by character or theme or action. The building of Chaucer's grammatical structures—the quality of Chaucer's language—has long been in the public domain; the aesthetic structure of many of Chaucer's individual tales has also been the object of scholarly concern for the past century. While the aesthetic design of the *Canterbury Tales* as a whole continues to elude us, that of the individual fragments has not generated much scholarly interest. I intend to focus upon the fragments, specifically, the intertextuality of the tales within each fragment.

I think Chaucer built the fragments as he did because the tales he chose to link together, especially in the two-tale fragments, are more like each other than they are like any other tale in the collection. Even when they do not share the same tone, point of view, narrator, or genre, they belong together because they share the same themes and types of characters and, most strikingly, the same architecture. The constant "contrast, cross-referencing, and the use of leit-motifs (of words and things)" that Besserman finds among the most important devices that unify the General Prologue (1986, 322) also unify all the fragments. These parallels are more than "local structuring" devices occasionally used for tale-bonding (Derek Pearsall 1985, 49); they pervade every fragment of the *Canterbury Tales*. They insist that certain tales, and no others, be joined to form a coherent, unified whole. While it may be oxymoronic to talk about a "whole fragment," it is also true that the links which bind tale to tale in a fragment are strong, finely and precisely detailed, and carefully wrought. Chaucer designed the fragments, such as they are, to be coherent units, parts of an uncompleted whole. To be sure, Chaucer may have had grand ideas for the unity of the whole when he composed the General Prologue and planned to write one hundred twenty stories, but he had to abandon much of that plan when he decided to write only sixty. He had to modify even that plan when he realized he would never get to write any more than the tales we presently have. The result is that each fragment, in its present state and regardless of its imagined position in an overall scheme which Chaucer never completed, is a finished work of art.

To pose the question of artistic unity in terms of the fragments instead of the individual tales or the collection as a whole acknowledges the essentially fragmentary nature of the *Canterbury Tales*. Many discussions of Chaucer's art concentrate on the skill with which Chaucer treats individual tales; others focus on the skill with which he orchestrates the whole of the *Canterbury Tales*. Few examine the fragments as artistic wholes.[9] Individual tales have long been analyzed from a variety of points of view, and indeed, as Benson notes, some of the most valuable criticism of the *Canterbury Tales* derives from individual tales treated in isolation (1988, 797). Nonetheless, in a clear and orderly manner Chaucer joined all but three of these individual tales into groups or fragments. Among the fragments, however, the order is not so clear. We usually read the fragments in one of two orders: that of the Ellesmere manuscript or that of the Chaucer Society. Although recent scholarly argument favors Chaucer's having worked on both and having entertained both,[10] we can only speculate about which one would have constituted his final arrangement.

Therefore, while individual tales may reveal the fine detail of Chaucer's art, the multitale fragments show the larger elements of Chaucer's craft in its least ambiguous and least contentious form. Unlike the *Canterbury Tales* as a whole, the individual fragments are finished; more than finished, they are polished. They reveal the principles of order, coherence, and propriety that Chaucer used to establish artistic unity. The tales that Chaucer wanted joined together in a fragment, he very carefully joined. He wrote links between the tales. He echoed words and phrases and attitudes. He established dramatic conflicts among the pilgrims to justify one tale following another. More than that, he revealed his own high degree of artistic consciousness by using one tale to comment upon another, to parody or develop it. All this is well-known. What this book proposes to make more well-known are the means which Chaucer employed to unify the fragments, to make them coherent in terms of structure, theme, and character.

Structure

We are accustomed to think of structure in large terms: quest, *entrelace*, and especially contrast.[11] But Chaucer reveals a far more precise conception of structure in the fragments. In one fragment, for example, he joins two tales that are completely different in genre, tone, meaning, significance, narrator, and psychological relevance of tale to teller. One is said to be among the best of Chaucer's tales, the other among the worst. Yet Chaucer has carefully organized the events in these two tales so that the order of events is actually identical in both. Both tales begin with self-descriptions followed by portraits of major figures; both interrupt the narrative at about the same point with admonitions that introduce important themes; both describe the primary impulse for action in approximately the same words; both define a conspiracy; both contain a confrontation scene in which a single defenseless individual faces overwhelming adversaries; both tales follow the confrontation scene with a discussion among the principal characters; both discussions end with a decision for death; people die in both tales; both end with a pardon; at the end of both tales Harry Bailly plays with the narrator; in both cases a representative of the *gentils* intervenes. No other Canterbury tale orders the events in exactly this way. For either one of these two tales to be replaced by any other Canterbury tale would completely demolish the architectural structure Chaucer had been at such obvious pains to build. These two tales—those of the Physician and the Pardoner—belong together and constitute a fragment (that is, a consciously designed, unified whole) because they share the same internal structure, unique to themselves.[12] They are structurally identical.

I take this as evidence of design—not because Chaucer does it so thoroughly in one fragment, but because he does much the same thing in all of the two-tale fragments and repeats elements of this patterning in the longer fragments as well. If the degree of correspondence or structural parallelism among the tales in a fragment were less precise or less extensive, we could dismiss it as chance or the ingenuity of the critic, but the very pervasiveness and consistency of the structural parallels with which Chaucer builds the fragments reveals his concern for the structure of the *Canterbury Tales*.

Moreover, parallels in the internal structure of the tales constitute only one principle of order in the fragments. These parallels are all-important in the two-tale fragments, of course, but Chaucer employs additional structural principles to organize the sequence of tales in the fragments composed of five and six tales. That is, Chaucer unifies such fragments not only by focusing upon parallels of internal structure, but also by establishing principles that determine the precise order in which the tales

Introduction   19

must occur in the fragment. We shall see these principles at work when we discuss Fragments I and VII.

Theme

Two recent books of Chaucer criticism, each splendid in its own right, reserve a chapter at the end to discuss some of the themes that run through the *Canterbury Tales*. P. M. Kean (1982) cites Fortune and Free Will, Marriage, and the Nobility of Man. Helen Cooper (1984) identifes Fortune, Providence, and Suffering; Felicity and Vision; Female Saints and Wikked Wyves; The Girl with Two Lovers; Brotherhood and Friendship; Tidings, Tales, and Voices. The multiplication of themes is endless.[13]

These general themes—and the many others, often so broad as to be all-encompassing—recur throughout the tales. They can be found in various states of development in every Canterbury tale because they indicate some of Chaucer's major intellectual concerns. They establish lines of unity that bind all the Canterbury tales together. They connect tales in different fragments and, like similarities of genre, establish multiple lines of coherence. As such, they have been well and fully examined by generations of scholars. Because of their very pervasiveness, no serious claims about the integrity of a single fragment can be based upon thematic concerns alone. Nonetheless, Chaucer also employs themes and motifs that are predominantly relevant only to a single fragment. These themes, often unique to the fragment in which they occur, appear in every tale of the fragment and even in its pilgrimage frame. My concern with theme, therefore, is primarily with those themes that achieve prominence by being shared with other tales in the fragment regardless of whether or not they also appear elsewhere in the *Canterbury Tales*. These may not always be the most important themes in the tales, but they are the ones that contribute to the fragment's integrity. And these have been studied less thoroughly.

Character

Chaucer also linked tales into a single fragment because, in addition to theme and structure, the characters are alike. Chaucer treats characters whom we would never confuse—like Walter and January, for example, or the merchant in the Shipman's Tale and

Chauntecleer—in shockingly similar ways. He uses the same language to describe them. He gives them the same history, attitudes, and modes of behavior. He shows them engaged in a sequence of particular activities which no other characters in the *Canterbury Tales* perform. He treats them in ways that he treats no other characters. Within a single fragment, we find similar or contrastive patterns of behavior, attitude, event, and language among the characters which distinguish them from all other characters in the *Canterbury Tales*, link them to each other, and thus contribute to the unity of the fragment.[14]

My interest, therefore, and the focus of this book is not to interpret or explicate individual tales or to argue for a specific way to read the *Canterbury Tales* as a whole. The first has been accomplished many times, and, as certain critics remind us, will continue to proliferate as long as there are readers of Chaucer. The second, given the unfinished state of the text, may never be accomplished to general satisfaction. Chaucer himself accurately defines the problem.

> Diverse folk diversely they demed;
> As many heddes, as manye wittes ther been.
> (V, 202–3)

My interest, rather, is to discover and define Chaucer's working concepts of organization and of artistic order as those concepts are revealed in the principles with which he unifies the fragments. I am interested in his methods: what he saw in the tales that led him to link them to form fragments; or, to put it another way, how he designed and built the tales to fit together with mutual congruence in order to create coherent fragments. What Chaucer knew or read or translated, what was current in the rhetoric or poetic theory of his time or available to him from antiquity can only explain how Chaucer arrived at his principles of order, but what Chaucer in fact *did* in the fragments reveals his working concept of organization, his principles of artistic order in action.

What follows, then, is not a comprehensive definition of Chaucer's artistry, his ability to adapt and metamorphose sources, his skill in portraying character or manipulating his audience, his adroit multiple definitions of narrator or recipient (the assumed, implied, ideal, or tertiary reader), his expression of his time and place in history, his culture, his religion, his thought. Rather, it is an excursus into Chaucer's narrative method in order to show the principles of artistic order he applies in constructing the fragments of the *Canterbury Tales*. It is a study designedly limited in critical theory either modern or medieval. In the spirit of liberal humanism that is supposed to characterize our profession, I trust that the Marxist, feminist, structuralist, poststructuralist, deconstructionist, and post-modernist critics will tend their gardens and allow me to tend mine. If, as Florence Ridley once remarked, the major thrust of modern Chaucerian criticism involves the effort to understand how the poet built his work, this study contributes to that thrust. And since medieval artists conceived of the job of making a poem as they thought of the job of building a house, this study examines Chaucer's methods of construction. I hope this will prove to be "useful criticism" that teachers can take into the classroom and scholars can debate and use for their own purposes. I intend it as criticism which offers (in language as clear as I can make it and argument as convincing as the evidence will allow) some insight into the way the individual fragments of the *Canterbury Tales* are constructed and thus some appreciation of the craft which Chaucer found "so long to lerne."

I have omitted from this discussion those tales which comprise a fragment by themselves: the Man of Law's Tale (II), the Manciple's Tale (IX), and the Parson's Tale (X). Since Chaucer did not connect them with any other tales, they can offer no evidence of his ideas on the artistic unity of a fragment. Perhaps the Manciple's Tale and the Parson's Tale were meant to share a fragment, but since the linkage is so problematic,[15] I have thought it better to omit them and to concentrate on the multiple tale fragments where Chaucer's ideas of artistic order are most apparent. In general, I allow Chaucer to speak for himself. Since each chapter is devoted to a single fragment, line references alone identify the quotations within the fragment under discussion; quotations from other fragments are located by fragment number as well. A text strewn with numbers can, of course, be irksome, but I felt that being able to locate lines quickly outweighed the disadvantage. I have followed the convenient practice of capitalizing the names of pilgrims and keeping in lower case the potentially confusing names of characters in the tales (the Canon and the canon in the Canon's Yeoman's Tale,[16] the Summoner and the summoner in the Friar's Tale, and so on). And since the two-tale fragments are simpler and more accessible than the others and since they establish principles which Chaucer develops elsewhere in the *Canterbury Tales*, let us begin with them before proceeding to Fragments III, I, and VII which contain three or more tales.

1
Fragment IV (Group E): The Clerk's Tale and the Merchant's Tale

> But ther been folk of swich condicion
> That whan they have a certein purpos take,
> They can nat stynte of hire entencion.
>
> (701–3)

Unique among the Canterbury fragments, the tales in Fragment IV explore the decision of two men to marry: when both Walter and January "have a certein purpos take, / They kan nat stynte of hire entencion" (702–3). But that sense of absolute commitment applies equally to Griselda, May, and Damian, all of whom take serious decisions (respectively to obedience, to self, and to lust) and abide by them with firm purpose. Only the fickle commons in the Clerk's Tale change their minds and reflect the background theme of mutability that runs through many fragments. The major characters are carefully matched, their similarities well-developed, and their contrasts purposeful. Chaucer works the themes these tales share into the fabric of the fragment as purposefully as he does the similarities and the contrasts among the characters. But the two tales are most strikingly related in terms of structure.

I. Structure

The Clerk's Tale and the Merchant's Tale present the same events in precisely the same order. They are, structurally, the same story; furthermore, they are more like each other than they are like any other tale in the Canterbury collection. Both begin by defining the main character's attitude toward marriage and follow with a sequence of councils devoted to the general topic of marriage. Both detail the marriage contract and celebrate the marriage feast. Both present a series of tests, explicit in the Clerk's Tale and implicit in the Merchant's Tale, and both end with a restoration scene. To be sure, each section does not receive the same length of treatment in each story, but that does not detract from the basic structural similarity that underlies both tales, justifies their architectural linkage, and reveals Chaucer's craft.

Clerk's Tale	Merchant's Tale
Walter's attitude	January's attitude
Councils	Councils
(1) Public: for people to announce intention (85–189)	(1) Public: for January to announce intention (1397–1576)
(2) Private: Walter communes with himself (232–45)	(2) Private: January communes with himself (1577–1610)
(3) Limited Public: to discuss problems of acceptance (297–371)	(3) Limited Public: to discuss problem of perfect joy (1611–90)
Marriage Agreement	Marriage Agreement
Feast	Feast
Three Tests: of Griselda	Three Tests: of May
Processional Visit from the Dead: Walter's Son and Daughter	Processional Visit from the Dead: Pluto and Proserpyna
Restoration Scene of Griselda of Walter	Restoration Scene of May of January

COUNCILS

Both tales begin by defining the attitudes of the principal lords followed by three clearly defined councils. In the Clerk's Tale, the narrator himself cites Walter's previous life and present attitude (his concern for "lust present" [80], his lack of consideration for the future, and his neglect in taking a wife) as the impetus for the people to address Walter on the topic of marriage. In the Merchant's Tale, the narrator describes January's previous life, and January himself reveals his present attitude toward marriage (in the long monologue, 1263–1392, with which the tale begins[1]) and so reveals the reason for his calling the first council.

Fragment IV

These councils are remarkable for their similarities. In the first council, for example, the people want to tell Walter their "trewe entente" (127). Aware of death, they encourage him to take a wife so that "a straunge successour sholde [not] take / Youre heritage" (138–39). They even offer to choose his wife for him and indicate what kind of wife they would choose (129–32)—an occupation that Walter denies them. January, too, calls a council to tell his friends "his entente" (1398). Aware of death, he, too, announces his intention to take a wife so that "myn heritage sholde [not] falle / In straunge hand" (1439–40). Unlike Walter, however, January gives his friends the task of finding a wife for him (1412–14) and indicates the kind of wife he would like them to choose. (Appropriate to the ironic connections between the tales in this fragment, the person January describes, both in his monologue and at this first council, is Griselda.) These first councils are alike, too, in the attitudes expressed by the counselors. Walter's people carefully insist that their role is purely advisory and that the ultimate decision on this, as on everything, is entirely his, "to doon right as yow leste" (105), "if it youre wille be" (110), "if that ye wole assente" (129). Placebo articulates the same attitude ("Dooth now in this matiere right as yow leste" [1517, and also 1490, etc.]), and so, surprisingly, does Justinus: "Ye mowe, for me, right as yow liketh do" (1554).

The subsequent, more private councils, in which Walter and January commune with themselves and consider the women they will marry, are the obverse of each other. Chaucer carefully orchestrates the contrast. Walter reflects soberly ("in sad wyse / Upon hir chiere he wolde hym ofte avyse" [237–38]); January enjoys "Heigh fantasye" (1577). Walter occasionally and by chance sees a single girl during the day; January consciously celebrates the romp of "many a figure" (1584) through his imagination every night (1580–81). Walter dismisses the "insight" of his people into "vertu" (242–43); January knows who has the "grettest voys" of the people and who stands most "in the peples grace" for "sadnesse" and "benyngnytee" (1590–92). Walter celebrates the more spiritual aspects of Griselda; January first delights in the physical aspects of May. Nonetheless, although Walter is not January, nor January Walter, both lords choose their future wives in precisely the same manner. The words used to describe January's choice—he "chees hire of his owene auctoritee" (1597)—apply with equal exactness to the way Walter makes his choice, and the attitudes that both men subsequently adopt toward their choices are also identical. Although the words are the Merchant's applied to January, they could with equal aptness be those of the Clerk applied to Walter.

> And whan that he on hire was condescended,
> Hym thoughte his choys myghte nat ben amended.
> For whan that he hymself concluded hadde,
> Hym thoughte ech oother mannes wit so badde
> That inpossible it were to repplye
> Agayn his choys.
>
> (1605–10)

At the third council both Walter and January announce their choices. Each lord insures that there will be no "repplye / Agayn his choys." At the end of the first council in the Clerk's Tale, Walter received both the assurance and the oath of his people that they "Agayn my choys shul neither grucche ne stryve" (170). To the same end, January opens the third council with the request "That noon of hem none argumentes make / Agayn the purpos which that he hath take" (1619–20). While he has called the council to announce his choice, January's real interest lies in receiving his friends' opinions on a point of theology which may be the single "obstacle" (1659) to his marriage and which so exasperates Justinus. Walter, on the other hand, removes the last obstacle to his marriage when he asks Janicula if he will accept his lord as his son-in-law and when he asks Griselda if she will agree with her father's decision. Notably, both Janicula and Griselda respond with the same attitude toward the ruler's judgment that Walter's people had revealed earlier and that Placebo best articulates.

THE MARRIAGE AGREEMENT

Both the Clerk and the Merchant define the marriage agreements in their tales much more carefully than do the Franklin or the Wife of Bath who, alone among the pilgrims who describe marriage, provide a marriage agreement comparable in any way with those that appear in Fragment IV. May's marriage to January is legalized by "sly [i.e., skillful] and wys tretee" (1692) agreed upon between May and January's friends. The agreement includes not only a great deal of valuable clothing but deeds and bonds by which she is put in possession of his land—all of which would take too long for the Merchant to tell in detail (1696–99). Shortly after his marriage, after January has been struck blind, he increases the marriage portion to include "al myn heritage, toun and tour" (2172) which allows her to convey everything into her posssssion according to charters that she herself shall design (2173). Walter is more circumspect. Instead of relying upon friends, he addresses Janicula and Griselda directly in a "collacioun" (325) that results in a "tretys" (331) whereby she promises to accomplish everything that he desires without complaining about it in any way (351–57). For his part, Walter agrees that she shall "be my wyf, and reule hire after me" (327). In both tales, then, the marriage agreement confers large properties and powers upon the wife.

Feasts solemnize the marriage agreement in both tales. Except for the one line referring to the feast solemnizing the marriage of Theseus and Hippolyta in the Knight's Tale (I, 883), the only other example in the *Canterbury Tales* of a feast celebrating a marriage occurs in the Man of Law's Tale, but it seems to occur sometime after Custance and the Sultan have been married (II, 412–15) and provides an occasion for the slaughter of the Christians, the assassination of the Sultan, and the banishment of Custance. No feast attends the marriage of Custance and Alla, Dorigen and Arveragus, Cecilia and Valerian, the crone and the knight in the Wife of Bath's Tale, but the wedding feast is important to Fragment IV. At the wedding in the Merchant's Tale Damian is burned by Venus's brand and falls in love with his lady May. The wedding feast is important to the Clerk's Tale because, at the beginning, it marks Griselda's elevation in her lord's grace, and, at the end, it celebrates the resurrection of her children and the public celebration of her own restoration to her proper place in the world. Although Chaucer had ample opportunity to refer to marriage feasts throughout the *Canterbury Tales*, the wedding feast is important only to the Clerk's and the Merchant's Tales and contributes to the cohesiveness of the fragment.

THE TESTS

Other female marriage partners—especially Custance, Dorigen, and Cecilia—undergo tests in the *Canterbury Tales*, but only that of Cecilia contributes to the unity of her fragment. It does so in a way completely different from what occurs here in Fragment IV. In Fragment VIII, as we shall see, the act and fact of testing rather than the testing of a marriage or a marriage partner connects the Second Nun's Tale with the Canon's Yeoman's Tale. But only in Fragment IV is a marriage or a marriage partner tested in all tales of the fragment. In the Clerk's Tale, Walter tests Griselda and finds her true; in the Merchant's Tale, both January and May are tested and found wanting.

Since Walter's testing of Griselda is obvious and central, it need not concern us overmuch here, but it is worth noting that Walter tests precisely those abstract qualities of "chiere" and "wommanhede" and "vertu" (238–40) which he appreciated in her from the very beginning. Specifically, he tests her "sadnesse" (i.e., steadfastness), her "pacience," and her "corage" in order to discover "If that she were as stidefast as bifoore" (789).[2] When he sees her "pacience," her "glade chiere," her "innocence," and her "stedfastnesse" (1044–50), the test is over. Clearly defined, exactly applied, the test of Griselda's abstract qualities accurately reflects the Clerk's concern for the abstract and the spiritual.

The tests implicit in the Merchant's Tale reflect January's contrastive concern for the physical, and their predictable results accurately reflect the Merchant's attitude toward women. The Merchant's Tale opens with an extended statement of January's assumptions about marriage. He announces those assumptions in the first council where Placebo confirms them. His subsequent marriage to May implicitly tests those beliefs, as the Merchant's marriage was the test of his own personal assumptions about marriage (which he identifies *post facto* as a "snare" into which he would never come again [1227]). Were January's assumptions measured against Griselda, she would pass, but May is made of more earthy stuff, and she fails the test of love or fidelity (in the sense that she does not measure up to January's assumptions) on the fourth day of her marriage when she determines to love Damian.

January also makes assumptions about the physical or sexual aspects of marriage. Once again he measures May against his assumptions. He looks forward to the "plesaunce" (1434) he expects to have with a young wife. At the first council he advertises his strength and ability "To do al that a man bilongeth to" (1459) and compares himself (with delicious irony that looks forward to the scene in the garden) to a blossoming tree "as grene / As laurer" (1465–66).[3] Unlike Walter, January responds first of all to the physical, to May's "fresshe beautee" and youth, especially as they are revealed by "Hir myddel smal, hire armes longe and sklendre" (1601–2).[4] At the wedding feast, he is eager to get that "myddel smal" into bed. In his heart he threatens to clasp her so tightly that he fears he may offend her and that she may not be able to endure "Al my corage, it is so sharp and keene" (1759). Nonetheless, he takes as many as eight aphrodisiacs "t'encreessen his corage" (1808).[5] But January's experience with May proves his assumptions wrong. Chaucer encapsulates January's entire misguided attitude toward the physical aspects of marriage in the image of his beard. Chaucer's emphasis upon its unpleasant aspects—with its thick bristles that are as unsoft as the skin of houndfish and sharp as briar—and his note that this is January's conscious creation reveal the limitations of January's sexual skill and the reasons for his failure. Justinus had predicted that January would not be able "to doon hire ful plesaunce" (1563) for three years; January fails on the first night, for May "preyseth nat his pleyyng worth a bene" (1854).[6]

January's most explicit test of May stems from his jealousy. After he is struck blind, he is overwhelmed by two related and "outrageous" (2087) desires. One is that May, after the eventual death of January, remain true as the turtledove to him, that she be no man's love or wife, and that she wear widow's weeds for the rest of her life. The second desire is that he always have a hand on her, no matter where she rides or walks, within the house or out (2077–91). Her triumph over the physical restraint and her triumph over January's desire that she be true to him (she has already assured Damian that she will be true to *him* [1983–84]) signal her ultimate victory over January[7]—or, which is the same thing seen from a different point of view, signal her failure to meet the tests January has implicitly set for her.

Unlike Walter, January is blind to the quality of the woman to whom he allies himself. Both men test their wives, but while Walter tests the spirit of the woman, January tests the degree to which she conforms to his own theory of marriage, her preferences in sexual activity, and her ability to outwit a cumbersome physical restraint and an unenforceable limitation upon her future activity. Unlike Griselda, May fails all her lord's tests.

THE RESTORATION SCENES

The restoration scenes which close the Clerk's and the Merchant's Tales are more akin to each other than they are to any of the other *Canterbury Tales* to which they might be compared (e.g., those in the Man of Law's Tale and the Franklin's Tale). Both follow processional visits from the land of the dead—Pluto and Proserpyna in the Merchant's Tale, Walter's son and daughter in the Clerk's Tale—which precipitate and guarantee the dénouement. Pavia is not the Otherworld, but Griselda does not know that. Indeed, in both tales, only the reader (and Walter) are aware of the visits from the Otherworld: January and May remain ignorant of those who share their garden with them, and Griselda is informed by Walter that the children, suddenly returned from the dead, had been secretly kept in Bologna. Once again, the two tales treat the same concerns in different ways. The restoration of Griselda invokes kisses, the affirmation from Walter that "Thou art my wyf" (1063), the apparent resurrection of her children, triumph over death, mutual gladness, the return of her proper clothes (the medieval badge of rank), the return to her proper place in society, and a feast to celebrate all.

How different are the kisses and embraces that January bestows upon May when she "leep doun fro the tree" (2411). He affirms their relationship by stroking her "on hir wombe" (2414) and leading her back within the palace. The action is ironic not only because we know, if he does not, that the womb which he strokes is now as accessible to Damian as it had been to January and that the home to which he leads her is not at all as secure as it was when he left. The action is ironic for another reason: the womb which January strokes, taken with May's earlier intimation of pregnancy, suggests the heir, the "leveful procreacioun / Of children" (1448–49) that was January's motive for marrying. The irony lies in our awareness that any child eventually born to May is as likely to be Damian's as January's—which adds an extra fillip to the irony implicit in May's final line: "He that mysconceyveth, he mysdemeth" (2410).[8] Instead of mutual gladness, only January is said to be glad (2412); we are not told if May is glad, though she clearly has much to be happy about: she has deceived her aged husband and prepared the way for future liaisons with her lover (2405–6). The scene at the end of the Merchant's Tale even echoes the concern for clothing in the Clerk's Tale, but instead of Griselda's rude and torn smock, Chaucer shows May's smock lying upon Damian's breast. No joyful feast celebrates the restoration of January's sight or the restoration of May—from "stronge lady stoore" (2367) to "my lief" (2391).[9] The Merchant's Tale is too dark and too ironic a tale to end in honest celebration.

II. Theme

At the beginning of the fragment, more often than not, Chaucer announces the internal connections that bind together the tales.

Even the prologues to the single-tale fragments (the Man of Law's Tale, the Manciple's Tale, and the Parson's Tale) introduce the themes that connect these tales to their pilgrimage frames. In the Prologue to the Clerk's Tale, Chaucer indicates the deliberateness of the fragment's organization by revealing the major concerns of the Merchant's Tale as well as the Clerk's. When Harry Bailly describes the Clerk as one who rides "as coy and stille as dooth a mayde / Were newe spoused, sittynge at the bord" (2–3), he accurately introduces, with this image, the basic story of the tales that occupy Fragment IV.[10] Both the Clerk and the Merchant tell tales of men who decide to marry. While other tales (the Manciple's or the Franklin's, for example) discuss the difficulties of being married, both the tales in Fragment IV—and only these tales—focus upon the decision to marry and the tribulations that attend that decision. Harry Bailly's introductory image resounds throughout both tales since, at central moments in their lives, both brides are characterized (as the Clerk had been) as "stille": Griselda "kneleth stille" (293) at the threshold of her father's house, and May is brought to her marriage bed "as stille as stoon" (1818). The wedding feast, implicit in "bord," occupies a major position in both tales, as we have seen above. But the subject and image of marriage are not the only contributions that the Clerk's Prologue makes to the unity of the fragment. The Prologue also introduces the themes of time, death, appearance/reality, and the conflict between experience and authority which permeate the tales told by the Clerk and the Merchant.

TIME

From the Host's point of view, a pilgrimage to Canterbury is an occasion for game and not for earnest. In his attempt to encourage the Clerk to participate in the game of the pilgrimage, Harry Bailly distinguishes between time appropriate for serious matters and time appropriate for play: "Salomon seith 'every thyng hath tyme'" (6). Since the Clerk does not engage in conversation, the Host assumes that he is considering "som sophyme" (5) and insists "It is no tyme for to studien heere" (8). He encourages the Clerk to tell a tale and to "Speketh so pleyn at this tyme" (19) so that all can understand. The triple reference to time in the Prologue to the Clerk's Tale suggests the importance of the theme to the fragment and its relevance both to Walter and to January.[11]

Time is relevant to our understanding of Walter not merely because of his youth and ancestry, but because "he considered noght / In tyme comynge what myghte hym bityde" (78–79). His concern for his "lust present" (80) and his disregard for time activate his people and embolden them to address him on the mutability of the human condition ("Ay fleeth the tyme" [119]) and to encourage him to marry. Their emphasis upon haste and their offer to select a wife for him as quickly as possible (130) reflect their concern for time. By marrying "as soone as evere I may" (151) and having children rather quickly (442), Walter does, of course, triumph over time, living "Ful many a yeer in heigh prosperitee" (1128) after which his son continues his line. Griselda, too, as a metaphor for human beings who uncomplainingly accept the will of God, also triumphs over time, indicated by the resurrection of her children and by her own festive restoration which echoes the joyful acceptance of the blessed into paradise (McCall 1966a, 263). In telling his story, the Clerk wittily adapts the Host's concern for time to his own more serious purposes by emphasizing the importance of time in the lives of Walter and Griselda.

The Clerk's Tale begins with Walter's disregard for time which motivates the people and provides the impetus for action. The Merchant's Tale begins with January's intense awareness of time, "he was passed sixty yeer" (1252), which impels him to want to marry. Though he considers himself white-haired and hoary (1400, 1461, 1464, and perhaps 1269), he emphasizes his own youthful vigor (1457–66) and the importance of having a young woman as his wife (1415–32). Speed, haste, and energy (1406, 1409, 1411) mark his search for a wife, and once he has wed her, they mark his eagerness to get her into bed (1765–67, 1805, 1813–15). As part of his argument for marriage, he refers to his age (1400), but he really does not think of himself as old (e.g., 1458 ff.) until after he is struck blind (2168, 2180) when even Pluto refers to his age (2259). Although Walter and Griselda and (through Griselda's example of obedience to God) all of us can triumph over time, January is the victim of time, too foolish, too careless of his youth, and too devoted to "his bodily delyt" (1249) to succeed in leading a life of "ese and hoolynesse" (1628) as Walter does (1129, 1132) until his death.

DEATH

The theme of death, like the closely related theme of time, also serves to unify the two tales, to connect them to their frame, and so to unify the fragment.[12] The Clerk himself introduces the theme of death in his Prologue. Not only is Petrarch "deed and nayled in his cheste" (29), but Lynyan also is dead. For the Clerk, however, as indeed for every serious Christian—especially those engaged in a holy pilgrimage to thank God through his blessed saint for their good health—the important thing is the working of death through time: "Deeth . . . wol nat suffre us dwellen heer / But as it were a twynklyng of an ye" (36–37). The result for every man and every thinking Christian is that "alle shul we dye" (38). This is a startling and remarkable line. The effect is the same as if I were to say that everyone who reads this line will die. It is true, of course, and inevitable, but to be reminded of one's mortality while cheerfully reading a book of Chaucer criticism is as shocking as being reminded of one's mortality while riding through the green English countryside on a lovely spring day listening to stories.

By allowing the Clerk to make this claim about human mortality, Chaucer affects both the unity of Fragment IV and of the *Canterbury Tales* as a whole. By turning the Host's game (Harry himself calls it "pley" [10, 11]) back into earnest, the Clerk reaffirms the sanctity of pilgrimage, refocuses the pilgrims' attention upon "oure olde synnes" (13), and reasserts the supremacy of *amor dei* over *amor*. His tale maintains that focus, but the Merchant's Tale subverts the pilgrimage once again to the earthly laughter that attends ferocious lust "Whan tendre youthe hath wedded stoupyng age" (1738). The tension between religious aspiration and secular intervention that began with Chaucer's description of spring in the first eighteen lines of the poem and continued in earnest with the Host's proposal of the storytelling game remains a central concern of the *Canterbury Tales* and is highlighted in the thematic unity of Fragment IV. Three references in the Clerk's Tale (609, 733, and 1175) to the distinction between earnest and game and a fourth reference in the Merchant's Tale (1594) emphasize Chaucer's reintroduction of the *amor/amor dei* dichotomy splendidly articulated by Arthur Hoffman (1954).

By allowing the Clerk to introduce the theme of death, Chaucer expands his characterization of the Clerk. He shows a man both playful in his treatment of the Host and serious in his religious awareness, one who sees the Host's limitations and objects to the secular turn the pilgrimage has taken. The Host has asked the Clerk to tell "som myrie tale" (9), "som murie thyng of aventures" (15), and specifically not to preach as friars do in Lent (12). While appearing to accept the host's instructions, the Clerk introduces the theme of death and relates an extended exemplum with connotations of a saint's life, designed to teach how every person should be "constant in adversitee" (1146) and receive without complaint everything that God chooses to send us. By professing one thing and presenting another, the Clerk disregards the Host with amused politeness.

We have already seen how Chaucer associates death with the theme of time in the Prologue to the Clerk's Tale. At the first council, Walter's people emphasize the Clerk's point in the Prologue by echoing his words when they say "we knowe echoon / That we shul deye" and that "deeth shal on us falle" (124–26). Their fear of Walter's death and "That thurgh youre deeth youre lyne sholde slake" (137) supports their argument in favor of Walter's marriage. The other occasions of death as a theme in the Clerk's Tale—the supposed death of the daughter and the son, the figural death by dispossession of Griselda, and the triumphant resurrection of all from death at the end—are too obvious to need further mention.

Chaucer works the theme of death more subtly into the Merchant's Tale. He keeps the image of death in the forefront of the tale with January's claims to be "on my pittes brynke" (1401) and the other references to his age, but most effectively with the references to illness. In the long monologue with which the tale begins, January thrice mentions the advantages to a sick man of having a wife (1288–90, 1291–92, 1381–82). It is ironic and appropriate too that sickness is attributed to Damian (1875, 1901, 1903) and that January is genuinely apprehensive that Damian might die (1908) when Damian is actually in love with May. From the moment that Damian first addresses her, the notion of death is made explicit: "For I am deed if that this thyng be kyd" (1943). With sophisticated irony Chaucer allows the Merchant to praise May's excellent generosity, which prevents her from allowing Damian to "sterven" (1991) and herself to be considered "an homycide" (1994). Finally, at the end of the Merchant's Tale, the theme of death reappears as an ironic echo of the Clerk's Tale when January, his sight restored, sees his wife in the tree with Damian and sets up a roaring "As dooth the mooder whan the child shal dye" (2365). Griselda did not roar when she thought her child would die.

APPEARANCE/REALITY

Of course this theme runs throughout the *Canterbury Tales* and appears in almost every fragment, every tale, but it may be

Fragment IV

worthwhile to note its particular formulation and the special emphasis it receives in Fragment IV.[13] The Host's misperception of the Clerk and his tale introduces the theme of appearance and reality to the fragment. Harry Bailly asks the Clerk to tell a tale in a manner "so pleyn . . . / That we may understonde what ye seye" (19–20), a tale in which the appearance and the reality congrue to create a meaning the other pilgrims will not misunderstand. The Clerk's tale is readily understandable but is not to be taken literally, as the Clerk himself explicitly announces at the end. The Clerk makes four points about the tale:

1) that the purpose of the tale, contrary to what may appear, is not to cause wives to emulate Griselda in patience, but to encourage all to be patient in adversity (1142–47);
2) that though God may seem to test our faith through adversity, he does not test those who are redeemed (nor does he have to test to know our qualities); God sends adversity to strengthen us (1149–61);
3) that patient wives of Griselda's quality virtually do not exist (1166–69); and
4) that married men should not misconceive the purpose of the tale by emulating and brutally testing their wives (1138–40, 456–62, 1149–51).

In doing so, the Clerk insists that one should not misconceive the purpose of things as they appear. The purpose of this tale is not as it seems, and the purpose of God's testing is not as it seems. Nonetheless at the end of the Clerk's Tale, in a stanza Chaucer subsequently canceled, Harry Bailly indicates that he has still missed the point and misjudged the tale by misconceiving its literal meaning.[14] Because the tale was a "legende" (1212 d) that ended happily, the Host applauds the Clerk's apt fulfillment of his request for "som murie thyng" (15) and commends him: "This is a gentil tale for the nones, / As to my purpose, wiste ye my wille" (1212 e–f).

The appearance / reality theme in the fragment as a whole may best be described by the last line that May speaks to January:

> Ful many a man weneth to seen a thyng,
> And it is al another than it semeth.
> He that mysconceyveth, he mysdemeth.
>
> (2408–10)

Almost every character in the fragment misconceives and misjudges or appears other than what he or she actually is. The evil-looking sergeant who withdraws Griselda's children is an obvious case in point, but even Walter, with all his "thoghtes wyse" (116), is just as guilty of "no parfit sighte" (2383) as is blind and foolish January. He tests his wife "whan that it is no nede" (461), for "He hadde assayed hire ynogh bifore / And foond hire evere good" (456–57). Griselda herself, as perfectly patient as she appears to be throughout the tale, also mistakes appearance for reality and actually reproaches her husband on two separate occasions. When Walter asks her to make way for his new wife, she renders her most passionate expletive and compares Walter's present with his former behavior:

> O goode God! How gentil and how kynde
> Ye semed by youre speche and youre visage
> That day that maked was oure mariage!
>
> (852–54)

She concludes that "Love is noght oold as whan that it is newe" (857). She reproaches him again when Walter, "as it were in his pley" (1030), introduces their daughter to Griselda as his new wife.

> O thyng biseke I yow, and warne also,
> That ye ne prikke with no tormentynge
> This tendre mayden, as ye han doon mo.
>
> (1037–39)

Both reproaches, of course, signal Griselda's misperception of her husband's motives and misjudgment of his behavior. Understandable as her misjudgment is—he has behaved with unspeakable cruelty—she still has mistaken the appearance for the reality.

The same is true throughout the Merchant's Tale. The Merchant himself reflects the theme in the Prologue to his tale when he admits to discovering two months after marriage that the appearance had been more attractive than the reality proved to be. January's confusion of the appearance and the reality of marriage is too comic and too famous to require further explication here. May hypocritically maintains a posture of love toward her husband while manipulating his servant to be her lover.[15] Damian's love-sickness masquerades as physical illness and generates a sequence of oxymoronic epithets from the narrator, all of which reflect the theme of appearance and reality (1783–86).

When Damian does recover, he serves January as docilely "As evere dide a dogge for the bowe" (2014). Placebo pretends to offer advice in his position as "brother" (1478) and counselor, but, as a matter of principle, his advice never contradicts the opinion of his lord. And Justinus, who seems to have a successful marriage to "the moost stedefast wyf / And eek the mekeste oon" (1551–52), has "wept many a teere / Ful pryvely" (1544–45). Even January's garden is not what it seems. The *hortus conclusus*, evoking the perpetual virginity of Mary, serves as an outdoor bedroom in the summer (2048–52).[16] Of all the characters in the Merchant's Tale, only Pluto and Proserpyna seem to be precisely what they are, though an argument can be made on the basis of their passionate disagreement in the garden that marriage is not what it appears to be even among the gods.[17]

AUTHORITY AND EXPERIENCE

By attributing the source of his story to Petrarch, the Clerk introduces the theme which contrasts authority and experience, a topic most dramatically articulated in the Prologue to the Wife of Bath's Tale and developed in various fragments throughout the *Canterbury Tales*.[18] But only here in the Clerk's and Merchant's Tales does Chaucer carefully and thoroughly develop the theme so that it emerges as a unifying device for the fragment as a whole. In the main, the Clerk's Tale emphasizes the supremacy of authority while the Merchant's Tale celebrates the validity of experience.

Chaucer discusses authority in the Clerk's Tale primarily in terms of the corollary theme of obedience to that authority.[19] Responding to the Host in the Prologue, the Clerk himself introduces the themes of obedience to authority. Because of the agreement made at the Tabard Inn in the General Prologue, whereby the Host was elected "governour" and "juge" and the pilgrims agreed to "reuled been at his devys / In heigh and lough" (I, 813–17), the Clerk acknowledges that he is under the "yerde" of the Host who "han of us as now the governance" (22–23). Because he recognizes the validity of the Tabard agreement and the importance of obedience to that properly constituted authority, the Clerk acknowledges his acceptance of that authority: "And therfore wol I do yow obeisance" (24). The whole sentence, with its double statement of fact followed by "And therfore," suggests a syllogism perfectly in character for the Clerk. But the Clerk, as logician and legalist and student preparing for the priesthood, carefully qualifies his acceptance of the foolish Host's authority. He emphasizes its temporal limitation ("Ye han of us *as now* the governance") and limits his own acceptance of that authority when he insists he will obey the Host only "As fer as resoun axeth, hardily" (25). He is not Griselda.

The Clerk's Tale begins by referring to Walter's "fadres olde" (61) and "worthy eldres" (65) both to establish the interest in heredity, which so concerns the people who will initiate the action of the tale, and also to establish the validity of Walter's authority. His is a well-run principality: "alle his liges, bothe lasse and moore" were "obeisant, ay redy to his hond" (66–67). Chaucer echoes the theme in the language by which the people recognize Walter's absolute authority at the first council: they do not actually advise; they merely provide an opinion. The people ask that Walter "accepteth" (96, 127) their "requeste" (172) for him to marry—which they refer to as "that blisful yok / Of soveraynetee" (113–14), an appropriate phrase because both "yok" and "soveraynetee" reflect the theme of authority, obedience, and control. Since Walter recognizes their "trewe ententente" (127, 148), he "wole assente" (150) to their request only if they "wole assente" (174) never to complain against the woman he chooses to be his wife. However, since their offer to find a wife for him infringes upon his authority, he quite properly rejects it.

To indicate either Walter's humanity or, which is more likely, to emphasize the theme of authority and obedience to authority, Chaucer also reveals the self-imposed limitations of Walter's power. Walter does not force himself upon his people. He asks their consent—especially in the matter of his marriage. To that end, Chaucer first shows Walter asking Janicula if he will allow Walter to marry Griselda and will accept him as a son-in-law and then shows the contract-scene with Griselda. Both scenes affirm Walter's supreme authority in almost the same words (319–22 and 361).[20] It is probably ironic, therefore, that Walter should claim that the influence of his "gentils" (480) and the "murmur" (628) of his "peple" (625, 800) "constreyneth" (800) him to remove the children and take another wife. Although Walter insists to Griselda that he is obliged to behave "Nat as I wolde, but as my peple leste" (490), the sergeant describes the lord's authority more accurately:

> lordes heestes mowe nat been yfeyned;
> They mowe wel been biwailled or compleyned,
> But men moote nede unto hire lust obeye.
>
> (529–31)

Throughout the Clerk's Tale, the authority of the ruler is affirmed. All the people "his comandement obeye" (194): his sergeant, his ladies (372–78), his wife, his sister and brother-in-law, the court of Rome (737). Nonetheless, a variety of details in the tale suggest that Walter is not the ultimate ruler. He himself insists that "Bountee comth al of God" (157) and that he trusts in God's bounty (159). The religious echoes of God's sending "His grace into a litel oxes stalle" (207), of Griselda's honoring her father, of Griselda at the well and kneeling at the threshold, of her making the sign of the cross over her child who shall "dyen for my sake" (560), of her final restoration, of the resurrection of her children, and so on, all suggest the ultimate ruler. These details properly prepare for the stanzas at the end in which the Clerk indicates that the tale is a metaphor and not a literal prescription for human action. The ultimate ruler is God in whom Griselda has been perfectly trusting and to whom she has been perfectly obedient throughout. He is the ultimate ruler of the Clerk's Tale, of the Clerk, and of the other pilgrims who journey toward Canterbury. To God the Clerk owes his total obedience without limitation as to time or "resoun" (25).

It is otherwise with the Merchant's Tale. Experience, not authority, is the benchmark of action. With regard to this theme, the tales link by contrast. In his Prologue, the Merchant affirms the validity of his own unpleasant experience with his wife. "I knowe ynogh," "I trowe that it be so," "For wel I woot it fareth so with me" (1214–17) emphasize the Merchant's experience. Precisely because of the Merchant's experience—"Syn ye so muchel knowen" (1241)—the Host calls upon him to tell the next tale. In linking a narrator (like the Clerk) who affirms the primacy of authority with a narrator (like the Merchant) whose tale reflects the validity of his own experience, Chaucer follows the contrastive pattern with which he unifies fragments throughout the *Canterbury Tales*.

Chaucer links the two tales in this fragment not only by echoing the last line of the Clerk's Envoy in the first line of the Merchant's Prologue, and not only by contrasting experience to authority, but also by comparing and contrasting the Merchant's own experience with that of Walter. Both Walter and the Merchant value their freedom. The Merchant says that if he were "unbounden," he "wolde nevere eft comen in the snare" (1226–27) just as Walter "rejoysed of my liberte / That seelde tyme is founde in mariage" (145–46). The Merchant insists that "We wedded men lyven in sorwe and care" (1228), which reflects Walter's reluctance to marry and his fears of "grucchyng," of bickering, and of a "frownyng contenance" which he specifically forbids Griselda in the marriage agreement (351–57). Chaucer contrasts the Merchant's two-months' experience with the many years of concord and of rest (1129) shared by Walter and Griselda. And finally, Chaucer employs a witty reference to the Clerk's Tale when the Merchant affirms that what he has to say about wives and marriage is true, "Assaye whoso wole" (1229). "Assaye" is precisely the word Chaucer uses many times (454, 461, 621, 697, 1054) to refer to Walter's testing of Griselda, which established beyond doubt the excellence of that particular patient wife.

In the Merchant's Tale itself, January's long introductory monologue (1263–1392) in praise of marriage is based more upon wish than upon experience.[21] Like Alice of Bath, he rejects the authority (Theofraste) that disagrees with his desire and cites the authority (four biblical women) that supports it. January relies upon his sixty years' experience with women when he defines for his friends the sort of woman he is eager to accept as his wife. He knows from experience that "olde wydwes"—any woman over thirty—know "muchel craft" and are already "half a clerk" (1423–28); younger women, he knows, are more pliable (1429–30).

One might expect January's advisers, Placebo and Justinus, to cite authority in the approved medieval manner. Placebo does, indeed, cite Solomon to the effect that one should "Wirk alle thyng by conseil" (1485), but then as a matter of principle derived from his many years' experience as a "court-man" (1492), he insists that only a foolish counselor assumes he knows more than his lord. Placebo redefines Solomon's "conseil" to mean uncritical approval of his lord's will. Although Justinus cites Seneca ("Men moste enquere" [1532]), most of his advice to January is based upon his own experience in marriage: his neighbors' high opinion of his wife belies his actual experience revealed by his secret tears; he "woot best where wryngeth me my sho" (1553).

Even the gods in the Merchant's Tale prefer experience to authority. Although Pluto knows "Ten hondred thousand [tales]" (2240) and refers to Solomon and to Jesus, *filius Syrak*, he emphasizes that "Th'experience so preveth every day / The tresons whiche that wommen doon to man" (2238–39). Proserpyna attacks all his authorities in general (2276, 2304–5) and Solomon in particular (2277–2302) and insists that "many another man" (2280) has found "Wommen ful trewe, ful goode, and vertuous" (2281) as Walter found Griselda to be. She encourages Pluto to base his judgment on his own experience: "Witnesse on hem that dwelle in Cristes hous" (2282). Indeed, his own experience with Proserpyna is sufficient for him to abandon argument, and with more will than grace, he capitulates and says, "I yeve it up" (2312).

III. Character

In addition to the rather remarkable similarities of theme and structure in the two tales, Chaucer fashions significant parallels among the characters as well. Although the characters are involved in action unique to their own tales, and behave in ways appropriate to completely different genre (Walter and Griselda appear in an extended exemplum or secular saint's life, and January and May in a kind of fabliau[22]), Chaucer has conceived of them as similar characters whom he treats in similar ways. More than that, Chaucer manipulates our response to these characters in a way that is also unique to this fragment.

WALTER AND JANUARY

Walter and January are neighbors, both born in Lombardy.[23] Indeed, according to some manuscripts which read "Pavye" for "Panyk," Walter's sister and brother-in-law, to whom he secretly sends his children for safekeeping, rule the very town where January was born. Both January and Walter are wealthy, both possess palaces, both convene councils which advise them on the proper conduct of their affairs, but this is really incidental to the larger connections between the two men. Because Walter is young and January old, we might well expect greater differences than we actually find. To be sure, we would never confuse the two men. Nonetheless, Chaucer has joined the Merchant's Tale to the Clerk's Tale because, among other things, the similarities between January and Walter far outweigh their differences. They are more like each other than they are like any other characters in the *Canterbury Tales*. Both men are bachelors and both men marry: one at the instigation of his people, the other "for hoolynesse or for dotage" (1253). As bachelors, the two men reveal similar characteristics. Walter thinks only of his "lust present" (80), which for him means "to hauke and hunte on every syde" (81). Similarly, January "folwed ay his bodily delyt" (1249), which for him means the pursuit of "wommen, ther as was his appetyt" (1250). Each chooses the girl he will marry "of his owene auctoritee" (1597) without benefit of council. January does so, we are told, "For love is blynd alday, and may nat see" (1598). Walter, too, is "blynd alday, and may nat see," though not in precisely the same way as January: Walter tests Griselda precisely because he cannot see and wants to learn the extent of his wife's steadfastness. No other fragment of the *Canterbury Tales* defines the major male figures of all the tales in precisely this way.

More telling, however, is the way Chaucer manipulates our response to each man. Although Walter and January differ in ways appropriate to the different genres in which they appear, Chaucer develops both characters in precisely the same way and so forces us to respond to them in analogous ways. In doing so, he reveals a unifying device unique to this fragment: no other characters in the *Canterbury Tales*, major or minor, are treated like this. For example, from the very beginning January's behavior is foolish and Walter's is unexpected or inexplicable. January's foolishness, characteristic of the *senex amans* in fabliaux, appears when he articulates his attitude toward marriage. Walter's inexplicable behavior, regardless of his possible origins among the demon-lovers of folklore, is revealed by his disregard for the continuation of his ancient line and by his subsequent choice of a peasant girl for a wife. From these beginnings, both men progress in their predominant characteristics: January becomes more foolish and Walter more strange. January becomes the increasingly fit object of our derision. At first, when he reveals his assumptions about marriage, he is merely the foolish *senex*. At the first council he reveals his blindness and stubbornness when he rejects Justinus's advice and accepts Placebo's; at the last council he reveals his supreme idiocy when he asks for advice about "parfite blisses two" (1638); and finally he becomes disgusting and ridiculous, the fit object of our derision and scorn, when we see him sitting up in bed on his wedding night.

Our sense of Walter's strangeness similarly increases: first, that he should ever develop the desire to test his wife; then that he should pursue it with such single-mindedness of purpose; then that he should actually remove his daughter from his wife by means of the frightening sergeant; and finally that he should do precisely the same thing again to his son and heir. Though some locate the nadir of Walter's reputation in his shameful dismissal of Griselda, the moment is actually articulated in the text as the time when "The sclaundre of Walter ofte and wyde spradde" (722) that he had murdered his children and that he had done so for having married a poor woman. As a result, the people who had earlier loved and feared him (69) as an absolute monarch, ruling a rich, obedient kingdom, come to hate him (731) as a cruel murderer and a man of evil reputation.

After showing Walter and January at their worst, Chaucer deliberately sets about restoring them. He manipulates our response by directing our attention to more positive aspects of their characters.

Walter's restoration occurs in three clear stages. The first occurs when the people, looking upon Walter's children and supposing the girl to be Walter's prospective wife, say that he "was no fool" and that it "was for the beste" (986–87) that he exchange Griselda for this new wife. They commend his governance (994). Although the more sober people in the city condemn this unstable and fickle attitude of the multitude, Chaucer has shown Walter in a more positive light. The next stage occurs when Walter calls an end to the testing of Griselda and reaffirms the wedding agreement which he has always and faithfully intended to implement (1065–67). He receives the final accolade when Griselda herself defends Walter to her children and to the populace assembled in the hall for the feast. She calls Walter his children's "benyngne father" (1097) and gives him credit equal to that of God for preserving them—God having done so "of his mercy" and Walter "tendrely" (1096–97). Thus, the restoration scene at the end of the Clerk's Tale includes not only the restoration of Griselda but that of Walter as well, both in the eyes of his people and in the more critical estimation of Chaucer's audiences. The tale could not end happily nor could we accept the judgment that the two of them lived happily "in concord and in reste" (1129) without the restoration of Walter.

Chaucer similarly manipulates our response to January. If January were to enter the garden at the end of the Merchant's Tale as completely the object of our derision as he is on his wedding night, then May's victory would be the empty triumph of a clever girl over a foolish, imbecilic old man who is ripe for gulling, and the Merchant's Tale would be little more than a fabliau. The tale is far more sophisticated than that, and part of the sophistication derives from Chaucer's decision to change our opinion of January, to generate some sympathy for him, and to raise him in our estimation—if only temporarily—so that his decision not to see what he has seen and his gently stroking May as he leads her back into the palace assume some of the pity generated by irony normally associated with tragedy and not with fabliau.[24] If no sympathy had been generated for January, the irony would be pointless and the end of the Merchant's Tale would not be as painful as it is.

Chaucer's restoration of January, like that of Walter, also occurs in three clearly defined stages. When January and May are eating in the hall after high mass, four days after their marriage, the narrator refers to January as "this goode man" (1897). The prime example of January's goodness is that he "Remembred hym upon this Damyan" (1898), asked the other squires about him, and indicated how sad it would be if Damian were to die of his illness (1907–8).[25] Our opinion of January improves in the second instance when Chaucer changes our response to May. At first, one tends to pity poor May for her marriage and to think of January as the rich and stupid *senex* who will deserve everything that he gets. However, once one sees that May is really no better than she should be, that she is quick to take a lover and break her marriage vows, that sexual hypocrisy lies well within her repertory, and that she disposes of a love letter in the "privee" (1954), pity for May evaporates, and some residual pity spills over onto January.[26] That pity increases when January is struck blind. His piteous weeping and wailing and his outrageous jealousy remind us that he is, after all, only a self-deluding, foolish old man, but his ultimate response to his affliction marks the third and most important stage of his restoration: "For whan he wiste it may noon oother be, / He paciently took his adversitee" (2083–84). Chaucer designed this attitude to gain our respect. It deserves our respect. Seen in the context of the Clerk's Tale, January actually exemplifies the moral point which the Clerk has carefully drawn from his tale: "wel moore us oghte / Receyven al in gree that God us sent" (1150–51). January's patience shows him capable of the same strength of character that Griselda has exhibited. As we admired patience and strength of character in Griselda, we must admire them in January.

Although our admiration for January is fitful and brief (he immediately tries to limit May's actions even more closely than before), it is this partially restored January who goes into the garden at the end of the Merchant's Tale. Because we think slightly better of him now than we had earlier, the irony is more biting, the betrayal more painful. January's laudable desire to satisfy the whim of his pregnant wife and his painful awareness of his limitations and vulnerability—"Allas . . . that I ne had heer a knave / That koude clymbe! Allas, allas . . . for I am blynd" (2338–40)—expressed when his knave Damian has already climbed into the tree successfully because January is blind, are all the more ironic and painful because we have seen January as something more than an idiotic *senex amans*.²⁷ For the same reason, his withdrawal from the truth—from "I saugh it with myne yen" (2378), to "me thoughte" (2386), to "if I have myssayd" (2391), to "I wende han seyn" (2393)—is lamentable though understandable.²⁸ And his final withdrawal into the palace with his beloved betrayer is ironic and painful because Chaucer allowed us to see for a moment the vestiges of Christian patience in an old and foolish man.

No where else in the *Canterbury Tales* does Chaucer treat characters the way he treats January and Walter, manipulating our response so that, as we see them in action, we come to despise them and then later to accept if not actually admire them. He contributes to the coherence of the fragment by reserving this treatment for Walter and January alone among the figures in the *Canterbury Tales*.

GRISELDA AND MAY

All of Chaucer's young women (with the possible exception of Malyne) are pretty. It is therefore no surprise to learn that Griselda and May are young and beautiful. Further, the genre of the story in which Chaucer's young women appear also affects the way in which he depicts them. Thus, to portray women in a saint's life (Cecilia) or in an extended exemplum with connotations of a saint's life (Custance, Virginia, and Griselda), Chaucer emphasizes their spiritual aspects: for Griselda, these are her "vertuous beautee," her "virginitee," her "rype and sad corage," her "reverence," "charitee," "obeisaunce" (211–31), and so on. To portray women in fabliaux (Alison, Malyne, the wife in the Shipman's Tale), which is perhaps the genre to which the Merchant's Tale belongs, Chaucer emphasizes the more physical aspects of their being: for May, "Hir myddel smal, hire armes longe and sklendre" (1602). But this evidence (with the possible exception of the implicit physical/spiritual contrast) does not convincingly support the claim that Chaucer deliberately set Griselda and May into the same fragment to unify it because they complement each other.

Other evidence, however, does support that claim. Griselda and May not only share some characteristics unique to the fragment in which they appear, but they also contrast with each other in ways that contribute to the unity of the whole. No other of Chaucer's ennobled women (Griselda marries a marquis; May marries a knight) come "of smal degree" (1625). Except for Emily who Palamon thinks is a goddess, no other of Chaucer's women is so beautiful and so excellent that she is thought to be otherworldly. Walter's people think Griselda is "hevene sent" (440, 406), appropriately because of her abstract and spiritual qualities; January's people think "it semed fayerye" (1743) to look at May, appropriately because of her physical beauty (1746–49) and her demeanor. While Griselda, by virtue of her virtue, calms strife and discord, May, by virtue of her nature, creates disagreement (between Justinus and January, for example) and mistrust (2343).[29] This fundamental opposition is found also in Griselda's exhibiting the virtue of patience and, by her example, teaching it to all of us, while May, driven by lust to love Damian (2094–95), only pretends to teach January "pacience" (2369). These similar and contrastive parallels exemplify Chaucer's design for coherence in the composition of the fragment.

One further aspect of Chaucer's craft deserves mention in the context of Griselda and May. Chaucer employs clothes, clothing, array to unify the fragment.[30] Clothing appears significantly in only one other fragment of the *Canterbury Tales*: in Fragment VIII, the Second Nun's Tale and the Canon's Yeoman's Tale, Chaucer uses clothing to articulate the theme of conversion and to contrast the spiritual and the worldly. One might have expected Chaucer to use clothing to good purpose in the Shipman's Tale where the narrator refers to clothing (VII, 1200–9), and the merchant's wife uses her clothing bill as an excuse to discuss a loan and its repayment (in a different coin) with the monk (VII, 1368–84), but in point of fact, clothing plays no very significant part in the Shipman's Tale or in Fragment VII as a whole. It is, however, quite important to the Clerk's and the Merchant's Tales.

In the Clerk's Tale clothing marks the progress of Griselda's elevation, humiliation, and restoration. In preparation for his marriage, Walter took the measure of Griselda "By a mayde lyk to hire stature" (257) so that she should have clothing appropriate to her marriage. (Chaucer describes the marquis' progress toward the wedding with echoes and puns on "array": 262, 267, 273, 275.) As is often the case in folklore, a change of clothing (372–85) celebrates Griselda's translation from poor girl to "markysesse." Walter refers to the point with a pun on "array" (467) when he announces the removal of his daughter, and Griselda makes the point once again and more explicitly when they discuss the removal of their son.

> "For as I lefte at hoom al my clothyng,
> When I first cam to yow, right so," quod she,
> "Lefte I my wyl and al my libertee,
> And took youre clothyng."
>
> (654–57)

Griselda's humiliating dismissal involves the return of the clothing Walter provided her (865–68), except for the simple "smok" (890) to cover her nakedness. When she returns to her former place and rank, her father appropriately covers her "with hire olde coote" (913). In order "The chambres for t'arraye" (961) in preparation for his supposed new marriage, Walter calls upon Griselda to help, regardless of the state of her clothing (his word is "array" [965]). The new wife impresses the fickle people with "hire array, so richely biseye" (984), unlike Griselda who is not at all embarrassed by the "rude" (1011–12) and shabby state of her own clothing which so astonishes Walter's guests (1019–20). In the final scene, Walter admits to having planned on testing Griselda "In greet estaat, and povreliche arrayed" (1055) and completes the restoration of his wife by removing "hire rude array" and having her dressed "in a clooth of gold that brighte shoon" (1116–17).

In the Merchant's Tale, May, like Griselda, receives "riche array" (1699) as part of her marriage portion. But whereas clothes reflect one's position in the world in the Clerk's Tale, clothes in the Merchant's Tale serve only as an "encombraunce" (1960) to January's sexual pleasure and must be removed. While Griselda strips herself down to her smock "Biforn the folk" (894), May in the privacy of her bedroom "strepen hire al naked" in order to provide "som plesaunce" (1958–59) to her husband. The same activity with its attendant stripping away of encumbering clothes is implicit "In somer seson" when January and May are alone in the garden and "he wolde paye his wyf hir dette" (2048–49). Chaucer articulates May's ultimate betrayal of her marriage vows and concomitant commitment to fleshly pursuits, explicit at the moment she takes Damian as a lover, in terms of the removal of clothing: the smock that Damian "Gan pullen up" (2353) and that January saw lying "upon his brest" (2395). Chaucer had carefully prepared for this scene earlier when May responds to January's implicit accusation by saying that if she is ever false to him he should "strepe me and put me in a sak, / And in the nexte ryver do me drenche" (2200–1). In May's choice of punishment—stripping off clothes (which occurs only in Fragment IV)—Chaucer ironically echoes the treatment of clothing that registers elevation and humiliation in the Clerk's Tale.

The importance of clothing to Griselda and May links the two women and affirms their formal similarity. No other of the Canterbury tales conceives of or defines its heroine in these ways. These parallels between Griselda and May, together with the parallels in conception and design that govern the treatment of Walter and January, fortify the connection between the Clerk's Tale and the Merchant's Tale and contribute to the unity of Fragment IV.

THE CLERK AND THE MERCHANT

Alone among the pilgrims whose tales have been linked into groups, the Clerk and the Merchant are also paired in the General Prologue to the *Canterbury Tales*. Their conjunction is probably accidental and not at all relevant to the unity of Fragment IV, but it is interesting, in the light of the many thematic and structural links that unify the fragment, to see how carefully the two portraits are linked.[31] For example, just as the Clerk's Tale emphasizes the value of an abstract virtue, patience, in ideal human behavior, and the Merchant's Tale shows the workings of ordinary lust in realistic human behavior, so the portraits distinguish between a man who is committed to the abstract, to "logyk" (I, 286) and "philosophie" (I, 295), and another who is committed to the realistic workings of the business world by means of usury ("bargaynes" and "chevyssaunce" [I, 282]) and the illegal involvement with foreign exchange (I, 278). Chaucer emphasizes the linkage by contrast. He describes the Merchant in terms of what he *has*: with a fashionably forked beard, he is dressed in "mottelee" and wears "a Flaundryssh bever hat" (I, 271–72) and boots beautifully fastened. Chaucer describes the Clerk in terms of what he *has not*: he is "nat right fat," looks "holwe," has no benefice, and is not so worldly as to have secular employment; his horse is "leene"; and his clothing is "thredbare" (I, 287–90). Chaucer develops the contrast. The Clerk does not speak much, not a word "moore than was neede" (I, 304), and he appears silent and preoccupied in the Prologue to his tale. When he does speak, "Sownynge in moral virtu was his speche" (I, 307). The Merchant apparently speaks constantly, "Sownynge alwey th'encrees of his wynnyng" (I, 275). Nonetheless, he presents himself in his tale as "a rude man" who "kan nat glose" (2351).

Although the two men are joined in terms of opposites, they do have one thing in common. Chaucer explicitly deflates the Merchant's portrait with the realistic observation that "Ther wiste no wight that he was in dette" (I, 280). Chaucer implies that the Clerk, too, is in debt since he has "but litel gold in cofre" and spends all that he can get from his friends on books and learning (I, 298–300). As the Merchant uses all his wit to buy and sell money and to improve his position in the world, the Clerk uses whatever money he can get in pursuit of the pure abstract. These are the complementary men who tell the tales in Fragment IV. As we shall see, Chaucer pairs his narrators with equal care only in Fragment VIII (the Second Nun and the Canon's Yeoman) and in Fragment VI (the Physician and the Pardoner).

By carefully crafting the Clerk's Tale and the Merchant's Tale to echo each other's structure, themes, and characters, Chaucer has created a fragment much greater than the sum of its parts. The structural parallels testify most graphically to the coherence of the fragment as a whole, and the resulting mutual interpenetration of tale by tale within the coherent fragment extends Chaucer's vision beyond the individual tale. Thus, January, to take the most obvious example, generates a predictable critical response in all of Chaucer's audiences who consider his appearance solely in the context of the Merchant's Tale. That critical response is complicated when January is evaluated in terms of Fragment IV as a whole, which includes the ethical point of the Clerk's Tale, the strange behavior of Walter, and the model of patience established by Griselda that January, to some degree, shares. Similarly, to take the least obvious example, Griselda herself receives different critical valuations when considered solely in terms of the Clerk's Tale and when considered in the context both of her more characteristically human counterpart, May, and of January's example of patience. By establishing lines of coherence in terms of structure, theme, and character, Chaucer has put together Fragment IV in a way that establishes the validity of the fragment as a coherent work of art.

2
Fragment VI (Group C): The Physician's Tale and the Pardoner's Tale

> I seye al day that men may see
> That yiftes of Fortune and of Nature
> Been cause of deeth to many a creature.
>
> (294–96)

These words of the Host to the pilgrims in the link between the Physician's and the Pardoner's Tales are often held to be the hinge which holds Fragment VI together—a fragment composed of the most vilified and the most celebrated of the *Canterbury Tales*.[1] Harry Bailly looks back to the Physician's Tale in identifying Nature's elaborate gifts to Virginia as being responsible for her fate: "Hire beautee was hir deth, I dar wel sayn" (297). And Chaucer wittily allows Harry Bailly to look forward to the Pardoner's Tale and foreshadow the death of the three rioters by referring to Fortune's gift of gold to them ("This tresor hath Fortune unto us yiven" [779]).[2] Gold also connects the narrators. In his portrait in the General Prologue, the Physician "lovede gold in special" (I, 444), and the Pardoner, who preaches against cupidity, only wants to "wynne gold and silver" (440). All this is obvious, but additional similarities connect the two narrators. Both are "leeches," both are protectors and preservers: one ministers to the body, the other ministers to the soul.[3] With consummate artistry and irony, Chaucer allows the one whose province is the body to tell a tale about the preservation of human values and the ability of noble human beings to transcend the flesh; and he allows the one whose province is the soul to tell a tale about three rioters immersed in fleshly delights.

As preservers of the body and the soul, the Physician and the Pardoner link in their common antipathy to death, and, as Harry

Fragment VI

Bailly's observation about the gifts of Fortune and of Nature indicates, the theme of death occupies a major place in the fragment. Together with the themes of governance and counterfeiting, death unifies Fragment VI. But perhaps the most persuasive argument for the integrity of the fragment comes from an examination of the structure of the tales, for Chaucer has carefully arranged the sequence of narrative events in a structural pattern that is almost identical in the two tales. The coherence of Fragment VI, like that of all the Canterbury fragments, requires that the interpretive access to one tale be made through the others in the same fragment.

I. Structure

No other narrative in the *Canterbury Tales* proceeds and develops in a way at all similar to the way shared by the Physician's and Pardoner's Tales. Throughout the *Canterbury Tales* Chaucer unifies fragments by repeating a sequence of events in a particular narrative order; he chooses a sequence unique to that particular fragment and unlike the sequence of events in any other tale or in any other fragment. The schematic presentation of Fragment VI below shows the parallel structural pattern shared by the two tales which creates the backbone of architectural unity within Fragment VI.

Physician's Tale	*Pardoner's Tale*
Before the Tale	Before the Tale
Nature: on Nature	Pardoner: on Pardoner
Portrait: Virginia	Portrait: Three Rioters
Interruption: Address to those who govern	Interruption: Sermon on sins of gluttony, hazardry, and blasphemy
The Tale	The Tale
Impulse for action: Apius: "This mayde shal be myn" (129)	Impulse for action: Three Rioters: "Deeth shal be deed" (710)
Conspiracy: Apius and Claudius	Conspiracy: Three Rioters
Confrontation Scene: Virginius	Confrontation Scene: Old Man
Discussion: Virginius and Virginia	Discussion: Three Rioters
Decision: Death	Decision: Death
Motive: Love	Motive: Gold

Death: of Virginia	Death: of Three Rioters
Pardon: Virginius of Claudius	Pardon: Christ's pardon
After the Tale	*After the Tale*
Host plays with the Physician	Host plays with the Pardoner
Gentils intervene	Knight intervenes

Let us examine these parallel items in order.

THE SELF-DESCRIPTIONS OF NATURE AND THE PARDONER

Chaucer begins the two tales of this fragment by having Nature and the Pardoner describe themselves and their characteristic action in the world. They are opposites. The Pardoner makes no pretense of being anything other than a fraud. In his defiantly self-revelatory Prologue, he delights in affirming that his primary activity is a "gaude" (389), that his preaching is mere "bisynesse" (399), and that even his voice is affected: "I peyne me to han an hauteyn speche" (330).[4] He saffrons his speech with Latin which he knows all by rote. His relics, which the people think are authentic, are actually "pigges bones" (I, 700) and "pilwe-beer" (I, 694) as we know from the General Prologue. He spits out his "venym under hewe / Of hoolynesse, to semen hooly and trewe" (421–22) though he proudly admits "I wol noon of the apostles countrefete" (447). Even his authority as a Pardoner is suspect. He may well have the seal of the local bishop on his patent to protect himself within that bishop's specific area of authority, but most scholars agree that it would be unlikely for him to have authentic "Bulles of popes and of cardynales, / Of patriarkes and bishopes" (342–43).

While the Pardoner exposes himself and all his activities as fraudulent, Nature presents herself and all her activities as genuine, authentic, unable to be duplicated or improved upon. No matter how the greatest artificers—Pigmalion, Apelles, Zanzis—attempt to imitate Nature's work, "Outher to grave, or peynte, or forge, or bete" (17), they can never succeed in counterfeiting what Nature does, because Nature, unlike the Pardoner, is God's perfect instrument: "My lord and I been ful of oon accord" (25). The Pardoner's "auctoritee" is granted to him "by bulle" (387–88); Nature's authority is direct and absolute. As the "vicaire general" of "He that is the formere principal," Nature forms and paints earthly creatures "Right as me list." Since everything under the moon is in Nature's "cure," "alle myne othere creatures" are, like Virginia, "made . . . to the worshipe of my lord" (19–27), in

Fragment VI

direct fulfillment of God's will. Unlike the Pardoner, who is guilty of the sin of avarice and preaches only "for coveitise" (424, 433) in order "for to wynne" (461), Nature works without avarice: "And for my werk right no thyng wol I axe" (24).

By joining the Pardoner's Tale to the Physician's Tale, Chaucer has carefully established the context in which to discuss the character of the Pardoner. While for a modern audience the Pardoner himself may share characteristics with the Wife of Bath and the Canon's Yeoman—and these connections contribute to the coherence of the *Canterbury Tales* as a whole—the primary access to the Pardoner's character for a medieval audience lies not only through the real pardoners that they saw in the world around them, but also through his contrast with the *Weltanschauung* generated by the characters and action of the Physician's Tale. His opposition to Nature only emphasizes that contrast.

PORTRAITS

Chaucer achieves architectural unity in the fragment not only by having portraits in both tales and by having them appear in the same position (see the schematic design) but also by designing the portraits of Virginia and of the three rioters to be the precisely balanced opposites of each other. The sins of the three rioters specifically counter Virginia's virtues.[5] Virginia is a modest virgin ("As wel in goost as body chast was she; / For which she floured in virginitee" [43–44]); the three rioters indulge in lust and lechery with the "tombesteres / Fetys and smale, and yonge frutesteres, / Syngeres," and so on who "kyndle and blowe the fyr of lecherye" (477–81). Virginia is temperate and abstinent (45–47); the three rioters are characterized "By superfluytee abhomynable" (471). Of Virginia we are told "Bacus hadde of hir mouth right no maistrie" (58); the three rioters "eten also and drynken over hir myght" (468). Virginia flees "the compaignye / Where likly was to treten of folye" (63–64); the three rioters comprise "a compaignye / Of yonge folk that haunteden folye" (463–64). Specifically, Virginia avoids "feestes, revels, and ... daunces, / That been occasions of daliaunces" (65–66); the three rioters seek "riot, hasard, stywes, and tavernes, / Where ... / They daunce and pleyen at dees bothe day and nyght" (465–67). Virginia's virtue is implicit in her going to pray at a "temple with hire mooder deere" (119); the three rioters' lack of virtue is explicit in their doing "the devel sacrifise / Withinne that develes temple" (469–70). While other portraits in the *Canterbury Tales* define saints and sinners, no other linked portraits are composed of precisely these contrary elements.[6] Chaucer contributed to the coherence of the fragment by conceiving and composing the portraits in Fragment VI as a balanced pair.

INTERRUPTIONS

Only one other fragment, Fragment III, which includes the Wife of Bath, Friar, and Summoner, contains structurally important interruptions in the narrative, but there the interruptions are all alike in being external: someone outside the tale disrupts the narrative. Here, in Fragment VI, the interruptions in the narrative are internally generated and thematically significant: in the Physician's Tale, the address to governesses; in the Pardoner's Tale, the sermon on gluttony, hazardry, and blasphemy. The interruptions in each tale define the controlling influence over that tale's principal characters: for Virginia that controlling influence is the governance of parents, governesses, and God; for the three rioters, the controlling influence is gluttony, hazardry, and blasphemy which lead to death. However, the tales of this fragment, like those of all the fragments, interpenetrate so that the claims of one modify the claims of the other. Thus, Virginia's governance leads to death, and the rioters' death derives from their lack of governance.

In the Pardoner's Tale the Pardoner's sermon on gluttony, hazardry, and blasphemy develops naturally from the portraits of the three rioters at the beginning of the tale.[7] Each of the three sins leads to death. Gluttony is the "original of oure dampnacioun"; "Corrupt was al this world for glotonye" (500–4); and he who seeks the delights of gluttony "Is deed" (548). Hazardry "is verray mooder of . . . manslaughtre" (591–93); and blasphemy or "fals sweryng" attends gambling, one of whose fruits is "homycide" which the Pardoner's sermon dramatizes: "By Goddes armes, if thou falsly pleye, / This daggere shal thurghout thyn herte go!" (632–57). And once the three have found the gold, they illustrate how these very sins, working in the lives of men, lead inevitably to death. They swear by "Goddes precious dignitee!" (782) [blasphemy]. They draw straws [hazardry] to decide which of them will go to town "And brynge us breed and wyn" (797) [gluttony]. They reveal themselves to be "enemys of Cristes croys / Of whiche the ende is deeth" (523–33).

Chaucer carefully designs the interruption in the Physician's

Tale so that it will precisely parallel that in the Pardoner's Tale in terms of position (after the portraits and before the tales) and of purpose (both introduce major themes). We know the Physician's address to the governesses to be Chaucer's creation because it does not appear in his sources: he wrote it specifically for the Physician's Tale. Chaucer develops the interruption quite naturally from the portrait of Virginia. But whereas the interruption in the Pardoner's Tale shows how sin leads inevitably to death, the interruption in the Physician's Tale focuses upon the preservation of virtue and the avoidance of death. The interruption therefore is addressed to "maistresses . . . / That lordes doghtres han in governaunce" (72–73) and to "Ye faderes and ye moodres eek also" who have "surveiaunce" of the children "under youre governaunce" (93–96). As the Pardoner's interruption defines and proscribes sin, the Physician's interruption defines virtue and encourages care. Governesses are encouraged "To teche hem vertu looke that ye ne slake," to "kepeth wel, for if ye wole, ye kan," and to "Looke wel that ye unto no vice assente" (82–87). Parents, too, are encouraged to protect and preserve their children "by ensample of your lyvynge" and by not being too lenient "in chastisynge" (97–98). Parental negligence is dangerous and can lead to death (99): "Under a shepherde softe and necligent / The wolf hath many a sheep and lamb torent" (101–2). Part of the dreadful irony in the Physician's Tale is that Virginia "kepte hirself" so well that "hir neded no maistresse" (106) and that in order to preserve her innocence, her father feels obliged to kill her. He had to kill her in order to "kep" her; the shepherd had to become the wolf.

IMPULSE FOR ACTION

After these interruptions, the tales begin in earnest with similar scenes that define the original impulse for the action which occupies the rest of the tale. Virginia's tale begins "upon a day" when she "wente in the toun / Toward a temple" (118–19). The three rioters are drinking "er prime" (662) in a tavern that had earlier been designated a "develes temple" (470). The action of the rioters' tale begins with the auditory sense: they hear the bell of a funeral procession as it passes. The action of the Physician's Tale begins with the visual sense: Apius sees the maid as she passes the spot where he stands. In both tales the effect is immediate. As for Apius: "his herte chaunged and his mood" (126). Chaucer dramatizes precisely the same change in the speech of one of the rioters as we see by comparing his first de-energized speech, "Go bet . . . and axe redily / What cors is this that passeth heer forby" (667–68), with his electrified enthusiasm when told about Death: "Ye, Goddes armes! . . . / Is it swich peril with hym for to meete? / I shal hym seke" (692–94). The rioter concludes with the emphatic statement that defines the impulse to action, "He shal be slayn" (700), which the narrator repeats a few lines later, "Deeth shal be deed" (710)—lines which syntactically parallel Apius's commitment to action, "This mayde shal be myn" (129).

At the moment Apius arrives at this conclusion, "the feend into his herte ran" (130). As the youngest of the three rioters goes toward town to buy the food and drink, "the feend, oure enemy, / Putte in his thought that he sholde poyson beye" (844–45). Only in Fragment VI does Chaucer account for the impulse to evil in both tales by having the devil enter the heart and the mind. Fiends impel the wicked to action elsewhere in the *Canterbury Tales*; it is a common medieval belief whose origin may lie in Judas's decision to betray Jesus (Luke 22:3). The "serpent Sathanas," who has his nest in the heart of Jews (VII, 1748–49), swells up and encourages the Jews to murder the clergeon in the Prioress' Tale. In the Man of Law's Tale, "Sathan . . . made a yong knyght" (II, 582–85) lust after Custance, and the Sultan's mother's iniquity is also attributed to Satan (II, 365–67). But only here do we see the fiend performing the same characteristic action in both parts of the fragment. It is not a major organizing device, but it is a unique and interesting detail which contributes to unity in the fragment.

CONSPIRACY

As soon as the villains decide upon their course of evil action, they create a conspiracy to help ensure their success. In his eagerness to avenge himself upon Death, the rioter who seems to be first among equals loudly proclaims "I shal hym seke" (694), but he has no intention of doing so alone. He enlists the aid of his companions who swear a mighty oath of brotherhood "To lyve and dyen ech of hem for oother" (696–704). Unlike the three rioters who are immediate, impetuous, and "al dronken in this rage" (705), Apius proceeds "by greet deliberacioun" and "In secree wise" (139–43). He calls upon the churl Claudius whom "he knew for subtil and for boold" (141), characteristics appropriate to the kind of attack he intends to make upon Virginia.

Fragment VI 57

Although a churl and a judge cannot share brotherhood, "yiftes preciouse and deere" seal their "conspiracie" which, like the rioters' sworn brotherhood, is redolent of death: Claudius "sholde lese his heed" (145–49) if he reveals Apius's plans.

Both the conspiracy of villains in the Physician's Tale and the conspiracy of rioters in the Pardoner's Tale appear all the more reprehensible in the context of the relationship between God and Nature that Chaucer established at the beginning of the fragment and humanized in the encomium to governesses. Moreover, the ideal relationship defined by God and Nature applies in equally human terms to the brotherhood of pilgrims wending toward Canterbury. The interpenetration of tales in Fragment VI penetrates the frame, too; the moral dimension of medieval literature addresses the behavior of that literature's audiences.

CONFRONTATION SCENE: VIRGINIUS AND THE OLD MAN

The scenes that follow are important to the plot of both tales. They are, in fact, confrontation scenes comparable to scenes of accusation, evaluation, and judgment elsewhere in the *Canterbury Tales* and especially in Fragment III. Although the two scenes are more alike in general than they are in specifics, the similar and contrastive details that they do share indicate Chaucer's craft. Virginius is accused of having stolen Claudius's servant; the Old Man is accused of being Death's spy. Virginius is not allowed to speak in his defense; the Old Man speaks at length. The three rioters call the Old Man a "false theef" (759); the narrator calls Apius a "false juge" (154, 158, 161). The rioters accuse the Old Man of being in league with Death, "For soothly thou art oon of his assent" (758); by contrast Claudius pretends not to be in league with Apius when he says "Lord, if that it be youre wille" (165). Claudius's basic claim against Virginius is that Virginia is not in her proper house: she is Claudius's servant "Which fro myn hous was stole upon a nyght" (184). Similarly, the Old Man is not in his proper house: he must constantly "knokke with my staf" upon "my moodres gate" and cry "Leeve mooder, leet me in" (729–31). Both scenes end in a judgment that directs the characters and the action of the tale toward death. When Apius decides "The cherl shal have his thral, this I awarde" (202), he puts Virginius on the road to Virginia's death ("Al wolde he from his purpos nat converte" [212]) just as certainly as the Old Man does the three rioters when he directs them "To fynde Deeth, turne up this croked wey" (761). At the end of the scene, Virginius "gooth hym hoom, and sette him in his halle" (207), which becomes the locus of death; in the Pardoner's Tale, "everich of thise riotoures ran / Til he cam to that tree" (768–69), which becomes the locus of their death.

The two scenes are significantly related in one other way. Because Virginia is "ful yong" (185) and the Old Man is "in so greet age" (719), they mark the beginning and the end of human life.[8] Chaucer has made an issue of age in the two tales of Fragment VI both to increase the pathos within the fragment (Virginia finds death while the Old Man seems to live forever) and to increase the irony (the Old Man who seeks death cannot find it while the young girl, who lives a virtuous and religious life, finds death all too soon). In all these ways, then, Chaucer contributes to the unity of the fragment by designing these two sophisticated confrontation scenes to be more like each other than they are like any other confrontation scenes in the *Canterbury Tales*.

DISCUSSION

Once Virginius arrives at home and the rioters arrive beneath the tree, they engage in discussions and reach exactly the same decision: death. Their motives differ, of course. In the Physician's Tale, Virginius decides "For love, and nat for hate, thou most be deed" (225). In the Pardoner's Tale, the two who remain behind decide to murder the third so that all the gold can be divided between the two of them, and the youngest decides to murder his two friends so that he can "Have al this tresor to myself allone" (841). Once decided upon a course of action, Virginius and the three rioters advance inevitably to their prospective murders.

DECISION: DEATH (OF VIRGINIA AND THE THREE RIOTERS)

In both tales the death scene contains some echoes of the Crucifixion. Virginius's purpose is the sacrifice of his daughter "For love" (225). Virginia's final words, "Dooth with youre child youre wyl, a Goddes name!" (250) are reminiscent of Jesus's words on Gethsemane: "Father, all things are possible unto thee; take away this cup from me: nevertheless, not what I will, but what thou wilt" (Mark 14:36). Claudius and Apius bear some distant resemblance to the two thieves crucified on either side of Jesus: like one of the thieves, Apius dies without salvation; the other thief goes to heaven that same day through the intercession of Jesus while Claudius goes free and into exile through the intercession of Virginius.

A similar argument exists that the scene in the Pardoner's Tale presents a blasphemous parody of the Crucifixion. According to a blasphemy current in the fourteenth century, the sacrifice of Jesus was accomplished by the other two members of the Trinity.[9] Details of the murder of the one rioter by the other two echo and parody the sacrifice of the Crucifixion. The "yongeste of hem alle" (804) goes to town to "brynge us breed and wyn" (797), an echo of the body and blood of Christ. When he returns, the others "ryve hym thurgh the sydes tweye" (828), an echo of Longinus's spear (John 19:34). The two remaining rioters plan to "pleye at dees" (834), which echoes the Roman soldiers casting lots for Jesus's seamless shirt (John 19:23–24). The metaphoric Crucifixion in the Physician's Tale—a sacrifice of love—is appropriate to the themes and purpose of that tale; the parodic Crucifixion in the Pardoner's Tale is appropriate to the Pardoner who himself parodies the divine function of pardon.

PARDON

The "goode men" (904) and the "wyves" (910) whom the Pardoner addresses at the end of his tale comprise the fictive audience in a church to whom the Pardoner has been imagining he has been preaching. With this example of his skills, he entertains the pilgrims on their way to Canterbury. The "sires" of l. 915 refers to those pilgrims, and it is to the pilgrims that the Pardoner addresses the famous lines about Christ's pardon:

> And Jhesu Crist, that is our soules leche,
> So graunte yow his pardoun to receyve,
> For that is best; I wol yow nat deceyve.
>
> (916–18)

The Pardoner's motive for saying this, especially since it follows his demonstration of how he sells fraudulent pardons to the fictional and obviously "lewed" audience he has ostensibly been addressing and also since it precedes his apparent attempt to sell the same fraudulent pardons to the Canterbury pilgrims, has been the passionate concern of many scholars since Kittredge identified the motive as "a very paroxysm of agonized sincerity" (1915, 217).[10] Regardless of the Pardoner's motive, his claims for Christ's pardon contribute to the unity of Fragment VI. The Pardoner provides a clear and unambiguous statement of Christian doctrine; the Physician shows that very same doctrine—the pardoning of human error out of love—at work in his own tale. On only one other occasion in the *Canterbury Tales* are sinners forgiven by those against whom they have sinned. In Chaucer's Tale of Melibee, Dame Prudence encourages Melibee to forgive his three foes and "lat mercy been in youre hert, / to th'effect and entente that God Almighty have mercy on yow in his laste juggement" which Melibee repeats in the same language at the end (VII 1868–71 and 1883–87). No other tale exhibits Christ's pardon in the way that the Physician's Tale does. That is one of the reasons why Chaucer joined it to the Pardoner's Tale.

At the end of the Physician's Tale, Apius is cast into prison and commits suicide; all others party to the conspiracy "were anhanged, moore and lesse." Only Claudius, condemned "for to hange upon a tree," is pardoned into exile because "Virginius, of his pitee, / . . . preyde for hym" (271–75). This is a remarkable demonstration of Christian love by a man who has just slain his daughter in part because of Claudius's behavior.[11] In the context of the Physician's Tale, the pardoning of Claudius is the ultimate act of charity, the working out of Christ's pardon in the world of men. Virginius's charity affirms God's governance of a frail and fallible world. He asserts the supremacy of love—that same love with which God loves the world and for which he grants his pardon; that same love for which he created Virginia as an example of how people ought to live. At the end Virginius assumes Virginia's *raison d'être*: he shows us how to live consonant with God's love for humanity. In doing so, he reveals toward Claudius the same pardon all Christians hope "Jhesu Crist, that is oure soules leche," will grant them on their judgment day. Ostensibly to be worthy of that pardon, certain pilgrims of our acquaintance journey toward Canterbury.

HARRY BAILLY'S GAME

After each tale in Fragment VI, Harry Bailly turns earnest into game as he plays with the narrator who has just finished speaking. The very straightforward game at the end of the Physician's Tale becomes much more complicated by the ambiguity of motives at the end of the Pardoner's Tale. The Pardoner either seriously offers his fraudulent relics to the pilgrims or (as seems more likely) he plays a game that is patently ridiculous by being excessive ("taketh pardoun as ye wende, / Al newe and fressh at every miles ende" [927–28]) and comic (lucky thing I've come among you in case one or two of you should fall off your horse and break your neck [931–40]). The Host responds either with serious outrage at having been singled out by the Pardoner as one "moost envoluped in synne" (942) or (as seems more likely) with comic excess in tune with the Pardoner's previous display of comic excess. One thing is certain: the Pardoner makes earnest out of game by taking the Host's response seriously and is driven to silence by his anger (956–57). If the Host had been serious, he tries to cover his gaffe by pretending he had been joking (958–59); or, if the Host had only been playing (as seems more likely), he identifies the joke as something not to be taken seriously when he says "I wol no lenger pleye / With thee" (958–59).[12]

Regardless of the complicated motives at the end of the Pardoner's Tale, Harry Bailly plays with the two narrators in essentially the same way. He refers to the elements of the narrators' professions with a familiarity that suggests knowledge which he actively delights in ("Seyde I nat wel?") though denies with comic modesty ("I kan nat speke in terme" [311]). For the Physician he refers to

> thyne urynals and thy jurdones,
> Thyn ypocras, and eek thy galiones,
> And every boyste ful of thy letuarie.
>
> (305–7)

He asks God to bless them and the "gentil cors" of the Physician whom he calls "a propre man" and likens to a "prelat" (304–10).[13] But with the Pardoner, who likes to think of himself performing "lyk a clerk" (391), the Host behaves differently. Instead of praising the Pardoner's manhood, he challenges it ("I wolde I hadde thy coillons in myn hand" [952]). Instead of blessing the Pardoner, he fears he will himself receive "Cristes curs" (946), and he refers with equal facility to the elements of the Pardoner's profession, his "relikes" and "seintuarie" (953) which he quite knowledgeably identifies as fraudulent—

> Thou woldest make me kisse thyn olde breech,
> And swere it were a relyk of a seint,
> Though it were with thy fundement depeint!
>
> (948–50)

—and as obscene ("shryned in an hogges toord" [955]). Although Harry Bailly occasionally plays with other narrators (the Clerk, Canon's Yeoman, Monk, and Nun's Priest), nowhere else in the *Canterbury Tales* does he play with all the narrators in the fragment in a pattern that is identical for all. Chaucer has carefully structured Harry Bailly's game in a way that contributes to the fragment's unity.

GENTILS INTERVENE

At the end of both tales, the *gentils* intervene to reestablish the orderly progression of events which had seemed momentarily to be getting out of hand. At the end of the Physician's Tale, the Host turns to the Pardoner and asks him specifically to tell "som myrthe or japes right anon." The Pardoner agrees, and the next item in the sequence of tales would seem to be the Pardoner's "ribaudye," except that "thise gentils" intervene and refocus the pilgrimage by insisting the Pardoner tell some moral thing. The Pardoner once again agrees, and the tales seem redirected upon more serious matters, the *gentils* having turned game into earnest. The same thing happens again, though in reverse, at the end of the Pardoner's Tale. The Pardoner's serious anger and Harry Bailly's serious response are not in keeping with the general tone, either religious or secular, of the Canterbury pilgrimage. For whatever reason (and many have been adduced), "al the peple lough" (961) at the conflict between the Host and the Pardoner. The Knight intervenes to turn earnest into game, to redirect the pilgrimage away from seriousness. He encourages the Pardoner to abandon his anger and to "be glad and myrie of cheere" (963), and he encourages the two adversaries in words that seem directed equally to all the other pilgrims as well, "And, as we diden, lat us laughe and pleye" (967).

II. Theme

We have seen how the banter between Host and Clerk in the Prologue to the Clerk's Tale introduces the major themes of Fragment IV. Similarly, the Physician's Tale (lacking a prologue) announces at the very beginning the major themes and the images which will develop the themes. Several themes unify Fragment VI, but the two most important are fraud and governance.

FRAUD

At the beginning of the Physician's Tale, Nature speaks:

> Lo! I, Nature,
> Thus kan I forme and peynte a creature,
> Whan that me list; who can me countrefete?
> Pigmalion noght, though he ay forge and bete,
> Or grave, or peynte; for I dar wel seyn,
> Apelles, Zanzis, sholde werche in veyn
> Outher to grave, or peynte, or forge, or bete,
> If they presumed me to countrefete.
>
> (11–18)

The repetition of "countrefete" (i.e., imitate) within six lines and the focus on other action verbs that connote copying or imitating—"forge," "bete," "grave" (i.e., engrave), and "peynte"—announce the theme of fraud or speciousness that both the Physician's Tale and the Pardoner's Tale will develop.

Chaucer defines Virginia by the absence of fraud. Her inner virtue and her outer beauty agree; she is "chast" (43) in body and in spirit. The appropriate superlatives describe her humility, abstinence, patience, bearing, discretion, and so on. Since she is genuine and honest, she has no need, we are told, to counterfeit language in order to seem other than what she truly is (51–54). Formed by Nature for the love of God, she has no need of art or fraud to remain God's perfect creation. The role of perfect creatures, devoted to God, in an imperfect world is to avoid corruption. In a world ruled by a corrupt judge and his corruptible minions, whose fraud, deceit, and moral counterfeiting focus upon the destruction of virtue, Virginia actively pursues virtue. Ironically, she does so by fraud. She avoids indecent company: "And of her owene vertu, unconstreyned, / She hath ful ofte tyme syk hire feyned" (61–62)—the appropriate metaphor for world-weariness. But that she should feign at all suggests her mastery of the world, her ability to use fraudulent but innocent means to achieve a good end (the preservation of virtue). In respect to fraud, Virginia is the obverse of Apius and the Pardoner, who use fraudulent means to a wicked end, and the thematic corollary of the reformed sinners among the governesses who must feign to teach virtue.

Once we see Virginia's goodness, Apius comes as no surprise.

His first action is lust, a sin of the eyes, which provides the single, clear, unambiguous motive for all his subsequent action. The "feend" who immediately rushes into his heart augments that lust by showing Apius how it can be satisfied through fraud or "slyghte" (131). Whether this fiend, like the one in the Pardoner's Tale, works the will of God or not (847–48) is secondary to the fact that the fiend transforms Apius from a powerful judge without piety into a malevolent force bent wholly to the perversion of God and Nature through their creature. Apius's lust inverts counterfeiting: he intends to transmute someone good and pure into someone base.[14]

Apius authors various kinds of hypocrisy and fraud. The suborning of Claudius is only the most noticeable. Twice Claudius performs an action (which we as audience know to be his actual desire) with the clause "if that it be youre wille" (165 and 189). No one is fooled by it—surely not Apius who designed it, nor Claudius who performs it, nor Virginius against whom it is directed, nor the populace in the consistory who witness it. The fraudulent and falsely hypothetical "if that it be youre wille" defines the relationship between governor and governed in its most pernicious form. We have seen this same relationship defined more honestly in Nature's statement "My lord and I been ful of oon accord" (25), and we are to see the ideal human approximation of this relationship when Virginia says "Dooth with youre child youre wyl, a Goddes name" (250).

Claudius's hypocrisy extends beyond his demeanor into his language. Contrary to popular scholarly opinion, the Physician's Tale is one of Chaucer's more carefully crafted poems. It contains little padding and few tags. It is extraordinary, therefore, to find a simple claim—"a knyght ... holdeth ... my servant"—expanded to eight lines of quasi-legalistic phrasing.

> To yow, my lord, sire Apius so deere,
> Sheweth your povre servant Claudius
> How that a knyght, called Virginius,
> Agayns the lawe, agayn al equitee,
> Holdeth, expres agayn the wyl of me,
> My servant, which that is my thral by right,
> Which fro myn hous was stole upon a nyght,
> Whil that she was ful yong.
>
> (178–85)

The passage actually represents *amplificatio* in the service of obfuscation and emphasizes that the hypocrisy of Claudius and

Apius, like that of the Pardoner, is one of word as well as action. The judge's fraud includes more than the manipulation of Claudius. He counterfeits when he adheres to the form but not the substance of justice. Apius claims he cannot give a definitive sentence until Virginius appears in court, but Virginius's appearance is pointless since he is not allowed to speak in his own defense. Ironically, Apius's hasty judgment denies the semblance of fair trial he himself has attempted to create.

The theme of fraud in the form of counterfeiting, misrepresentation, duplicity, and pretense also occupies a major place in the Pardoner's Tale. The two rioters who remain with the gold intend to murder the third by counterfeiting a game ("Arys as though thou woldest with hym pleye" [827 and 829]). The third rioter gains the poison by misrepresenting the purpose for which he needs it. Indeed, even in the link between the tales, Harry Bailly plays with the Physician by pretending to command medical terms. He protests his inability to "speke in terme" and yet is particularly proud of having done so ("Seyde I nat wel?" [311]). As we know from his apparent creation of the word "galiones" (306) and his mispronunciation of *cardiacle* as "cardynacle" (313), he pretends to greater knowledge than he actually possesses.[15]

The Pardoner himself is the most fraudulent creature of all, a "self-confessed purveyor of deceptions."[16] His duplicity, from his "hauteyn speche" (330), his pretense to Latin, his phony patents, warrants, and relics, his posture "lyk a clerk" (391), his misrepresentation of "entente" (403–4, 432–33), his hypocrisy (421–22), and his refusal to "countrefete" (447) any of the apostles, are all too well-known to require explication. His fraud appears all the more objectionable contrasted with the "prototype of integrity" (Amoils 1974, 18) Chaucer carefully creates in the Physician's Tale with Virginia's portrait and Nature's declaration of authenticity. One point, however, does deserve comment. I agree with those scholars who believe that at the end of his tale the Pardoner only pretends to offer his "relikes and pardoun" (920) to the Canterbury pilgrims. He is making a joke when he asks the pilgrims to "taketh pardoun as ye wende, / Al newe and fressh at every miles ende" (927–28), and he expects the pilgrims to be amused by his ridiculous and comic pretense. Chaucer's irony intensifies when he shows the literal-minded Host responding to the pretense as if it were serious. Whether the Host himself is serious or (as seems more likely) only playing at this point is irrelevant, since the effect is precisely the same: he publicly pierces the Pardoner's ultimate pretense to normalcy with his lewd joke about the Pardoner's "coillons" (952). The master counterfeiter has had his most transparently counterfeit performance ironically accepted as true and valid. When the truth beneath the fraud is revealed, the Pardoner's only response, like that of Iago in the last scene of *Othello*, is silence.

GOVERNANCE

In Fragment VI alone of all the fragments in the *Canterbury Tales*, Chaucer defines all the major characters in both tales in terms of the governor-governed relationship. He begins in the Physician's Tale by describing increasingly inclusive levels of governance—in the individual, in the family, in the body politic, and in the cosmos—before he begins the main action of the tale. Chaucer defines governance at the cosmic level as the relationship between God and Nature and then again between Nature and sublunary creation. At the national level, Apius, as the governor of "that regioun" (122), controls the full spectrum of society and dictates the fortunes both of the churl, Claudius, and of the knight, Virginius. Virginius's control at the level of the family is equally absolute, but Chaucer also discusses the familial aspect of the theme in terms of the relationship between governesses and children. Virginia most clearly represents the theme at the level of the individual.

The poem had begun with the familial relationship—Virginius, his wife and daughter. Nature then intervenes to celebrate Virginia's uniqueness and introduces two more governor-governed relationships—those between Nature and God and Nature and creation. The relationship between God and Nature is perfect. Nature is the "vicaire general" of God. Although endowed with some degree of freedom to form and paint earthly creatures "Right as me list" and to hold everything "in my cure" (22), Nature is involved in creation for the greater glory of God. As Nature says of Virginia, "I made hire to the worshipe of my lord" (26). Nature defines the ideal relationship between governor and governed: "My lord and I been ful of oon accord" (25). The same claim can be made of the other governor-governed relationships, but it takes on ironic proportions both when applied to Claudius and Apius, where the "oon accord" is evil, and when applied to Virginia and Virginius, where the "oon accord" leads to martyrdom.

Most students of the poem find the Physician's address to

governesses and then parents an inappropriate digression,[17] but Chaucer has carefully crafted the passage, which does not appear in his sources, to reflect the tale's and the fragment's concern for fraud and honesty in governors. Only two kinds of people may serve best as the parents' "vicaire general" in the governance of children: those who have kept their honesty and those who have sinned and reformed. Throughout the passage the concern for counterfeit and fraud among governors appears in the tension between those who govern well and those who betray innocence. The lines which encourage governesses to behave virtuously are directed primarily to those who have known the "olde daunce" (79) and have reformed. The Physician recognizes here a special tension between what governesses are capable of doing and what they ought to do. They must govern themselves well. They must constantly be on guard so that they "unto no vice assente" (87), and they must camouflage those aspects of character they have had to reform. To them especially the Physician addresses his famous lines on traitors: "Of alle tresons sovereyn pestilence / Is whan a wight bitrayseth innocence" (91–92).

Virginia epitomizes the individual who governs herself well. Nonetheless, she has governors enough: the mother who escorts her to the temple, the father who slays her, the judge who rules her, and finally the God who loves her. But Virginia "neded no maistresse" (106) because she is the one person in the tale actively seeking a direct relationship to God. In applying to God, she overleaps the governance of family and judge. In behaving according to her relationship to God, she is the quintessentially moral person in the tale. Consequently, she governs her own life. Virginia adheres to her father's wishes at the end of the tale not because he governs or rules her, but because she willingly commits herself to God through him. "Blissed be God that I shal dye a mayde!" she says. "Dooth with youre child youre wyl, a Goddes name" (248–50). It is the active and willing sacrifice of a saint who delivers her body to the temporal arm.

By design and by contrast with the multiple governing forces in the Physician's Tale, the narrator and characters of the Pardoner's Tale are governed almost exclusively by their appetites. The very first words the Pardoner speaks in the link articulate this development in the theme of governance. Before he tells a tale, the Pardoner insists that "heere at this alestake / I wol bothe drynke and eten of a cake" (321–22). He is the only Canterbury pilgrim whom Chaucer shows so completely governed by his appetites that he must stop for food and drink. Unlike Virginia and her commitment to virtue and to temperance, the Pardoner defines his own *raison d'être* as that of one who "wol drynke licour of the vyne, / And have a joly wenche in every toun" (452–53). The domination of his spirit by his flesh and his enslavement to appetite infect his intellectual life as well, indicated by the very fact of his profession and by the topic he chooses to preach in order to succeed in that profession. He twice proclaims his "theme is alwey oon, and evere was" (333 and 425); he twice proclaims what that theme is (334 and 426); and he twice proclaims "I preche of no thyng but for coveityse" (424 and 433). He admits to being guilty of the sin of avarice (428–29) and to being "a ful vicious man" (459). His viciousness takes the form only of acquisitiveness: he gathers "moneie, wolle, chese, and whete" (448) and carelessly disregards the effect that satisfying his appetite might have upon "the povereste page" (449) or "the povereste wydwe" even though "hir children sterve for famyne" (450–51).

The three rioters, of course, share the Pardoner's commitment to satisfying their fleshly appetites. Conceived and defined as exempla of the sins central to the Pardoner's sermon, they have little dramatic existence beyond exhibiting their governing sins of drunkenness, gambling, and swearing. Their homicidal avarice is the logical intensification of the Pardoner's appetite for acquisitiveness and reveals their own bondage to their appetites. They are all "so glad" when they discover the gold that they sit down immediately to enjoy visual possession of "the floryns . . . so faire and brighte" (773–74). The "worste of hem" whose "wit is greet" uses that wit to determine how their own appetites can best be satisfied so that they can live their lives "In myrthe and joliftee" (776–80). Though found treasure belongs to the king, he insists twice that "al this gold is oures" (786 and 779).[18] He designs the plan that will allow them to avoid the accusation "that we were theves stronge," to escape from death by hanging, and to carry the gold home so they can live "in heigh felicitee" (787–90). He proposes how they shall be provisioned. The "breed and wyn" (797), which in the Christian context sustain the soul, appear in this context as the means to satisfy their bodily appetites. The youngest rioter, governed like the others by the desire to possess, employs his wit to win the gold for himself alone. He fabricates a story about "vermyn that destroyed hym by nyght" (858) in order to convince the apothecary to sell him poison, and he convinces another man to loan him "large botelles thre" (871). Such cleverness in the service of such greed wins him only death.

Death governs the Pardoner's Tale. The governing roles occupied by God, Nature, Apius, Virginius, parents, and governesses in the Physician's Tale are occupied by Death in the Pardoner's Tale. Dozens of references to Death appear in both tales.[19] Death provides the corpse with which the Pardoner's Tale begins: it "hath a thousand slayn" and "al the peple sleeth"; it lives nearby "withinne a greet village"; and it hovers over the landscape as "this pestilence" (676–87). Death energizes the three rioters: the search to slay Death provides the primary action of the tale, and the triumph of Death over the rioters represents the orthodox Christian judgment on the wages of sin.

Only one moment in the history of the three rioters denies the primacy of Death. The Old Man's benediction in greeting the three rioters ("Now, lordes, God yow see" [715]), and his double benediction when attempting to leave them ("God be with yow" [748] and "God save yow" [766]) affirm God's primacy. The Old Man acknowledges the supremacy of God in two ways: first, the duration of his life is absolutely in God's governance since he must "han myn age stille, / As longe tyme as it is Goddes wille" (725–26); and then as long as it is God's will, he is immune from Death who "wol nat han my lyf" (727) even though Death kills "Bothe man and womman, child, and hyne, and page" (688) elsewhere in the world of the story. The Old Man ironically accomplishes what the three rioters are eager to accomplish and fail to do: triumph over Death. The Old Man is the only character in the Pardoner's Tale, including the Pardoner himself, who takes God's governance of the world as seriously as Virginia does in the Physician's Tale. Since he parallels Virginia in this respect, he contributes to the unity of the fragment.

Although only in this fragment are two principal characters killed by knives, curiously much more is made of hanging. The three rioters want to bring the treasure home by night in order to avoid being hanged as thieves (789–90). Claudius is condemned "for to hange upon a tree" (271); others in the conspiracy "were anhanged" (275). Perhaps these references are one with the oak tree under which the three rioters find gold and death. Or perhaps they are the secular opposition to the religious tree upon which Christ died. Though the cross is not referred to as the tree in this fragment, there are many clear references to the crucifixion of Christ who "for us dyde" (658) or "boght us with his blood agayn" (501) or "with his precious herte-blood thee boghte" (902), all of which suggest Christ's sacrifice and imply "Cristes croys" (532), the tree upon which Christ was "anhanged" and suffered death for the salvation of mankind. Governed by their appetites which can only lead to death, the three rioters and the Pardoner have abrogated salvation; governed by her devotion to God, Virginia has earned it.

3
Fragment VIII (Group G): The Second Nun's Tale and the Canon's Yeoman's Tale

>Trouthe is a thyng that I wol evere kepe
>Unto that day in which that I shal crepe
>Into my grave, and ellis God forbede.
>
>(1044–46)

We generally agree about the dating of the two tales which compose Fragment VIII.[1] The Second Nun's Tale is held to have been composed early in Chaucer's career before he began active work on the *Canterbury Tales*. The speaker's reference to herself as an "unworthy sone of Eve" (62) suggests a speaker other than the Second Nun even though the line recalls a line from the antiphon to Mary, *Salve Regina* ("Ad te clamamus exules filii Evae"), which the Nun sang every day.[2] The formality of the Prologue and perhaps that of the stanza form in the Tale itself suggest composition for a public occasion more formal than simply inclusion in the *Canterbury Tales*. And most significantly, because Chaucer refers to "the lyf . . . . of Seynt Cecile" in the Prologue to *The Legend of Good Women* (426), a poem generally assigned to 1385–86, the Second Nun's Tale is said to antedate the *Canterbury Tales*. On the other hand, the Canon's Yeoman's Prologue and the first part of his Tale seem to have been composed well after Chaucer was seriously at work on the *Canterbury Tales*. Nonetheless, the references to "worshipful chanons religious" (992) and the lines that follow (to 1011) at the beginning of part two, suggest to some that Chaucer had a different audience in mind. If so, then he wrote part two of the poem outside the framework of the *Canterbury Tales* and subsequently worked it into the *Canterbury Tales* by composing the Prologue and first part of the Tale.

The important question, however, is not whether one or both of the tales, in whole or in part, were composed before or after Chaucer began to work on the *Canterbury Tales*, nor why he decided to assign one to the Second Nun and to create a new character, the Canon's Yeoman, to narrate the other. The more important question, to my mind, is why did Chaucer decide to join just these tales together? Since he had the Second Nun's Tale already at hand, he could have joined it to other tales he also had at hand or in the planning stage. He could have joined it to the Man of Law's Tale or to the Clerk's Tale to make a fragment of saintly women. He could have joined it to the Wife of Bath's Prologue and Tale to show by contrast the disparate potentialities of women.

The same kinds of question arise with the Canon's Yeoman's Tale. Whether he had written the Canon's Yeoman's Tale, part two, before or after he had begun to work on the *Canterbury Tales*, why did he decide to write the Canon's Yeoman's Prologue and the first part of the Canon's Yeoman's Tale in order to join the Canon's Yeoman's Tale, part two, to the Second Nun's Tale? He could have joined it to other tales already written or planned (the Friar's and Summoner's Tales, for example, to make a fragment of tricksters); he could have written other tales to go with it. But instead of these more obvious and seemingly more sensible choices, he went to quite a good deal of trouble—inventing the Canon and his Yeoman, inventing a reason for them to join the pilgrimage, inventing a reason for the Canon to leave, writing 252 lines of poetry—just to join the Canon's Yeoman's Tale, part two, to the Second Nun's Tale. What similarities or contrasts link these two tales? What structural patterns and thematic parallels did he see that led him to just this conjunction? What aesthetic dimension could this seemingly disparate pair of tales contribute to the *Canterbury Tales* as a whole?

These questions are not new. Over the years scholars and students of Chaucer have delighted in finding similarities between the two tales. We have concentrated upon the alchemical details that appear in both tales: the alchemical symbols that attend Cecile's marriage, for example; or the canon's crucible and Cecile's bath; or the image of "mortal mannes power" as nothing more than "a bladdre ful of wynd" (438–39) and the active attendance of the Canon's Yeoman to the Canon's fire as a metaphor for the futility of alchemical research; or the fire prepared for Urban, feared by Tiburce, and experienced by Cecile. References to gold and to "philosophres" and to "ocular proof"[3] (of angels, crowns, stone idols, silver) appear in both tales. And we have concentrated, more importantly, upon theme. Much has been made of vision and blindness (both Almache's and the priest's), of Cecile's "grete light / Of sapience" (100–1), her wisdom or spiritual sight, and the spiritual blindness, with its attendant darkness, of the others. Images of vision and verbs of perception abound in both tales as do images of darkness or blindness and, especially in the Canon's Yeoman's Prologue and Tale, trickery designed to deceive the eye. Constant reference to the visible and the invisible, to the corporeal and the spiritual, to the false and the true, to the magical and the miraculous, to being free and being ensnared, to the work of the Devil and the work of God, to the work of an alchemist (with its failure and loss) and the business of a saint (with its success and increase) infuse both tales, link them together, and unify the fragment. Others of us have argued for a more philosophical linkage in terms of unifying contraries such as the doctrines of Charity and Cupidity or of reason and revelation. And others still have suggested unity in terms of a contrast of textures: Chaucer wanted to set some hard details of life in the real world of modern London against the disembodied details of a saint's life in ancient Italy.

Much has been written to establish the basic lines of thematic coherence that join the tales in Fragment VIII. The similarities in structure between the two tales, however, have gone almost completely unrecorded.

I. Structure

Glending Olson is the only scholar who has directly addressed the problem of structure in the fragment. He argues, quite convincingly, that the basic structure of Dante's *Purgatorio* "is to present first examples of a virtue, then a meeting with those guilty of the opposite vice, then examples of the vice" and that the organization of Fragment VIII "is structurally the same" except that "Chaucer has substituted full-length narratives for the brief references to stories that appear in Dante" (1982, 228). While Professor Olson accurately describes the skeletal structure of the fragment as a whole in these general terms, a closer examination of the parallel development in the two tales shows a different kind of structural organization. The same items appearing in the same order reveal the way the tales interpenetrate and provide the basis for the coherent architecture of Fragment VIII.

Second Nun	Canon's Yeoman
"feithful bisynesse" (24)	sweaty activity
Invocation: to Mary	Invocation: to Canon's Yeoman
Interpretation: Cecile	Explanation: Alchemy
Tale	Tale
three conversions:	three conversions:
Valerian	"bechen cole" (1160)
Tiburce	"holwe stikke" (1265)
Maximus (tormentors and ministers)	"coper teyne" (1324)
Almache: tests idol	priest: tests silver
Final Preaching: Second Nun	Final Preaching: Canon's Yeoman

Since contrast rather than similarity dominates structure as well as theme in Fragment VIII, many items in the parallel structural pattern oppose rather than duplicate each other. The beginnings of the two tales provide a case in point. The Second Nun translates the "lif and passioun" (26) of St. Cecile in order to engage in "leveful bisynesse" and "feithful bisynesse" and so avoid "slogardye" and "slouthe" which can place her soul in danger. The Canon's Yeoman's Prologue, however, begins with frantic riding "lik as he were wood," "more than trot or paas" for the remarkable distance of "miles three" (561–76). Horses are flecked with foam[4] and the Canon himself is drenched with sweat and breathless, as the very rhythm of his greeting to the pilgrims indicates: "'God save,' quod he, 'this joly compaignye! / Faste have I pricked,' quod he, 'for youre sake'" (583–84). But while the Second Nun, like Cecile herself, achieves her aim and triumphs over idleness and sloth, the Canon, for all his noise and sweat, fails to join the pilgrims. He had come for "desport" and for "daliaunce" (592), but "He fledde awey for verray sorwe and shame" (702).[5] He fails in this as he fails in alchemy. Unlike St. Cecile, all his frenetic activity and sweaty expense of energy in this world are vain.

INVOCATION

Details of the introductions to both tales echo one another and suggest that Chaucer designed the two prologues to be more like each other than like any other prologues in the *Canterbury Tales*. They belong together. Mary and the Canon, for example, are

Fragment VIII

conceived as contrasting opposites. Mary is "humble, and heigh over every creature, / . . . [she] nobledest . . . oure nature" (39–40); the Canon is "a passyng man" (614). Mary is a "meeke and blisful faire mayde" (57); the Canon is "a man of heigh discrecioun" (613) and "over-greet a wit" (648). To know Mary is to know a "welle of mercy, synful soules cure" (37); to know the Canon "wolde be for youre prow" (609). The Canon, we are told, can turn the Canterbury road "up-so-doun, / And pave it al of silver and of gold" (625–26); Mary has only "wan thurgh hire merite / The eterneel lyf and of the feend victorie" (33–34). Through Mary, God clothes his Son in "blood and flessh": "Withinne the cloistre blisful of thy sydis / [God] Took mannes shap" (41–44); the Canon is "sluttissh" (636). Mary provides the "wit and space" (65) that allow the Second Nun to "be quit from thennes that most derk is" (66); the Canon lurks "in hernes and in lanes blynde" (658) where robbers and thieves have their fearful secret residences. All in all, Mary is successful, the Canon is a failure.

Chaucer carefully shapes the two narrators to convey opposing attitudes with regard to experience and authority. The Second Nun speaks from authority. She cites Bernard of Clairvaux and Jacobus de Voragine. She acknowledges that she has both "the wordes and sentence / Of hym that at the seintes reverence / The storie wroot" (81–83) and that her only function in translating the glorious life and passion of St. Cecile is to "folwen hire legende" (83). Nonetheless, she asks Mary for help and asks her audience to forgive her for not expressing herself "subtilly" and to "amende" (79–84) what is amiss in her work. The Yeoman, on the other hand, speaks only from his own experience ("Al that I kan" [704], "Swich thyng as that I knowe" [719]).[6] He brags of future success and acknowledges constant failure. He prays to God that his own "wit myghte suffise / To tellen al that longeth to that art" (715–16). The Second Nun had indicated how the devil catches men "in his trappe" (11); the Yeoman admits how he is ensnared in alchemy and can never abandon it. The Yeoman's experience with the Canon and with alchemy provides material for "game" (703); the Second Nun's work of translating authority expresses her "feith" (64).

Read by themselves, the Second Nun's Tale affirms the virtues of St. Cecile, and the Canon's Yeoman's Tale belittles alchemical practice and speculation. But each read in the context of the other—precisely what Chaucer established by linking the two tales in Fragment VIII—the Second Nun's Tale affirms the primacy and success that attends adherence to the divine will while the Canon's Yeoman's Tale denigrates the vanity of worldly success through the metaphor of striving for gold.

INTERPRETATION AND EXPLANATION

With Chaucer's usual care in ordering the details of structure in parallel patterns, the Yeoman explains alchemy in a passage that parallels the Second Nun's explanation of Cecile's name. The Yeoman's explanation comes after a brief self-portrait (720–49); Cecile's parallel portrait begins her tale (120–40). From her acknowledged authority, the *Legenda Aurea* of Jacobus de Voragine, the Second Nun provides five separate possible interpretations of the name Cecile. These are clear and straightforward and need no longer concern us.[7]

There are no simple, clear-cut divisions of the Yeoman's explanation as there are of the Second Nun's *Interpretacio*, no doubt because the topic is secret and murky and does not easily lend itself to casual explication. Moreover, the character of the Yeoman—his energy and enthusiasm, his lack of discipline, or his inability to concentrate on a single idea and develop it carefully—together with his freedom from the Canon's restraint and his speaking from his own experience rather than from the authority of a written text all conspire to complicate his explanation of alchemy.[8] Nonetheless, Chaucer structures the four parts of the Yeoman's alchemical explanation in similar ways: each part has a topic however fuzzily announced; each part includes a list; and, since the Yeoman intends to admonish others and to hold himself up as an example not to be followed, each part ends with a warning of failure or loss.

1) The Yeoman starts with "Oure termes [that] been so clergial and so queynte"; then he lists the "thynges whiche that we werche upon," "poudres" and such; then he mentions apparatus like "pot and glasses"; and he concludes with the warning of failure: "we kan nat conclude," "Noght helpeth us, oure labour is in veyn," "no thyng us availle," and so on (752–83).
2) The second part in his explanation includes "ful many another thyng / That is unto oure craft apertenyng" which he lists "as they come to mynde" (784–88). After again listing various materials and apparatus, he adds a metaphysical dimension in "The foure spirites and the bodies sevene" (820), before concluding with the warning of failure: "He shal no good han," "He lese shal," "Al is in veyn," "it wol nat bee," "they faillen bothe two" (831–51).

Fragment VIII

3) The third part begins with an erratic listing of the "names" of material that he "forgat" to include earlier. Although he admits to having "yow toold ynowe / To reyse a feend" (Cecile, of course, told Valerian enough to raise an angel), he remembers something else he forgot and refers to "the philosophres stoon, / Elixer clept," which, since it "wol nat come us to," leads him to conclude with the warning of failure: the inevitable destruction of "good hope" and expectation ("futur temps"), and the loss of "muchel good" and "al that evere they hadde" (852–76).
4) The fourth part of the alchemical explanation starts out as a description of the Canon demonstrating an experiment before friends, but "The pot tobreketh" (907). It concludes with a list of diverse explanations for the failure of the experiment given by the Canon, the Yeoman, and the alchemical friends.

Finally, the Yeoman observes that it makes no difference why this particular experiment failed. They all fail: "we concluden everemoore amys. / We faille of that which that we wolden have" (957–58). He refers to alchemists as raving madmen and concludes his explanation of alchemy with a series of maxims on the confusion that attends the way things appear and the way things actually are (962–69). Chaucer contrasts the mad confusion and messiness of the Canon and the Yeoman's devotion to "That slidynge science" (732) and that "elvysshe craft" (751) with the clarity and neatness of the Second Nun's devotion to the "cleernesse hool of sapience, / And sondry werkes, brighte of excellence," that men may see in Cecile as easily as they see the sun and moon and stars in the sky (107–12).

Once again, by developing the Canon's Yeoman's Tale in the context of the Second Nun's Tale, Chaucer modifies our understanding. Read by itself, the Yeoman's explanation of alchemy is a chaotic, mind-numbing recitation which reveals his own confusion or his desire to obfuscate or both. However, by setting it against the clarity of the Second Nun's explication of St. Cecile's name, Chaucer affirms the validity of metaphysical speculation over manipulation of the physical world.

THE TALES

In both the narratives spoken by the Second Nun and the Canon's Yeoman, Chaucer places the tale itself after the interpretation/explanation and before the final lesson. These tales share the same internal organization: they both describe three attempts at conversion—spiritual conversion in the Second Nun's Tale and physical conversion in the Canon's Yeoman's Tale—and they both end with a discussion and a test. No other of the Canterbury tales shares this pattern. In the Second Nun's Tale, the first two conversions, those of Valerian and Tiburce, are connected because the two men are brothers. In the Canon's Yeoman's Tale, the first two conversions, those of the beech coal and the hollow stick, are connected because the two tricks are variants of a single trick: both coal and stick are hollow, both are filled with silver filings and stopped with wax, and both are burned above the crucible into which they release the silver. The third conversion—that of Maximus, the tormentors, and Almache's ministers in one tale, and that of the copper in the other—evolve out of the previous conversions. In the Second Nun's Tale, for example, Valerian and Tiburce are converted by Cecile but educated and christened by Urban and (Valerian at least) by the old man.[9] Maximus and the tormentors, on the other hand, are not converted directly by Cecile; they are converted by Valerian and Tiburce, and they are christened by priests who come with Cecile (380). Similarly, in the Canon's Yeoman's Tale, the success of the copper conversion does not depend directly upon the melting of silver filings as in the first two conversions but upon a substitution prepared for by some sleight of hand accomplished during the earlier beech-coal conversion.

Chaucer designed the final discussion scenes, involving Almache and the priest, to be alike in both tales. The testing of the stone idol and of the silver ingots is only the most obvious similarity. Almache's idol is truly stone, and he mistakenly believes it God; the priest's silver is truly silver, and he mistakenly believes the process good by which he received it. Almache is duped by what is false (the stone idol is not God); the priest is duped by what is true (the silver is actually silver). Both are "byjaped and bigiled" (1385). What they understand as success is actually failure. Almache's order to "Brenne hire right in a bath of flambes rede" (515) does not accomplish her death since "She sat al coold, and feelede no wo" (521). The executioner who inflicts the ultimately fatal wounds helps release the miracle both of her continuing to preach for three more days and so extend the faith and also of her final elevation to heaven as a martyr. Just so, the priest who thinks he has bought a powder and a recipe to "mortifye" (1126) quicksilver "And make it as good silver and as fyn" (1128) has actually bought something that "wolde nat be" (1384).

Other parallels link the scenes and contribute to the unity of the fragment. Cecile's words to Almache, "Ther lakketh no thyng to thyne outter yen / That thou n'art blynd" (498–99), apply with equal appropriateness to the priest since he is as blind to what is true in the physical world as Almache is blind to what is true in the spiritual world. Almache resists every attempt to reach an accommodation with Cecile in contrast to the priest who is eager to reach an accommodation with the canon for the secret. The priest is "sotted" (1341); Almache is foolish ("O nyce creature!" [493]). The priest is "gladder" (1341) than a bird in the morning; Almache "weex wroth" (513). The canon has worked "To brynge folk to hir destruccioun" (1387) which in the priest's case means the loss of "fourty pound" (1361); Cecile, of course, works to bring folk to salvation and succeeds with all except Almache whose refusal means the loss of his immortal soul.

One final irony deserves mention. Cecile is a saint; the canon is a crook.[10] Cecile offers what is true in a Christian context; the canon offers what is false in a Christian context (1476–78). Almache rejects Cecile's truth as false; the priest accepts the canon's falsity as true. These parallel contrasts and similarities reveal Chaucer's skill in establishing lines of coherence between the two disparate tales that comprise the fragment.

FINAL PREACHING

Both narrators end their tales by returning to the concern which motivated them to tell a tale in the first place. For the Second Nun, that is "feithful bisynesse" (24)—no longer for her the propagation of the faith as it was for St. Cecile, but rather the presentation of Cecile as a Christian saint worthy of emulation. To be sure, the tale ends with Cecile's preaching for three days and continuing "the feith to teche" (538), but what is more to the Second Nun's point is the example of Christian living that St. Cecile provides for the Nun's audience. On her deathbed, Cecile generously "yaf her moebles and hir thyng" (540) to "The Cristen folk, which that aboute hire were" (535), commended them all to Pope Urban (perhaps for the continuation of their Christian education [538–39]), and finally bequeathed "myn hous perpetuelly" (546) to serve as a church "In which, into this day, in noble wyse, / Men doon to Crist and to his seinte servyse" (552–53). The Second Nun presents in St. Cecile an example for every Christian soul to follow.[11]

The Canon's Yeoman presents in himself an example for every Christian soul to avoid. In the last ninety-four lines of his Tale, the Canon's Yeoman reiterates, often more than once, every major admonitory point of his Prologue, explanation of alchemy, and Tale: that the alchemical concern for "multiplying" (1391) blinds people; that the language of alchemical discourse is misty; that no one can ever learn the craft which always ends in failure; that joy turns into sorrow; that money is squandered; that it is better to abandon the attempt before one loses everything and is ultimately blinded to the impossibility of ever succeeding. Only at the very end does the Canon's Yeoman add the weight of authority—Arnold of the Newe Toun and Plato—to the validity of his own experience in affirming that the "secree of the secretes" (1447) cannot possibly be discovered and that anyone who attempts to do so "maketh God his adversarie . . . [and] never shal he thryve" (1476–78). Since God was Cecile's ally and the reason for her success, Chaucer continues the pattern of contrasting items to the very end of the fragment.

Moreover, to the extent that the Second Nun's Tale articulates an ideal[12] and the Canon's Yeoman's Tale articulates the deterioration or opposite of that ideal, Fragment VIII describes the contrastive pattern of degeneration and decay that Chaucer will use to build other fragments of the *Canterbury Tales*.

II. Theme

In the fragments we have discussed heretofore, Chaucer presents the parallels in theme and structure by balancing similarities and contrasts, sometimes emphasizing one over the other. In this fragment, contrast predominates. Chaucer carefully crafts the tales to parallel each other, but he has designed them to emphasize opposition rather than congruence.

CONVERSION

One of the more obvious contrasts that links the Second Nun's Tale with that of the Canon's Yeoman is the contrast between the spiritual and the physical. Both the Canon in the Prologue and the first part of the Tale and the canon in the second part work exclusively with the physical; Cecile's commitment is to the spiritual. But, unlike the Physician and the Pardoner, Cecile and the Canon are not concerned with ministering to their respective interests; they are concerned with changing and multiplying them.[13] The Canon, as alchemist, wants to convert base metal into gold and never doubts "That of a pound we koude make tweye" (677); Cecile, as saint, wants to convert base pagans into Christians "And nevere cessed hem the feith to teche" (538).

Chaucer develops the theme of conversion with the sophisticated distinction between conversions that are fraudulent and those that are genuine. The Canon in the Prologue and part one engages in a genuine though unsuccessful attempt at conversion while the occupation of the canon in part two is fraudulent. But the theme of conversion in the Canon's Yeoman's Tale need not concern us here except to point out that the only successful transformation occurs, strangely enough, in the Yeoman himself. Chaucer dramatizes it in the Yeoman's behavior and pictorializes it in the Yeoman's clothing (as we shall see) and in his complexion ("And wher my colour was bothe fressh and reed, / Now is it wan and of a leden hewe" [727–28]). The Yeoman appears in the Prologue first as the dutiful servant who warns his lord when the pilgrims ride because he knows the Canon "loveth daliaunce" (592) and is eager to join them. He praises his lord who knows a great deal about "murthe and . . . jolitee," who can take upon himself "many a greet emprise," and who knows how to turn the Canterbury road "up-so-doun, / And pave it al of silver and of gold" (600–26). Nonetheless, as he speaks, the Yeoman admits the fraudulence of such puffery: "we blondren evere," "faille of oure desir," and always "lakken oure conclusioun" (670–72). Although he helps the Canon to "doon illusioun" (673), he knows that regardless of what people believe, "Yet is it fals" (678). Abandoned by the Canon, the Yeoman changes from a person eager to preserve his lord's secrets ("But al his craft ye may nat wite at me" [621]) to one eager to reveal them ("Al that I kan anon now wol I telle" [704]). From an accomplice-deceiver, the Yeoman becomes a truth-teller: "Swich thyng as that I knowe, I wol declare" (719). The tale he tells bespeaks the genuineness of his conversion.

The Second Nun dramatizes the same disparity between genuine and fraudulent conversion. The conversions to Christianity are all genuine as the ultimate martyrdom of the converts testifies. Valerian converts not only from pagan to Christian but also, as Urban notes, from "fiers leoun" to one who is "As meke as evere was any lomb" (198–99). Tiburce is "chaunged . . . al in another kynde" (252) by smelling the invisible crowns of rose and lily. Though more reluctant than Valerian, Tiburce too is ultimately and permanently converted to "Goddes knyght" (353). Maximus, the tormentors, and Almache's ministers are all separated from "The false feith" (378) and converted, some by Valerian and Tiburce and others by Cecile (414). Maximus himself "converted many a wight" (404). The attempt at fraudulent conversion in the Second Nun's Tale occurs when Almache pressures the Christians to "reneye" (458–59) their faith. These attempts to convert the true to the false in the spiritual domain fail, as do all the attempts in the physical domain, both genuine and fraudulent, in the Canon's Yeoman's Tale. In Fragment VIII, only genuine spiritual conversions succeed.

CLOTHES

Chaucer articulates one aspect of the theme of alchemical conversion, of finding the gold among the dross, in terms of clothes.[14] In the Prologue to the Second Nun's Tale, he presents the central mystery of Christianity, God become man, as the act of clothing the divine in flesh and blood. Mary so ennobled the nature of humanity that God did not disdain "His Sone in blood and flessh to clothe and wynde" (42). Chaucer repeats the idea of something precious, something gold or divine, hidden beneath or contained within something mundane and transitory when he describes Cecile's clothes. But Cecile turns worldly values "up-so-doun" and affirms Christian values: "Under hir robe of gold, that sat ful faire, / Hadde next hire flessh yclad hire in an haire" (132–33). The hairshirt, which mortifies the flesh and exalts the spirit, is the divine and precious thing hidden beneath the mundane and transitory "robe of gold" ordinarily prized in the world. In Christian terms, the outer golden show is dross; the true gold, contained within the dross, celebrates the triumph of the spirit over the flesh. A further expression of the same theme occurs when Valerian finds the "hooly olde Urban" (185) and "An oold man, clad in white clothes cleere" (201) carrying "a book with lettre of gold" (202) "Among the seintes buryeles lotynge" (186). The holy men, the saving book, and the golden letters all reflect the spirit that here is hidden within the catacombs, which, by their very nature, affirm the transitoriness of the flesh and this world.

The Canon's clothes show the same contrast of the spiritual and the worldly. Like the old man in the catacombs, the Canon wears a "whyt surplys" (558) but it is underneath his "clothes blake" (557). The condition of the Canon's clothes indicates his disregard for his mortal state, for his spirit encased in the physical and in the worldly. "His overslope nys nat worth a myte, / . . . It is al baudy and totore also" (633, 635) and the ensemble is "sluttissh" (636), which accurately reflects both his lack of success in the world and his shabby spiritual condition. Moreover, he has contaminated the Yeoman. The change in the Yeoman's clothing, the contrast between his former and his present attire, articulates the loss he has suffered in dwelling seven years with the Canon. Before that, the Yeoman was "wont to be right fressh and gay / Of clothyng and of oother good array" (724–25), but now, instead of a hat or a hood or some other medieval head-covering appropriate to his station or indicating fashionable apparel, he only wears "an hose upon myn heed" (726) which advertises the shabbiness of his earthly goods and may suggest a parallel shabbiness in spiritual state as well.[15]

When the Yeoman explains that alchemists generally appear in "threedbare array" (890) in order to avoid discovery and the concomitant danger that "Men wolde hem slee by cause of hir science" (896), he connects the theme of deception to that of clothes. Such deception lies behind the Canon's having sewn his hood and his cloak together. The pilgrim Chaucer reflects the degree to which the Canon's attire deceives the pilgrims. Because of the Canon's clothing, Chaucer is confused about what sort of man approaches them pell-mell after the Second Nun's Tale. He says "in myn herte wondren I bigan / What that he was," and he reaches a decision only after "I had longe avysed me" (569–72). He decides the man must be some sort of canon only when he "understood / How that his cloke was sowed to his hood" (570–71). Regardless of whether a canon was supposed to wear a hood or not, was supposed to wear it sewn to his cloak or not, Chaucer's realization that the man does have a hood but that it is sewn to his cloak finally resolves his doubt and leads to the Canon's identification.[16] And, of course, in the tale itself clothing and deception are closely allied. The canon uses his clothes to deceive the priest when he takes "A teyne of silver" "out of his owene sleeve" (1224–25), shapes it into an ingot, hides it again in his clothing, and later slips it from his sleeve into a pan of water. Clothing that is so clear in the Second Nun's Tale—Christ clothed in flesh, Cecile's spirit wrapped in worthless gold—develops into a public expression of a spiritual condition and a means of deception in the Canon's Yeoman's Prologue and Tale.

SMELL

No other fragment of the *Canterbury Tales* is so concerned with the way things smell. To be sure, the Manciple objects to the "cursed breeth" (IX, 39) of the Cook in the Manciple's Prologue; Alison's "mouth was sweete as bragot or the meeth" (I, 3261) and Absalon censes the ladies in church and "cheweth greyn and lycorys, / To smellen sweete" (I, 3690–91), but Chaucer does nothing further with smell in the first fragment.[17] The gorgeous gardens in which Emily, Canacee, the monk and wife in the Shipman's Tale, and January and May disport themselves are odorless. Only Dorigen's garden bears "The odour of floures" (V, 913), one among many descriptive details. Chaucer is characteristically less receptive to the smell of things than he is to the way they look, but the absence of smell elsewhere in the *Canterbury Tales* makes its appearance in both tales of Fragment VIII all the more striking.[18]

In the Prologue to the Second Nun's Tale, we learn that Cecile's name derives from lily and that she herself possessed the symbolic characteristics of the flower, including "of good fame / The soote savour" (90–91). In the Tale itself, of course, the divine crowns of rose and lily provide the primary smells. The smell is more important than the flower, for while the flowers may never rot, nor ever "lese hir soote savour" (228–29), it is the smell of the flowers which pierces Tiburce's heart and leads to his ultimate conversion. Once Tiburce enters, with Valerian, upon the path to martyrdom, God prepares floral crowns for the brothers, but instead of mentioning the colors and the names of the flowers, Chaucer here describes the flowers only as "wel smellynge" (279).

Smelling good comes from being busy about God's work, multiplying the faithful and extending the faith; smelling bad comes from being busy about the Devil's work, learning to "multiplie" (669, 835, 1401, 1479) in the alchemical search for gold. In a splendid passage, the Canon's Yeoman describes the stench that constantly attends alchemists which, together with their threadbare clothes, constitutes a defining characteristic of the breed.

> And everemoore, where that evere they goon,
> Men may hem knowe by smel of brymstoon.
> For al the world they stynken as a goot;
> Hir savour is so rammyssh and so hoot
> That though a man from hem a mile be
> The savour wole infecte hym, trusteth me.
>
> (884–89)

Chaucer unifies the fragment by contrasting two ways of working in the world, the saint's and the alchemist's, in terms of smell.

The question implicit in the fragment's concern for odor is this: Does one want to smell like a flower or to smell like hell? The answer to that question depends upon how well one has been taught.

TEACHERS

Like many another fragment in the *Canterbury Tales,* Fragment VIII is concerned with teachers. Cecile, the angel, Urban, the old man, the Second Nun, the Canon, the Canon's Yeoman, and the canon in part two of the tale are eager to impart information. They teach the same thing from different points of view: the Second Nun's Tale focuses on how to smell good; the Canon's Yeoman's Tale focuses on how to avoid smelling bad. Or, to put it another way, the Second Nun's Tale provides "a lesson on how to regard the physical world from a spiritual point of view" and the Canon's Yeoman's Tale "looks at the physical world from a physical point of view" (Cook 1987, 38).

In the Second Nun's Tale, the primary teacher is Cecile. She shows "the wey to blynde" because "she ensample was by good techynge" (92–93). The "Ensample of [her] goode and wise werkes alle" (105) allows all the people to see the magnanimity, wisdom, and good works that reside in faith (109–12). She "corrected" (162) Valerian, who "was taught by his lernynge" (184) from her how to find Urban and what to say to him. The old man instructs him in the creed, and Urban christens both Valerian and later Tiburce whom he also makes "Parfit in his lernynge" (353). The angel of God instructs Valerian, and both Valerian and Cecile instruct Tiburce on the vanity of idols, the value of martyrdom, and the composition of the Trinity. In the trial scene, Cecile repeatedly attempts to correct the errant Almache whose blindness prevents him from seeing the truth about idols—a point she had already argued successfully with Tiburce. And in the three days between her execution and her death, Cecile "nevere cessed hem the feith to teche" (538).

The Second Nun herself is equally active as a teacher. The stanzas on "ydelnesse," which begin the Prologue, establish the principle that underlies her eagerness to teach. Her reference to "we" and to "us" in parallel statements of obligational imperative unites us with the other pilgrims as the proper audience for her active teaching: "Wel oghten we to doon al oure entente, / Lest that the feend thurgh ydelnesse us hente" (6–7) and "Wel oghte us werche, and ydelnesse withstonde" (14). In translating the life of St. Cecile, she performs her own "feithful bisynesse" (24) and so offers herself as an active example of the imperatives she teaches. With the example of her own activity as well as with the example of the saint, the Second Nun instructs us in how best to live our lives and how best to avoid the devil's "trappe" (11).

The Canon's Yeoman instructs us in how not to lead our lives in order to avoid a different sort of devil's trap. Unlike everyone else in the *Canterbury Tales*, the Yeoman does not know that the pilgrims are engaged in a storytelling contest to win a supper at the Tabard Inn on their return to London from Canterbury. Indeed, we have no way of knowing whether he and the Canon are even pilgrims. His motive for telling a tale, therefore, is not to win the game but to instruct, to present himself as an example of what is to be avoided: "Lat every man be war by me for evere!" (737).[19] After seven years in the Canon's service, the Yeoman knows that alchemy is wasted effort and squandered money. He describes the canon's activity in part two only "To th'entente that men may be war therby" (1306). He wants his audience to "taak heede of this chanons cursednesse" (1101) so they will know what to avoid, and should any of his listeners already be ensnared in alchemical endeavor, he advises them to abandon it "Lest ye lese al" (1410). With the example of his own activity as well as the example of the canon, the Yeoman instructs the pilgrims on how *not* to lead their lives and what to avoid.

Indicative of the priest's foolishness and guillibility in part two is his eagerness to have the canon "techen me / This noble craft and this subtilitee" (1246–47).[20] The canon, out of apparent generosity and the desire to repay the priest's kindness in originally loaning him money, tutors the priest "pleynly" (1057), teaching him to put the quicksilver into the crucible by himself, to blow the fire, and to take the silver out himself, all the while pretending to do things before the priest's very eyes. Nonetheless, he still manages to deceive the priest about alchemical conversion of quicksilver into silver and to teach the priest an expensive lesson about the futility of alchemical endeavor.

The Yeoman interrupts his narrative to register his outrage at the canon's "false dissymulynge" (1073) by citing the proverbial "Ful sooth it is that swich profred servyse / Stynketh" (1066–67). The point would hardly be worth mentioning were it not that the Second Nun addresses exactly the same point and teaches her audience precisely where proffered service *is* welcome. One of the qualities which the Second Nun finds to praise in the *Invocacio ad Mariam* is that Mary

> Nat oonly helpes hem that preyen thee,
> But often tyme, of thyn benygnytee,
> Ful frely, er that men thyn help biseche,
> Thou goost biforn, and art hir lyves leche.
>
> (53–56)

The difference in response to freely proffered service characterizes the two tales and their narrators and suggests the contrastive connection that unifies the fragment. The Second Nun celebrates Mary's freely given service which leads to the soul's salvation; the Yeoman decries the canon's freely proffered offer to teach which leads to the priest's beguiling, losing money, and endangering his soul.

SECRECY

The teachers in the Second Nun's Tale differ from those in the Canon's Yeoman's Prologue and Tale in their attitude toward secrecy. The Yeoman's Tale is full of secrets. From the moment he starts talking with the Host in the Prologue, the Yeoman indicates his concern with secrecy, revealing not only that he possesses secrets but also that he is willing to disclose them privately if the Host will "keepe it secree" (642–43). The Canon abandons the pilgrims he had seemed so eager to join because the "Yeman wolde telle his pryvetee" (701) and "discoverest that thou sholdest hyde" (696).[21] The canon in part two of the Tale pretends to reveal his "pryvetee" (1052) which becomes "Oure pryvetee" (1138) when he includes the priest. There are actually several secrets. The priest thinks he is learning the canon's secrets of conversion. The canon's actual secret is that the secret which the priest thinks he is learning is nonexistent and forms part of the canon's secret attempt to gull the priest and bilk him out of forty pounds. Once sold, the secret must be "kept . . . cloos" and "secree" (1369–70). Since we know what the priest does not, we are in a better position to delight in Chaucer's irony: the priest thinks he is learning a secret that the canon, in fact, hides from him and that the Yeoman reveals to us.

In the Second Nun's Tale, on the other hand, secrets exist to be revealed. Cecile is "right fayn" to tell Valerian the "conseil" (145–46) that will lead to his conversion to Christianity and to the translation to heaven that will follow his martyrdom—all implicit in Urban's "secree nedes and . . . good entente" (178). For the same motive, Valerian is anxious to reveal the secret to Tiburce so that he too may "knowe the trouthe" (238). In a tale which emphasizes light, clarity, and spiritual vision, Cecile is eager to reveal the secret truth to Tiburce "al open and pleyn" (284) and to reveal Almache's blindness and falsehood "al openly" (478). In the Prologue to the Canon's Yeoman's Tale, the revelation of secrecy banishes the fraudulent and false (the Canon leaves); in the Tale itself, the revelation of secrecy ironically supports fraud, conceals the truly secret, and deceives the gullible; and in the Second Nun's Tale, the revelation of secrecy reveals the truth and multiplies the faithful. This serious concern with secrecy, like the concern for conversion, clothes, smell, and teaching, establishes lines of coherence that unify the fragment thematically.

III. Character

Chaucer designed the Second Nun and the Canon's Yeoman, Cecile and the Canon (and the canon), and Almache and the priest as similar and contrastive pairs. This pairing has been apparent throughout much of the previous discussion of the fragment's coherence where we discussed parallels of character at the same time as parallels of theme and structure. What follows, then, are additional parallels that contribute to the unity of the fragment.

VALERIAN AND THE PRIEST

Valerian and the priest are both the objects of attempts at conversion, and both convert. Valerian changes from a pagan Roman, capable of threatening his new wife with murder, into a Christian martyr; the priest changes from a pleasant and generous man, capable of lending a "marc" (1030) or "a noble, or two, or thre, / Or what thyng were in my possessioun" (1037–38), into a "sotted preest" (1341) bilked out of forty pounds. But the more important similarity between the two is that of all the characters in the *Canterbury Tales*, they alone require "ocular proof." Not even Dorigen in the Franklin's Tale, whose marriage and happiness depend upon proof of the rocks' disappearance, distrusts the courtliness of Aurelius enough to go to the coast and actually see for herself if the rocks are gone. Valerian insists that Cecile must "Lat me that aungel se and hym biholde" (164). Cecile sends Valerian to Urban to be purged of sin: "Thanne shul ye se that angel" (182). The priest, too, insists on "ocular proof." The canon is anxious to show the priest what he "shul wel seen at ye" (1059). As part of the patter designed to deceive the priest, the canon emphasizes what the priest sees and experiences for himself (1120, 1125–27, 1154–55, 1205, 1215, and 1242). Indeed, one of the splendid ironies in the fragment is the contrastive function of "ocular proof" in the two tales. For Valerian, "ocular proof" leads to salvation and to martyrdom; for the priest, "ocular proof" leads to loss and confusion.

ALMACHE AND THE CANON

Although Almache shares characteristics with both the priest and the canon, most of these are not particularly significant in unifying the fragment. They seem to be details more of accident than design, similar to Cecile asking God "To han respit thre dayes and namo" (543) and the canon's asking the priest to loan him money "but dayes three" (1026). "Three days"—like a year and a day—is such a common temporal designation in the Middle Ages that it can not serve as serious evidence for Chaucer's craft. The "folye" of the priest (1085) and of Almache (428, 463, 493, 495) falls in the same category as does also their parallel blindness (1077–78 and 498–504).

Of somewhat greater weight, however, is that both Almache and the canon consciously destroy Christian faith. The canon "everemoore delit hath and gladnesse . . . / How Cristes peple he may to meschief brynge" (1070–72). The same is true for Almache and not simply because the plot calls for him to persecute Christians and so release the miracle of martyrdom. Although Almache knows the Christians to be innocent (452), he puts "on us a cryme and eek a blame" (455) "and with a wood sentence / Ye make us gilty, and it is nat sooth" (450–51). Only in the Prioress' Tale and the Man of Law's Tale do we find a similar animosity, but both of those attacks against Christians are prompted by "Sathan" (II, 365 and VII, 1748). In Fragment VIII, however, Satan does not directly motivate attacks upon Christianity: Almache seems to delight in his legal obligation (444–48 and 470–72), and the canon seems to find an easy mark among churchmen.

CECILE AND THE CANON (AND THE CANON)

The parallels between Cecile and the Canon who flees and the canon in the Yeoman's Tale are more telling of design than are those between Almache and the canon. The canon's greed reflects a worldly concern that contrasts with Cecile's generosity in distributing her worldly possessions among Urban and the other Christians. The canon's "fraude and deceite" (1367) contrast with Cecile's "honestee . . . / And . . . conscience" (89–90). Although Cecile swears Valerian to secrecy just as the canon swears the priest to secrecy, both Cecile and the canon reveal "conseil" (145) and "pryvetee" (1052) and offer to establish the validity of their secrets with experiential and visible proof (170 and 1059, for example). Both Cecile and the canon must "send out" in order to create the conditions to verify their secret claims: Cecile sends Valerian out to find Urban on the Via Appia, and the priest sends his servant out to bring back "quyksilver . . . ounces two or three" (1103–4) and coals for a fire.

Cecile's similarities to the Canon of the Prologue are more indicative of design. Although Palamon misperceives Emily and the three rioters question the Old Man, no characters in the same fragment of the *Canterbury Tales* other than Cecile and the Canon have their identities seriously questioned. As we have seen (p. 83), as the Canon approaches the pilgrims, Chaucer the pilgrim wonders "What that he was" (570) which parallels Almache's opening question in the trial scene, "What maner womman artow?" (424). The summoner in the Friar's Tale, although he has greater cause, does not actually put that question to the devil he meets, and even Chaunticleer responds instinctively to the fox he has apparently never seen before without wondering in his heart what sort of beast it was.

Another similarity is that Cecile and the Canon alone are said to be worthy of reverence. The Second Nun's attitude in the Prologue and her celebration of Cecile's activities in the Tale express that reverence; the Yeoman's insistence that "men sholde hym reverence" (631) expresses his parallel attitude toward the Canon. But Chaucer undercuts the Yeoman's professed reverence with irony. Although proclaiming that his lord the Canon has a reputation for performing experiments skillfully, the Yeoman describes an experiment that fails (905–21)—nothing to reverence there. He excuses his lord's shabbiness by claiming it is a disguise to avoid the animosity of men intent upon learning his secrets. The ironic result is that we never learn the Canon's name, which renders him difficult to reverence, while Cecile, whose name the Second Nun expounds in detail in the Prologue, is renowned "into this day" (552).

Perhaps we are now in a better position to see what Chaucer

saw in an early tale he had on hand and a late tale he was in the process of writing that led him to build Fragment VIII as carefully as he did. The contrastive dichotomy between spiritual and physical would have proven attractive as would have the opportunity to employ the technical language of alchemy in a witty way: literally in the Canon's Yeoman's Tale and metaphorically in the Second Nun's Tale.[22] Given the nature of the two tales, Chaucer could easily play aesthetic language games with vision and blindness, gold and dross, success and failure. In addition to these and with equal care, Chaucer arranged to tell the Canon's Yeoman's Prologue and Tale in a manner structurally congruent with the Second Nun's Prologue and Tale. He could order the events in one tale to parallel the events in the other. He saw that the characters of one tale shared details of behavior and attitude with those in the other. He also saw ways that the two tales shared themes—conversion, clothes, smell—that would both support their integrity as individual texts and contribute lines of thematic coherence to the intertextualization both of the fragment and of the *Canterbury Tales* as a whole. Seen in the context of Chaucer's artistic practices, the answer to the question "Why did Chaucer join the Canon's Yeoman's Tale to the Second Nun's Tale?" is clear: since no other combination of tales was as aesthetically satisfying, no other combination was possible.

4
Fragment V (Group F): The Squire's Tale and the Franklin's Tale

> For in this world, certein, ther no wight is
> That he ne dooth or seith somtyme amys.
>
> (779–80)

Part of what makes the *Canterbury Tales* exciting as literary game and intellectual construct is the complexity of theme and allusion that Chaucer uses to bond tales to each other in building the fragments. Especially in Fragment V that complexity has tended to blur the very clear lines which join the Squire's Tale to the Franklin's Tale, and to seduce readers into privileging the many connections these tales share with tales elsewhere in the *Canterbury Tales* rather than those which bind the two together.

Alone among the fragments of the *Canterbury Tales*, only Fragment V contains two thoroughly pagan tales. The Squire's Tale opens in southeastern Russia and begins with a portrait of Cambyuskan containing qualities and characteristics appropriate to any Christian king. But Cambyuskan is not Christian. He professes an unspecified heathen religion into which he was born and to which he is absolutely faithful (17–18). The only religious service referred to in the poem occurs in a "temple" (296), a word Chaucer uses primarily to refer to a place of pagan worship, and in the context of the Squire's Tale, no other meaning is possible. The Franklin's Tale is similarly devoid of specific Christian allusion.[1] The Christian narrator distinguishes between the present time of the tale's telling and "thilke dayes" when the events of the tale occurred and when "hethen folk useden" (1293) astrological calculations to create deceptive illusions (see also 1132–34). When Aurelius seeks Dorigen, he knows he will find her in a "temple" (1306). He himself prays to Apollo, and Dorigen's la-ment refers only to classical and pre-Christian heroines who choose death over dishonor. There is not a single Christian martyr. When Dorigen questions that "Eterne God" (865), whose providence rules the world and who unreasonably created the black rocks, it would be comfortable to think that she intends the Christian God (whose presence, no doubt, lies behind the references to God in the tale), but actually the God to whom she refers is more likely the same generic First Mover to whom Theseus refers in his famous speech at the close of the pagan Knight's Tale or the "formere principal" (VI, 19) that Nature lauds in the Physician's Tale. The reference to "Nowel" (1255) in December is surely a Christian allusion, but it is the only one in the tale, and, since the sun is referred to as Phebus (1245) and the year as Janus (1252) in the same context, the Christian allusion reveals Chaucer's inevitably anachronistic historical sense more than it does his attempt to infuse Christianity into the tale. The same is true for Aurelius's brother and the Orleans magician who are anachronistically Christian "clerkes" in an essentially pagan world. Nonetheless, as we shall see in discussing the chiasmic structure of the fragment, the Christian dimension is important to unity.

The fragment is also unique in the contribution of dance to unity. To be sure, dance appears elsewhere in the *Canterbury Tales*: Virginia avoids dances as "occasions of daliaunces" (VI, 66), folly, and immoral behavior; perhaps for precisely those reasons, dance is important to the Wife of Bath. But only in Fragment V does dance contribute to theme by being suffused with dangerous deceptions. On the afternoon of Cambyuskan's birthday, Canacee dances with the strange knight, which allows Chaucer to define the character of dance in general:

> Who koude telle yow the forme of daunces
> So unkouthe, and swiche fresshe contenaunces,
> Swich subtil lookyng and dissymulynges
> For drede of jalouse mennes aperceyvynges?
>
> (283–86)

In precisely this way Aurelius dances before Dorigen. His behavior, too, is marked by "subtil lookyng and dissymulynges," but whereas at Cambyuskan's dance, the surreptitious exchange of glances may be designed to avoid the perception of jealous husbands, the glancing in the Franklin's Tale is more direct, more obvious, and totally ineffective. Aurelius "looked on hir face / In swich a wise as man that asketh grace" (957–58), but Dorigen, immersed in her own misery, is completely unaware of what he is doing.

Thus dance serves to characterize Dorigen. Her inability to perceive Aurelius's double intentions contributes to our perception of her naivete, sometimes called her "moral blindness" (dramatized by her questioning divine order and her address to the rocks), and testifies to the tenacity of her love for Arveragus. It is one of many themes that establish the lines of coherence in Fragment V.

I. Theme

ASTROLOGY

Chaucer uses astrological references in two completely different ways in both tales of the fragment. If we dismiss the astrological references that Chaucer's age commonly accepted as a scientific description of the time of day or the season of the year,[2] the important astrological references which remain are associated with the expression of magic and the marvelous. In the Franklin's Tale, for example, Aurelius's prayer to Phebus asks for an extended astrological opposition that will generate tides to cover the rocks; the Orleans clerk-magician studies "magyk natureel" (1125, 1155) based upon the "moones mansions" (1154, 1129–31) "and swich folye / As in oure dayes is nat worth a flye" (1132); and the magician's ultimate illusion is expressed in just those arcane astrological terms which the Franklin professes not to know (1273–93). Chaucer does not confine this association of astrology and magic to the Franklin's Tale. The Squire refers to a magician every bit as clever and as dependent upon astrological conjunctions as the magician in the Franklin's Tale. The magician who created the brass horse knew the craft of magic and depended on astrological omens; he had to wait for the proper conjunction of constellations before he could devise the horse and seal (or bond) the magic effectively (or perhaps permanently) (128–31).[3]

One further point needs to be made about the magicians as they function to unify the fragment. Both tales refer—and no others in the Canterbury collection do—to the regular appearance of magicians at feasts.[4] In wondering about the brass horse, some people claim it is only "An apparence ymaad by some magyk, / As jogelours pleyen at thise feestes grete" (218–

19). Aurelius's brother, too, refers to "diverse apparences" which "thise subtile tregetoures" create "ofte at feestes" (1140–42), and he goes on to describe the wonders that he has heard magicians can create and cause to vanish. No other tales use magicians in just this way; no other fragment is unified by the existence of magicians in all its tales; and no other fragment uses astrology to describe magical events in arcane terms.

MARVEL/MAGIC

Miracles or, in the pagan context of Fragment V, the marvelous works of gods and magicians occupy a central place in the fragment because of the illusion produced by the Orleans clerk to deceive Dorigen. But different kinds of marvel occur in the two tales, and Chaucer shows the characters responding to them in ways important to our understanding of the tale's action and of the fragment's coherence.

Because the Franklin's Tale, in large measure, concerns Dorigen's failure of perception, all the magical activity in that tale involves vision. The Orleans clerk entertains Aurelius and his brother before supper with a series of visions, a "sighte merveillous" (1206), while they sit in his study. Of course he merely creates an illusion to make "It [seme] that alle the rokkes were aweye" (1296). Aurelius's response to the marvel is symptomatic of the response that all characters in the Franklin's Tale make to the magical. He does not care how the "myracle" (1299) is performed; he merely celebrates its occurrence.[5] Dorigen, too, neither questions nor wonders about the marvel. Her lack of foresight or inability to speculate ("She wende nevere han come in swich a trappe" [1341]) allows her only to declaim against the "monstre or merveille" which is "agayns the proces of nature" (1344–45) and to accept it sorrowfully. Even Arveragus is defined as not being "ymaginatyf" (1094), not given to speculate about the world—specifically, whether anyone might have spoken to his wife about love while he was away from home for two years. All the characters in the Franklin's Tale lack imagination in the sense that they neglect to ask important questions.

Chaucer also shows characters in the Squire's Tale confronting something magical and all responding in the same way. But whereas the characters in the Franklin's Tale lack inquisitiveness, the characters in the Squire's Tale are filled with wonder. To be sure, the marvels are not tricks of vision; they are concrete as well as visible: a brass horse that flies, and a magical sword, mirror, and ring.[6] Chaucer presents these wonders in fifty-two lines (115–67) and then, quite remarkably, devotes another eighty-two lines (180–262) to describing the response of the people. As each marvel was presented and described individually, so each is wondered about individually. Those who wonder so desperately about the magic gifts are probably the common people, called the "prees" (189), the "peple" (201), the "lewed peple" (221), and the "folk" (236), although the crowd also contains aristocrats.[7] Cambyuskan holds his birthday feast surrounded by his nobility (77). These people join Cambyuskan when the king, "with al a route / Of lordes and of ladyes hym aboute" (303–4), rises from his feast to see the brass horse and specifically asks the strange knight to explain the "vertu," the "myght," and the "governaunce" (310–11) of the horse. So, not only does the miraculous have its place in both tales, it contributes in two entirely different though complementary ways to the coherence of the fragment: the concrete generates wonder in the Squire's Tale, and the illusory generates belief in the Franklin's Tale.

ILLUSION

Illusion occupies a major place in the Franklin's Tale. At the very beginning, Dorigen and Arveragus design their relationship so that it appears to be an ordinary marriage in which he maintains "the name of soveraynetee . . . for shame of his degree" (751–52) when actually it is a courtly love relationship in which he will "hire obeye, and folwe hir wyl in al" (749).[8] Aurelius, too, appears to be a good neighbor when actually he is the viper in Dorigen's garden and the source of her discomfiture. Finally, Dorigen misperceives Aurelius's intentions (959, 981–82) just as she misperceives the danger of the rocks in nature. They "semen . . . a foul confusion" (869) rather than the sensible creation of a prescient God whose works Dorigen mistakenly questions. Confused by the appearance of nature and not able to perceive the reality, she attributes to the rocks a danger to her happiness when the danger actually arises from the elegant garden, "so curiously / Arrayed" by the "craft of mannes hand" (909–10). The primary expression of illusion in the tale, however, involves the apparent disappearance of the rocks. Aurelius's brother remembers the "diverse apparences" (1140) with which magicians delight and deceive men's sight. The Orleans clerk provides just such a sequence of marvelous illusions in his study, and he produces the ultimate "myracle" (1299) of illusion in nature which seems to win Dorigen for Aurelius.

Illusion would not be a significant force for the unity of Fragment V were it not employed to similar good effect in the Squire's Tale. Of the four gifts, themselves a source of wonder because of the discrepancy between what they appear to be and what they are, the mirror most aptly reflects this theme because of its facility to determine truth beneath "tresoun" and "subtiltee"—especially in love and especially during "this lusty someres tyde" (139–42) when people are most likely to fall in love. The lovers in the Squire's Tale are birds. Like Aurelius, the tercelet "semed welle of alle gentillesse; / Al were he ful of treson and falsnesse" (505–6). The falcon's weepy tale is full of recriminations against the tercelet who, from the falcon's point of view at least, appeared to be, time and again, something that he was not.

TROTH

In the link between the two tales, Harry Bailly reminds the Franklin that he must tell a tale "or breken his biheste" (698). Although the Franklin is overly unctuous in his eagerness to please the Host and fulfill his pledge (700–8), he tells a tale in which everyone breaks his or her promise. In both tales the issue of one's troth is central.[9] In the Franklin's Tale the precise nature of Dorigen's commitment (whether what she has promised "in pley" is more or less binding than her marriage vows, especially since Aurelius fulfilled neither the spirit nor the letter of her conditions for loving him) has interested scholars more than it interested Dorigen: she assumes her word is binding as does Arveragus at the end when he sends Dorigen to the winter garden in apparent fulfillment of her summer's promise. Arveragus pledges his troth at the beginning of the tale (745) and Dorigen responds in kind (759). Although aware that people may sometimes err in pledging their word (779 ff.), the Franklin approves Dorigen and Arveragus's mutual commitment (787–90) as an expression of their "Pacience" (773), "temperaunce" (785), and "governaunce" (786)—virtues all. The magician swears that he will not do the job for less than a thousand pounds, and Aurelius swears "by my trouthe" (1231) that the magician shall be truly paid.

The remarkable thing about the pledges in the Franklin's Tale is that not a single one of them is fulfilled. The magician does the job for nothing; Aurelius does not well and truly pay him; Arveragus, who swore to "take no maistrie" (747), commands Dorigen "up peyne of deeth" (1481) not to tell anyone of the adventure; and Dorigen, who had sworn to be Arveragus's "humble trewe wyf" (758), finds herself pledged to love another man and, in the event, escapes from that pledge as well.

In the Squire's Tale, pledges are as frequent and as central as they are in the Franklin's Tale, but the world of the Squire's Tale, though more exotic, is simpler: all the pledges are honored. Cambyuskan is defined as a man "Sooth of his word" (21); sworn to keep the law under which he was born, "He kepte his lay" (18). Canacee swears as "a kynges doghter trewe" (465) to help the falcon—and she does. Only the tercelet, as the "god of loves ypocryte" (514) betrays his troth in the Squire's Tale, but the deviation from his pledged word is only temporary since we are told he eventually returns repentant to the falcon (654–55). In Fragment V, then, the theme of troth progresses from simple adherence (Cambyuskan, Canacee) through temporary rejection (the tercelet), to ultimate betrayal (Arveragus, Dorigen, Aurelius, the magician) of one's pledged word.

Perhaps as the necessary corollary to the theme of troth, Chaucer focuses upon the way people speak and the language they use. Chaucer's concern for language in this fragment goes beyond referring to the Squire's insufficiency and the "burel" Franklin's command of English, Latin, and the Breton tongue.[10] When the strange knight rides into Cambyuskan's hall, the Squire recognizes the peculiarities of "the forme used in [the strange knight's] langage" (100) and indicates his own limitations in not being able to imitate the style of the strange knight's speech (105). We are told twice (94 and 103) that the strange knight's bearing and speech were appropriate to the occasion, a rhetorical stratagem also employed by the tercelet and described in almost exactly the same words (561). Aurelius succeeds in masking his love from Dorigen because, unlike the tercelet and the strange knight, his words do not conform to his behavior: "no thyng dorste he seye" (943) except sometimes at dances he would look at her "as man that asketh grace; / But nothyng wiste she of his entente" (958–59).

DEATH AND WOUNDS

And language can kill, so Aurelius claims (975). While we should not take courtly lovers' protestations of imminent death too seriously, Fragment V is unusually rich in references to death and wounds that have nothing to do with lovers' attempts to gain the sympathy of the beloved.[11] As we might expect in a fragment so devoted to illusion as this one, the wounds and threats of death tend to be more illusory than real. Dorigen's complaint to God about the rocks ("An hundred thousand bodyes of mankynde / Han rokkes slayn" [877–78]) and the magician's vision of the deer slain by arrows and dogs and the heron slain by hawks are cases in point.

Ironically, and in contrast to the courtly lovers in the Knight's Tale and the mock courtly lovers in the Miller's Tale, the women and not the men are wounded or threatened with death in both tales of Fragment V. Although Aurelius rather predictably claims that Dorigen's refusal of his suit will be the death of him, she is the one who "causelees . . . sleeth hirself, allas" (825), who is threatened by "hire derke fantasye" (844), whose heart suffers "bittre peynes smerte" (856) and is slain by fear of the rocks (893), and who, whether seriously or not, contemplates suicide. Dorigen's mental suffering contrasts with the falcon's physical suffering. Not only has the falcon beaten herself "so pitously / With bothe hir wynges" (414–15) that her blood runs down the tree, but she has also pricked herself with her beak (418).[12] The falcon swoons "for lak of blood" (440, 443) just as Dorigen "nas a drope of blood" "In al hir face" (1340) when Aurelius reveals the rocks are gone. Both Dorigen and the falcon are cured: the falcon by "salves" (639) and "plastres" (636), Dorigen by Arveragus's decision and Aurelius's *gentillesse* in withdrawing his suit. But, unlike other women who are the object of courtly lovers' affection in the *Canterbury Tales*, only Dorigen and the falcon are actually threatened by death or bodily harm.

GENTILLESSE

In the link between the Squire's Tale and the Franklin's Tale, the Franklin praises the Squire for acquitting himself "gentilly" (674) and laments his own son's disinclination "to comune with any gentil wight / Where he myghte lerne gentillesse aright" (693–94). The Host doesn't give a "Straw for youre gentillesse" (695) and urges the Franklin to tell a tale.[13] Considering the importance of *gentillesse* in the link and the amount of scholarly interest it has generated, it is somewhat surprising then to discover that the theme of *gentillesse* functions in completely different ways in the two tales.[14]

In the Squire's Tale, the issue of *gentillesse* does not arise until the second part, and there it functions rather predictably in the falcon's tale. Although the Squire describes the falcon as having "gentillesse / Of shap" (426–27), the *gentillesse* of the tercelet in his role as a courtly lover is the issue. He "semed welle of alle gentillese" (505) and behaved "So lyk a gentil lovere" (546) that all his behavior "sownen into gentillesse of love" (517), but even "Though he were gentil born" (622), "No gentillesse of blood ne may [him] bynde" (620). The falcon's misery is directly proportional to the expectations she had of her courtly lover based upon his apparent *gentillesse* and to her ultimate disappointment in him when he fails to remain as *gentil* as he professed to be. As she says to Canacee, "gentil herte kitheth gentillesse," "As wel by werk as by auctoritee" (482–83), and in abandoning her, the tercelet shows his lack of *gentillesse*. *Gentillesse*, then, is a façade for disillusion, a metaphor for the attractive but illusory expectation that precedes disappointment—like the Squire himself or the Squire's Tale.

In the Squire's Tale, *gentillesse* functions as a measure of a lover's courtliness: the word appears only in the falcon's tale and primarily in conjunction with the tercelet. *Gentillesse* has nothing at all to do with courtly love in the Franklin's Tale, and this is surprising since Aurelius is, in many ways, Chaucer's most complete and most completely described courtly lover. Except for a moment at the beginning of the tale, when Dorigen recognizes Arveragus's "gentillesse" (754) in offering her free rein in their relationship, the term and the concept do not arise until the last hundred lines when Dorigen meets Aurelius on her way to the winter garden. Aurelius realizes he had better desist from his lust for her and not force her to fulfill her promise which is "Agayns franchise and alle gentillesse" (1524). He recognizes Arveragus's "gret gentillesse" (1527) and, in releasing Dorigen, insists "Thus kan a squier doon a gentil dede / As wel as kan a knyght" (1543–44), which opens the contest among the principals as to who can be "the mooste fre" (1622).[15] *Gentillesse* in the Franklin's Tale is almost universally held to be a mark of nobility and generosity; in the Squire's Tale it is a measure of courtly love—and a deceptive measure at that. In both senses it contributes to the unity of the fragment.

II. Structure

The fundamental structure of Fragment V is chiasmus, the AB:BA organization of items in classical rhetoric which Chaucer learned from the medieval rhetoricians.[16] Specifically, the Squire's Tale begins with the generous giving of gifts to Cambyuskan by "The kyng of Arabe and of Inde" (110) and ends with the courtly love adventure of the unhappy falcon; the Franklin's Tale begins with the courtly love adventure of unhappy Dorigen and ends with a competition in generosity which, especially in the Christmas season, reflects the gift from a different king of his only begotten son to the world.

	Squire's Tale		Franklin's Tale	
A	B	:	B	A
gifts	falcon's courtly love adventure	:	Dorigen's courtly love adventure	gifts

The fragment begins and ends with gifts, but they are gifts of a fundamentally antithetical nature. Cambyuskan's gifts come to him on "the feest of his nativitee" (45), while the gifts at the end of the Franklin's Tale are exchanged at a time that celebrates the feast of Christ's nativity implicit in "Nowel." The gifts in the Squire's Tale are tangible—horse, mirror, ring, and sword—and contribute to mastery over nature. The generous gifts in the Franklin's Tale have no physical presence and reflect mastery over one's spirit. If one adds to this the Christian gift implicit in "Nowel," then God's generous gift of his son to the world affirms the triumph of spirit over nature and of life over death in the orthodox Christian scheme.[17] The gifts exchanged at the end of the Franklin's Tale reflect the spirit and the nature of God's gift. They also invert the Chaucerian pattern of deterioration that we saw in the previous three chapters and will see again when we discuss Fragment I. Instead of describing the decay of the ideal, the basic movement here in Fragment V, epitomized by the gifts, is from disorder to order, from narrative dispersal to narrative focus, from physical to abstract, from the concern with the material of this world to concern with the spiritual.

Within this general pattern of chiasmus in the fragment, other chiasmic details of plot emerge. Chaucer manipulates time in order to create the chiasmus. For example, the tercelet's absence from and betrayal of the falcon causes the falcon's misery, but Chaucer inverts the presentation of these events and shows us the effect before the cause, the misery before the betrayal. The same events in the Franklin's Tale, Arveragus's departure and then Dorigen's sadness, are presented chronologically. When Chaucer joined the Squire's Tale to the Franklin's Tale, therefore, the misery of the falcon precedes the absence of the tercelet while the absence of Arveragus precedes the misery of Dorigen to create the following chiasmic pattern:

	Squire's Tale			Franklin's Tale	
A	B	:	B	A	
misery of falcon	absence of tercelet	:	absence of Arveragus	misery of Dorigen	

To develop the chiasmus even further, the Squire's Tale ends with an indication that the tercelet will return and that the falcon will get her love again; the Franklin's Tale begins with Arveragus and Dorigen "in blisse and in solas" (802).

	Squire's Tale			Franklin's Tale	
A	B	:	B	A	
absence of tercelet	tercelet and falcon together	:	Dorigen and Arveragus together	absence of Arveragus	

The central scene in the Franklin's Tale, the scene in which Dorigen "in pley" (988) promises to love Aurelius if he rids the coast of rocks, lies at the very heart of a chiasmus. The scene had begun with Aurelius's request that Dorigen have mercy upon him or else "ye wol do me deye" (978). Dorigen responds in a clear negative ("Ne shal I nevere been untrewe wyf / In word ne werk" [984–85]) which emphasizes her married state ("I wol been his to whom that I am knyt" [986]). After her promise, she provides an even more emphatic negative ("No, by that Lord . . . that maked me!" [1000]) and again refers to her married state (1003–5). The scene ends with Aurelius complaining once again "of sodeyn deth horrible" (1010). Schematically it sets as follows:

A	B	:	B	A
Aurelius's death	Dorigen's "No" and reference to her marriage	[Dorigen's Promise]	Dorigen's "No" and reference to her marriage	Aurelius's death

Concurrently with the chiasmic structure, Chaucer organized the fragment along temporal lines. No other two-tale fragment contains so many references to time.[18] The fragment moves forward through the year; the seasons are clearly pointed. The Squire's Tale begins on March 15 and is cut off two months later, about May 15 (671–72).[19] Dorigen goes to the garden on "the sixte morwe of May" (906), and her tale ends in December. Janus sitting by the fire and every lusty man crying "Nowel" (1255) suggest the Christmas season and the depths of winter. In order to unify the fragment in terms of the temporal progression, Chaucer carefully compares the pagan spring of Cambyuskan's birthday with the Christian winter of Christ's birthday in terms of the changes in Phebus.[20] Cambyuskan's feast begins in

> The laste Idus of March, after the yeer.
> Phebus the sonne ful joly was and cleer,
> For he was neigh his exaltacioun
> In Martes face and in his mansioun
> In Aries, the colerik hoote signe.
> Ful lusty was the weder and benigne,
> For which the foweles, agayn the sonne sheene,
> What for the sesoun and the yonge grene,
> Ful loude songen hire affecciouns.
> Hem semed han geten hem protecciouns
> Agayn the swerd of wynter, keene and cold.
>
> (47–57)

The only other extended evocation of the season in the fragment describes the time of year at which the magician makes the rocks disappear, three days after which Arveragus sends Dorigen to Aurelius in the winter garden. Chaucer again focuses upon Phebus, but this time in

> The colde, frosty seson of Decembre.
> Phebus wax old, and hewed lyk laton,
> That in his hoote declynacion
> Shoon as the burned gold with stremes brighte;
> But now in Capricorn adoun he lighte,
> Where as he shoon ful pale, I dar wel seyn.
> The bittre frostes, with the sleet and reyn,
> Destroyed hath the grene in every yerd.
> Janus sit by the fyr, with double berd,
> And drynketh of his bugle horn the wyn;
> Biforn hym stant brawen of the tusked swyn,
> And "Nowel" crieth every lusty man.
>
> (1244–55)

The parallels between the two passages insist that Chaucer composed each with the other in mind and that in doing so he thought of them as establishing lines of coherence between the Squire's Tale and the Franklin's Tale that contribute to the unity of the fragment.

Squire's Tale	Franklin's Tale
March	Decembre
Phebus . . . ful joly was and cleer	Phebus wax old and hewed lyk laton
exaltacioun	declynacion
Martes . . . Aries	Capricorn
hoote signe	hoote declynacion
Ful lusty was the weder and benigne	The bittre frostes, with the sleet and reyn
foweles	swyn
sonne sheene	shoon ful pale
yonge grene	Destroyed . . . grene
songen	crieth
lusty . . . weder	lusty man

Perhaps the conclusions to these passages suggest another parallel more in keeping with the general temporal movement in the fragment from pagan past to Christian present and the general concern in the *Canterbury Tales* for the tension between *amor* and *amor dei*. The animals on the one hand, in this case the birds at the end of the passage in the Squire's Tale, celebrate nature and the season—the sun and the "yonge grene"—by singing as though doing so enables them to accumulate "protecciouns" against the bitter cold and implicit death of winter. Human beings on the other hand, in this case "every lusty man" at the end of the passage in the Franklin's Tale, celebrate the birth of Christ by crying out "Nowel"; in doing so they acknowledge their ultimate protection against winter and death. What is death for nature is life for human beings. The irony of Christ being born in the dead of winter for the redemption and resurrection of man—what seems most dead in natural or temporal terms is actually most alive in Christian or eternal terms—appears in two ways at the end of the poem. First, winter is the season of Dorigen's deception. She who trusted in Nature (1345) instead of God (865 ff.) is ironically deceived by nature. Second, although it seems to be the worst time of the (natural) year, Dorigen ironically meets Aurelius "right in the quykkest strete" (1502) with, as one critic has said, God's grace abounding (Gerhard Joseph 1966, 30–31). This Christian dimension is the appropriate conclusion to an otherwise essentially pagan fragment.

III. Character

Most of the scholarly comparisons made among characters in Fragment V concern the relationship between Aurelius and the Squire. The portrait of the squire Aurelius in the Franklin's Tale echoes certain words and attitudes used in the portrait of the Squire in the General Prologue. These echoes generally support claims that the Franklin, in evoking the Squire in the squire, is attempting to correct the Squire's adherence to courtly love or to teach him something. Chaucer unifies the fragment by echoing characters within the tales as well.

Since all courtly lovers are more or less interchangeable, nothing can be proven by comparisons among Arveragus, Aurelius, and the tercelet. Nonetheless, Chaucer does provide some interesting lines of coherence among the characters. For example, the knight Arveragus does not much resemble the pagan king Cambyuskan with his splendid array, lavish feasts, and three children, and yet Chaucer carefully points out that both are true to their word (21 and 1479). What joins Aurelius and the tercelet is not simply that both are fond courtly lovers, but that both—somewhat strangely as far as details are concerned—are neighbors to the women with whom they fall in love (504 and 961). Arveragus and the tercelet are both successful courtly lovers and both abandon their beloved for similar reasons: Arveragus, after living with Dorigen "A yeer and moore" (806), arranges to go to England "To seke in armes worshipe and honour" (811); the tercelet, after living with the falcon "lenger than a yeer or two" (574), decides to go somewhere else (577–78) "For his honour" (592).

Dorigen and the falcon provide the more unifying connection between the tales, and their differences are more telling than their similarities. Like typical courtly ladies, both Dorigen and the falcon choose to accept their courtly lovers because of their apparent worthiness and their "meke obeysaunce" (739 and 562, 515). And, of course, the two courtly ladies reveal their misery in similar ways, but there the similarity ends. Of the two, the falcon is perhaps the more characteristically courtly. When she takes the tercelet to be her love, "my wyl was his willes instrument; / This is to seyn, my wyl obeyed his wyl" (568–69). The relationship between Dorigen and Arveragus is perverse in medieval terms since he will "hire obeye, and folwe hir wyl in al" (749).[21] While the falcon enters the courtly love relationship interested in "Kepynge the boundes of my worshipe evere" (571), Dorigen and

Arveragus are lovers who masquerade as marrieds or marrieds who masquerade as lovers: they are interested not so much in the true limits of their worship as they are in creating the illusion of rectitude with Arveragus maintaining the "name of soveraynetee, / That wole he have for shame of his degree" (751–52).

Canacee, more than any other female in the fragment, represents the norm against which the falcon and Dorigen are to be measured: of Canacee we are told "She was ful mesurable, as wommen be" (362). To be sure, she weeps immoderately and must be upbraided by the falcon (496–97), but that is as much an expression that "pitee renneth soone in gentil herte, / Feelynge his similitude in peynes smerte" (479–80) as it is evidence of excess. Measured against Canacee's norm, the falcon rather surprisingly appears the nobler of the two courtly ladies. When the tercelet leaves the falcon, she behaves nobly and "mesurable": "I made vertu of necessitee, / And took it wel, syn that it moste be. / As I best myghte, I hidde fro hym my sorwe" (593–95). Only after she discovers that he "hath his trouthe falsed" (627) and that she has lost his love (626) does her response become the characteristically excessive response of the betrayed courtly lover. Dorigen, on the other hand, responds excessively almost from the moment Arveragus leaves. "She moorneth, waketh, wayleth, fasteth, pleyneth" (819) not from loss of love but from "Desir of his presence" (820) even though Arveragus constantly reveals his love for her by sending "hire lettres hoom of his welfare" (838).

If, then, the Franklin's Tale is held to be the Franklin's response to the excesses of the Marriage Group, of the Squire's untrammeled narrative style, and of courtly despair, then Chaucer has ironically undercut the seriousness of the Franklin's instruction by showing the falcon to be more "mesurable," more in control, than the heroine of the Franklin's Tale. It is one of the many ways Chaucer employs parallels of theme and structure and character to establish artistic order in the fragments of the *Canterbury Tales*.

5
Fragment III (Group D): The Wife of Bath's Prologue and Tale, the Friar's Tale, and the Summoner's Tale

> What wiste I wher my grace
> Was shapen for to be, or in what place?
>
> (553–54)

    Because of the antagonism between Friar and Summoner that erupts in the Prologue to the Wife of Bath's Tale and continues through the Prologues to the other tales, no one doubts that Chaucer consciously designed Fragment III as a coherent artistic whole. Though we cannot be certain, most scholars cautiously agree that Chaucer wrote what we now call the Shipman's Tale for the Wife of Bath and then subsequently assigned it to the Shipman when he found a better tale for Alice to tell. Whether the Wife of Bath's new Prologue and Tale actually introduce the Marriage Group or not is less important to this discussion of Chaucer's craft in the individual fragments than is the basic question of why Chaucer joined the Wife of Bath's Prologue and Tale to those of the Friar and Summoner. He has done so with art aforethought. With premeditation Chaucer introduces the antagonism between Friar and Summoner; with equal care he establishes strong similarities of structure and coherently develops themes which contribute to the unity of the fragment.

    Minor parallels and echoes enrich Fragment III. All the tales involve deception: Alice deceives her husbands, the crone deceives the knight, the devil deceives the summoner, Thomas deceives the friar, and so on. All the tales are concerned with riddles or mysteries: what women most desire, how the devil can shift his shape, how to divide and distribute the sound and savor of a fart, perhaps even whether a woman can be married more than once. Both the old crone in the Wife of Bath's Tale and the devil in the Friar's Tale have long been recognized as equally magical shape-shifters and the only ones in the *Canterbury Tales*. Both are discovered in the magical twilight zone "under a forest syde" (990 and 1380) between the open plowed fields on one side and the dark woods on the other. The devil hunts for souls, as the hunting imagery throughout the Friar's Tale suggests; the friar in the Summoner's Tale fishes for "Cristen mennes soules" (1820).¹ The lord's wife says to the friar in the Summoner's Tale that "a cherl hath doon a cherles dede" (2206), which echoes the crone's statement to the knight in the Wife of Bath's Tale that "he is gentil that dooth gentil dedis" (1170). The "book of wikked wyves" (685) from which Alice rips three pages in her Prologue appears in different guise as "the erchedeknes book" (1318) in the Friar's Tale and again as a book of women wicked in a different sense whose names the summoner intends to "striken . . . out of oure lettres blake" (1364); the friar in the Summoner's Tale does the same when "He planed awey the names everichon / That he biforn had writen in his tables" (1758–59). This friar claims that the poverty of his order may cause them to sell their books (2108). In no other fragment do books appear with such consistency; nowhere else are they treated with such disrespect.²

A great deal of activity in the *Canterbury Tales* occurs in bed. The beds in Fragment III radiate lines of coherence within the fragment that extend throughout the *Canterbury Tales*. The wedding-bed and the sick-bed are the central scenes for the action in the Wife of Bath's Tale and in the Summoner's Tale: the friar sits beside Thomas's sick-bed and lectures him until he receives Thomas's gift; and the knight sits beside his wedding-bed listening to the old crone lecturing him until she urges him to "Cast up the curtyn" (1249). Curiously, both Thomas's wife and Alice of Bath describe in similar words bed-activity which appears nowhere else in the *Canterbury Tales* so explicitly stated. Alice "wolde no lenger in the bed abyde, / If that I felte his arm over my syde" (409–10), and Thomas's wife, for other reasons, also finds no joy in bed when she "over hym leye my leg outher myn arm" (1828). In the Wife of Bath's Prologue, the bed is a place for debate (273), for murder (766 and cf. 578–79), for danger (87–89), and for joy (508). Only the Friar's Tale lacks a bed, though the "lecchours" (1310) whom the archdeacon stings for "fornicacioun" (1304) and the "bawdes" (1339), "approwours" (1343), and "wenches" (1355) whom the summoner employs all imply characteristic bedroom activities. The scene between the summoner and the old widow contains specific reference to all the beds in the *Canterbury Tales*: the sick-bed (1592), the marriage-bed (1621), and the fornicator's bed (1583, 1616).

References to sickness and death also reverberate through the fragment.[3] Thomas, of course, is sick in the Summoner's Tale, and the old widow in the Friar's Tale has "been syk, and that ful many a day" (1592). Thomas's wife mentions that her child died within the past two weeks (1852); the friar in the same tale describes "Irous Cambises" (2043) murdering a lord's child in an act of drunken illogic (2068) and a judge who irrationally condemns three knights to death (2034–42). The old widow in the Friar's Tale is apprehensive about going to the archdeacon's court for fear that "I be deed, so priketh it in my syde" (1594) and, since her husband has already died, she is a "widwe" (1619). The Wife of Bath, of course, is also a widow who has buried five husbands.

These incomplete parallels and complicated echoes are all decidedly minor contributions to the unity of the fragment. So too are the parallels among characters within the tales. More convincing parallels exist between the characters within the tales and the pilgrims. The degree to which Chaucer interpenetrates levels of fictionality—characters in the fiction of the Canterbury pilgrimage penetrating characters in the fictional tales that the pilgrims tell—distinguishes Fragment III from the other fragments in the *Canterbury Tales*. But, as with the other fragments, theme and structure also establish lines of coherence. The thematic component is particularly rich, and parallel patterns of organization in the structure of the tales are characteristically unique to the fragment.

I. Structure

If the Wife of Bath's Prologue is treated as a part of the fragment equal to the three tales, it shares with those tales exactly the same structure and pattern of development that characterize all parts of the fragment.[4]

Wife of Bath's Prologue	*Wife of Bath's Tale*	*Friar's Tale*	*Summoner's Tale*
Introductory Portrait: Alice of Bath Advertisement for herself	Introductory Description: Locus of Action	Introductory Portrait: Archdeacon and summoner	Introductory Portrait: friar
	Attack on Friar	Attack on Summoner	Attack on Friar
Interruption by Pardoner (163–92)	Interruption by Wife of Bath (931–82)	Interruption by Summoner (1332–37) Host cries "Pees" (1334)	Interruption by Friar (1761–64) Host cries "Pees" (1762)
Tale: Wife of Bath in action: quest for a husband	Tale: knight in action: quest for an answer	Tale: summoner in action: quest for money	Tale: friar in action: quest for money
Double Conclusion	Double Conclusion	Double Conclusion	Double Conclusion
End of Anger (822)	End of Anger (1239)	End of Anger (1634)	End of Anger (2195)
Link: Friar and Summoner	Link: Friar and Summoner	Link: Friar and Summoner	
Host cries "Pees" (850)	Host cries "Pees" (1298)		

Fragment III

INTRODUCTORY MATERIAL

All tales must begin in some way. Generally, Chaucer's tales begin with portraits of people whom Chaucer then shows in action. The introductory material which begins each tale in Fragment III, however, is more complicated than usual because, unlike material that introduces every other Canterbury tale, each introduction to a tale here has both an interior and an exterior focus. We shall see the same double focus repeated in the conclusion to each tale. Chaucer has designed this introductory material not simply to introduce the tale which follows but also to penetrate the frame of the pilgrimage by referring to matter outside the tale. The portrait of the friar which begins the Summoner's Tale, for example, describes the hypocritical, acquisitive main figure of the tale in terms which the pilgrim Friar understands as personally applicable to him or professionally applicable to friars in general. His interruption, "Nay, ther thou lixt, thou Somonour" (1761), indicates that he accepts the Summoner's fictional description up to a point ("ther") where he begins to take offense at a portrait which he no longer accepts as true of him or of friars in the world of the pilgrimage. Similarly, the portrait of the summoner which begins the Friar's Tale describes the archdeacon's sly boy (1322) in terms that suggest a devil (Mandel 1976) and apply specifically and explicitly to the pilgrim Summoner: "For though *this* Somonour wood were as an hare, / To telle *his* harlotrye I wol nat spare" (1327–28, my emphasis). The material which introduces the Wife of Bath's Tale does not portray a figure in the tale but describes the moral order of the world in which the tale occurs, the old days of King Arthur. It has long been noted that this description (857–81) also constitutes a subtle attack upon the pilgrim Friar who had presumed to control the Wife of Bath by interrupting her Prologue. The material which introduces us to Alice of Bath not only introduces the voice and character which dominate her Prologue and reveal her history, but also introduces a person whose easy and open celebration of sexual activity advertises her interest in a sixth husband wherever he may be found among the pilgrims or out in the world.

INTERRUPTIONS

Several tales in the *Canterbury Tales* are interrupted, but all the tales of Fragment III are the only ones that are interrupted and continued. The Host interrupts Chaucer's Tale of Sir Thopas, but instead of resuming it, Chaucer continues with Melibee. The Monk's Tale is interrupted and abandoned. The Squire's Tale may or may not be interrupted; it is not continued. The tales in Fragment III are not only all interrupted and resumed, but are all interrupted at approximately the same point in the development of the tale: after the introductory material and before the tale itself.

Furthermore, the interruptions share similar language. When the Friar interrupts the Summoner, the Host cries "Pees" (1762) and encourages the Summoner to disregard the Friar, to "Tel forth thy tale, and spare it nat at al" (1763). When the Summoner interrupts the Friar, the Host cries "Pees" (1334) and encourages the Friar to disregard the Summoner, to "telleth forth . . . / Ne spareth nat" (1336–37). When the Pardoner interrupts the Wife of Bath's Prologue, she cries "Abyde!" (169), and the Pardoner eventually encourages her to disregard everyone and "as ye bigan, / Telle forth youre tale, spareth for no man" (185–86). Since no one on the pilgrimage has the temerity to interrupt Alice of Bath (once they have heard her savage the Friar), Chaucer wryly allows her to interrupt herself. Her voice, as that of the narrator, is resonant throughout the tale, of course, but at one point in the tale she interrupts the voice of the narrator with the voice of the pilgrim. She interjects herself and the women of her time as the proper objects of the Arthurian knight's quest, disregarding the historical distinction she had earlier, in her position as narrator, been at pains to establish (857–81). The repetition of the first person plural pronouns ("we," "us," "oure") fifteen times in twenty-one lines (929–50), which occurs at no other point in her tale, affirms the interruption; the digression on Midas (952–82) emphasizes it—especially since that interruption begins with a formal acknowledgment of the audience of pilgrims ("wol ye heere the tale?" [951]) and ends with an equally disruptive bibliographical note that if the pilgrims want to hear the rest of the tale of Midas they should "Redeth Ovyde, and ther ye may it leere" (982).[5]

THE TALES

Despite differences in plot and genre, the tales of Fragment III are all stories of a quest involving a character in spite of him or herself. The Friar tells a tale of a summoner's quest for money. In spite of his overweening self-assurance and desire to help his "brother," the summoner is thwarted in his search and ironically becomes the devil's "preye" (1455) when he only wanted to give the devil an "ensample" (1580). The Summoner tells about a hypocritical friar's quest for money or goods. In spite of his previous success in the same place (1766–67) and his continued glib hypocrisy, the friar is thwarted in his attempt to win either Thomas's money or the sympathy of the local lord. The Wife of Bath's Tale concerns a knight's quest for the answer to a life-and-death question posed by the queen. In spite of his senseless rape of the maid and his resistance to the old crone, the knight wins both love and marriage. Alice of Bath, in spite of her previous experience of the "wo that is in mariage" (3), actively searches for a sixth husband wherever she can find him (45). No other fragment contains tales which all share both of these characteristics. Though one could argue that the Pardoner's Tale describes the quest for death and Sir Thopas the quest for an elf-queen, they do not share that element of plot with the other tales in their fragments, and they do not rely upon a character in spite of himself. No other fragment is rendered coherent by the consistent emphasis upon the quest as is Fragment III.

THE DOUBLE CONCLUSION

Chaucer ends the three tales and the Wife of Bath's Prologue with a double conclusion composed of a statement that caps the tale—often a blessing—and then an additional statement, irrelevant to the tale, which penetrates the frame of the pilgrimage. In the Friar's Tale and the Summoner's Tale, the addition takes on the character of an epilogue which advertises the speaker's learning. Fragment III is chockablock with teachers and preachers who create a particular tone characteristic of this fragment. Chaucer brought together three narrators who share the same attitude toward their fellow pilgrims and who, in advertising their control over the material they elucidate or would have liked to elucidate, affirm their superiority over their audience. The act of instruction presupposes the superiority of the instructor and so reflects the theme of mastery.

Much of the comedy and irony in the Friar's Tale derives from the summoner's attempt to teach the devil his business both with the carter and with the old widow. And, of course, the devil at the end plans on teaching the summoner hell's secrets so well that he will be able to lecture on the topic better than Vergil or Dante (1519–20). After the summoner is whisked off to hell, the Friar turns to the pilgrims with a conventional blessing (1642–44) similar to that which concludes other tales. Then, in an epilogue addressed to the "Lordynges" (1645) on the pilgrimage, the Friar extends his discourse beyond the false ending marked by the conventional blessing to advertise the kinds of learned things he might have spoken about were he not embroiled with the antagonistic Summoner. The Friar has been prevented from teaching the pilgrims something "After the text of Crist, Poul, and John, / And of oure othere doctours many oon" (1647–48).

Chaucer ends the Summoner's Tale with a similar internal and an additional external focus. The story concludes with the bemused lord calling the company to return to their meal and flippantly cursing Thomas for posing such a problem to the friar (2240–42). Jankyn's epilogue provides the second conclusion to the tale. Through Jankyn the Summoner continues his attack upon the pilgrim Friar by attributing to a squire and to a churl the qualities of wit and learning that the Friar claims for himself (1270–77). While the Friar would like to have spoken "After the text of Crist, Poul, and John" (1647), Jankyn speaks "As wel as Euclide [dide] or Protholomee" (2289). And Thomas shows the "subtiltee / And heigh wit" (2290–91) which the Friar implies he himself was prevented from displaying. Indeed, Jankyn's solution is more characteristic of the scholastic learning normally exhibited by medieval friars than that usually attributed to the less learned summoners of the time (cf. the portrait of the Summoner in the General Prologue, I, 637–45). Part of Chaucer's ironic treatment of the Friar derives from his placing that learning in the mouth of a squire who is himself, in the fiction of the *Canterbury Tales*, the created character of a Summoner. Or perhaps we should see the subtlety and high wit as the Summoner's who thus advertises himself every bit as learned as the self-important Friar.

Alice of Bath is a famous teacher. Not only does her tale turn upon the answer that the crone "taughte" (1050) to the knight,[6] but the Pardoner denominates her "a noble prechour" (165) and urges her to "teche us yonge men of youre praktike" (187). Chaucer ironically shows her teaching "wise wyves" (225) how she governed her first three husbands and "chidde hem spitously" (223). Surely that is not what the Pardoner had in mind. Although learning occupies a place at the end of Alice's Prologue and Tale (Jankyn's book and the crone's curtain speech), the external focus in the conclusion to the Wife of Bath's Tale does not advertise her learning as those of the Friar and Summoner had done; it advertises her experience. The Wife of Bath penetrates the frame of the pilgrimage at the end of her tale when she advertises her own preference in men by including herself among the "us" to whom she wants Jesus to send "Housbondes meeke, yonge, and fressh abedde" (1260). The Wife converts the conventional blessing, which often closes the tales, into a curse when she prays that Jesus shorten the lives of husbands "That noght wol be governed by hir wyves" (1262) and that God send the plague to niggardly husbands. These husbands, unlike the newly educated knight, are not in Alice's fiction but in the external world of the pilgrimage.

THE END OF ANGER

In addition to the double conclusion and the echoes of learning which characterize the ends of the tales in Fragment III, all the tales end with the same announcement: that the anger which occupied the characters within the tale is, or should be, now at an end. Fragment III is the most contentious fragment. Alone among the multitale fragments that comprise the *Canterbury Tales*, Fragment III is unified by anger. In no other fragment does the animosity among the pilgrims so threaten Harry Bailly's control of the pilgrimage that he is obliged to shout "Pees!" as he does not once but four times and only in this fragment (850, 1298, 1334, and 1762). The animosity between Friar and Summoner that begins in the Wife of Bath's Prologue, and the naked anger that appears in the links and generates their respective tales need not detain us—they are too obvious to require comment.

Interestingly, Alice of Bath, who seems removed from the angry exchange between Friar and Summoner, is the only one of the three described in the General Prologue as angry: if any wife preceded her to the offering, "so wrooth was she, / That she was out of alle charitee" (I, 451–52). Chaucer reveals Alice's anger in the Prologue to the Tale, too. The long example of how she controls her husbands (235–378) actually describes mock anger consciously designed and cautiously applied to achieve mastery. Only twice does she feel genuine rage: once with her fourth husband whom she makes fry in his own grease "For angre, and for verray jalousye" (488) because he had a mistress; and the second time with Jankyn over the book. Alice of Bath resolves her disagreement with Jankyn and marks the end of anger at the conclusion to her Prologue when she says that "We fille acorded by us selven two" (812) and that "After that day we hadden never debaat" (822).

Chaucer develops the theme of anger in the Wife of Bath's Tale by concentrating upon the knight who discovers himself the victim of his own rash boon and trapped into marrying the old crone. He laments ("Allas and weylawey!" [1058]); he resists ("chees a newe requeste! [1060]); he calls her his "dampnacioun" (1067) for having "so foule disparaged" (1069) a man of his birth. To no avail: he is constrained to marry her in a ceremony characterized by "hevynesse and muche sorwe" (1079) and by "the wo the knyght hadde in his thoght" (1083). All this reflects his anger which he articulates in action as "He walweth and he turneth to and fro" (1085) and prays that "God myn herte wolde breste!" (1103). The crone accurately defines his anger when she says "Ye faren lyk a man had lost his wit" (1095). The knight's anger dissipates only at the end of her reasoned and passionless curtain speech when she reveals her magic and says "Kys me . . . we be no lenger wrothe" (1239), which generously includes herself in the passionate anger that her husband alone has exhibited and which is now at an end.

Only the devil is passionless and calm in the Friar's Tale. He recognizes that the carter's anger at his horses is not heartfelt, and he intercedes in the angry exchange between the summoner and the widow when he recognizes that she sincerely damns the summoner. As part of the pattern of anger that thematically binds the fragment, the summoner had boasted to the devil that he did not care how angry the old woman became (1576); he was going to get money from her and show the devil how to "Wynne thy cost" (1580). In the splendid scene which follows, Chaucer carefully records their increasing anger and animosity in the rising volume of their voices until the woman begs for charity and the summoner wrathfully curses himself in refusing her (1609–11). Only when he angrily steps beyond the border of reason and unjustly accuses her of infidelity, does she actually become angry ("Thou lixt!" [1618]) and genuinely curse the summoner who, in his state of aroused anger, refuses to repent to save his soul.[7] With what gentle irony does Chaucer allow the devil to intercede and say to the angry summoner, "Now, brother, . . . be nat wrooth" (1634). He should not be angry with the old widow who, after all, gives him the chance to repent (1629); he should not be angry with the devil who, after all, takes only what people will give him (1430); and he should not be angry with himself for, after all,

Fragment III

he has done only what he intended to do and taught the devil how to win his cost (1580). It marks the end of anger in the Friar's Tale.

The contribution of the Summoner's Tale to the unifying theme of anger is more obvious and the irony less subtle than in the other tales of the fragment. Thomas's ill-health has left him cranky and "as angry as a pissemyre" (1825); the friar's hypocrisy has made him "wel ny wood for ire" (2121). Ironically, the friar, who preaches a sermon against anger (1992–2093) becomes enraged himself when he discovers himself insulted by Thomas and thwarted in his attempt to get money. The lord encourages the friar to "Distempre yow noght," be patient, and "Tel me youre grief" (2195–98). But the hypocritical friar, who speaks so glibly about the ill-effects, disadvantages, and sinfulness of anger, seems incapable of abandoning his own anger. His final speech (2210–15) plots vengeance against Thomas. The anger dissipates at the end of the tale nonetheless when the lord completely disregards the friar and Chaucer simply turns away from the friar's anger to focus on the comic and dramatic solution proposed by Jankyn.

LINKS

Of the six principal arguments which develop among the pilgrims in the links between the Canterbury tales, only that between the Friar and the Summoner contributes to the unity of the fragment in which it appears. When the Host interrupts Chaucer's Tale of Sir Thopas, Chaucer portrays himself as momentarily put out (VII, 2116–18), but once the Host justifies his displeasure, Chaucer "gladly" (VII, 2126) goes on to tell a different tale. When the Knight, supported by the Host, interrupts the Monk and encourages him to tell something more "gladsom" (VII, 3968), the Monk demurs saying he has "no lust to pleye" (VII, 3996). To be sure, the disagreement between the Manciple and the Cook contributes a clever comic extension to our understanding of the Manciple's Tale, but since the fragment is composed only of that one tale, it falls outside the scope of this work. Perhaps there is some disagreement between the Franklin and the Squire (it depends upon whether one understands the Franklin's words as interrupting the Squire or as following a Squire's Tale that Chaucer may have planned but never completed), but Chaucer makes nothing of it. Only the argument between the

Miller and the Reeve affects structure by ordering the sequence of tales, but it is a limited effect, pertaining only to two of the four tales in that fragment.

Alone among those fragments in the *Canterbury Tales* which have multiple links, Fragment III has the same two pilgrims present or implicit in all of the links. The argument between the Friar and the Summoner, which will focus the remainder of the fragment, begins in the link between the Wife of Bath's Prologue and her Tale. Each threatens to discredit the other. The Friar promises to "Telle of a somonour swich a tale or two / That alle the folk shal laughen in this place" (842–43); the Summoner promises to tell two or three tales of friars that "shal make thyn herte for to morne" (848). In the link between the Wife of Bath's Tale and the Friar's Tale, the Friar once again threatens that he "wol yow of a somonour telle a game" (1279), and the Summoner retorts that he will "hym quiten every grot" (1292) with tales of the Friar's crimes and his office (1295–97). In the final link between the Friar's and the Summoner's Tales, only the Summoner speaks to tell an obscene story about friars in hell, but the friar within the story has a speech and the Summoner specifically exempts "this cursed Frere" (1707) from the blessing with which he ends his Prologue.

II. Theme

WANDERING

No other fragment in the *Canterbury Tales* is so concerned with wandering. In Fragment III, Chaucer interpenetrates frame and tale: the external condition of pilgrimage becomes the internal focus of the tales. Indeed, except for the Man of Law's Tale, that of Sir Thopas who "wolde out ride" (VII, 1940), and perhaps that of the Pardoner whose three rioters do not seem to get very far from the tavern anyway, all of the Canterbury tales other than those in Fragment III describe close-to-home, local sorts of events that occur in bedrooms, gardens, woods, and nearby courts or consistories of the world in which the tale is set. Perhaps because Chaucer in the General Prologue remarks that Alice of Bath has been to Jerusalem (three times), to Rome, Bologne, Cologne, and St. James of Compostella, and "koude muchel of wandrynge by the weye" (I, 467), all of the tales in Fragment III emphasize search, quest, and wandering.[8] And they are all bound together by a line of coherence that I have used as the epigraph to this chapter: no one in the fragment knows what his or her fate is going to be, nor where it will be found.

The same restlessness which prompted the far-ranging activity that Chaucer uses to characterize Alice in the General Prologue, Alice reveals when describing the quality of her life in Bath in her own Prologue. As a matter of principle, she affirms that "We love no man that taketh kep or charge / Wher that we goon; we wol ben at oure large" (321–22), which for her means the freedom to visit "a gossib or a freend" (243) either at his house (245) or in the fields (549 and 564). She wanders about by day or night (397), from house to house (547 and 640), in any season (546) visiting vigils, processions, preachers, pilgrimages, miracle plays, and marriages (555–58) in order to see, to be seen, and to play (551–52). Her disclaimer that she is not interested in Jankyn who "squiereth me bothe up and doun" (305) fools no one but her husbands, and when Jankyn himself reads her proverbs which advise that "Man shal nat suffre his wyf go roule aboute" (653), she disregards him as cavalierly as she had disregarded her former husbands: "And walke I wolde, as I had doon biforn / From hous to hous, although he had it sworn" (639–40).

While the Wife of Bath in her wanderings may seek friendship or love, the knight in her Tale must "wende" (915) "A twelfmonth and a day, to seche and leere" (909) an answer to the question posed by the queen in order to preserve his life. His worldwide search requires that "He seketh every hous and every place / Where as he hopeth for to fynde grace" (919–20). Like Alice, he does not know "wher my grace / Was shapen for to be, or in what place" (553–54). Nor does the summoner in the Friar's Tale. Though he does not intend to ride far (1387–90), he actually goes all the way to hell with the devil who himself not only comes from a great distance (1397) "fer in the north contree" (1413), but eagerly rides "Unto the worldes ende for a preye" (1455). The friar in the Summoner's Tale wanders about his limited area of southern Yorkshire in order "To preche, and eek to begge" (1712). "In every hous he gan to poure and prye" (1738) advancing "hous by hous, till he / Cam til an hous ther he was wont to be / Refresshed moore than in an hundred placis" (1765–67), little realizing that his "grace / Was shapen for to be" of a sort quite different from what he expected.

ACQUISITIVENESS

People wander in Fragment III to win or acquire something. Alice is looking for a sixth husband (no one has ever suggested that her penchant for pilgrimage expresses a profound religious commitment); the knight requires an answer;[9] the summoner seeks a "brybe" (1378); the devil searches for "a preye" (1455); the friar has a long list of food, money, and cloth (1739-53) he is eager to accept. Of course the desire for something and the lust for power appear in one form or another in most of the tales, but Chaucer foregrounds acquisitiveness in the characters and actions of Fragment III. These people are almost exclusively concerned with money, possessions, riches, and with buying and selling or bartering or trading in order to satisfy their acquisitiveness. Alice of Bath, to take an obvious example, endures much "For wynnyng" (416). As she puts it in her famous statement of principle, "al is for to selle" (414), including what she calls "The bren" (478) and her *"bele chose"* (447). To be sure, she claims to marry Jankyn "for love, and no richesse" (526), but in order to win her other husbands' land and treasure (204, 212) she will "suffre hym do his nycetee" (412). In a metaphor common to the Middle Ages in the Christian West, she refers to sexual intercourse between husband and wife as the payment of "dette" (130, 153, 155) or of "raunson" (411). Whether or not the desire to acquire riches was Jankyn's primary motive in marrying Alice, he does come to possess "al the lond and fee" (630) which she had gathered from her former husbands until she realizes her mistake and wins back "the governance of hous and lond" (814).

In the Wife of Bath's Tale, the errant knight offers to pay the old crone if she can help him acquire an answer he has been searching the world to discover (1008). The crone, too, reveals her acquisitiveness in demanding that the knight agree to perform "The nexte thyng that I requere thee" (1010). When she requires marriage, the horrified knight attempts to buy her off with all his goods (1061), but she will not agree "for al the metal, ne for oore" (1064) that is above or below the ground. Her curtain speech decries all such riches and possessions and concludes that "He that coveiteth is a povre wight" (1187), a maxim as applicable to the friar and summoner in the following two tales as it is to the Wife of Bath. In the world conceived by Alice, where everything is for sale, the knight's relinquishing the alternatives offered to him by the crone acknowledges that he has suppressed his worldly appetite and his desire to assert mastery over women—

epitomized by the rape with which his adventure began. In allowing her to choose, he not only grants her sovereignty in marriage, but he withdraws from the acquisitive hurly-burly that characterizes Alice's world; ironically, he achieves everything he ever hoped to acquire.

The Friar's Tale is rife with acquisitiveness, the getting and taking of things, mostly money. The archdeacon applies "pecunyal peyne" (1314) to those of his parishioners who want to preserve their money or goods for themselves by proffering only small tithes and making small offerings to the church. The best part of the summoner's income derives from "briberyes" (1367) with which he manages "to fille his purs" (1348); he keeps for himself half the amount due his lord (1352). The devil appeals to the summoner's acquisitiveness when he offers him "gold and silver" (1400), all of which will be his when the summoner comes into the devil's country. The desire to learn "Som subtiltee" whereby he "may moost wynne" (1420–21) motivates the conversation between the two, for the devil too "wol entende to wynnyng, if I may" (1478). They ride together about the process of acquiring things, each taking his part of "what that men wol thee yive" (1531). Since the devil knows he wins nothing from the carter, the summoner will show him how to "Wynne thy cost" from the old widow who herself thinks in acquisitive terms ("This wyde world thogh that I sholde wynne" [1606]). The scene is rich in the language of acquisition—"profit" (1600, 1601), "Twelf pens" (1599, 1603, 1607), "hoold" (1607), "dette" (1615), "payde" (1617), and a double pun on gilt and guilt suggested by the old woman's proclamation of innocence, "I have no gilt" (1612, and cf. 1096, 385, 387)—and ends with the devil acquiring both body and pan. Ironically, the summoner articulates his blind refusal to repent in terms of acquisitions: he will not repent "For any thyng that I have had of thee. / I wolde I hadde thy smok and every clooth" (1632–33).

The importance of acquisitiveness in the Summoner's Tale requires little explication. Acquisitiveness defines the friar's character.[10] In church he exhorts the people "to yeve" (1717), and when everyone "had yeve him what hem leste" (1735), he wanders about his territory searching for more. Though the friar vilifies worldly possessions (1923–28), both Thomas and we recognize his "false dissymulacioun" (2123) and his greed. Thomas gives gold and goods away (1949–51, 1963–65) without apparent interest in acquiring something in return, though one can also argue that in return for his generosity he expects either a physical (1948–53) or a spiritual (2095–98) benefit. Even Jankyn, the lord's squire and servant, reveals his acquisitiveness when he offers to solve the riddle of division "for a gowne-clooth" (2247).

Chaucer discusses the theme of acquisitiveness not only as the activity of acquiring things but the attendant acts of division and distribution. In the Wife of Bath's Prologue, for example, Alice acquires land and treasure from her three good husbands without great expense of love. She acquires and holds everything, but Jankyn she "took for love, and no richesse" (526). She explicitly states that she gave him alone "al myn herte" (599) as well as "al the lond and fee / That evere was me yeven therbifoore" (630–31). She does not allow any of her other husbands to "Be maister of my body and of my good" (314), and they certainly do not possess her love. Although she repents "ful soore" (632) of her generosity to Jankyn, she retrieves only part of her gift to him, "the governance of hous and lond" (814). The other part—her love—he retains. Throughout her long monologue filled with curses and imprecations, denial of priestly authority, and disregard of aged husbands, Jankyn is the only man she honestly blesses—and she blesses him twice (504 and 827).[11]

In the Wife of Bath's Tale, the same concern for division occurs when the knight distinguishes between his body and his goods (1061). The choice that the old crone offers the knight in the curtain speech involves an improper division of what would delight him. He would be (and ultimately is) delighted by having "a trewe, hymble wyf" who is also "yong and fair." What he is offered, however, is a choice between a true wife who is "foul and old" (1220–23) or a beautiful young wife of whose virtue he could never be certain and whose effect upon the honor of his house he could never predict. He solves the dilemma by not choosing; and she satisfies his "worldly appetit" (1218) by re-dividing his choice, amending the real world that could not be amended, and giving herself to him "bothe fair and good" (1241).

In the Friar's Tale, the summoner and the devil swear true brotherhood, which means that each shall go about acquiring what he can (1530–32), "And if that any of us have moore than oother, / Lat hym be trewe and parte it with his brother" (1533–34). The tale provides no evidence that the devil divided his day's winnings with the summoner, since the summoner's body and the widow's pan went off with him to hell that night. In the Summoner's Tale, Chaucer brings to a point of comic delight the motif of division. The division of "Ful many a pound" (1951), "a ferthyng" (1967), and Thomas's gaseous "somwhat" (2129) prepare for the scene of division and distribution dramatically realized by Jankyn in his solution. Jankyn, as many have realized, as the lord's "kervere," is the appropriate member of the lord's household to solve a problem in division and distribution.

MASTERY/CONTROL

Mastery or control, especially in its form as sovereignty in marriage, has long been recognized as a central theme in the Wife of Bath's Prologue and Tale and in the *Canterbury Tales* as a whole.[12] Kittredge's seminal article on the theme of sovereignty in marriage (1911–12) argues that the Friar's and Summoner's Tales interrupt the Marriage Group that the Clerk's, Merchant's, and Franklin's Tales complete. I have no interest in joining the debate about the Marriage Group; I am more interested in determining why Chaucer joined the Wife of Bath's Prologue and Tale with the Friar's and Summoner's Tales. Seen from this point of view, the theme of mastery or control appears in all the tales of Fragment III and contributes to its coherence. Specifically, the theme involves the various answers to a question implicitly posed by Alice of Bath: Who shall "Be maister of my body and of my good"? (314). Each tale provides a different answer for "who" and for "what."

The Wife of Bath retains control both of her body and of her goods with four of her five husbands, and she retrieves that control from her fifth husband to whom she had carelessly relinquished it for love. The same concern for control over both body and goods appears in her Tale when the knight declares "Taak al my good and lat my body go" (1061). Both Alice and the crone get "maistrie" (818 and 1236) to "Do as thee lust" (820) or "as you liketh" (1235), and both become more attentive to their husbands (823–25 and 1255) though scholars disagree on the quality of that attentiveness for each woman. In the Friar's Tale, although the primary concern of the archdeacon and the summoner appears to be the acquisition of goods, the more important concern is actually the control of body. The summoner's spies, bawds, and wenches help him "somne" (1347, 1361, 1586) both the innocent and the evil to the archdeacon's court, but he willingly relinquishes this control over their bodies in order to accept bribes of money or goods. The summoner is fascinated by the "mannes shap" and "figure . . . determinat" (1458–59) that the devil assumes, and the devil promises him that he will ultimately learn the secrets of mastery over bodily shape (1514). The carter, who has difficulty controlling his horses, damns them "body and bones" (1544), while the old widow, who claims ever to have been "of my body trewe" (1621), earnestly damns the summoner's "body" (1623) to the devil who thus achieves ultimate control over the summoner's body (and the widow's pan). In the Summoner's Tale, on the other hand, the more important concern is the control of goods. While the friar claims control over the souls in hell (1729) and professes to pray for the speedy return to health of Thomas's "body" (1947), his primary concern is actually to acquire goods (1746–53) and Thomas's money. Ironically, Thomas thwarts the friar's lust for goods with a gift from his body. The irony is then compounded when Jankyn's solution to the problem, posed by Thomas's gift to the friar, involves the body of Thomas himself brought into the hall "with bely stif and toght" (2267).

The theme of mastery and control interpenetrates frame and tales in Fragment III when Chaucer involves the pilgrims who tell the tales. The antagonism which breaks out between Friar and Summoner at the end of the Wife of Bath's Prologue reflects the attempt of each to assert mastery over the other. Their behavior in the links between the tales—the Friar's "maner louryng chiere" (1266) and the Summoner's standing high in his stirrups (1665)—reveals their attitudes in their action and demeanor, and the tales they tell, by denigrating their adversary, reveal their desire for personal victory. The Friar interrupts the Wife of Bath in order to control the direction of her discourse—which she coyly recognizes when she pretends to ask the Friar's permission to continue (855). However, when she begins by savaging friars in the first twenty-four lines of her Tale, she reveals the futility of the Friar's attempt to control her.

In Fragment III, we cannot say whether the Friar or the Summoner wins the argument. We can say, however, that of the three pilgrims, Alice of Bath seems most in control. She alone retains mastery over both her body and her goods in her Prologue and, if the crone is the psychological extension of the Wife as Holland has claimed, in her Tale as well.[13] While Alice affirms her control, Chaucer shows that Alice of Bath does not at all control her own mind and body. She loses control in a variety of ways. At the beginning of her Prologue she introduces Solomon as an example of someone having many wives, but she loses the point of her comparison and drifts off to muse about his sexual accomplishments (35–43). She begins to discuss her fourth husband and drifts off to the joys of wine (453–68). She loses the concatenation of ideas: "But now, sire, lat me se what I shal seyn? / A ha! By God, I have my tale ageyn" (585–86). Three times she starts to tell the story of why Jankyn boxed her ears and why she was "beten for a book" (712). Finally the dramatic act of ripping three pages from Jankyn's book itself depicts a momentary loss of control over her body and her temper which the rest of the scene shows her reclaiming.

CONTRACT: BROTHERHOOD, SISTERHOOD, MARRIAGE

Though "contract" and its corollary, the acknowledgment of obligation among individuals (brotherhood, sisterhood, marriage), occupy an important position throughout the *Canterbury Tales*, it is ironic that Chaucer makes so much of it in a fragment so devoid of it.[14] Anger, not brotherhood, dominates Fragment III, and anger implies dissention.

The most formal contract for brotherhood, which implies mutual obligation, occurs in the Summoner's Tale. Though the friar refers to Thomas as "oure ͛ ᴜther" (1944) and "leeve brother" (2089), Thomas wants to know "how that I am youre brother" (2126). The "lettre with oure seel" (2128), which the friar claims to have given Thomas's wife, would have registered Thomas as a lay member of the friar's religious house. The friar had referred to that particular brotherhood earlier in the tale when he mentioned the "sexteyn" and "fermerer" who "han been trewe freres fifty yeer" (1859–60). The same brotherhood appears again in Jankyn's solution as the "covent" (2259) of friars brought into the lord's hall to partake in the division of Thomas's gift. Thus, as a formal brother in a relationship confirmed by a letter and a seal, Thomas is willing to give a gift to the friar on the famous "condicion" that he "swere on thy professioun" to "departe it" (2132–35) equally among the brotherhood.

Brotherhood is established and contracts formed in two less formal ways in Fragment III. One way involves the exchange of a handclasp; the other merely pledging one's word. When the friar agrees to Thomas's condition, "his hand in his he leith" (2138). The same act marks the knight's contract with the old crone in the Wife of Bath's Tale: the crone wants the knight to "Plight me thy trouthe heere in myn hand" (1009). Pledging with a mutual handgrip also joined the summoner and the devil: "Everych in ootheres hand his trouthe leith, / For to be sworne bretheren til they deye" (1404–5). Perhaps as a statement of his absolute sincerity (a matter of some consequence in the Friar's Tale) the summoner also pledges his word repeatedly: "My trouthe wol I holde to my brother, / As I am sworn" (1527–28, and 1525). Their "bretherhede" (1399) originates in recognizing that they share the same occupation, that of bailiff. It develops through an act of swearing fidelity each to the other (1404–5, 1521–29) and culminates in the contractual agreement that should one win more than the other, he will "parte it with his brother" (1534). He does not.

Chaucer describes other contracts and obligations in the fragment which are confirmed by pledge alone. Before the queen will allow the knight to leave court for a year-and-a-day to discover what women most desire, she requires some sort of "suretee" (911) or collateral that he will return, his "body for to yelden in this place" (912). The knight's word alone (1024) is apparently sufficient because he is allowed to leave the court and begin his search. The knight's pledge of his "trouthe" to the old crone leads inevitably to a different and unexpected sort of contractual arrangement when she requires him to marry her. The marriage contract obliges her, too, for after the knight allows the crone to decide between the two choices she had offered him, she decides "by my trouthe" to be "bothe fair and good" (1240–41). Perhaps her later decision to obey him in everything also derives from her marriage pledge. Chaucer had referred to the marriage contract earlier in the Wife of Bath's Prologue. The accord (812) between Alice and Jankyn, which ends their dramatic fight over the book, is simply a revision or realignment of the "statut" by which all her husbands "were bounden unto me" (198–99).

One final organization requires notice in Fragment III, the least formal and most successful of all. Alice of Bath's Prologue refers to a network of women in support of women, marked by mutual trust and mutual confidence, which Orme denominates "the female freemasonry of deception and seduction" (1981, 41).[15] It is a permanent relationship unformalized by pledge or contract, a sisterhood whose informal obligation is the furtherance of its members. First there is Alice's "gossib" (529), also named Alisoun, to whose house she "often tymes" (544) went before her marriage to Jankyn (who boarded at this gossib's house [528–29]), and whom she intends to continue visiting after her most recent marriage (639–40). This Alisoun "knew myn herte, and eek my privetee, / Bet than oure parisshe preest" (531–32). She was the person to whom Alice confided all her secrets (533) and all her husband's secrets as well (538).[16] In addition to Alisoun, the Wife of Bath was on equally intimate terms with "another worthy wyf,

/ And my nece, which that I loved weel" (536–37). These women support each other in various ways. Like the brotherhood of the summoner and the devil, which involves the exchange of subtleties (1418–20), all members of this sisterhood also exchange subtleties. When Alice leads Jankyn to believe that "he hadde enchanted me" (575), she willingly admits "My dame taughte me that soutiltee" (576) and that in matters of seduction or dream interpretation "I folwed ay my dames loore" (583).[17] Alice also affirms that women will lie in support of each other (227–28). Should any woman "mysavyse" (230) and be caught or suspected of improper behavior, she need only argue against her husband "And take witnesse of hir owene mayde / Of hir assent" (234–35). The maid will inevitably support her mistress.

The sisterhood continues to exercise its power in the Wife of Bath's Tale. The "queene and other ladyes mo" (894) rise in support of the raped maiden and beg the king to place the knight's fate in their hands.[18] A dance "Of ladyes foure and twenty, and yet mo" (992) supports the old crone. The knight appears before the queen's court composed of "many a noble wyf, and many a mayde, / And many a wydwe . . . / The queene hirself sittynge as a justise" (1026–28). When the old crone asks this court to support her claim upon the knight, this court constrains him to marry her. Chaucer creates the sisterhood of women as Alice of Bath's answer to the brotherhood of men. With irony, Chaucer shows in this fragment that the sisterhood provides more support to its members than does the brotherhood of men which, in the Friar's and the Summoner's Tales, is characterized by perfidy, deceit, broken oaths, and disloyalty.

6
Fragment I (Group A): The General Prologue, the Knight's Tale, the Miller's Tale, the Reeve's Tale, and the Cook's Tale

> For nature hath nat taken his bigynnyng
> Of no partie or cantel of a thyng,
> But of a thyng that parfit is and stable,
> Descendynge so til it be corrumpable.
>
> (3007–10)

The first fragment of the *Canterbury Tales* is Chaucer's most polished fragment. The dramatically sensible impetus that defines the tale-telling game and joins the General Prologue to the first tale, the logical transitions between the subsequent tales, the contribution to the drama of the pilgrimage by the tensions between characters that develop in the links, and the comments made by subsequent tales of Miller, Reeve, and Cook upon the preceding tale or teller suggest Chaucer's craft and the care he took to unify the fragment.

Care and craft were necessary. We have no way of knowing how many of the tales Chaucer had on hand before he started to assemble the *Canterbury Tales*. It is relatively easy to construct a fragment out of two tales written from scratch: one can conceive the unity of the whole before beginning to write. It is only slightly more complex to construct a fragment out of two tales, one of which is already at hand: one can shape the second tale to reflect and develop the themes, characters, and structure of the first and so establish the unity of the whole. Fragment I is complex not only because the story of Palamon and Arcite existed at least in manuscript before Chaucer conceived of it as the Knight's Tale and the first in the *Canterbury Tales*,[1] but also because, once

Chaucer had chosen a pilgrimage to be the frame for the *Canterbury Tales*, he was obliged by the demands of his fiction to create introductory material (the General Prologue) which, by its very nature, was different from and unrelated to any of the subsequent tales.

Nonetheless, Chaucer unifies the fragment in many ways. He repeats words and phrases (e.g., 545 and 3469) and even whole lines ("Allone, withouten any compaignye" [2779 and 3204] is the most famous). He shows people weeping (the Prioress [144], Venus [2664–66], Absolon [3759], and Malyne almost [4248]), which he does only rarely elsewhere. He uses the same device—a hole—to further the plot in all the tales: Palamon sees Emily through a window; John's servant peeps in at Nicholas through a hole which the cat was accustomed to use; Absolon's serenade, insult, and revenge all occur at the "shot-wyndowe"; and moonlight shines through a hole in the Reeve's Tale by which light Symkyn's wife mistakes her husband for a clerk and knocks him down. But Chaucer's real success in unifying this fragment, as in unifying all the other fragments, occurs in theme and structure. They testify to his craft.

I. Structure

At the beginning of the *Canterbury Tales*, Chaucer creates his world out of the stuff normally available for these purposes in the Middle Ages: air ("Zephirus," "sweete breeth," "Inspired"); earth ("droghte," "roote," "holt and heeth"); fire ("the yonge sonne"); and water ("shoures soote," "bathed," "licour"). In this world, suggestive of Eden, of new birth and young life, nature and supernature function quite as they should: "smale foweles maken melodye" and people long to express their devotion to God as is appropriate in any well-constructed Christian universe.[2] However, with the acknowledgement that Fortune or chance operates in the world ("Bifel," "by aventure"), Chaucer commits himself to showing that well-made world going askew. The most immediate indication of a world—built of the best materials and peopled by seekers after holiness—going askew appears in the very portraits of the pilgrims, not because they are in any sense grotesque or aberrant, but because they are quintessentially human. Though often the best of their kind, they are born in time after the Fall and are therefore less than Edenic. The second indication of a world askew comes when Harry Bailly affirms the importance of chance ("Now draweth cut") after he transforms the nature of the pilgrimage from a religious observance, in which one thanks God through his "hooly blisful martir," into a game, an occasion for "disport" designed for "confort," "myrthe," and "pleye" (772–75). However, the most important indication of a world askew is expressed in the very structure of Fragment I.

In Fragment I two structural principles are at work simultaneously: (1) the structure of the individual tales, which reveals their similarity, and (2) the structure of the fragment as a whole, which describes the organizational principle governing the relationship among the tales within the fragment. The attached scheme expresses each of these in a different way: (1) the Distribution of Characters by Generation shows the similarity in structure of the individual tales, and (2) the Distribution of Characters by Function shows the principle of decay which describes the relationship among the tales.

We have long recognized that the Miller's Tale parodies the Knight's Tale, retelling the story and recasting the characters. The Miller transforms a story of courtly love among the nobility in ancient Athens into a story of quite common lust among ordinary people in contemporary Oxford. In the Reeve's Tale and what exists of the Cook's Tale, Chaucer again repeats the structural pattern among the characters of the Knight's story: the triadic relationship of two men to one woman. As the Distribution of Characters by Generation indicates, all the tales in Fragment I contain a member of an older generation and three members of a younger generation, a group for the most part composed of two men and a woman, whose relationships threaten the various ideas of order represented by the older generation. The stories all show how the younger generation upsets the order by deceiving and tricking or manipulating the older generation with varying degrees of success.[3]

The structure of these individual tales remains consistent throughout the fragment and contributes to its unity. But a principle of decay governs the relationship among these tales, describes the organization of the whole, and contributes to the structural unity of the fragment. Chaucer articulates that principle most clearly in the First Mover speech which I have taken as the epigraph for this chapter: "Descending so til it be corrumpable" (3010). The Distribution of Characters by Function most clearly describes this principle of deterioration and decay of the world gone askew. The tales within this fragment descend from

Distribution of Characters by Generation: The Similarity in the Structure of Tales

	Knight's Tale	Miller's Tale	Reeve's Tale	Cook's Tale
Older Generation	Saturn (Jupiter)[a] (Egeus) Theseus	John ( )	(Priest) Symkyn	Master ( )
Younger Generation	Venus Mars Diane	Nicholas Absolon Alison	John Aleyn Malyne and Symkyn's Wife[b]	Perkyn Friend Wife

Distribution of Characters by Function: The Principle of Decay in the Relationship of Tales

	Knight's Tale	Miller's Tale	Reeve's Tale	Cook's Tale
Beloved	(Diane)[c] Emily	Alison	Malyne and Symkyn's Wife	Wife
Adversary (Pilgrims)	Palamon Arcite Theseus	Nicholas Absolon John	John Aleyn Symkyn	Perkyn Friend Master
Authority (Host)	Venus Mars Saturn			

[a] The less important figures among the older generations appear in parentheses. They occupy only minor positions in the Knight's and Reeve's Tales and are absent from the Miller's and Cook's Tales.
[b] Splitting one character into two is a common phenomenon known as "fission."
[c] Perhaps this slot should be blank since Diane is not the object of the adversaries' attention. She appears in this scheme only to complete the pattern and because she does represent Emily's ideal.

the ideal to the real, from the "parfit . . . and stable" (3009) to the flawed and chancey, from the divine to the merely ordinary, from the eternal to the "corrumpable." Tracing the deterioration of a particular group of characters—the beloved, the adversaries, the figure of authority—through the fragment describes this principle at work.

Significantly, Chaucer did not wait until the end of the Knight's Tale to introduce the principle. The General Prologue illustrates precisely this principle of deterioration in the idea of pilgrimage which, by beginning as an exercise in religious devotion (albeit qualified by Chaucer's irony) and descending to a game, deteriorates from the ideal to the "corrumpable." The portraits of the pilgrims follow the same principle, beginning with the Knight and Squire and ending with five thieves and the mundane Host who perverts the purpose of pilgrimage by transforming earnest into game.

PROGRESSIVE DETERIORATION OF THE BELOVED

The decay in the conception of the woman from Emily to the wife of Perkyn Revelour's friend marks the descent from the ethereal to the mundane and mirrors the organizational principle of the fragment.[4] The contrast between Emily and Alison has long been in the scholarly public domain. Emily's portrait is of airy nothing built. She is "fairer" and "fressher" and probably "fyner" (1035–39) than various flowers and has only one distinguishing physical characteristic: "Hir yelow heer was broyded in a tresse / Bihynde hir bak, a yerde long" (1049–50). This insubstantial wraith resists the contamination of the flesh, preferring "to ben a mayden al my lyf, / Ne nevere wol I be no love ne wyf," nor "be with childe," nor "knowe the compaignye of man" (2305–11). Her ideal is the divine Diane the chaste. Alison's famous portrait, on the other hand, emphasizes her barnyard associations and animal appetites. She seems to have been designed for the joys of the flesh to be shared with "any lord" or "any good yeman" (3269–70). The repeated adjective "any" suggests her lack of discrimination and marks a moral as well as a spiritual decline from Emily.

Alison does not represent the last word in corruption. While Alison "atte laste" (3290) commits herself to loving Nicholas with its attendant joys, Malyne and her mother's involvement with the two clerks is both unpremeditated and unexpected. Unlike Alison's affair with Nicholas, Malyne's involvement with

Aleyn is an unplanned and isolated experience offering no possibility of continuation. Her mother's involvement with John is equally the result of accident and happy chance. Chaucer does not indicate her interest in cuckolding her husband or even that she knows she has been in bed with anyone other than Symkyn, though she ultimately may suspect.[5] The fact that she enjoys her bed-partner without knowing who he is looks forward to the wife of Perkyn Revelour's friend, a woman whose profession demands repeated and premeditated sexual play with various unknown johns for money.

The descent from Knight's Tale to Cook's Tale describes a movement from simplicity to multiplicity, from unique love to indiscriminate love. At first Emily utterly rejects love, men, and marriage.[6] Only at the instigation of the prince and with the confirmation of his parliament does she finally marry. The standard of resistance established by Emily deteriorates among the other women as the fragment develops: Alison puts up only a mock refusal before capitulating; Malyne and her mother do not refuse at all; and the wife of Perkyn's friend, as a professional, readily accepts everyone.

As part of the decay from simplicity to multiplicity, the love relationship becomes increasingly complicated. In this sense, the Miller's Tale is more complicated than the Knight's Tale because, unlike Emily, Alison is married to one man and in bed with another. The relationships depicted both in the Knight's and in the Miller's Tales appear concurrently in the Reeve's Tale. The situation of Symkyn's wife echoes that of Alison; Malyne's bedtime relationship echoes that of Emily since it depicts two unmarried people and is decorated with the language of courtly love; and the wife of Perkyn's friend is married to one man and in bed with everyone else. If the numerical progression means anything, Fragment I deteriorates from love between two (Palamon and Emily) to sexual involvement among three (John, Alison, and Nicholas), four (Aleyn and Malyne, John and Symkyn's wife) or five (if one adds Symkyn), and finally to what masquerades as love between a married prostitute and her numberless clients.

To mark the decline from the spiritual, Chaucer emphasizes the physical aspects of lovemaking as the number of people involved in the activity increases. In terms of the principle which governs the structure of Fragment I, the quality of love deteriorates as the fragment develops. The lovers in the Knight's Tale never touch, never immerse love in flesh. The courtly conception of love at a distance, uncontaminated by mutual awareness or mutual response, defined by the courtly love code of selfless service, never descends to the physical or even the personal, as Theseus points out with amusement in his speech on "The god of love" (1785–1844). For Palamon and Arcite, love is visual: Palamon "cast his eye upon Emelya" (1077) and Arcite "gan espye" (1112) her. Chaucer couches the question of love with which the first part ends in terms of sight: "That oon may seen his lady day by day, / . . . That oother . . . / . . . seen his lady shal he nevere mo" (1349–52). Love is more physical in the Miller's Tale as the emphasis upon Nicholas's hands suggests. But when the lovers are abed, Chaucer retreats behind the indefinite "bisynesse of myrthe and of solas" (3654). The Reeve's Tale, which is, in general, a more athletic tale than the others, is far more specific than they about the physical aspects of love. Aleyn "priketh harde and depe as he were mad" (4231), and John worked so hard all night long while he "Swyved the milleres doghter bolt upright" (4266) that he says his "heed is toty of my swynk to-nyght" (4253). We have no way of knowing how Chaucer would have treated the sexual activity of a professional who "swyved for hir sustenance" (4422) in the unfinished Cook's Tale, but the treatment of the preceding relationships shows a clear pattern of development.

The conception of marriage changes in line with the general deterioration that characterizes the structure of the fragment. In the Knight's Tale, the marriage between Theseus and Hippolyta expresses one aspect of Theseus's excellence; his success in love and in war provides an ideal to which the other knights aspire. The marriage of Palamon and Emily more explicitly defines the ideal relationship that Chaucer repeats elsewhere in the *Canterbury Tales*. They live "in blisse, in richesse, and in heele"; Emily loves him "tendrely"; Palamon serves her "gentilly" so "That nevere was ther no word hem bitwene / Of jalousie or any oother teene" (3102–6). The only indication that marriage can be less than ideal occurs in Arcite's prayer to Mars when he refers to the time that Vulcan caught Mars lying by his wife. In the Miller's Tale, jealousy and adultery weaken marriage: the jealousy that Palamon and Emily never felt completely dominates John's attitude toward Alison, and the adultery that the Knight reserves for the gods becomes the common activity for the Miller's more earthly characters and so vitiates the ideal of marriage. For the Reeve, marriage is even more debased. He defines it as the commercial alliance of appropriate ranks. Only the Reeve mentions dowry. Symkyn marries his wife "To saven his estaat of yomenrye" (3949). The parson of the town was anxious "that

Symkyn sholde in his blood allye" by marrying his daughter, and therefore he provided as dowry "ful many a panne of bras" (3944–45). In order for Malyne to marry "Into som worthy blood of auncetrye," her grandfather will provide her, too, with a significant dowry "of his catel and his mesuage" and other of "hooly chirches good" (3979–83). The Cook's Tale, again, is too incomplete to provide any firm evidence for the continued deterioration of the ideal of marriage, though the apparent commercial exploitation of a wife as a prostitute seems yet another step in that direction.

PROGRESSIVE DETERIORATION OF THE ADVERSARIES

To the extent that the *Canterbury Tales* is drama and the essence of drama is conflict, the idea of adversary relationships pervades every tale and fragment of the poem, affecting both characters and pilgrims.[7] In Fragment I, the relationship among the pilgrims deteriorates so that people who are initially fellow travelers become adversaries. In the General Prologue Chaucer carefully describes the ties which bind the pilgrims together and then shows the forces which break those ties in the links between the tales. The pilgrims begin their journey as a "compaignye / Of sondry folk" come together by chance but unified "In felaweshipe" by their common commitment: "and pilgrimes were they alle" (24–26). As a group they admit Chaucer to their fellowship. As a unified company they agree to start early in the morning, and they make another agreement, confirmed by oaths, to tell tales on the way to and from Canterbury and to let Harry Bailly be their governor and judge. The Knight confirms this ideal of amity and fellow-feeling when he shows his willingness "To kepe his foreward by his free assent" (852).

The rivalry among the pilgrims quickly dissipates the friendship and apparent singleness of purpose that unites them. Neither love nor lust nor the desire to win the supper at journey's end motivates the antagonism among the pilgrims; they are moved by ordinary human perversity. The Miller thwarts the Host because he has a different idea of what it means to "werken thriftily" (3131) and wants to "quite" the Knight's Tale with a "noble tale" that reflects a completely different order of reality. The Reeve attacks the Miller on personal grounds with professional overtones; the Cook attacks the Host on professional grounds with personal overtones.

Having established in the frame the idea that rivalry is a fundamental pattern of human behavior, Chaucer develops the idea in the Knight's Tale and the Miller's Tale. He shows its pervasiveness when he brackets the noble rivalry of Palamon and Arcite from above and below with parodic antagonism in heaven and in Oxford. The conflict between Palamon and Arcite arises out of genuine differences in their conception of friendship and out of genuine rivalry over Emily. The animosity between Venus and Mars parodies that between Palamon and Arcite by being a childish fuss over preeminence and having nothing at all to do with friendship or with love. It develops out of silly pique by two selfish gods unaccustomed to having their wills thwarted or their promises denied. Just so, the battle between Absolon and Nicholas parodies that in the Knight's Tale by having nothing at all to do with friendship or with love. The diminution in social scale from courtly knights to common clerks is only part of the parody. No matter how fine the language in which Absolon and Nicholas dress their feelings, courtly love is only common lust, too easily won (3288–93) and too quickly abandoned (3754–57). Moreover, their antagonism does not spring from any genuine differences. The eager young men do not even know they are adversaries: Nicholas does not consider Absolon an obstacle in his conquest of Alison, and Absolon does not know about Nicholas until he hears Nicholas's joyful cry "A berd! a berd!" after Alison "clapte the wyndow to" (3740–42). The battle itself, of course, fought at night in private with deception, a hot coulter, and air, parodies the public daytime conflict of two hundred knights fighting with more conventional weapons.

John and Aleyn are adversaries of another sort. They compete with each other only to determine who shall appear less foolish when the day's events are related among their friends. Motivated by vengeance and pride, they share a mutual antagonism to Symkyn, but they compete with each other only for reputation. They do not even argue over a woman: two women are available, and both clerks succeed. Aleyn sleeps with Malyne for "esement" (4186) and the opportunity to crow over John for being a coward; John sleeps with Symkyn's wife so that he will not "been halde a daf, a cokenay" (4208), when the story is told. The diminution appears on the social scale as well: both are slightly below the clerks in the Miller's Tale. Nicholas has already completed his study of the trivium, and Absolon is already a parish clerk; neither lives in college. John and Aleyn, however, are in the midst of their studies and continue to live in college, at Solar Hall in Cambridge.

And Perkyn Revelour and his compeer, as apprentices in the "craft of vitailliers" (4366) (if that is what "of his owene sort" [4419] means in addition to meaning as riotous as Perkyn), are one step below the clerks on the social scale. We cannot know whether Perkyn and his friend would become rivals for the apparently generous favors of the friend's wife since the tale is incomplete, but Chaucer had prepared for that possibility by continuing the pattern of a triadic relationship from the Knight's Tale into the Cook's Tale.

PROGRESSIVE DETERIORATION OF THE OLDER GENERATION

The figures of authority in all the tales of Fragment I quite naturally represent the older generation. These figures of established accomplishment affirm the moral order of the world they inhabit. The descent from Theseus to Symkyn follows the same principle of deterioration from the ideal to the corruptible that we have seen throughout the fragment. Though the best of the lot, Theseus still lives in the post-Edenic real world where perfection is not attainable. He is far from ideal. He is quick to take offense (905–6), excessive (1024), punctilious (1704–13), quick to anger (1762), and quick to judge (1747). He is also quick to pity (952–64), generous (1205), reasonable (1766), and compassionate (1770). His changeableness appears most publicly on the morning of the tournament when his herald announces the changes in the rules for the combat: "Wherfore, to shapen that they shal nat dye, / He wol his firste purpos modifye" (2541–42). Theseus is thwarted in this as he is in so many other things. His inconstancy is not caprice,[8] but it does reflect an orderly universe subverted by chance more often than the First Mover speech might lead us to believe possible. Like Theseus, who is the epitome of success in war and love, John the carpenter succeeds in work and money. He is both rich and active in his craft (3400, 3665–68). Though John himself is honest, his universe is subverted by deception. Symkyn, however, is fundamentally dishonest. He represents a decayed world more corrupt and farther from the ideal than that of the Miller's Tale. Stealth and violence ("sleighte" and "force" [4011]) subvert this world. The master in the world of the Cook's Tale does not continue the descent from the ideal to the corrupt. His release of the riotous apprentice and his desire to preserve order by eliminating one "roten appul" bespeak an intelligence and a moral view superior to that of Symkyn.

Other than this master of the fragmentary Cook's Tale, whose ultimate success we have no way of measuring, the most successful ruler in Fragment I is Saturn. His powerful influence, defined in terms of death, vengeance, treason, and deception (2454–69), works capriciously in the world to frustrate human endeavor. The capricious death of Arcite, arranged by Saturn to settle a squabble among the gods and to favor his granddaughter Venus, contradicts in spirit and substance the Boethian view of cosmic order propounded by Theseus in the First Mover speech.[9] Theseus's view, which describes an ordered world of ideal authority, and Saturn's view, which describes a world controlled by chance and sublime special interest, reflect a tension between the ideal and the real which energizes both this fragment and the *Canterbury Tales* as a whole.

In the frame, Harry Bailly himself assumes, with the consent of the other pilgrims, a position of control and authority. Everyone agrees that "we wol reuled been at his devys" and "been acorded to his juggement" (816–18), but the reality of pilgrimage and the effect of drink upon the Miller quickly subvert the Host's ideal of order, of what it means to "werken thriftily" (3131). By refusing to allow the Host to proceed according to his idea of order and by threatening to abandon the fellowship, the Miller undermines Harry Bailly's authority and affirms a different, more capricious idea of order. The Host can only capitulate. He attempts to reimpose his authority when he speaks to the Reeve "as lordly as a kyng" (3900). He attempts to resurrect his idea of order by establishing two principles with which to proceed thriftily in the future. One is time: "Sey forth thy tale, and tarie nat the tyme" (3905–8). The other is estate or position in society: "The devel made a reve for to preche" (3903). The Reeve may proceed to tell a tale if he will do so quickly and assume his proper estate in society, which means that he speak like a reeve and not like a priest. When the Cook comes to tell his tale, he asks Harry Bailly for permission (4340–41), which Harry eagerly grants twice (4345 and 4353), but his authority has long since been undermined, and he never quite gains control of the pilgrimage again.

Chaucer describes the decay of order in the *Canterbury Tales* in many ways: the deterioration among the characters in the older generation and of Harry Bailly in the frame, which we have just seen, are only the most obvious. But Chaucer's craft in the *Canterbury Tales* shows him unifying the fragments by multiplying parallels. The idea of order "Descendynge so til it be corrumpable" appears in more subtle and sophisticated ways throughout the fragment.

Ceremony, procession, and purposeful journey objectify the idea of order in the fragment. They appear in every tale in Fragment I although, as Cooper notes, this is unusual for Chaucer who "very rarely makes a journey the structural basis of a work" (1984, 129). The Christian ideal of a purposeful journey, of course, is the pilgrimage, both as a journey to Canterbury and as a metaphor for the soul's journey to the heavenly Jerusalem. In the Knight's Tale, the journey takes the form of Theseus's wedding procession, the advance of the army against Thebes, the return to Athens after the tournament, the return of the tournament participants to their homes, and the procession of mourners to Athens after Arcite's funeral—all of which reflect, in one way or another, the twin themes of love and war.[10] These processions which open Fragment I—religious devotion, love, and war—deteriorate as the fragment progresses. In the Miller's Tale, Alison goes to church "on an haliday" (3309) which connotes procession, but she goes with a shiny forehead which suggests a motive less serious than religious devotion; John goes to Osney to work and Absolon goes "With compaignye, hym to disporte and pleye" (3660). Nicholas describes the victory over the flood as a procession of tubs floating through a hole in the gable. Symkyn precedes his wife to church on holidays and threatens anyone else "that wente by the weye" (3957) who would treat her with disrespect, thus vitiating the religious motive with violence and pride. And Perkyn eagerly joins every procession "whan ther any ridyng was in Chepe" (4377). He also partakes of the procession when he was "somtyme lad with revel to Newegate" (4402). Since the paradigm of an ordered procession and purposeful journey is the pilgrimage with which the poem begins, the final procession of Perkyn to Newgate suggests how much the ideal order has deteriorated in the fragment, from Canterbury to Newgate, from the cathedral which points the soul's way to heaven to the prison which incarcerates the flesh.

Chaucer establishes a progressively less stable world for each tale in Fragment I; chance and chaos become stronger in each.[11] The Knight's Tale defines the order of the universe in two ways. In the First Mover speech, Theseus affirms the existence of a stable and eternal Prince who binds the world with a "faire cheyne of love" (2988) and holds it under his conscious control: "Wel wiste he why, and what thereof he mente" (2990). Palamon and Arcite provide quite a different view. Arcite emphasizes the uncertainty of the world: he sees that human beings are as "dronke . . . as a mous" and acknowledges that "to a dronke man the wey is slider" (1261–64). Palamon recognizes that cruel gods govern this world and questions their ability to do so: "What governance is in this prescience[?]" (1313). Both Palamon and Arcite, who have defined the world as uncertain and basically lacking in order, behave as though they were living in Theseus's well-ordered universe. Their prayers to the gods indicate that they see the gods as able to arrange and rearrange the world. Theseus, on the other hand, who has posited an ordered, purposefully governed universe, behaves as though he were living in an uncertain one. His contradictory and shifting demands indicate his desire to control that uncertain world and ironically contribute to its uncertainty, and his depression at the seemingly pointless death of Arcite reflects his inability to accept the world's disorder.

In the Miller's Tale, John enunciates the uncertainty of the universe in which he lives: "This world is now ful tikel, sikerly" (3428) and "A man woot litel what hym shal bityde" (3450). Like the characters in the Knight's Tale, John believes one way and acts in another. Despite his attitude toward clerks and learning, he accepts Nicholas's explication of "Cristes conseil" (3504) and, in releasing the servants, gathering the tubs and provisions, and building the ladders, John behaves as though the world were more ordered than he has indicated he believes it to be. The Reeve's Tale, on the other hand, has no explicit statement of the world's order, but the emphasis in the tale on truth (3924), philosophy (4059), law (4179), time (3906–7), and social order (3903) imply an ordered universe. The universe is not so benevolently ordered, of course; instead, chance or malevolence actually control the world of the Reeve's Tale. Chance and malevolence ultimately thwart human attempts to manipulate the world signaled by Symkyn's thievery and the clerks' stratagems.

In the fragmentary Cook's Tale, the actions of the master suggest a logical, ordered world which is abandoned by the characters whose behavior would have formed the tale. More directly than in the preceding tales Chaucer here posits a world where chance dominates. Chaucer's image for this is "dys," and Perkyn is master of the game: "nas ther no prentys / That fairer koude caste a paire of dys / Than Perkyn koude" (4385–87). His compeer, too, "lovede dys" (4420), and they would often gather with their friends "To pleyen at the dys" (4384). The result is rot, riot, waste, theft, and deception—all aspects of chaos and a long descent from a world "that parfit is and stable" (3009).

Chaucer carefully orchestrates the decay of order in the fragment by showing the members of the older generation, the representatives of authority and accepted social norms, as victims of deception overcome by trickery. Arcite, himself deceived by Mercury, deceives Theseus by adopting the name Philostrate in order to be admitted to the royal household.[12] The Miller's Tale depends upon Nicholas's elaborate deception of John. Chaucer develops the decay of order through deception with Alison's trick upon Absolon at the shot-window, with Absolon's desire to avenge himself by promising a ring but delivering a hot coulter instead, and with Nicholas's plan to "amenden al the jape" (3799). Symkyn is a "sly" (3940) thief and trickster who reflects the moral untidiness and instability which rule the world of the Reeve's Tale. At first he deceives "curteisly" and then he deceives "outrageously" (3997–98). Although John and Aleyn's first courteous attempts to enforce the miller's honesty by standing above and below the mill do not deceive Symkyn at all ("This millere smyled of hir nycetee" [4046]), their later, more outrageous attempts to redress their grievance by sexual assault upon Symkyn's family succeed. Appropriately in such a world, "a litel shymeryng of a light" (4297) deceives Symkyn's wife; when she attacks her husband who normally defends her, she contributes to the topsy-turviness of the world. In the Cook's Tale, the wife of Perkyn's friend disguises her primary occupation by keeping a shop "for contenance" (4421), but the decay of order through deception stops with her. Perkyn's behavior does not deceive the master who "yaf him acquitance, / And bad hym go, with sorwe and with meschance" (4411–12).

Characters among the younger generation also contribute directly to the decay of order in the world. They subvert the authority of the older generation and try to manipulate or vitiate the order of the world by attempting to discover secret things, "pryvetee."[13] The characters in the Knight's Tale actually contribute least in this regard. Palamon, Arcite, and Emily only want to know or influence the will of the gods. Unaware of "The destinee, ministre general, / That executeth in the world over al / The purveiaunce that God hath seyn biforn" (1663–65), they each address their favorite deity in order to discover the secrets of the future and to affect the outcome of the tournament. But the Miller says that "An housbonde shal nat been inquisityf / Of Goddes pryvetee, nor of his wyf" (3163–64). Though John also believes that "Men sholde nat knowe of Goddes pryvetee" (3454), he is duped by Nicholas's interest in astrology (a way of knowing

God's secrets) into believing Nicholas's claims about the coming flood. Nicholas appeals to John's credulity by refusing to divulge God's secrets ("I wol nat tellen Goddes pryvetee" [3558]) with regard to saving the servants although he has already done so with regard to the flood. Nicholas's refusal to divulge God's secrets implies that he knows them.

That is the last attempt, either real or fraudulent, to discover God's secrets in the fragment. After this point in the Miller's Tale, people are interested only in discovering each other's secrets or in disguising their own. It marks a descent from a kind of ideal (perception of the divine plan) to rather ordinary nosiness. John tells Alison his "pryvetee" (3603), works "pryvely," and hangs the tubs in the roof "in pryvetee" (3622–23). Absolon asks a cloisterer about John "Ful prively" (3662) and decides to arouse Alison by knocking at the window "Ful pryvely" (3676). And when Nicholas wants to improve on Alison's joke, he raises the window "And out his ers he putteth pryvely" (3802). Unlike God's privity, all these secrets are discovered. The discovery of God's secrets is never an issue in the Reeve's Tale where Malyne reveals Symkyn's secret (the location of the "cake of half a busshel" [4244]), and Aleyn reveals the secret that he has "Swyved the milleres doghter bolt upright" (4266) to the wrong person. For that reason the Cook draws the moral that "Wel oghte a man avysed for to be / Whom that he broghte into his pryvetee" (4333–34) and tells a tale about a man who "was free / Of his dispense, in place of pryvetee" (4387–88). What began as the noble inquiry into divine secrets and the way God works in the world in the Knight's Tale has decayed to a platitude about keeping one's own counsel in the Cook's Prologue and the locus of perhaps immoral activity in the Cook's Tale.

A final gauge of the decay of order is reflected in the confusion of earnest and game which occupies a more important place in this fragment than in any other.[14] The antagonism between Palamon and Arcite begins precisely on the issue of whether Arcite responds to Emily "in ernest or in pley" (1125). Theseus contributes first by turning the "heigh folye" (1798) of the two lovers into a serious "bataille" (1853) between two hundred knights in official lists and then by turning the "mortal bataille" (2540), which had earlier been referred to as a "game" (2108), into a game indeed, a tournament that does not involve "destruccion of blood" (2564). Nicholas's "pleye" (3273) with Alison has the serious object of deceiving her husband and getting her into bed. Once committed to Nicholas, Alison dismisses Absolon's advances "And al his ernest turneth til a jape" (3390). His earnest desire to kiss her at the window turns into a joke (" 'Tehee!' quod she" [3740]) which Absolon turns back into earnest when he arms himself with the hot coulter. Chaucer dramatizes the conflict between earnest and game in the scene between the playful Gervais and the serious Absolon. Even John's pain turns "unto a jape" (3842). Symkyn, of course, makes earnest out of a game when he threatens to kill anyone who "dorste rage or ones pleye" (3958) with his wife, and he makes game out of earnest when he jokes about the clerks' adversity and their ability to expand space by argument (4120–26). John and Aleyn, ever "lusty for to pleye" (4004), are eager to turn the manciple's perhaps fatal malady (3993–94) into a game to trick Symkyn. When he seems to have gotten the better of them, they turn game into earnest and then back into game by seeking a complicated revenge that is both "a wikked jape" (4201) and "a noble game" (4263).

Chaucer articulates the decay of order by turning earnest into game in the frame of Fragment I as well as among the characters of the tales. Harry Bailly introduces the theme at the Tabard Inn when "after soper pleyen he bigan" (758) and convinces the pilgrims to transform the earnest spiritual exercise of a religious pilgrimage into a tale-telling game with a flesh-satisfying supper as its prize. By the very tale he tells, the Miller makes a game out of earnest when he makes a "cherles tale" (3169) and "harlotrie" (3184) out of the "noble storie" (3111) that the Knight had told. But the Miller can also make earnest out of game, as he does when he interrupts the order of the Host's game and insists that he will "go my wey" (3133) if he is not allowed to tell the next tale. The Reeve, of course, makes earnest out of game as his anger both before (3144–49) and after (3859–63) the Miller's Tale indicates. The Host warns the Cook about taking a joke seriously and becoming angry even though "A man may seye ful sooth in game and pley" (4355). In doing so, he echoes Chaucer's famous interjection at the end of the Prologue to the Miller's Tale when he addresses his audience directly and says "men shal nat maken ernest of game" (3186). Although the warning applies immediately to the tale the Miller is about to tell, it also applies in the larger sense to all of the Canterbury tales that Chaucer is in the process of telling.

DETERIORATION OF LANGUAGE

One final observation should be made about the principle of deterioration that defines the structure of Fragment I: it concerns the descent of language from the elevated to the parochial that is limited and arcane. This is a matter different from that which insists "The wordes moote be cosyn to the dede" (742). Twice in the fragment—once in the General Prologue (720–42) and again in the Prologue to the Miller's Tale (3167–86)—Chaucer comments on quality of language. In doing so, he justifies speaking "pleynly" (727) and keeping his own language "as ny as evere he kan" (732) to that of the teller and of the tale so as not to "falsen som of my mateere" (3175). Chaucer also uses language as a unifying device in quite a different sense in Fragment I. In addition to the relationship between teller and tale, Chaucer shows the deterioration of language from tale to tale as the fragment progresses.[15] Indeed, Chaucer himself demonstrates how language will deteriorate in the course of the fragment by demonstrating the deterioration of language in the first forty-two lines of the General Prologue.[16] The first eighteen lines of the poem are written in "Heigh style" (IV, 18) with elevated language appropriate to the beginning of a serious poem. Lines 19–29, however, relate facts in a descriptive narrative style unadorned by a single poetic image. Lines 30–34 break the fiction of the narrative by foregrounding the narrator—the "I" (31, 32, 34) who is aware of an audience ("yow" [34])—and by assuming an aesthetic principle of economy ("shortly" [30]). Lines 35–42 focus on the audience, freeze the temporal progression of the narrative, and emphasize the fiction of the fiction ("this tale" [36]). By the time Chaucer begins to describe the pilgrims, his language has descended from the lofty and elegant to the work-a-day, the directly realistic, and the ironic—the linguistic mode in which he appears most comfortable.

The same process of deterioration marks the language of the tales in Fragment I. The rich language of the Knight's Tale, appropriate to a courtly romance, appears to good effect in the descriptions: Theseus's advance upon Thebes; the portraits of Emily, Lygurge, and Emetreus; the temples of the gods. Nothing so elegant appears in the Miller's Tale where people are "somdeel squaymous / Of fartyng" (3337–38), "may blowe the bukkes horn" (3387), "leet fle a fart" (3806), "pisse" (3798), and kiss either "hir ers" (3755) or "his ers" (3800). Nicholas's address to Alison in the language of courtly love is parodic and fraudulent. Absolon's address to Alison in the language of the Song of Songs is empty hyperbole and counterfeit courtly language.[17] John himself reduces language to nonsense with the "nyght-spel" (3408) he pronounces over Nicholas. In the Reeve's Tale the two clerks speak a language both precious and arcane, a Northern dialect of English that Garbaty (1973) has shown was comic to Chaucer's audience. At one point even the horse speaks, "wehee" (4066). We cannot guess what Chaucer had planned for the Cook's Tale, but the Cook knows at least one foreign phrase (" 'sooth pley, quaad pley,' as the Flemyng seith" [4357]) and the setting of his tale in London among foreign communities, riotous apprentices, inhabitants of Newgate, and prostitutes suggests that "heigh style" was not in the offing.[18] Like many other things in Fragment I, the language itself descends until it is "corrumpable."

II. Theme

Because of the General Prologue, Chaucer's artistic problem in Fragment I is slightly more complicated than it is elsewhere in the *Canterbury Tales*. In fragments composed entirely of tales and a bit of connecting frame, Chaucer develops themes particularly relevant to the tales and echoes them in the frame to give cohesiveness to the fragment. In Fragment I, however, the General Prologue has the prominence of a tale but not its development of character or plot. Chaucer's artistic problem, therefore, was to design themes for the General Prologue and tales of Fragment I that were relevant both to the pilgrims who tell the tales and to the characters within them.

HERBERGAGE (LODGING)

Having chosen the frame of pilgrimage, Chaucer is committed to the fiction of pilgrims as his storytellers. These pilgrims, gathered at the Tabard Inn in Southwerk, provide the most obvious connection among the tales in Fragment I: not only are they all lodgers themselves, but they all tell tales about lodgers. Unless one counts the monk who is an occasional guest in the Shipman's Tale or the strange knight who comes bearing gifts to Cambyuskan in the Squire's Tale, both unlikely candidates, nowhere else in the *Canterbury Tales* does Chaucer use lodgers as major characters and no where else do lodgers tell tales about lodgers.[19]

Both Chaucer and the pilgrims lodge overnight at the Tabard where "The chambres . . . weren wyde, / And wel we weren esed atte beste" (28–29). Palamon and Arcite, as Theseus's perpetual prisoners, find lodgings less congenial in "The grete tour, that was so thikke and stroong" (1056). When Arcite returns from Thebes to Athens, he falls in with Emily's chamberlain and eventually becomes "Page of the chambre of Emelye the brighte" (1427)[20] until Theseus "hath taken hym so neer, / That of his chambre he made hym a squier" (1439–40). Both Palamon and Arcite, together with Emetreus, Lygurge, and the other knights who come to the tournament, are "inned . . . everich at his degree" (2192) by Theseus. In the Miller's Tale, Nicholas is one of the "gestes heeld to bord" (3188) by the carpenter and refers to John's house as "this in" (3547). His "chambre . . . in that hostelrye" (3203) is pleasantly decorated with sweet herbs. John and Aleyn beg Symkyn "Of herberwe and of ese" (4119). Even though his "hous is streit" (4122), Symkyn grants them lodging in his own chamber; they find their "ese" by themselves. Perkyn Revelour is the only lodger to be evicted. At first he "with his maister bood" (4399) until his master dismisses him; then "he sente his bed and his array" (4418) to his married friend at whose house he takes up lodging. With the possible exception of Palamon and Arcite's prison lodgings (which might have been more sumptuous than the rooms at the Tabard or a student's room in a carpenter's cottage), the accommodations trace a descent from "wyde" in the Tabard to "streit" in Symkyn's house and therefore conform to the general pattern of deterioration characteristic of Fragment I.

Although the Cook has only Symkyn in mind when he quotes Solomon about the dangers of having lodgers ("'Ne bryng nat every man into thyn hous' / For herberwynge by nyghte is perilous" [4331–32]), the observation actually applies to all the other tales in the fragment as well. We cannot speculate about Perkyn's conduct in his friend's house, but his master compares him to a rotten apple who will contaminate all the other apples in the barrel. John and Aleyn avenge themselves upon Symkyn by committing adultery and fornication with his wife and daughter before they "beete hym weel and lete hym lye" (4308). Nicholas seduces John's wife and makes him a public laughing stock. The lodgers in the Knight's Tale, like lodgers in fabliau, are equally dangerous: Palamon, with a friend's help, drugs a guard and breaks out of prison, which suggests the limitations of Theseus's power. When he separates Palamon and Arcite in the forest, Theseus discovers one former lodger who is his "mortal foo" (1724) living in his house as Philostrate, and another former lodger who is also his "mortal foo" (1736) armed and free in the countryside.

Finally, the pilgrims in the General Prologue are lodgers and therefore perilous, but in a slightly different sense. They pose no immediate threat to the proprietor of the Tabard Inn, though as the pilgrimage progresses they become occasionally recalcitrant and troublesome (as in the Prologue to the Miller's Tale, the Prologue to the Manciple's Tale, and the conclusion to the Pardoner's Tale). But the pilgrims are not dangerous to the other characters whose plane of reality they share; they are dangerous to Chaucer's audience, and that means they are dangerous to us. Chaucer warns us twice that the very act of reading or listening to the *Canterbury Tales* is perilous to our well-being. Once at the end of the General Prologue, Chaucer warns us of an impending affront to our sensibilities when he appeals to our "curteisye" that we not attribute any "vileynye" to him for plain-speaking "rudeliche and large" (725–34). Tongue firmly in cheek once again in the Miller's Prologue, Chaucer warns "every gentil wight" (3171) that he is about to tell a ribald tale which may prove offensive to those of us in the audience who prefer "storial thyng that toucheth gentillesse, / And eek moralitee and hoolynesse" (3179–80). In doing so, Chaucer indicates that the pilgrims who lodge at the Tabard Inn and eventually tell the Canterbury tales will prove to be as perilous, as dangerously disruptive to us as the lodgers within the tales will be to their hosts. Just as the lodgers within the tales disturb established relationships and arrangements, these pilgrims will disturb the comfortable opinions of Chaucer's audience and encourage us to look again at people whom Chaucer describes as among the very best of their kind in the world.

MEAT AND DRINK

No other fragment is quite so concerned with food.[21] By agreeing to Harry Bailly's suggestion that the prize for the storytelling competition be "a soper at oure aller cost" (799), the pilgrims acknowledge the importance of meat and drink. In the General Prologue, Chaucer defines some pilgrims (e.g., the Knight, Prioress, Monk, Franklin, Physician, Cook, and Summoner) in terms of their relationship to food, but meat and drink serve an adhesive function by reappearing in various forms throughout the fragment. To be sure, the minor references to food—e.g., Theseus's feasting the knights at the tournament (2736)—should not concern us. Of greater importance are the "mete and drynke" (1615) that Arcite brings to Palamon in the forest because they suggest Arcite's gentility and celebrate the *amicitia* which has been tested by their competitive love. Nicholas brings "Bothe mete and drynke for a day or tweye" (3411) to his chamber to prepare for gulling John and insists that John "Fecche me drynke" (3492) before he reveals God's secrets. To survive the flood, they must have "vitaille suffisant / But for a day" (3551–52) which means "breed, and cheese, and good ale in a jubbe" (3628). Nicholas and Alison find a different food to sustain them, but Absolon, ironically, can only dream he "was at a feeste" (3684). The only sustenance he has is "greyn and lycorys, / To smellen sweete" (3690–91). He claims, in any event, that he has such a love-longing that he "may nat ete na moore than a mayde" (3707). When John cuts the cord that holds his tub and plummets to the floor, Chaucer describes the speed of his descent with an image about food: "he foond neither to selle / Ne breed ne ale, til he cam to the celle / Upon the floor" (3821–23). When John and Aleyn in the Reeve's Tale beg Symkyn for "mete and drynke" (4132), he sends Malyne into town "For ale and breed, and rosted hem a goos" (4137). It is his undoing, for while "They soupen . . . / And drynken evere strong ale atte beste, . . . / Wel hath this millere vernysshed his heed" (4147–49). The Cook, of course, deals in meat and drink. When Harry Bailly upbraids him for selling food twice hot and twice cold, he threatens to tell a tale later about a "hostileer" (4360) and then begins his tale of an apprentice who was "of a craft of vitailliers" (4366).

Chaucer's emphasis upon food is particularly appropriate to the first fragment. It has the effect of foregrounding the concerns of the flesh at the expense of the concerns of the spirit and so affirms in different thematic terms the deterioration of the pilgrimage from earnest to game, from a spiritual journey to a physical adventure, from the call of the saint to the pull of nature.

LAW: CONTRACT

We have seen how the theme of contract, with its attendant theme of obligation, contributes to the coherence of Fragment III. Law and contract also contribute to the unity of Fragment I.[22] The "foreward" (829) by which all agree to the storytelling contest and to be ruled by the judgment of Harry Bailly is the most obvious expression of the idea in the General Prologue. There had been another agreement earlier when Chaucer had been admitted into the fellowship of pilgrims and then all had "made forward erly for to ryse" (33). Various pilgrims are characterized in terms of their relationship to law: the Monk (173), Man of Law

(315, 327), Manciple (577), and Summoner (646); one can also argue for the Parson (527–28) and the Plowman as being completely obedient to God's law.

Equally diverse references to law appear throughout the fragment. The patina of order created in the Knight's Tale by the role of Theseus and by the important First Mover speech is enhanced by the various occasions when the rule of law appears. It is implicit in Theseus's returning the bones of their husbands to the grieving widows, and explicit in Theseus's "forward" (1209) with Arcite, and in Palamon's fear that Arcite may win Emily as his wife by "some tretee" (1288). Ironically, Palamon and not Arcite wins Emily by treaty when, with the advice of his parliament, Theseus agrees to ally Athens with Thebes and seal the alliance with marriage. The point is doubly ironic since both Palamon and Arcite, as lovers, are outside the law according to "the olde clerkes sawe, / That 'who shal yeve a lovere any lawe?'" (1163–64). They demonstrate their lawlessness when Arcite breaks his "forward" with Theseus by returning to Athens and when Palamon breaks out of prison.

The Miller is equally lawless. He breaks the agreement sworn to in the General Prologue when he gainsays the Host's desire to "werken thriftily" (3131) and thwarts the Host's judgment as to who shall tell the next tale. Out of ignorance John the carpenter disregards the rule "That bad man sholde wedde his simylitude" (3228). Nicholas explains to John God's "ordinance" (3592) which insists that he and Alison hang their tubs far apart in order to avoid sin during the night of the flood. John and Aleyn justify their vengeance upon Symkyn by quoting "a lawe that says thus: / That gif a man in a point be agreved, / That in another he sal be releved" (4180–82). And Perkyn's "papir" (4404) of apprenticeship is a legal document which binds him to his master who legally releases him by giving him "acquitance" (4411). Perkyn also has been a lawbreaker, as the fact that he was "somtyme lad with revel to Newegate" (4402) indicates.

WEAPONS

This is among the bloodiest fragments; it is certainly among the most violent. The blood, as we might expect, appears mostly in the Knight's Tale, both in the tournament and in the fight between Palamon and Arcite in the wood, but the Prioress weeps if she should see a bleeding mouse, and both Absolon and the Cook know how to "laten blood" (3326, 4346), though perhaps it is a sign of deterioration from the noble to the mundane in the fragment that the Cook's doing so only means that he knows how to draw off the gravy. The violence in the fragment is directly proportional to the number of people bearing arms. In no other fragment of the *Canterbury Tales* does Chaucer concentrate so much upon weapons.

While a sword had been considered a badge of rank at various times in various places throughout the Middle Ages, by Chaucer's time the distinction between who could and who could not wear a sword had fallen into disuse. Many of the most ordinary sorts of people carried weapons—usually knives—more as a mark of fashion than a badge of rank, though such was the violent tenor of medieval life that even the most peaceable of creatures may have felt more comfortable with a knife at his belt for self-defense. It was as characteristic of a man as the distaff was of a woman (VII, 3096–97).

Among the pilgrims in the General Prologue, we might well expect the two professional soldiers, the Knight and the Squire, to be well-armed, but ironically either they are not carrying weapons or Chaucer chooses not to describe them. Their servant, the Yeoman, carries weapons appropriate to his rank: a bow and arrows, a sword and buckler, and a "gay daggere" (113). The Shipman carries a concealed weapon which, together with other details, suggests that he may be a pirate. The Franklin and the Tradesmen bear arms more for fashion than for use. The epicurean and sybaritic Franklin carries an "anlass" (357), a short two-edged dagger, on his belt. The Tradesmen carry knives "chaped noght with bras / But al with silver" (366–67), indicating they are more for domestic than military use, more for decoration than for defense. The Miller carries "A swerd and a bokeler" (558), arms both for attack and defense, which appropriately reflect his pugnacious character, and the Reeve carries a "rusty blade" (618), an old sword for an old man.

The tales in Fragment I are unusually rich in arms. Their appearance in the Knight's Tale in the fights between Palamon and Arcite, in the portraits of Mars, Diane, Lygurge, and Emetreus, in the description of Cupid, in the prayers at the temples, in the tournament, and in Arcite's funeral obsequies (he lies upon the bier with a sword in his hand) connote the incipient violence that lies beneath the smooth surface of the romance. Although no one in the Miller's Tale is armed, Absolon in the climactic battle scene converts a hot coulter into a weapon. Everyone is armed in the Reeve's Tale. Symkyn bristles with arms—"panade," "swerd," "poppere," "thwitel," "knyf," and "boidekyn" (3929–32, 3960)—which serve him not at all in his battle with the clerks. John and Aleyn carry their meal to be ground "With good swerd and with bokeler by hir syde" (4019), which they carry with them all the time and lay down only when they dash off to the fens to catch their horse. In the final battle, Symkyn's wife arms herself with a staff that she finds against a wall and uses to smite her husband by mistake.

Chaucer's unique emphasis upon weaponry in Fragment I ironically foregrounds a completely worthless means of human preservation. In the context of pilgrimage, no "thwitel," no matter how sharp or dexterously manipulated, can supplant the "hooly blisful martir" in the only confrontation of any significance to the Christian soul: the defense of the spirit before the judgment of God. Chaucer's display of medieval cutlery, therefore, only sharpens our sense of the deterioration from the saintly to the secular and from the spiritual to the physical concurrently suggested by the theme of meat and drink.

MUSIC

This is the most musical fragment. Perhaps because the fabliau is connected to young love or because the pilgrimage occurs in spring, when "smale fowcles maken melodye," almost all of the characters in the tales and many of the pilgrims are connected to music.[23] The Squire, of course, is singing or fluting all day and knows how to compose songs. The Prioress sings the divine service well. The Monk's bridle jingles. The Friar sings and plays a "rote" (236, 266). The Miller plays the bagpipes, and the Pardoner and Summoner join in part-singing "Com hider, love, to me" (672–73), though the Pardoner is much better at singing "an offertorie" (710). Chaucer makes a point of separating the two most serious pilgrims, the Parson and the Clerk, from music. Although singing the daily services would have been part of any Parson's job, Chaucer distances the Parson from music by describing the Parson's relationship to music in the negative. To emphasize the Parson's devotion to his flock, Chaucer tells us that he did not run off to St. Paul's in London "To seken hym a chaunterie for soules" (510), and by reporting the Clerk's preference for books at the head of his bed instead of a "fithele, or gay sautrie" (296), Chaucer emphasizes the Clerk's seriousness.

The world of the Knight's Tale rings with music from the "melodye" (872) that attends Theseus's wedding journey to the "blisse and melodye" (3097) that attend Palamon's marriage to Emily. Emily's singing "hevenysshly" (1055) as she wanders in the garden on a May morning contrasts with Palamon's "compleynynge of his wo" (1072) as he paces in a tower chamber. Later when Arcite wanders in the woods, "loude he song ayeyn the sonne shene" (1509) much like the "bisy larke [who] ... / Salueth in her song the morwe gray" (1491–92). Away from Emily, of course, he cannot bear the sound of song or instrument. Later still, when Palamon hears the lark singing, he goes to worship at the temple of Venus where he would have seen depicted musical "instrumentz, caroles, daunces" (1931) and the goddess herself with "A citole in hir right hand" (1959). The music in the temple of Mars is more ominous, full of "chirkyng" (2004) and rumblings. To indicate that Arcite's prayer will be answered, "The statue of Mars bigan his hauberk rynge" (2431), and both the rings on the temple doors and the doors themselves clatter. With similar clattering Diane indicates that Emily's prayer will be answered, and she quenches a fire with "a whistelynge" (2337). Although Theseus hunts in the woods with horn and hounds and Emetreus's voice is "as a trompe thonderynge" (2174), which suggests his value on a medieval battlefield, the tournament provides the most obvious occasion for music. Minstrelsy and song mark the feast, and the tournament itself is punctuated by "Pypes, trompes, nakers, clariounes, / That in the bataille blowen blody sounes" (2511–12, 2565, 2600, 2671). Indeed, the "mynstralcie and noyse" (2524) awaken Theseus from sleep on the day of the tournament.

In the Miller's Tale the clerks' devotion to music and to musical instruments suggests the degree to which they deviate from the ideal defined by the Clerk. Nicholas's "gay sautrie" (3213) lies above the shelves at the head of his bed. Not only does he make the chamber ring with melody every night as he sings *Angelus ad virginem* and "the Kynges Noote" (3213–17), but when properly inspired, he "pleyeth faste" (3306). Absolon knows how to "pleyen songes on a smal rubible" and a "giterne" (3331–33). His voice, a high treble which he trills or quavers like a nightingale, is described both as a "loud quynyble" (3332) and as "gentil and smal" (3360) when he serenades Alison as she is lying in bed with her husband. Alison, too, has a song that is both "loude and yerne" (3257) as one might expect from a young woman of her energy and disposition; her husband John only knows how to snore: "he routeth, for his heed myslay" (3647). On one of those few occasions when Chaucer uses music as a metaphor (the others are 830, 1838, 3387, and 3896), he describes the joyful fornication of Nicholas and Alison as "the revel and the melodye" (3652) which is interrupted only quite early in the morning when "the belle of laudes gan to rynge, / And freres in the chauncel gonne synge" (3655–56).

In the Reeve's Tale Symkyn demonstrates no musical talent though he knows how to play the bagpipes (3927). (The detail is merely the Reeve's attempt to suggest a similarity between his fictional miller and the Miller on pilgrimage who he thinks has insulted him.) Most of the music in the Reeve's Tale is both dissonant and comic. The only human song is hardly human and scarcely a song. Symkyn "fnorteth in his sleep" like a horse (4163). His wife, like the Summoner in the General Prologue, takes the bass part and "bar hym a burdon, a ful strong" (4165); the two of them can be heard two furlongs away. To this cacophony must be added the sound of Symkyn's flatulence, since "Ne of his tayl bihynde he took no keep" (4164). The clerks provide the appropriate judgment when Aleyn pokes John and says "Herdestow evere slyk a sang er now?" (4170). Neither the bell at lauds nor the singing of friars calls these clerks from their nocturnal exertions. They endure "This joly lyf . . . / Til that the thridde cok bigan to synge" (4232–33).

In the Cook's Tale, Perkyn Revelour, who is not a clerk, is quite an accomplished musician. Not only does he know how to "pleye on gyterne or ribible" (4396), but "At every bridale wolde he synge and hoppe" (4375). His musical skills and accomplishments mark him as a ne'er-do-well: should any procession pass down Cheapside, he would abandon his master's shop and follow it until he had seen everything "And daunced well . . . / And gadered hym a meynee of his sort / To hoppe and synge" (4380–82). On most occasions a master benefits from the skills of his apprentice, but this master gains nothing because his apprentice is skilled in music; on the contrary, he ultimately has to pay for it since the time spent in music means that much less work is done in the shop. In Fragment I, Chaucer shows music drawing people away from the serious concerns of life. It is a trivial pursuit, appropriate to birds, lovers, and degenerate apprentices.

One can trace the decay of the world through the music in Fragment I. What begins as the heavenly singing of Emily, the lark's call to lovers, the prophetic noises of the gods, and the musical celebration that attends feast and festival in the Knight's Tale deteriorates to a more natural and more human level in the Miller's—the musical invitation and accompaniment to seduction and the "thonder-dent" of Nicholas's fart. The degeneration continues in the Reeve's Tale, where the cacophony is less human and more bestial, and in the Cook's Tale where music gathers unruly apprentices, disturbs civil order, disrupts commerce, and causes loss of work and money. By weaving the theme of music through all the tales and the frame, Chaucer not only bonds the General Prologue to the tales and contributes to the unity of the fragment, but he describes in theme the degenerative principle that defines the structure of the fragment.

ANIMALS

Throughout the *Canterbury Tales*, Chaucer compares people to animals, but nowhere is the comparison so consistently applied as in Fragment I.[24] Chaucer's portrait of Alison in terms of animals and barnyard imagery is the most famous for the sinewy softness it grants her and for the physical appetites it suggests; the comparison of Palamon and Arcite to lions and tigers and boars is the most obvious and predictable. Knights in romance are always as brave as such beasts, and it comes as no surprise when Emetreus is compared to a lion or Lygurge to a "grifphon" (2133). Chaucer is more original artistically when he allows his two heroes to couch philosophical generalizations about the nature of man in terms of animal comparisons. Arcite describes the blindness of human endeavor with a proverbial expression, "We faren as he that dronke is as a mous" (1261), and Palamon describes the helplessness of human beings before the cruel gods who govern this world by comparing people to "sheep that rouketh in the folde" (1308). Arcite describes his competition with Palamon for the lovely Emily in the least romantic terms when he says "We stryve as dide the houndes for the boon" (1177), a comparison by which Chaucer deftly undercuts the hackneyed imagery of the empty courtly love tradition he partly holds up to ridicule in this tale.

Neither Theseus nor Emily is ever compared to animals—and neither, rather surprisingly, is Nicholas. Absolon is compared rather thoroughly to an animal. His eyes are "greye as goos" (3317), and he sings like a nightingale. Chaucer compares his attraction to Alison as that of a cat for a mouse. Absolon compares himself to a lamb and a turtledove, but to no avail: Alison "maketh Absolon hire ape" (3389). John, too, is like a bird: Nicholas compares him, with a curious sex-change, to a "white doke [swimming] after hire drake" (3576). In the Reeve's Tale,

Malyne, like Nicholas, has no animal comparison; everyone else does. Symkyn is as proud as a "pecok" (3926), bald as an ape (3935), "fnorteth" like a horse (4163), isn't worth a "flye" in Aleyn's estimation (4192), and rolls on the floor like a pig. His wife is as "peert as is a pye" (3950) and as "jolyf" "As any jay" (4154). Both the clerks return from chasing their horse "Wery and weet, as beest is in the reyn" (4107). John thinks of himself as swift as a roe, and though Aleyn calls him a "swynes-heed" (4262), it is actually Aleyn who wallows with Symkyn "as doon two pigges in a poke" (4278).

In the General Prologue, the Pardoner's "glarynge eyen . . . as an hare" (684), "voys . . . as smal as hath a goot" (688), and sexual deviation *qua* spiritual state ("a geldyng or a mare" [691]) have long been noted. The Friar is compared to a puppy (257), and the Miller's hair is as red "as any sowe or fox" (552). The more interesting comparison associates both the Summoner and the Squire with birds. The Summoner is as "lecherous as a sparwe" (626, and cf. 642); the Squire "sleep namoore than dooth a nyghtyngale" (98). The association of pilgrims with birds is significant for two reasons: one is that it continues the connection to animals that contributes to the thematic unity of the fragment, but the other and more interesting reason is that it implies Chaucer's judgment and displays Chaucer's craft. Chaucer's birds almost invariably diminish human concerns and make them comic. Those whom Chaucer wants to denigrate, if not actively treat with contempt, and those whom Chaucer holds up for amused scrutiny, he depicts as birds. In the tales of Fragment I these include John the carpenter, Alison, and Absolon, and Symkyn and his wife in addition to the Squire and Summoner from the General Prologue. To these we must add Arcite. Perhaps our first indication in the Knight's Tale that Arcite will fail in his suit for Emily occurs when Chaucer attributes to him the mindless joy of a bird: he leaves the temple of Mars "As fayn as fowel is of the brighte sonne" (2437).

It is one thing to depict characters as birds and quite another to depict pilgrims as such. The most subtle example of Chaucer's irony (most subtle because it does not involve language or situation but the value of a particular image and therefore requires multiple exposure to the meaning of that image before the irony is disclosed) occurs toward the end of the General Prologue when the Host awakens the pilgrims to begin the journey. Chaucer refers to Harry Bailly as "oure aller cok" (823) and, in the next line, to all the pilgrims as a "flok" (824). In this context, the flock can only be of birds and not of sheep—the traditional Christian metaphor for a congregation. The "sondry folk" who gathered in the Tabard the previous evening have all been metamorphosed into a "flok" of birds when the Host makes a joke out of what is serious and transforms the pilgrimage from earnest into a game. In perverting the purpose of pilgrimage, Harry Bailly changes the pilgrim seekers-after-holiness into rather silly birds. By depicting the pilgrims as birds, Chaucer judges the human condition before his human comedy properly begins. At the very same time, Chaucer here brings theme and structure together: the deterioration of the pilgrims from people at the beginning of the General Prologue into birds at the end reflects the general principle of decay and deterioration that marks the fragment's structure. The splendid complexity of the association and the grace with which it succeeds show Chaucer's art at its finest.

7

Fragment VII (Group B₂): The Shipman's Tale, the Prioress' Tale, the Tale of Sir Thopas, the Tale of Melibee, the Monk's Tale, and the Nun's Priest's Tale

>   . . . ther nas no remedie
>
>   (1993)

If conscious construction characterizes the first fragment in the *Canterbury Tales*, lack of finish, lack of polish, and lack of tidiness characterize the seventh. Obvious imperfections and infelicities mar the whole. The Shipman's Tale, for example, seems originally to have been written for the Wife of Bath and was transferred to the Shipman when Chaucer designed Fragment III. Remnants of the original feminine narrator remain to disturb the tale. The Host's enthusiastic response to the Tale of Melibee (1893 ff.) corresponds closely to his enthusiastic response to the Clerk's Tale (IV, 1212ᵃ⁻ᵍ). Chaucer may have intended to cancel one. Similarly, the Host addresses the Monk in language he later uses to address the Nun's Priest ("Thou woldest han been a tredefowel aright" [1945 ff. and 3451 ff.]). No doubt one or the other was meant to be canceled. The Prologue to the Nun's Priest's Tale exists in two versions. The shorter version omits reference to the tale of Croesus at the end of the Monk's Tale, which suggests the Nun's Priest's Tale may have been written for some other fragment of the *Canterbury Tales* and that Chaucer rewrote the Prologue when he decided to place it after the Monk's Tale. In some manuscripts the Host interrupts the Monk; in others, the Knight interrupts. The very order of tragedies in the Monk's Tale differs in various manuscripts: in some, the modern tragedies appear at the end; in others, they appear between Zenobia and Nero.

Because it has the tidiness of an attic or a junkyard—two unfinished tales (the Monk's and Sir Thopas), two polished tales (the Prioress' and the Nun's Priest's), one confusingly and imperfectly realized narrator (the Shipman), and the translation of a French tract (the Melibee)—Fragment VII appears, on first blush, to be an *omnium gatherum* of disparate tales imperfectly fitted to each other; it seems to lack the coherence and unity of the other fragments. The evidence of incompleteness and untidiness both in the construction of individual tales and in the relationships and connections among tales, makes it comfortable to assume this was the last fragment Chaucer worked on, trying to put together something coherent and workable from the tales that remained, not quite polishing everything, not quite able to read through the whole and to cancel the duplications, exhausted and frustrated by the intractability and the unwieldiness of it all. But, of course, it is not so. Even in its unfinished state, Fragment VII exhibits the same complexity of theme and delight in structure that characterize the other fragments of the *Canterbury Tales*. It is only longer, larger, more complex, and more sophisticated— though less finished—than the other fragments.

But why did Chaucer join just these six tales and fragments of tales together? What principle of artistic order arranges the tales within the fragment? What consistent themes and structural parallels establish lines of coherence among the tales? We can best answer these questions by pointing to an anomaly in the fragment: the Tale of Melibee. The Tale of Melibee is more finished than the incomplete tales, those of Sir Thopas and the Monk; it is generally dated earlier than the two polished tales, those of the Prioress and the Nun's Priest. But there is nothing else quite like it in all the *Canterbury Tales*. It is not like the Parson's Tale with which it shares a few obvious similarities. The Parson's Tale joins a sermon on Penitence to a treatise on the Deadly Sins; since the precise sources are unknown, we can not know exactly what changes Chaucer made. The Tale of Melibee, on the other hand, is a close translation of a known French text. It is a close translation, not a creation. Neither structure nor theme are his. Idea, structure, theme, character, development—all derive from the French text he translated. Why is it in the *Canterbury Tales* at all? After all, it can stand alone, like the *Treatise on the Astrolabe* or the *Book of the Duchess*. No one has suggested that Chaucer purposely translated the Tale of Melibee in order to include it in the *Canterbury Tales*. It seems to have been something that Chaucer was working on at various times in his life, but it is not his own in the sense that every other Canterbury tale is his own.

Why, then, did Chaucer decide to bring the Tale of Melibee into the *Canterbury Tales*? Why did he decide to narrate the Tale of Melibee himself? Why did Chaucer place it at the very center of Fragment VII and surround it with just the tales that he did? Or, to put it another way, what part does the Tale of Melibee, which is fundamentally different from every other Canterbury tale, play in the unity and coherence of Fragment VII? Ultimately, we shall see that the Tale of Melibee determines the design and structure of the fragment, dictates the order of the tales, and articulates the dominant theme. Although the unproveable implication is that the Tale of Melibee was written first and the rest of the fragment constructed around it, what is both clear and proveable is that the Tale of Melibee belongs in Fragment VII because it lies at the very heart of the fragment. It belongs in the *Canterbury Tales* because it echoes every other tale in the collection, because it radiates ties to every other fragment, and because it articulates a Christian truth important to Chaucer.

Part of what makes the structure of Fragment VII so complex to describe is that the order in which the tales appear can be defined and described in two completely different ways. On the one hand, the six tales of Fragment VII are organized upon the rhetorical principle of chiasmus which links the first tale to the sixth, the second to the fifth, and the third to the fourth. On the other hand, Fragment VII shares with other fragments in the *Canterbury Tales* a fundamentally sequential order whereby each tale is purposefully linked by theme and structure to the tale or tales immediately contiguous to it.

One purposeful thematic link that binds the tales in Fragment VII is that they all address an implicit question: What is the remedy for misfortune? I have taken as the epigraph to this chapter the Monk's answer, "ther nas no remedie" (1993), repeated on several occasions throughout the fragment (427, 2132, 2784). From the Monk's point of view, no one can escape misfortune. Nonetheless, part of what unifies the fragment is that Chaucer describes alternatives to the Monk's attitude. These remedies contribute lines of coherence to the fragment and testify, once again, to Chaucer's craft.

GEOFFREY CHAUCER
The Order of the Tales (I): Chiasmic Order

The familiar medieval rhetorical pattern, chiasmus, distributes its elements in the AB:BA pattern. Applied to the six tales of Fragment VII, that pattern is only slightly more complex: ABC:CBA.[1]

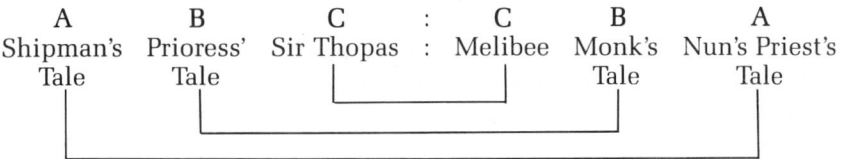

Specifically, the Shipman's Tale and the Nun's Priest's Tale, disparate as they are, share more characteristics with each other than they do with any other tales in the fragment. The same is true for the Prioress' Tale and the Monk's Tale. The tales of Sir Thopas and Melibee also share characteristics, and because they are at the very heart of the fragment in this schematic way of looking at the order, they also contain elements that radiate throughout the fragment and touch the most distant corners both of the fragment and of the whole *Canterbury Tales*. Let us begin with the first and last tales of the fragment.

THE SHIPMAN'S TALE AND THE NUN'S PRIEST'S TALE

Chaucer pairs the Shipman's Tale with the Nun's Priest's Tale in the chiasmic order of Fragment VII because these two tales share parallels of form, structure, character, imagery, and theme. The parallels of structure and character are particularly telling of Chaucer's design because they are unique to these tales. Nowhere else in the fragment and nowhere else in the *Canterbury Tales* as a whole does Chaucer repeat these parallels.

The tales share a similar poetic form. The fragment begins and ends with tales written in rhymed couplets that Cooper identifies as "riding rhyme" (1984, 161). The Prioress' Tale is in seven-line stanzas, the Tale of Sir Thopas in six-line stanzas (mostly), the Monk's Tale in eight-line stanzas, and Melibee begins as metrical prose (decasyllabic verse) that eventually loses its meter and becomes plain prose. Only the Shipman's Tale and the Nun's Priest's Tale share the iambic pentameter rhymed couplet form that is Chaucer's most often employed mode of poetic expression throughout the *Canterbury Tales*.

Fragment VII

The two tales share structural as well as formal aspects. They both begin with scenes that contrast a raised, secure place with a dangerous garden—similar to the tower and the garden at the beginning of the Knight's Tale. The raised place for the merchant is his "countour-hous" (77) which, since both he and his wife must go up to it (77, 212), is on an upper floor of his house and secured by a locked door. Chauntecleer's raised place is his perch "that was in the halle" (2884) and sufficiently elevated to be among the beams of the house. These high places of comfort and security contrast with the dangerous garden where the monk and the merchant's wife plot the arrangement whereby she prostitutes herself and cuckolds her husband while the monk dishonors his vow of chastity. Chauntecleer's dangerous garden, to which he "Was wont, and eek his wyves, to repaire" (3220), is the yard which hides the fox.[2]

The structural parallels extend beyond the tower and the garden. Before prime in both tales and before the characters go to breakfast, they engage in conversations which begin in similarly innocent ways and which end on a highly sexual note. Pertelote is surprised to discover that Chauntecleer has awakened so early from his sleep and asks "What eyleth yow[?]" (2890). The merchant's wife places the same question to the monk: "What eyleth yow so rathe for to ryse?" (99). Chauntecleer has been frightened by a dream which he describes to Pertelote, but the monk deflects the wife's concern (100–1) and registers his own concern for her with a reference to the sexual activity he assumes occupied her "sith the nyght bigan" (108). Their conversation culminates in the arrangement for the same sexual activity between the monk and the wife that the monk assumed had occupied the husband and wife overnight. The conversation between Chauntecleer and Pertelote culminates in the very sexual activity between Chauntecleer and Pertelote that the narrowness of their perch had prevented them from enjoying overnight: "He fethered Pertelote twenty tyme, / And trad hir eke as ofte, er it was pryme" (3177–78).

Both Chauntecleer and the merchant descend from their towers to eat breakfast. The merchant "richely" feeds the monk his "dyner" (that is, breakfast, 253–54) while Chauntecleer graciously shares his morning "pasture" (3185) with his wives. In both tales this occurs about prime (88 and 3197).

Time is a matter of great concern in these two tales, but not in the other four tales of this fragment. It is one of the thematic parallels by which Chaucer emphasizes the similarity between these two tales in the chiasmic patterning of the fragment. I count over forty temporal references in the Nun's Priest's Tale and over twenty-five in the Shipman's—a total almost three times the number of temporal references in the remaining four tales of the fragment put together. Although Harry Bailly (in the Introduction to the Man of Law's Tale) and Chaucer himself (in the Prologue to the Parson's Tale) indicate their concern for time and recognize the hour by the position of the sun, only the monk and Chauntecleer, of all the characters in the *Canterbury Tales*, are associated with clocks. The monk has a "chilyndre" by which he knows that "it is pryme of day" (206); Chauntecleer's crowing is more accurate than "a clokke or an abbey orlogge" (2854).[3]

Pertelote and the merchant's wife resemble each other more than they resemble any other female characters in the fragment, and they differ from most other women in the *Canterbury Tales*. Chaucer calls them "compaignable" (4 and 2872), a term he applies to no other characters in all of the *Canterbury Tales*. They are the only two women overtly concerned about their husband's health. (Thomas's wife in the Summoner's Tale is concerned about her husband's disposition.) Pertelote adopts the courtly beloved's function as Love's Physician when she prescribes "som laxatyf" (2943) to cure Chauntecleer's fear of dreams, and the merchant's wife shows similar concern for her husband's health (which may or may not be sincere) when she urges him to stop his work and break his fast (215–23).[4] Pertelote and the merchant's wife share with each other (and with Alice of Bath) the same criteria for a husband. The merchant's wife wants a husband to be "Hardy and wise, and riche, and therto free, / And buxom unto his wyf, and fressh abedde" (176–77); Pertelote wants a husband "hardy, wise, and free, / And secree—and no nygard, ne no fool" (2914–15). The song that Pertelote sings with Chauntecleer, "My lief is faren in londe" (2879), is both pleasantly ironic (since Chauntecleer generally does not travel into the country at all) and foreshadows his rather unexpected journey toward the woods on the fox's back. Could the merchant's wife sing, and we have no evidence that she would sing except her ebullient good spirits at the prospect of sexual activity (especially 373–81 and 400–26), her song would no doubt be the same, since at least one of the men she considers "lief" actually does travel throughout the country as part of his occupation and the other travels "out of this toun" (361) in the company of his abbot. The obscene puns on "taille" (416) and "Taillynge" (434) become more pointed and comic when we see the merchant's wife's sexual activity in the context of the treading and feathering of Pertelote who does, actually, have a tail.[5]

Parallels of imagery also bind these two tales. Chaucer compares everyone in the merchant's house to a bird: the merchant himself is "murie as a papejay" (369 and cf. 38); his wife is "jolif as a pye" (209); and his entire household is as glad of the monk's coming "As fowel is fayn whan that the sonne up riseth" (51). Chaucer subtly strengthens the connection between the two tales when he reveals the monk's mastery over birds. He shows the monk contributing wild fowl ("volatyl" [72]) to the celebrations at the merchant's house.

The monk shares this attitude toward birds—that they are to be captured and consumed—with the fox in the Nun's Priest's Tale, and indeed, the two share other characteristics as well. Both claim close family ties and long friendship with their victims (31–32 and 3285): the monk claims "cosynage" (36) to the merchant, and the fox claims that Chauntecleer's mother "Han in myn hous ybeen to my greet ese" (3297). Both affirm the relationship for their own advantage. Both abandon the relationship when they have their prey within their grasp. The monk denies to the wife his relationship to the merchant (149–50), the more easily to seduce her; and the fox's action in grabbing Chauntecleer by the "gargat" (3335) at once denies and ironically affirms his ambiguously professed relationship to Chauntecleer's family. Both the monk and the fox flatter their adversaries, the monk by indicating his concern for the merchant's health and offering his services in the merchant's absence (260–68) and the fox by praising Chauntecleer's father and urging Chauntecleer to imitate him. Both are duplicitous and traitorous, and both succeed. Neither Chauntecleer nor the merchant is sensitive to the treason that surrounds him. The two victims are ravished by flattery and done in by their own misplaced trust.

Fragment VII begins in sin and ends in salvation, yet Chaucer defines the world in the first and last tales as essentially amoral. No one is punished. Fortune and not moral law rules this world. The monk and the wife on the one hand and Chauntecleer on the other escape the vagaries of Fortune by wit, not by virtue. Their successes provide one answer to the basic question ("What is the remedy for misfortune?") that underlies all the tales and contributes to the thematic unity of the fragment. In the Shipman's Tale, ironically, the merchant does not even recognize his misfortune. He believes that Fortune favors him, "For he was riche and cleerly out of dette" (376), but he has been deceived by his desire to be among the two-of-twelve who shall thrive (228), by his measuring success in terms of money, and by his own acquisitiveness. His wife acknowledges that he has sufficient money: "Ye have ynough, pardee, of Goddes sonde" (219). She employs the same language in sexual play: "'Namoore,' quod she, 'by God, ye have ynough!'" (380). When she translates sex into money and affirms that she "wol nat paye yow but abedde" (424), "This marchant saugh ther was no remedie" (427) for him but to accept the commercialization of his marriage.[6]

In doing so, he adopts the attitude of the pilgrim Monk toward misfortune. But for the wife and the monk in the Shipman's Tale, as for Chauntecleer later, wit and cleverness comprise a remedy to deflect the brunt of ill-fortune. This shared remedy to misfortune emphasizes the chiasmic connection of the Shipman's Tale and the Nun's Priest's Tale; we shall see that no other tales in the fragment provide just this emphasis upon wit as the answer to misfortune. The Tale of Sir Thopas and the Tale of Melibee describe other remedies to misfortune, and the Prioress' Tale, the one most closely linked chiasmically with the Monk's Tale, describes a remedy different from the others and one that specifically counters the Monk's overwhelmingly depressive and hopeless view.[7]

THE PRIORESS' TALE AND THE MONK'S TALE

The chiasmic pattern of tales in Fragment VII links the Prioress' Tale with the Monk's Tale. For one thing, they are the only pair of tales in Fragment VII in which people actually die.[8] In response to these clear statements of absolute misfortune—the loss of life—they provide equally clear answers to the question of remedy for misfortune which dominates the fragment. For the Monk, "ther nas no remedie" (1993) when "Fortune list to flee" (1995). He reiterates the point seventeen times.

The Prioress describes a totally different remedy. For her, the single, clear, and ultimate source of evil and misfortune in the world is "Oure firste foo, the serpent Sathanas" (558), and the single, clear, and ultimate remedy for the boy's death and the widow's misfortune is God. By calling "evere on Cristes mooder meeke and kynde" (597), the widow indicates the orthodox Christian attitude in the face of misfortune. "Jhesu of his grace" (603) reveals to her the general location of the pit into which her son has been cast (604–6), and the "greyn" (665) that Mary placed on the child's tongue allows him to sing *O Alma re-*

demptoris mater, which leads to the discovery of the crime and the punishment of the criminals. Mary gets the credit for the miracle, but it is actually Jesus who allows the child to speak and to sing both so "that his glorie laste and be in mynde, / And for the worship of his Mooder deere" (653–54). Like the seventeen figures of tragedy in the Monk's Tale, the young clergeon suffers the same sudden and fatal reversal of fortune that they do, but unlike most of them, the little clergeon benefits from the remedy to misfortune offered by God's bounty.

God's bounty, which reflects God's absolute control of the world and constitutes the central theological point of the Prioress' Tale, is not so important an element in the Monk's world. Most of the Monk's tragic figures, like Hercules, accept death "whan he saugh noon oother remedye" (2132). Some, like the little clergeon, suffer misfortune without apparent justification; others suffer misfortune through their own pride or misgovernance or through the treachery of others. Only three of the seventeen tragic figures benefit from the remedy to misfortune offered by God and described by the Prioress, and all three of them are, rather surprisingly, involved with the Jews who, in the Prioress' Tale, are the villains. Chaucer's attitude toward the Jews, expressed through the Monk here and in his own voice in the Tale of Sir Thopas (863–65), ameliorates the Prioress' negative portrait of the Jews.[9] Nebuchadnezzar conquered Jerusalem and castrated "The faireste children of the blood roial / Of Israel" (2151–52), but because of his pride and arrogance (2167), God made a beast of him. Only toward the end of his life, did God restore his wit. Nebuchadnezzar "thanked God" (2179) and "knew that God was ful of myght and grace" (2182), a point that Daniel reiterates to Balthasar (2215–22). Antiochus, too, hated the Jews (2588, 2593) and wanted to destroy Jerusalem, but "God for his menace hym so soore smoot" (2599, 2609, 2615) that his body corrupted and filled with worms and stank. Just before his death, he "knew God lord of every creature" (2622). And Sampson, the great warrior of the Jews, "consecrat" "to God Almyghty" (2017), prays for God's pity and help which God provides by sending him water to drink at a crucial moment.

THE TALE OF SIR THOPAS AND THE TALE OF MELIBEE

Chaucer is the only Canterbury pilgrim who tells two tales. The Host asks the Monk and (in the Introduction to the Manciple's Tale) the Cook to tell a second tale, but the Monk demurs and the Cook is too drunk to comply. Thus the unique situation of two tales with the same narrator lies at the heart of Fragment VII. They are further tied together by their both claiming to be merry tales. Chaucer complies with the Host's request to "Telle us a tale of myrthe" (706) by relating the Tale of Sir Thopas, a tale "Of myrthe and of solas" (714) which is "Murier than the nyghtyngale" (834). He advertises the Tale of Melibee, too, as a "murye tale" (964) though his earnest request that he not be interrupted in this tale as he had been in that of Sir Thopas (966) suggests his awareness that the tale may not be as merry as the Host would have liked.

The tales of Melibee and Sir Thopas are surprisingly alike in initial situation and development. At the beginning, both characters are rich young men; both suffer an unexpected outrage in that both are attacked without clear cause (Sir Thopas directly and Melibee through his helpless family); both threaten vengeance; both declare a desire to fight; both gather advisers, both are eager to go to war. To this point, Chaucer has designed his Tale of Sir Thopas and his Tale of Melibee to be more like each other than they are like any other of the *Canterbury Tales*, but there the similarity ends. Melibee is serious and Sir Thopas is silly. Although Sir Thopas's first response, like that of Melibee, is to fight, his first action is to flee. The council Sir Thopas calls, unlike that of Melibee, does not advise him but entertains him: he calls his "myrie men . . . / To make hym bothe game and glee" (839–40), and his "mynstrales, / And geestours for to tellen tales" (845–46). The last we see of Sir Thopas, he is riding along, fully armed and perhaps overdressed, ostensibly on his way to fight "a geaunt with hevedes three" (842).[10] No doubt Sir Thopas's adversary is Chaucer's different imaginative configuration of Melibee's adversaries, the three "olde foes" (969) who attack his family.

The Tale of Melibee continues where the Tale of Sir Thopas ends. The tales are congruent up to the point where Melibee, like Thopas, decides by himself "to doon vengeaunce upon his foes, and sodeynly desired that the werre sholde bigynne" (1009). At this point, the only remedy that both Sir Thopas and Melibee can offer to human beings afflicted by misfortune is to go to war, to take vengeance, and to try to redress their grievances and their losses by bloody conflict. Chaucer does not allow us to applaud that remedy. He presents it in verse described as "verray lewednesse," "drasty speche," and "rym dogerel" (921–25). The prime exemplar of that attitude is the silly Sir Thopas, and while

Chaucer shows Sir Thopas's preparations, he does not show Sir Thopas's success.

Instead, Chaucer presents the Tale of Melibee which argues and demonstrates that vengeance and war cannot succeed, that they are no remedy for human misfortune.[11] In effect, Chaucer takes one step back and convenes for Melibee the serious council that Sir Thopas neglected to convene for himself. In the course of that council, Prudence teaches the single, clear, unambiguous Christian remedy for misfortune in this world. Prudence teaches Melibee that he must learn to suffer and be patient (1504–5), that he must avoid excess and outrage (1529), and, most important of all, that he has "noon oother remedie but for to have youre recours unto the sovereyn Juge that vengeth alle vileynyes and wronges" (1458). Prudence's attitude toward human misfortune resembles that articulated in the Prioress' Tale, but the differences are large and important. In the Tale of Melibee Chaucer presents a more sophisticated version of the Prioress' naive faith: Prudence buttresses her belief with wisdom.

The council which Melibee calls to advise him, in the context of which Prudence leads him to wisdom, is central to the structure as well as to the theme of the fragment. It is central to the theme, as we have seen, in that Prudence affirms the fundamental orthodox Christian remedy to human adversity and to the vagaries of Fortune in this world by directing attention to the "sovereyn Juge" (1458). It is central to the structure of the fragment in that the council itself invokes and echoes each of the six tales that comprise the fragment. Melibee convenes six groups of advisers. At first (1010–49), each group advances to define its attitude and reveal its position. Each group of advisers represents one of the six tales; the advisers speak in the same order in which the tales they represent appear in the fragment. Later (1265 ff.), Prudence reevaluates many of these positions and, in doing so, provides subtle criticism of the other tales in the fragment and of the remedies they propose.

The surgeons, who speak first, reflect the Shipman's Tale: "whan twey men han everich wounded oother, oon same surgien heeleth hem bothe" (1013). When "twey men," the merchant and the monk, are wounded by love and lust for the merchant's wife, "oon same surgien," that same merchant's wife, acting as Love's Physician, "heeleth hem bothe." The surgeons say "we do no damage" (1012), and the Shipman's is the only tale in the fragment in which no one is hurt or in danger of physical harm. The surgeons are nonjudgmental, finding little to praise and little to blame: "unto oure art it is nat pertinent to norice werre ne parties to supporte" (1014). Just so, the Shipman's Tale is the only fabliau in the *Canterbury Tales* in which no one is punished or made to look ridiculous. The characters who articulate the great issues of the tale—a monk who betrays a friend, abandons his vows for lust, borrows money to buy "certein beestes" (272); a merchant who places money before God and accepts the prostitution of his wife to himself; and a sexually satisfied woman who reveals her *demesure* by going out of her way for more—all remain curiously unjudged and unpunished because the Shipman, like the surgeons, supports no parties.

The physicians, who speak second, add only "a fewe woordes moore" (1016) to what the surgeons had said, but these are enough to identify them with the second tale in the fragment, the Prioress'. The physicians declare: "right as maladies been cured by hir contraries, right so shul men warrishe werre by vengeaunce" (1017). Later, Prudence asks Melibee how he understands this, and he responds "that right as they han doon me a contrarie, right so sholde I doon hem another. / For right as they han venged hem on me and doon me wrong, right so shal I venge me upon hem and doon hem wrong; / and thanne have I cured oon contrarie by another" (1280–82). Melibee describes the action of the Prioress' Tale in which the Jews "venged" themselves by murdering the little clergeon, and the Christians avenged themselves upon the Jews and thus "cured oon contrarie by another." In pointing out how Melibee has misunderstood the physicians' words, Prudence criticizes the seemingly orthodox attitude expressed through the action of the Prioress' Tale. She points out that "wikkedesse is nat contrarie to wikkednesse, ne vengeaunce to vengeaunce, ne wrong to wrong, but they been semblable. / And therfor o vengeaunce [the murder of the clergeon] is nat warrished by another vengeaunce [the death of the Jews], ne o wroong by another wroong" (1285–86). Prudence's advice to Melibee here constitutes subtle criticism of the Prioress' Tale.[12] Prudence affirms that the wickedness of the Jews should be answered by good, war by peace, vengeance by sufferance (1289), for "certes, wikkednesse shall be warisshed by goodnesse" (1290) which is a more tolerant and enlightened Christian attitude (which Prudence supports by reference to St. Paul) than that expressed in the Prioress' Tale.

Melibee's "neighebores ful of envye" (1018), false friends, and flatterers speak next and reflect the next tale in the fragment, the

Tale of Sir Thopas. They begin by "preisynge greetly Melibee of myght, of power, of richesse, and of freendes" (1019). With as much sincerity as Melibee's false flatterers, Chaucer praises Sir Thopas who "bereth the flour / Of roial chivalry" (901-2) when compared to Childe Horn, "Ypotys," Bevis of Hampton, Guy of Warwick, Sir Lybeux (Lybeus Desconus), and "Pleyndamour." Melibee's untrustworthy neighbors advise him that "he anon sholde wreken hym on his foes and bigynne werre" (1020) which is precisely the decision Sir Thopas comes to himself, without the benefit of council. The Tale of Melibee ultimately argues forcefully against this position, by which means Chaucer subtly criticizes this thoughtlessly bellicose response to adversity which the Tale of Sir Thopas puts forward.

The lawyers and "othere that were wise" speak next in the person of an "advocat" (1021), an "olde wise man" (1035). Since he occupies the same position in the sequence of advisers that the Tale of Melibee occupies in the fragment, he not only reflects the attitudes finally affirmed in the Tale of Melibee, but he is also validated by Prudence.[13] The advocate advises Melibee to protect his person diligently, to garrison and provision his house adequately, and not to decide on war or vengeance lightly. The advocate requires lengthy deliberation: "But certes, for to moeve werre, ne sodeynly for to doon vengeaunce, we may nat demen in so litel tyme that it were profitable. / Wherfore we axen leyser and espace to have deliberacion in this cas to deme" (1028-29). When Prudence later evaluates the advice of the advocate, she only clarifies the first two points (that Melibee should trust in Jesus Christ to keep his body [1298 ff.] and that he should defend his house with true friends and the love of his people [1335-40]), and she agrees wholeheartedly with the third point: "I trowe that they seyden right wisely and right sooth" (1343). This is the only point Prudence approves in all the advice offered by the six groups of counselors. And, of course, the rest of the tale is devoted to examining "with greet diligence and greet deliberacioun" (1342) the topics of vengeance and war before Melibee decides, with Prudence's help, to forego both.

The "yonge folk" (1035) who follow the lawyer correspond to the next tale in the fragment, the Monk's Tale. In the Monk's Tale, when Fortune turns against an individual, she works almost exclusively through treason and misgovernance. The tragic figure is either the hapless victim of external forces (treachery) or the victim of his own lack of self-control (misgovernance). Both characterize the young folk who insist upon immediate retribution, vengeance, and war. Dame Prudence, when she later evaluates this position (1352 ff.), concludes that "alle tho that conseilleden yow to maken sodeyn werre ne been nat youre freendes" (1364). Prudence lumps the young folk with Melibee's "olde enemys reconsiled" and his "flatereres" (1350–51). These are among the advisers whom Prudence specifically forbids (1172–99) because they think of themselves first; they place their own interests above those of their lord (1186–87 and see 1173). In doing so, they act treacherously. The young folk, scorning the old man and making noise while he talks, reflect the "mysgovernaunce" (2012) explicitly attributed to Adam and implicitly a contributing cause to the fall of many other tragic figures in the Monk's Tale. Thus, treachery and misgovernance connect the young folk to the Monk's Tale.

The "olde wise" (1037) who speaks last corresponds to the Nun's Priest's Tale. This speaker argues against the young folk's insistence upon war by pointing out the difficulty of ever knowing how the war will turn out: "but certes what ende that shal therof bifalle, it is nat light to knowe" (1040). One can never be certain of victory, for even at the moment of greatest success—racing toward the woods with the cock upon his back—the fox discovers "Lo, how Fortune turneth sodeynly" (3403). Therefore, before they go to war, "men moste have greet conseil and greet deliberacion" (1042).

Since the young folk are even more disruptive in shouting down this speaker than they had been in interrupting the old lawyer, the speaker breaks off with two maxims: "For soothly, he that precheth to hem that listen nat heeren his wordes, his sermon hem anoieth" (1043) and "as muche availleth to speken bifore folk to which his speche anoyeth, as it is to synge biforn hym that wepeth" (1045). The Nun's Priest's Tale appropriately echoes these maxims by beginning with the great deliberation between Pertelote and Chauntecleer on the interpretation of dreams. While not the same thing as deliberating war, it ultimately involves a life-and-death situation for Chauntecleer. Nonetheless, since Chauntecleer "list[eth] nat heeren" Pertelote's argument (as his attitude toward laxatives indicates), her sermon annoys him: "Madame, . . . graunt mercy of youre loore" (2970).

One final word about the centrality of the Tale of Melibee to Fragment VII and its importance to the *Canterbury Tales* as a whole. Throughout the fragment, and most pointedly in the Monk's Tale, we are told "ther nas no remedie" (1993) for human disaster brought on by the instability of Fortune. Nonetheless, the various tales assay various remedies: wit, war, miracle, and acceptance. But in the Tale of Melibee, Chaucer defines, in a tale he takes as his own, the best human response to adversity and the vagaries of Fortune: patience, deliberation, sufferance, mercy, and trust in God.[14] All Chaucer's serious heroes and heroines possess these virtues; all his villains deny them.

This response to adversity is important in a larger sense. Prudence educates Melibee not only so that he will know how to respond to the specific outrage which initiates the tale; she educates him for the salvation of his soul. Specifically, she asks him to be Christ-like in his mercy: "Wherfore I pray yow, lat mercy been in youre herte, / to th'effect and entente that God Almighty have mercy on yow in his laste juggement" (1867–68). Melibee's final address to the three adversaries who attacked Sophie and Prudence reflects the triumph of wisdom and prudence that he articulates as Christ-like mercy. Melibee also defines the appropriate attitude of the repentant Christian who hopes to achieve God's mercy.

> Al be it so that of youre pride and heigh presumpcioun and folie, and of your necligence and unkonnynge, / ye have mysborn yow and trespassed unto me, / yet for as muche as I see and biholde youre grete humylitee, / and that ye been sory and repentant of youre giltes, / it constreyneth me to doon yow grace and mercy. / Wherfore I receyve yow to my grace, / and foryeve yow outrely alle the offenses, injuries, and wronges that ye have doon agayn me and myne, / to this effect and to this ende, that God of his endelees mercy / wole at the tyme of our diynge foryeven us oure giltes that we han trespassed to hym in this wrecched world.
>
> (1876–84)

This speech has more than local applicability. It speaks as much to the pilgrims on pilgrimage as it does to Melibee's three old foes; and it speaks as much to the courtiers in Chaucer's first audience as it does to the pilgrims. Consequently, it speaks to us. Fragment VII asks a serious question relevant to all Chaucer's audiences: What is the remedy to misfortune? Some tales respond with the Monk's depressive answer, "ther nas no remedie." Others offer equally unsatisfactory alternatives. The Tale of Melibee provides an answer which I understand as Chaucer's answer. The Tale of Melibee not only lies at the heart of this fragment; it lies at the heart of the *Canterbury Tales* as a whole.[15]

The Order of the Tales (II): Sequential Order

In addition to ordering the tales in Fragment VII according to the principle of chiasmus, Chaucer also linked the tales sequentially. Although Chaucer connects the tales in very definite and precise ways, I find no single principle (like that of deterioration and decay in Fragment I) which describes the sequential order—unless, as has been suggested, that principle is variety.[16] In joining the tales sequentially in Fragment VII, Chaucer rarely uses the same predominant method of linkage twice. He links the tales by contrast, by parody and diminution, by similarity, by theme, and by summary or recapitulation. Of course, as he does elsewhere in the *Canterbury Tales*, Chaucer also binds the two tales in sequence by emphasizing similarities and contrasts of theme, of character, and of situation, but his doing so only contributes to the variety of sequential linkage in the fragment.

FROM THE SHIPMAN'S TALE TO THE PRIORESS' TALE

When Harry Bailly swears "by corpus dominus" (435) in the link between the Shipman's and the Prioress' Tales, he does more than make a comic error in Latin: that is, he thinks he calls upon the body of the Lord (which would be *corpus domini*), but in fact he refers to a body (*corpus*) and to God (*dominus*) and so articulates the contrast between the physical and the spiritual that links the first two tales of Fragment VII.[17] His tone supports the contrast: he is brash and imperative when he addresses the Shipman who, in transporting goods, ministers to physical needs, but he is courteous and supplicative when he addresses the Prioress, who ministers to spiritual needs. The Shipman's worldliness, articulated in the tale by expansiveness (the feasts, the travel, the play), contrasts with the Prioress' spirituality, articulated in her tale by diminutiveness (the "litel scole" [495], "litel clergeoun" [503], "litel child" [516], and so on).[18] The Prioress dismisses as "foule usure and lucre of vileynye" (491) the Shipman's worldly attitude toward money. The merchant's "largesse" (22) and the monk's generosity (43) focus upon this world and contrast with those of the Virgin Mary, who is the true "roote / Of bountee" (465–66) and who acts for the spiritual benefit of people even before they ask for it (477–80 and cf. the Prologue to the Second Nun's Tale, VIII, 50–56).

Chaucer develops the contrast between the worldly and the

spiritual, which unites these first two tales in Fragment VII, by focusing upon the mass and upon the abbots who appear in both. In Fragment VII, the mass appears only twice: the Shipman dismisses the mass as something to be said "hastily" so that his characters can "spedily" set the table and "spedde" themselves "faste" to the "dyner" (251–53) by which they satisfy their physical needs; the Prioress concentrates upon the length of a mass for the dead (635–36) after which the abbot and his monks "sped hem" (638) to bury the little clergeon, which leads to the second occurrence of the miracle. Haste in the Shipman's Tale satisfies physical needs; haste in the Prioress' Tale brings on a miracle of the Virgin. Chaucer continues to contrast the worldly and the spiritual in his treatment of the abbots. Abbots appear only twice in active roles in all of the *Canterbury Tales*: both appearances are in Fragment VII.[19] The Shipman's worldly abbot allows the monk "out for to ryde" (65), which releases the monk into the world and exposes him to the attractions of the merchant's wife; the Prioress' abbot, on the other hand, is a holy man who performs the act that releases the murdered child's soul to heaven. The Prioress carefully distinguishes between worldly and spiritual monks (642–43, and cf. 456).

The relationships among the characters within these two tales are remarkably similar, more so than they are to those in any other tales of the fragment. In the Shipman's Tale, two men claim kinship on the basis of acquaintance and having been "yborn in o village" (35). In the Prioress' Tale, two boys claim fellowship (525) on the basis of their shared religion and common school. It can be said that each male group shares a lady in common: the monk and the merchant share the merchant's wife in a carnal or physical sense; the two Christian children share "our blisful Lady fre" (532) in a religious or spiritual sense. Both male groups emphasize secrecy. The older boy teaches the little clergeon "prively" (544), and the monk insists that his financial arrangement with the merchant "be secree" (277).

Finally, as scholars have long noted, the Shipman's Tale has a great deal of swearing on saint's names, breviaries, bones, and brotherhood, as well as much calling upon God to witness, defend, and preserve—the abundant and careless profanity of ordinary, secular people. Nothing similar appears in the Prioress' Tale. In her Prologue, the Prioress calls upon Mary to support her in telling her tale; and within the story, the widow earnestly calls upon Mary to help her find her lost child. In spite of all the swearing and calling upon God, God does not appear in the Shipman's Tale, but devoutly addressed, both Jesus and Mary perform miracles in the Prioress' Tale.

The pointed contrast between the physical and the spiritual that Chaucer develops in so many ways throughout the Shipman's Tale and the Prioress' Tale emphasizes their similarity and supports their juxtaposition. No other tales in Fragment VII address precisely these issues. No other tales balance just these relationships among the characters. Chaucer has joined the Shipman's Tale with the Prioress' Tale because they are opposite sides of the same coin. Their conjunction, their careful opposition of the physical and the spiritual, and their balance of characters all show Chaucer's craft. The two tales belong together because in this respect, they are more like each other than they are like any other tales in the fragment.

FROM THE PRIORESS' TALE TO THE TALE OF SIR THOPAS

The relationship between the Tale of Sir Thopas and the Prioress' Tale differs completely from the relationship between the Prioress' Tale and the Shipman's. Whereas the Shipman's Tale contrasts with the Prioress' Tale, the Tale of Sir Thopas diminishes and parodies certain elements of the Prioress' Tale.

The Prioress tells a story of a boy born far away "in Asye, in a greet citee" (488); Sir Thopas, too, was born "in fer contree, / . . . al biyonde the see" (718–19). Both comparisons are rendered ridiculous: the great city is the tiny town of "Poperyng" and the distant country is only Flanders. The little clergeon, "That nevere, flesshly, wommen . . . ne knewe" (585), goes before the Lamb (579–85); Sir Thopas, too, "was chaast and no lechour" (745), but he goes before "many a wilde best, / Ye, bothe bukke and hare" (755–56). The clergeon adores the Queen of Heaven; Sir Thopas adores an elf-queen, and, by wanting her to "slepe under my goore" (789), seems to desire the flesh of a spirit. He almost finds her "in a pryve woon" (801) just as the little clergeon is murdered in "a privee place" (568) and his body ultimately found in a "wardrobe" (572) which is a privy of a different sort. Both Sir Thopas and the widow call upon "Cristes mooder" (597) "Seinte Marie" (784) to aid their search, and God's grace operates in both tales: Jesus "of his grace" (603) lets the widow know where her son's body lies, and Sir Thopas escapes from Sir Olifaunt "thurgh Goddes gras" (831). The "white lylye flour" (461), emblematic of

Mary in the Prioress' Tale, appears again ridiculously sticking out of a tower on the crest of Sir Thopas's helmet (906–7). The great gems of spiritual defense, "This gemme of chastite, this emeraude, / And eek of martirdom the ruby bright" (609–10), appear as the "charbocle" (871) which is only painted on Sir Thopas's shield.[20] The "greyn" which lies upon the clergeon's tongue is echoed only in Sir Thopas's complexion which is "scarlet in grayn" (727). The "hooly water" (638) that unleashes the miracle the second time is echoed only in the "water of the well" (915) that Thopas drinks. Perhaps, too, the liberality of Sir Thopas's father, "a man ful free" (721) reflects the liberality of the lord who allows the Jewry to remain or the liberality of the clergeon in expressing his adoration of Mary; surely it continues the liberality of merchant and monk in the Shipman's Tale. In connection with the Shipman's Tale, it is amusing to see that the great medieval fair-town of Bruges, to which the merchant travels in the Shipman's Tale, is the source of Sir Thopas's hose (733). These are the only two references to Bruges in the *Canterbury Tales*.[21]

So many accurate echoes, precise contrasts, repetitions, and inversions all in the service of parody and diminution suggest the purposeful linking of these two tales. Chaucer's design for the unity of Fragment VII is far more complex than it is for other fragments. His linking of the Shipman's Tale to the Prioress' Tale by contrast and then linking the Prioress' Tale to the Tale of Sir Thopas by diminution and parody testify to the complexity and sophistication of that design.

FROM THE TALE OF SIR THOPAS TO THE TALE OF MELIBEE

In the sequential order of Fragment VII, the Tale of Melibee follows the Tale of Sir Thopas. The connection between the two tales, as we have already seen in our discussion of the chiasmic order of the fragment, is close: a single narrator tells the two "murye" tales that lie at the heart of the chiasmus and at the heart of the fragment. Sir Thopas and Melibee share certain characteristics; they also share similar misfortunes and arrive, at least initially, at similar remedies to misfortune. We need not repeat the details of that connection. But what is interesting from the point of Chaucer's craft in the sequential order of the fragment is that Chaucer binds the Tale of Melibee to the Tale of Sir Thopas in a way different from any he has used heretofore in the fragment: contrast binds the Shipman's Tale to the Prioress' Tale;

parody and diminution bind the Tale of Sir Thopas to the Prioress' Tale; and now similarity—extending even to the narrator—binds the Tale of Melibee to the Tale of Sir Thopas.²²

FROM THE TALE OF MELIBEE TO THE MONK'S TALE

Chaucer carefully links the Tale of Melibee to the next tale in the sequential order, the Monk's Tale, in two ways: the first emphasizes the themes that the two tales share; the second begins to recapitulate the entire fragment, a process Chaucer perfects in the Nun's Priest's Tale. The thematic connection is most obvious. The Tale of Melibee and the Monk's Tale directly address the question of what constitutes the remedy to misfortune that binds the fragment, and they arrive at different answers. Harry Bailly makes the immediate connection in the link between the tales when he compares his own wife, Goodelief, with Dame Prudence, but where Prudence cautions Melibee to be patient, to suffer, to forbear, and to trust in God as remedies to misfortune, Goodelief incites Harry Baily to war ("False coward, wrek thy wif!" [1905]) against both Harry's "knaves" (1897) and his "neighebor" (1901). She reflects an attitude similar to that first advocated by Sir Thopas and initially adopted by Melibee. Prudence's advice provides the remedy that the Monk feels does not exist to counter the ill-effects of unstable Fortune. Another theme which binds the tales concerns the counsel of women. The Tale of Melibee introduces the relationship between husband and wife, especially as regards taking the counsel of women, which the Prologue to the Monk's Tale, the Monk's Tale itself (in the example of Sampson, 2091–94), and the Nun's Priest's Tale (especially 3252–66) continue and develop.

Finally, the two tales are bound by the theme of tragedy. The Monk's Tale is about tragedy, and Melibee himself exemplifies an incipiently tragic figure, as the Monk defines the term (1992–94). Melibee recognizes the gifts that Fortune has bestowed upon him in the past and he intends to test Fortune in the future: "I bithenke me now and take heede how Fortune hath norissed me fro my childhede and hath holpen me to passe many a strong paas. / Now wol I assayen hire, trowynge, with Goddes help, that she shal helpe me my shame for to venge" (1445–46). Prudence's advice—"ye shul nat assaye Fortune by no wey. . . . Trusteth nat in hire, for she nys nat stidefate ne stable, / for whan thow trowest to be moost seur or siker of hire help, she wol faille thee and deceyve thee" (1447 and 1451–52)—affirms the central attitude of the Monk's Tale toward Fortune (1995, 1997, 2136, 2140–42,

2239–46, 2765–66, etc.) and in effect prevents Melibee from becoming another example in the Monk's list of tragic figures. In terms of the sequential order of tales in Fragment VII, the Monk's Tale shows what happens to people who share Melibee's initial attitude (e.g., Sir Thopas) but lack the kind of good advice that Prudence provides.

The second way by which Chaucer joins the Monk's Tale to the sequential order of the fragment has larger implications for the unity of the fragment as a whole. Chaucer uses the Monk to recapitulate the fragment. The Prologue to the Monk's Tale refers, with greater or less specificity, to all the tales in Fragment VII. Harry Bailly's reference to his own wife and that of Melibee is the most obvious, but the Monk's taking Harry's ribaldry "al in pacience" (1965) also evokes Melibee and Prudence. The Host's curious and inexplicable attempt to explain why "oure wyves wole assaye / Religious folk" (1959–60) recalls the Shipman's Tale where the merchant's wife assays the monk. The protestation of ignorance (1990) and the threatened death of young boys (1899) recall the Prioress and her Tale. The description of the Monk (1931) suggests Sir Thopas, and the Monk's sexuality in a religious man is the obverse of Sir Thopas's virginity in a worldly man. In suggesting that the monk is a "tredefowel aright" (1945), the Prologue to the Monk's Tale looks forward to the Nun's Priest's Tale where both Chauntecleer and the Nun's Priest are treadfowls.

FROM THE MONK'S TALE TO THE NUN'S PRIEST'S TALE

Chaucer links the Monk's Tale to the Nun's Priest's Tale in two ways, similar to those which joined the Monk's Tale to the Tale of Melibee: the first is thematic; the second, retrospective and recapitulative. The Nun's Priest's Tale continues the theme of tragic story introduced and developed in the Monk's Tale.[23] The story of Chauntecleer, while not exactly preserved in "olde bookes" (1974), does tell "Of hym that stood in greet prosperitee, / And is yfallen out of heigh degree / Into myserie" (1975–77). Even though Chauntecleer does not "endeth wrecchedly" (1977) as do most of the figures in the Monk's Tale, his story is one of pride, deception, betrayal, and treason, marked by sudden shifts of Fortune. Both tales warn against trusting in Fortune (1995–96 and 3403). Both tales instruct with a variety of morals equally applicable to both.[24] The maxims that end the Nun's Priest's Tale, for example, encourage Chaucer's audience to beware of how

Fortune turns against the hope and pride of her enemy (3403–4), to be vigilant against treachery (3429–32), not to be "undiscreet of governaunce" (3434), and to be careful not to be tricked by flattery (3436–37). This "fruyt" (3443) is also the fruit of the Monk's Tale.

The second way that Chaucer links the two is retrospective.[25] Just as the Prologue to the Monk's Tale referred, often obliquely, to the other tales in the fragment, so the Nun's Priest's Tale refers, not once but twice, to all the other tales in the fragment. The first recapitulation appears at the beginning of the Nun's Priest's Tale and refers to all the other tales in the order in which they appear in the fragment. The Nun's Priest's Tale begins with the widow's poverty and Chauntecleer's rich array, which recall the merchant's lavish feasts and his wife's concern for clothes in the Shipman's Tale. Chauntecleer's splendid singing voice recalls that of the clergeon in the Prioress' Tale. The courtly love treatment of Pertelote recalls the attitude of Sir Thopas to the elf-queen. The debate between Chauntecleer and Pertelote recalls that between Melibee and Prudence. The tragedies of those who disregard dreams recall the Monk's tragedies and, like his, are also preserved in "olde bookes" (2974; cf. 1974).

At various moments elsewhere in his tale, the Nun's Priest recapitulates the other tales a second time in a more precise and explicit manner. I have already indicated the parallels between the Nun's Priest's Tale and the Shipman's Tale (the rich men, good providers, who come down to breakfast from their perch or counting-house; the tales of misplaced trust, flattery, and treason) and the parallels in tragic form between the Nun's Priest's Tale and the Monk's Tale. They need no repetition. But the Nun's Priest recapitulates all the other tales in the fragment with equal care. Chauntecleer's first exemplum (2984–3062) explicitly recapitulates the Prioress' Tale.[26] The two fellows who go on pilgrimage parallel the little clergeon and his fellow who meet on their journey to school. The two pilgrims must separate to sleep, just as the clergeon and his fellow must separate. Only the clergeon goes through the ghetto. Furthermore, one from each group is slain and then buried in similarly unsavory places: one in a privy, the other in a dung cart. Both call out supernaturally: the dead pilgrim calls to his fellow in dream; the dead clergeon sings "O Alma." The widow goes to the Jews who claim not to have seen the child; the other pilgrim goes to the inn where the innkeeper says his fellow has already departed. The pilgrim remembers his dream; Jesus puts the thought of where the boy is buried into the widow's mind. The Christian folk rush in to see what is happening; the "peple out sterte" (3047) to help the pilgrim. The carter and the innkeeper, like the Jews, are tortured and hung. Both the Prioress and Chauntecleer declare "Modre wol out" (576 and 3057). Finally, in comparisons appropriate to the degree of each, the princely Chauntecleer refers to St. Kenelm, the martyred son of "the noble kyng" (3111) Cenwulf of Mercia, and the Prioress compares her widow's son to the commoner Hugh of Lincoln.

The Nun's Priest recalls the Tale of Sir Thopas the second time with similar precision. Only Sir Thopas and Chauntecleer, among all the characters in Fragment VII, are introduced with a description of their person and their attire. Both are colorful, both richly arrayed. Both are surprised by animal adversaries: one is a fox; the other evokes an elephant. If Sir Thopas's speedy withdrawal from combat with Sir Olifaunt indicates his cowardice, then Sir Thopas is guilty of behavior that Pertelote finds reprehensible in Chauntecleer: "fy on yow, hertelees! . . . / I kan nat love a coward" (2908–11). They are the only two characters in the fragment so implicated.[27] Both tales parody medieval romance, though they do so in entirely different ways: the Tale of Sir Thopas parodies the form of medieval romance; the Nun's Priest's Tale parodies romantic attitudes toward courtly love. Sir Thopas, who is "chaast and no lechour" (745), finds no woman in the world worthy to be his mate; by contrast, Chauntecleer is surrounded by "Sevene hennes . . . / Whiche were his sustres and his paramours" (2866–67). Sir Thopas and Chauntecleer are the only characters in the fragment who dream: Sir Thopas dreams of an elf-queen and is attacked by Sir Olifaunt; Chauntecleer dreams of a fox and is attacked by a fox. Both escape.

Finally, the Nun's Priest's Tale recalls and parodies the Tale of Melibee. To be sure, both involve the counsel of women and both cite authorities,[28] but the most telling detail involves the only dramatic moment in the conversation between Prudence and Melibee. Melibee accuses Prudence of not loving "myn honour ne my worshipe" (1681), and Prudence "bigan . . . to maken semblant of wratthe" (1687). The Nun's Priest's Tale reiterates the moment. Pertelote's initial anger with Chauntecleer ("Avoy! . . . fy . . . Allas . . . How dorste ye seyn, for shame, unto youre love / That any thyng myghte make yow aferd?" [2908–19]) is also "semblant of wratthe"; in the rest of her speech she moderates her anger and ends on a positive note ("Be myrie, housbonde, for youre fader kyn!" [2968]). Chauntecleer responds to Pertelote's argument and disregards her anger; Melibee responds to Prudence's "semblant of wratthe," begs her forgiveness (1698), and capitulates entirely by placing himself completely under her control: "I am redy to do right as ye wol desire" (1702). Melibee has come a long way from his initial attitude toward taking advice from his wife. He had four clear and compelling reasons supported by authority for not doing so (1055–61). Chauntecleer has only one, and it is personal: "I ne telle of laxatyves no stoor, / . . . I hem diffye, I love hem never a deel!" (3154–56). Melibee abandons his reasons; Chaunteleer does not. Melibee is educable; Chauntecleer is not.

The Tale of Melibee shares with the Nun's Priest's Tale this tendency to evoke the entire *Canterbury Tales*. The Tale of Melibee was such a storehouse of recorded wisdom for Chaucer that he repeated lines from the Tale of Melibee in ten of the Canterbury tales and evoked almost all the other tales.[29] Most of those repeated lines are proverbs or scriptural quotations, but even a line as important to the Miller's parody of the Knight's Tale as "alloone withouten any compaignye" appears in the Tale of Melibee (1560). And most of the evocations are rather straightforward and obvious. Prudence's discussion of ire, for example, evokes that in the Summoner's Tale, and her discussion of covetousness evokes the Pardoner's Tale. I mention the point here only to support the notion that the Nun's Priest Tale contributes to the unity of Fragment VII by reiterating all the tales in the fragment. Chaucer employed the same summary device in the Tale of Melibee where he recalls the *Canterbury Tales* as a whole.

* * *

In the course of discussing the various patterns of order and structure in the fragment, I concurrently discussed the various themes that contribute to the unity of the whole. Of these, perhaps the concern for "remedie" is the most consistently developed theme and the one most conducive to coherence in the fragment. Chaucer develops the themes of treason and the counsel of women with almost as great consistency, though he omits both from the Tale of Sir Thopas and neglects to develop the second (although it appears in the tragedy of Sampson) in the Monk's Tale. Other themes which appear fitfully throughout the fragment—governance, honor, brotherhood—seem not to have been developed at all beyond the local linking of two or three of the six tales. But in a fragment so structurally sophisticated as Fragment VII, it might be gratuitous to insist upon a broad spectrum of fully developed themes to solidify a unity already so patently present.

Fragment VII begins, as the *Canterbury Tales* begins, with the fundamental dichotomy of the physical and the spiritual, *amor* and *amor dei*, the call of the bird and the call of the saint. This beginning not only defines the parameters of discussion for the fragment as it does for the whole, but it indicates the human interpenetration of each by the other, incarnation and transfiguration, the worldliness of the spiritual and the divinity of the physical worked out in completely different ways in the Shipman's and the Prioress' Tales and in the Tale of Sir Thopas. However one arranges the fragments of the *Canterbury Tales* between the clearly labeled first and tenth fragments, all the individual tales in all the individual fragments celebrate the issues joined in Fragment VII: the flesh (Shipman's Tale), the triumph of the spirit (Prioress' Tale), silliness, parody, and comic optimism (Sir Thopas), wisdom (Melibee), and tragic defeat and the instability of Fortune (Monk's Tale, Nun's Priest's Tale). Nonetheless, Fragment VII ends in affirmation. Although Chauntecleer falls from prosperity in this world, he also gains a high place. The source of Chauntecleer's salvation is a tree,[30] emblematic of the cross upon which Christ was crucified to save mankind, most of whom are as confused about the spirit and the flesh as are most of Chaucer's pilgrims and most of the characters in the tales they tell. Fragment VII makes a basic Christian statement: by showing the salvation of a bird as silly, proud, uxorious, careless, and human as Chauntecleer, it holds out the possibility of salvation to all of Chaucer's audiences. To that end, Chaucer's pilgrims journey toward Canterbury. To that end, we join them. We may not travel the road to their Canterbury, but we take them and their tales with us as we journey toward whatever judgment, whatever salvation awaits us.

8
Conclusion

> . . . here is God's plenty.
>
> —Dryden

Dryden delights in the splendid variety of Chaucer's characters, in "the various manners and humours . . . of the whole English nation in his age. Not a single character has escaped him. All his pilgrims are severally distinguished from each other; and not only in their inclinations, but in their very physiognomies and persons." The serious characters are distinguished from each other "by their several sorts of gravity." "Even the ribaldry of the low characters is different," as are the tales they all tell and the ways they tell them (Dryden 1700, 262). Every age adds to Dryden's list. Every age finds in Chaucer's verse a gorgeous variety of whatever interests it. We have found the classical tradition, the Italian tradition, the French tradition, and the English tradition. We are quite comfortable with claims that the *Canterbury Tales* is an encyclopaedia of genre, style, tone, learning, source, mood, character, idea, and so on. We are in the process now of finding the reader(s) in the text, defining various reader responses, and applying feminist, deconstructionist, modernist, and postmodernist literary theory to Chaucer's medieval texts. We rejoice with Dryden in Chaucer's richness and his plenitude.

Variety, in itself, is not a mark of genius in a poet; it is not even a mark of excellence. However, the ability to control that variety measures a poet's mastery of his craft. As much as he admired Chaucer, Dryden thought that Chaucer occasionally "runs riot . . . and knows not when he has said enough" (265). Modern readers of Chaucer less willingly acknowledge his limitations, in part because we are constantly discovering new areas of his excellence and control. The present excursus into Chaucer's artistic methods, our examination of the parallels in structure, theme, and character with which he established lines of coherence in the fragments of the *Canterbury Tales,* is only another event in the continuing effort to understand the working of Chaucer's imagination, the extent of his excellence and control. All of us who have seen something new and interesting in the work of Geoffrey Chaucer agree with Dryden when (in a slightly different context) he says of his own efforts to perpetuate Chaucer's memory among his countrymen: "I must at the same time acknowledge, that I could have done nothing without him" (268). We discover new and interesting and often amazing things in Chaucer's work not because we are clever but because Chaucer is. He put them there.

In this book I have shown that Chaucer's control of his craft extends to one of the more neglected aspects of the *Canterbury Tales,* the joining of the tales in the building of the fragments. We all agree that Chaucer designed every one of the individual tales to stand alone, a self-contained, coherent artistic whole. We also agree that when he began to build the *Canterbury Tales,* Chaucer had an idea of a different coherent artistic whole: he projected one hundred twenty stories linked together, told by pilgrims, and set in the framework of a pilgrimage to Canterbury. Somewhere between 1387 when he began to work on the *Canterbury Tales* and his death in 1400, Chaucer modified his plan, reducing the stories to sixty and introducing a narrator who was not one of the original storytellers, and who may not even have been a pilgrim (the Canon's Yeoman). Sometime in the process of putting together the *Canterbury Tales,* either early or late, Chaucer started to group the tales that he wanted to be read together either in the one-hundred-twenty-story plan or in the sixty-story plan—or perhaps he grouped the tales in the daunting knowledge that he would never write many more stories than the ones he already had on hand and so would never satisfy even the limited 60-story plan. In building the fragments, Chaucer consistently adhered to principles of artistic order which he invented, defined for himself, or discovered among the writers that he read. In the characters, themes, and organization of narrative events in disparate stories, Chaucer saw parallels which he decided belonged together. Then he wrote prologues and links and manipulated the structure, themes, and characters of the tales to justify bringing them together. He consciously crafted the fragments, unified them, and integrated all the parts so that they would coalesce to form what he considered a coherent, artistic whole—something often unknown and seldom defined in the literary theory of his day. Upon these he lavished his imagination, ingenuity, and care.

I am not arguing here what Chaucer thought he was doing or intended to do (the intentional fallacy). In order to enlarge our awareness of the richness and fecundity of Chaucer's creative imagination, I am showing inductively from the evidence of the fragments what Chaucer in fact did to join the individual tales into the multitale fragments. His imagination was not limited to retelling or inventing tales in poetry, creating characters and situations, and articulating human behavior with compassion, irony, and wit. He is also among the very first in English literature to have an idea of the whole, a sense of the congruence of parts, and an imagination both vast and particular enough to deal with the great and small details of artistic creation. He is also among the very first to have a fully developed and coherent aesthetic imagination sufficiently comprehensive to embrace a single long work like the *Troilus* and sufficiently sophisticated to embrace all the details of a complicated, multifocal/multivocal work like the *Canterbury Tales*. Everything is important in Chaucer. As Robert Frank, Jr., once remarked, "These similarities, contrasts, and variations . . . [are] the work of a comprehensive imagination which transformed his experience and reading into marvelously complex, varied, ironic, playful, and penetrating clusters of narratives in which human assumptions, aspirations, follies, and, sometimes, agonies were presented to us that we might appreciate more completely and wonderingly how winding and wonderful, how treacherous and teasing, how farcical and exalting that pilgrim's road from original sin to final judgment was."

Structure

I do not believe that Geoffrey Chaucer built the fragments of the *Canterbury Tales* with mathematical precision. One must "draw the line between art and algebra" (Muscatine 1957, 222). But I do believe, and it has been the purpose of this book to show, that Chaucer's imagination worked in such a way that he consistently and very carefully joined together those tales that, regardless of their differences, were alike because they shared the same themes, characters, and order of narrative events. Order is crucial; order defines structure. Chaucer joined the Second Nun's Tale with the Canon's Yeoman's Tale to form Fragment VIII, for example, because they involved the same narrative events—invo-

Conclusion   185

cation; interpretation and explanation; a tale involving three conversions; testing; final preaching—in the same order in both tales. No other tale shares this sequence of narrative events. For Chaucer to have joined the Second Nun's Tale or the Canon's Yeoman's Tale with a tale that presents different events in a different order—one of the tales in Fragment III, for example (the Wife of Bath's Tale, the Friar's Tale, or the Summoner's Tale)— would have satisfied no aesthetic principle except that of "variety." All the tales in Fragment III have an introductory portrait with an interior and an exterior focus; an interruption originating outside the tale; a tale of quest; a double conclusion with an interior and an exterior focus; and a passage describing the end of anger. Nothing in the structure of a tale from Fragment III justifies its sharing a fragment with a tale from Fragment VIII. While they may share any variety of themes and motifs with each other and with tales elsewhere in the *Canterbury Tales*—an aesthetic principle which contributes to the coherence of the work as a whole—they lack the similarities of structure that we have seen Chaucer manipulating in all the fragments. To link a tale from Fragment VIII with a tale from Fragment III would be structural chaos, not artistic order.

Chaucer's imagination delights in contrast as well as similarity. The relationship between the Second Nun's Tale and the Canon's Yeoman's Tale is fundamentally contrastive; although the sequence of narrative events is the same in both tales, comparable events are the inverse, obverse, and opposite of each other. Contrast dominates. But whether parallel narrative events link by similarity or by contrast, the tales within a two-tale fragment share essentially the same structure unique to that fragment. Consequently, every tale is precisely where it should be in the *Canterbury Tales*. No tale could be moved to another fragment without compromising and destroying the structural integrity of that fragment.

In addition to this pattern of parallel events that establishes the structural integrity of each fragment, Chaucer uses other principles to determine the specific order of the tales in the larger fragments. In Fragment III, that principle is external to the tales. Because of a disagreement among the pilgrims in the frame, the order of tales after the Wife of Bath's is determined by the dramatic antagonism between the Friar and the Summoner. In Fragment I, on the other hand, the organizational principle is internal. Regardless of the antagonism between the Miller and the Reeve, the tales follow an order that traces decay and deterioration in accordance with the principle announced by Theseus in the First Mover speech. All matters within the tales—theme, character, relationships, even language—contribute to the pattern by adhering to the principle of decay.

The principles which govern the order of tales in Fragment VII, the longest and most complex in the *Canterbury Tales*, are also the most complex and varied. Chaucer determines the order of tales by applying three principles unique to Fragment VII. The first is antimetabole or the chiasmic arrangement of six items (ABC:CBA). Although Chaucer had employed chiasmus to order events within the tales of Fragment V (the Squire's Tale and the Franklin's Tale), only in Fragment VII does he employ antimetabole to order the tales themselves. The second principle is recapitulation. In the Tale of Melibee, in the Monk's Tale, and twice in the Nun's Priest's Tale, Chaucer carefully refers to all the tales in the fragment. The third principle is sequence. As he has in the two-tale fragments, Chaucer links each of the six tales in Fragment VII with its neighbor. The manners of linkage—contrast, parody, similarity—are not unique to this fragment; what is unique is the number of tales involved. The ironic cap to this sequential ordering occurs at the end of the fragment when the last tale, that of the Nun's Priest, links with the first, that of the Shipman, by chiasmus.

One final point: our description of the structural integrity of the individual fragments describes what is. It neither describes nor predicts what might have been Chaucer's final arrangement had he completed the sixty-story version of the *Canterbury Tales* and so linked all the disparate fragments into a single coherent whole. Such speculation on our part would be particularly barren. The *Canterbury Tales* is not finished. With twenty-four tales—including three or four incomplete tales and two long prose pieces not originally intended for inclusion in the *Canterbury Tales*—we have barely one-third of even the projected sixty-story shortened version. Trying to predict the coherence of the whole from the fragments that we have is like trying to predict what Canterbury Cathedral would look like from fragments of various sizes taken at random from the body of the building. Or, to use a more modern and perhaps more apt comparison, it would be like trying to design the rest of La Sagrada Familia in Barcelona from what is presently on site, knowing that Gaudi's architectural blueprints, plans, sketches, and drawings for the cathedral are lost and that he was actively changing the plans as he went along. And since Chaucer has already made changes in his original plans (creating narrators, reassigning tales, introducing new characters), any attempt to predict how he might have planned to join the disparate fragments together into an integrated coherent whole—if that was ever his dream—would be futile.

Theme

In addition to the themes which form the major concern of individual tales and the themes which radiate lines of cohesion throughout the *Canterbury Tales,* Chaucer employs themes and motifs specifically designed to establish coherence within the fragments themselves. Chaucer enriches these themes by developing them differently. Similarity and contrast are the most obvious ways. In the Clerk's Tale and the Merchant's Tale, for example, Chaucer treats time in the same way by showing the similar attitudes of Walter and January, but in the Second Nun's Tale and the Canon's Yeoman's Tale Chaucer treats smell in contrastive ways. *Gentillesse* in Fragment V measures courtly love in the Squire's Tale and is a mark of nobility in the Franklin's Tale. The Second Nun reveals secrets; the Canon's Yeoman professes to keep them hidden (and ironically reveals them). Clothes which measure rank in the Clerk's Tale and suggest sexual activity in the Merchant's Tale are connected to spiritual conversion by the Second Nun and to fraud by the Canon's Yeoman.

Character

We have seen with what skill Chaucer links and balances characters in order to unify the fragments of the *Canterbury Tales.* Chaucer primarily emphasizes similarities of manner, action, attitude, and history in establishing connective relationships among the characters. The most elaborate and complicated similarities occur in Fragment VII where Chaucer uses parallel characters to support both the chiasmic and the sequential order from the Shipman's Tale to the Nun's Priest's Tale. Perhaps the most sophisticated treatment of similar characters is his parallel portrayals first of the deterioration and then the restoration of Walter and January. Chaucer also joins and balances the characters by contrast: Griselda and May, Virginia and the rioters, the Second Nun and the Canon's Yeoman. In addition to balancing characters with characters within the tales and pilgrims with pilgrims within the frame, Chaucer constantly crosses the boundary that separates the fiction of the pilgrimage from the fiction of the tales when he pairs pilgrims with characters: Walter and the Merchant, the Friar and the friar (in the Summoner's Tale), the Summoner and the summoner (in the Friar's Tale), Aurelius and the Squire, the Reeve and the carpenter (in the Miller's Tale), and the Miller and the miller (in the Reeve's Tale) all testify to Chaucer's imagination in unifying the fragments vertically as well as horizontally.

Dryden's enthusiasm for Chaucer's skill in capturing the character "of the whole English nation in his age" is an instance of Dryden's pardonable exuberance and not a literal measure of Chaucer's achievement. Of course Chaucer did not capture every "single character," even if we use the term in Dryden's limited sense of humours and manners, but he made the most of those he did depict by rarely repeating any of them. The variety of Chaucer's women has long been a critical commonplace. Let us consider, instead, those of Chaucer's men who are lovers.[1] Some are married and some are not. If, at first, we look only at Chaucer's married lovers, we see three separate groups whose members Chaucer depicts in completely different ways.

Among the young marrieds are Walter, Arveragus, Valerian, Jankyn (Alice's fifth husband), the young knight in the Wife of Bath's Tale, and, from among the pilgrims, the Merchant. All of these men are in the process of coming to terms with their recent marriages, and all do so in different ways: Walter tests; Arveragus leaves; Valerian threatens and ultimately obeys; Jankyn ridicules and fights; the knight resists, listens, and learns; and the Merchant bewails.

Among the married men who seem comfortably middle-aged when we meet them are Theseus, Symkyn, the merchant (in the Shipman's Tale), Melibee, Chauntecleer, and, from among the pilgrims, Harry Bailly. With these men, Chaucer presents various ways of dealing with the married state. Theseus, Symkyn, and the merchant take their wives for granted and occupy themselves with other things. Theseus rules; Symkyn steals; the merchant makes money. Their marriages and their wives (Hippolyta hardly appears in the Knight's Tale at all) are at the periphery of their lives. The result of this attitude can be disastrous as it is for the merchant, whose wife sells herself to him, and for Symkyn, whose wife knocks him down. For Melibee, Chauntecleer, and the Host, however, the married state is more central to their lives:

Conclusion

all take advice from their wives; all are affected in different ways. Melibee thrives because of his wife; Chauntecleer survives in spite of his wife; Harry Bailly is driven by his wife (VII, 1913–22).

Finally among the married men are the old lovers who are also among the most recently married: January and John the carpenter. Since they are a medieval type, the *senex amans*, they must share the characteristics of the type: foolishness, uxoriousness, pride in their vigor, humiliation. Nonetheless, Chaucer carefully develops the different possibilities within the type. January relies upon learned authority to support his decision to marry; John derides learning. January sleeps and naps; John is active, travels to Osney, and works at his profession. January's marital humiliation is private; John's is public.

Among Chaucer's unmarried male lovers, the largest group is that of the courtly lovers, both those of the appropriate rank who take courtly love seriously and those of the lower rank who do not. Although a courtly lover, like a *senex amans*, is a medieval type, Chaucer depicts them all with splendid diversity. Perhaps Damian resembles Nicholas somewhat in approaching his lady directly and perhaps Aurelius resembles Arcite somewhat in taking to his bed before actively attempting to win his lady, but Nicholas is more clever than Damian, and Aurelius is more successful than Arcite. The other courtly lovers—Palamon, the tercelet, Absalon, Sir Thopas—emphasize different aspects of the courtly attitude they all represent: Palamon waits faithfully; the tercelet abandons and betrays his beloved; Absalon loves the idea of being in love; and Sir Thopas represents the active knight in quest of his beloved.

Chaucer depicts other groups of men, both married and unmarried, who love in the *Canterbury Tales*. We may dismiss Thomas and the lord in the Summoner's Tale as well as Perkyn Revelour's friend—married men about whom Chaucer provides no relevant information. Those who remain are the uncourtly seducers, John and Aleyn, whose motives for love render their behavior reprehensible. The monk in the Shipman's Tale, though involved in mutual seduction between consenting adults, is Chaucer's most venial cleric in a tale; his religious status makes his behavior reprehensible, too. Apius is Chaucer's most criminal lover, a man willing to pervert the order of the world to satisfy his lust. Three other men complete the panorama of Chaucer's lovers. What distinguishes them from all other of Chaucer's lovers is not their relationship to their wives or their beloved, but their relationship to their children. Janicula and Virginius (and the Roman emperor in the Man of Law's Tale) all love their daughters: one gives his daughter to his lord; one gives his daughter to extend the Christian faith; and one kills his daughter to prevent her contamination.

Dryden's sense of Chaucer's variety is certainly well-founded with regard to Chaucer's characters (which is all Dryden had in mind); it is equally well-founded with regard to Chaucer's themes and structures. Aware of the difficulty of Chaucer's language and the importance of preserving the *Canterbury Tales* for his age, Dryden posed a question as relevant to the twentieth century as it was to the seventeenth: "How few are there who can read Chaucer, so as to understand him perfectly?" (267). Dryden was justifying his translation, but the fact remains that no one reads Chaucer perfectly. No one can consider everything that Chaucer built into the *Canterbury Tales*. Therefore everyone who approaches the *Canterbury Tales* must be open to surprise. The surprises are there, waiting to be found. They are aspects of Chaucer's imagination and Chaucer's art, of the craft that he found "so long to lerne" (*Parliament of Fowls*, 1). No one denies that Chaucer learned his craft. We are constantly discovering how well he did so. This book has been one step in that continuing process of discovery.

Appendix: Temporal References in the Squire's Tale and the Franklin's Tale

Squire's Tale

twenty wynter (43)
yeer to yeer (44)
Idus of March, after the yeer (47)
a someres day (64)
pryme (73)
los of tyme (74)
the space of o day natureel (116)
someres tyde (142)
Phebus hath left . . . (263–65)
til men to the soper dresse (290)
by day (297)
At after-soper (302)
ful soone (333)
the day bigan to sprynge (346)
tyme to lye adoun (351)
pryme (360)
eve (364)
morwe (366)
er that the sonne gan up glyde (373)
Thus erly (379)
. . . the yonge sonne That in the Ram is foure degrees up ronne (385–86)
er that it were nyght (468)
Whil that I have a leyser and a space (493)

Franklin's Tale

a yeer or tweyne (809)
two yeer (813)
nyght and day (824)
a day, right in the morwe-tyde (901)
the longe day (905)
sixte morwe of May (906)
a tyme abyde (923)
Two yeer and moore (940)
To ech of hem his tyme and his seson (1034)
yeres tweyne (1062)
thise yeres two (1068)
nyght and day (1070)
longe tyme (1081)
Two yeer and moore (1102)
in oure dayes (1132)
a wowke or two (1161)
it was tyme (1203)
to-morwe (1233)
nyght (1236)
day (1239)
Decembre (1244)
nyght and day (1262)
wayten a tyme (1263)
yeeris (1275)
thilke dayes (1293)
a wyke or tweye (1295)
nyght and day (1299)
tyme (1308)

many a day (536)
a yeer or two (574)
nyght and day (612)
day to nyght (641)

a day or two (1348)
a day or tweye (1457)
thridde nyght (1459)
to day (1473)
tyme (1558)
yeer by yeer (1568)
dayes (1575)
Two yeer or thre (1582)
that day (1600)
good day (1619)

Notes

The notes to each chapter, except for the Introduction and Conclusion, begin with a Bibliographical Note that establishes the context for discussion. It sets out the various arguments about the coherence of the fragment that is the subject of that chapter, and it cites those arguments that connect individual tales within the fragment to tales elsewhere in the *Canterbury Tales*. I have limited my references to those which bear directly on the topic of the fragments.

Introduction

1. Derek Pearsall (1985, 11). The integrity of Ellesmere has been defended by Kane (1984b). Charles Owen distinguishes "at least three different plans for the whole work" (1977, 7).

2. See Donaldson (1970b especially 203), Howard (1976), Benson (1987, 795–97; and 1981), David (1976), Dean (1985), and Zacher (1976)—and Derek Pearsall's splendid review and sensible solution to the problems in his chapters on "Date and Manuscripts" (1985, 1–23) and "Plan and Order" (1985, 24–51). He concludes that "the Ellesmere order is not Chaucer's order" and that "indeed there is no Chaucerian order," but that "the Ellesmere order is the best available, and . . . this is the one that the modern editor must accept" (1985, 22). Charles Owen, however, prefers Hengwrt's order (1982).

3. The earliest responses to Chaucer are collected in Burrow's useful book (1969). Twentieth-century work on Chaucer is reviewed by Baugh (1951) for the first fifty years of this century; Markman (1966) updates to 1965. Early notions of unity emphasized "la comedie humaine," the idea of pilgrimage, devotion to Venus, the Seven Deadly Sins, and the like. See Richard Hoffman (1968, 52–53) and Mehl (1986, 143–56).

4. Allen and Moritz affirm that "the organizational principles recognized and used in the Middle Ages have not been taken into account in modern efforts to understand the plan of Chaucer's story array" (1981, 4–5). They emphasize organizational principles that include "natural, magical, moral, and spiritual" (22) groups of tales. Their conclusion that Ovid's *Metamorphoses* and Chaucer's *Canterbury Tales* are "identical to one another" (15) and therefore that Ovid is the "formal precedent" (16) for Chaucer has not been generally accepted.

5. Stroud (1981, 33 n. 10). Mehl, too, celebrates "Chaucer's unorthodox delight in experimental diversity, extending to the field of literary genres and narrative methods" (1986, 148).

6. Kane (1984a, 2–3). For discussions of these critical theories, other influences upon Chaucer's poetry, and useful bibliographies, see Payne (1968), Mustanoja (1968), Robert Jordan (1968), and Rowland (1968).

7. Preston adequately describes the critical theory available to Chaucer (1952, 91–118). On Chaucer's indebtedness to Geoffrey de Vinsauf, see also Atkins (1943, 99). Chaucer's mistranslation of *praemetitur* (measures out) as *praemittitur* or *praemittetur* (will be sent out) may have derived from a faulty manuscript. See Benson (1987, 1030).

8. See Morgan (1986, 287). Gaylord refers to Chaucer as "architect and artist" (1967, 235). Hult has shown that for vernacular writers of the twelfth and thirteenth centuries, the idea of poetic individuality "had considerably more to do with the treatment and organization of plot or subject matter than it did with the actual precision of poetic expression" (1986, 853). For the artist as Pygmalion, see Kean (1982, 179).

9. Robert Jordan's argument (1967) that medieval books were as formally disjunctive and complexly structured as Gothic cathedrals and that medieval authors did not seek unity in any modern sense both supports and denies aspects of the argument for unity in the fragments that I shall present below. In his review of Cooper's book, Minnis presents a plea for evaluating the fragments as artistic wholes: "Once again, it may be protested that we are dealing not with a structure but with structures, and that each structure should be given its due. Why not develop an 'aesthetic of the unfinished,' an approach which would focus directly on the alternative patterns both between and within the groups of tales and celebrate these phenomena rather than minimizing or ignoring them?" (1985, 267). The two most important discussions are Cooper's chapter titled "Links within the Fragments" (1984, 108–207) and Howard's chapter titled "The Tales: A Theory of Their Structure" (1976, 210–332). Neither Cooper nor Howard nor any of the several articles which focus on the unity of individual fragments makes the claims or examines the fragments from the point of view I shall present in the chapters which follow.

10. See especially Benson (1987, 796; and 1981); Donaldson (1970b); and Cooper (1984, 56–71).

11. Although Richard Hoffman warns against applying Hegelian dialectic too strictly to the contrast of tales (1968, 68), both John Gardner (1977, 223–24) and Mehl (1986, 149) identify contrast as the central dramatic principle of the tales which both define in terms of "debate." Lumiansky sees the contrast of contiguous tales in terms of "a principle of contrast in the personalities of the successive storytellers" (1955, 176). Patterson argues that the principle of contrast derives, rather, from "bipartition or binarism" which he identifies as "one of the most common of medieval narrative structures" (1978, 375). Chaucer's "engrained tendency to see oppositions everywhere" (1973, 13) became the topic of Elbow's notable book. The earliest mention of a binary pattern that I have found with regard to Chaucer is that of Markman, who was interested in binary rhythm, "an alternating pulse, a crisp oscillation from narrative to lyric, from lyric to narrative" (1966, 98). Howard sees the dominant structure of the *Canterbury Tales* as "a system of pairs within groups" (1976, 216); Norton-Smith calls the same arrangement "recurring pairing arrangements indicating that some of the tales have been deliberately written in contrasting 'twins'" (1974, 97). Regardless of the derivation of the form the contrast takes, significant pairing is one of Chaucer's aesthetic games.

12. Surely it is "inconceivable that a series of stories could be other than closely related if they have similar plot structures and motifs" (Silvia 1967, 235). Interestingly, Beidler (1969) employs the same principle to justify the pairing of the Franklin's Tale with the Physician's Tale. While he does not argue

for their sharing a single fragment, he does imply that the Ellesmere order, in which Fragment V (which includes the Franklin's Tale) is followed by Fragment VI (which includes the Physician's Tale), is superior to the Chaucer Society order which separates them. I have not seen Lawler (1979).

13. Richard Hoffman provides a more comprehensive list of Chaucer's themes: "The stories, tragic and comic, treat of knighthood, chivalry, love, war, and death; cuckolding and adultery; gentility; marriage and 'the battle of the sexes'; the swearing of oaths and the dangers of literalism; hypocrisy and anger; patience; spiritual blindness; honor and the fulfillment of promises; virginity and sacrifice; *cupiditas,* riotous living, and the plague; deception, martyrdom; prudence and morality; biblical, ancient, and modern tragedy; predestination, free-will, the interpretation of dreams, and the secular-regular controversy; alchemy; jangling; sin, contrition, confession, and penance; and scores of minor themes" (1968, 51). To this list, Markman adds that "the emotional (and intellectual) core of this fiction is love" (1966, 98). Woo and Matthews agree and add that the primary purpose of the *Canterbury Tales* is to justify the ways of God to men (1970, 97, 98). Chamberlain (1981) is best on the contribution of musical signs and symbols to the thematic coherence of the *Canterbury Tales.* See note 23 in chapter 6 below for further discussion of music in Chaucer. Most recently, Williams has argued that Chaucer succeeds in "raising the theory of poetry to the level of the theme of his work" (1987, 74). For others who focus on the thematic unity of the *Canterbury Tales,* see Benson (1987, 797).

14. Lumiansky was reflecting an older critical tradition when he affirmed that Chaucer's narratives were "vehicles for character portrayal" (1955, 3), an attitude resurrected in more acceptably modern dress by Kane (1984a, 54). More recently, criticism tends to differentiate between the nominal and the real teller of Chaucer's tales. "It is rather unlikely that the individual tales were conceived as an expression of complex personalities . . . or that they were primarily intended to contribute to the portraits of their respective narrators" (Mehl 1986, 144). Or "To put it bluntly: the 'I' of narration is demonstrably not the 'I' of the ostensible teller" (Lawton 1985, 96). See also Morgan (1986, 287–88). My primary concern with Chaucer's characters is to point out the convincing parallels that Chaucer created between characters within tales though I occasionally do make comparisons between narrators and between narrators and characters when it seems clear that Chaucer designed such comparisons to contribute to the coherence of the fragment.

15. Since the Manciple's Tale is followed by the Parson's Tale in all manuscripts where both appear and Chaucer refers to the Manciple's Tale in the first line of the Parson's Prologue, some readers tend to consider these separate fragments, IX and X, as linked. To do so they must overlook a serious temporal problem: the short Manciple's Tale begins in the morning, and the Parson's Tale follows it late in the afternoon.

16. Baldwin (1962) is alone in arguing (against the Yeoman's explicit statement to the contrary) that the Canon of the pilgrimage and the canon of the tale are the same person.

Chapter 1. Fragment IV (Group E)

Part of this chapter appeared in *Hebrew University Studies in Literature and the Arts* 16 (1988): 27–50, as part of a tribute and memorial to Morton W. Bloomfield. I am grateful to the editors for allowing me to reprint it here.

BIBLIOGRAPHICAL NOTE

Most scholarly opinion has drawn attention to the connections that the Clerk's Tale and the Merchant's Tale share with tales elsewhere in the *Canterbury Tales*. The Clerk and his Tale have most often been connected with Alice of Bath, especially since Kittredge's famous article on the Marriage Group (1911–12). See also Hinckley (1917), Clawson (1951), Slaughter (1950), Lumiansky (1955, 141), Carruthers (1983), and Longsworth (1974). Baker (1962a) argues that the theme of *gentilesse* links the Wife of Bath's Tale with the Clerk's Tale; Alford finds their conflict "rooted in the recurrent tension between two modes of discourse, rhetorical and philosophical" (1986, 109)—the Clerk is "Logic personified" and Alice is "Dame Rhetoric herself" (1986, 110); and Axelrod (1974) argues that Alice has her eye upon the Clerk as her sixth husband. The Merchant's Tale, on the other hand, is most often connected with the Franklin's which follows it in the Hengwrt MS. See Holman (1951), Patch (1939, 220 and 226), Chute (1947, 289), and Tatlock (1936). Muscatine connects the Clerk's Tale with the Knight's Tale (1957, 190) and the Merchant's Tale with the Miller's (1957, 237). Huppé reads the Merchant's Tale with reference to the Parson's Tale (1964, 152–58); Derek Pearsall connects it to the Miller's and Reeve's Tales (1985, 193–97) and to the Franklin's Tale (1985, 195–96); and Mehl relates it to the Manciple's Tale (1986, 184). Howard cites allusions to seven or eight tales (1976, 261–62, nn. 54 and 55). These valuable discussions emphasize the connections among the fragments of the *Canterbury Tales*.

Of those who discuss the unity of the fragment itself, Hardman (1980) and John Gardner (1977, 287) see the Merchant's Tale as a parody of the Clerk's Tale; Heninger (1957) argues that the Merchant "proceeds to illustrate the Clerk's ironical envoy" (395); Traversi finds both the Clerk's Tale and the Merchant's Tale connected to the Wife of Bath's Tale by the subject of marriage (1983, 122); Cherniss finds them "interlocked thematically and verbally" (1972, 235); Levy (1977) emphasizes *gentilesse* as the connecting link. Allen and Moritz make the interesting observation that "Walter's proposed January–May marriage to his own daughter, which is of course pure pretense, becomes in the *Merchant's Tale* the serious basis of the narrative" (1981, 195). Donaldson does not see the Clerk's Tale as a story of marriage at all (1958, 920) and argues that the Merchant wants to destroy "the fiction of the Clerk's lovely idea of women . . . and . . . replace the idea with his own vile one" (1958, 921); Knight, on the other hand, anticipates one of my points in arguing that both tales are about "a decision to marry and its results" (1986, 112). Cooper emphasizes the "precise thematic contrast . . . of the tales of the patient and the unfaithful wife" (1984, 134); Brewer agrees that the tales are connected by contrast (1984, 221); and Howard finds that the tales "complement each other—both are accomplished displays of rhetoric which set realities against ideals. But the Clerk has a feeling for the old ideals and takes an ironic view of present realities; the Merchant heaps contempt on the ideals and takes a bitter view of realities" (1976, 264). Thus, the Merchant's Tale follows the Clerk's Tale "answering its idealism with disillusionment" (1976, 152, n. 32). John Gardner, placing the fragment in a larger context, argues that "every one of the tales in Fragments II–V . . . is a tale which comments directly or indirectly on the interrelated ideas *constancy* and *patience*. . . . In Fragments II–V, the real subject is 'headship' or proper authority" (1977, 267). None of these views recognizes the basic structural identity of the two tales in the fragment.

1. In his notes to Wilhelm Hertzberg's *Canterburyerzählungen*, a reissue of Hertzberg's 1866 translation of the *Canberbury Tales* into German, Koch first argued that January speaks these lines instead of the Merchant. While most scholars believe the Merchant is speaking ironically here (e.g., Donaldson 1958, 923; Howard 1976, 261), Huppé believes "the thoughts are clearly January's" (1964, 150), and Lumiansky sees "January's argument here with himself" (1955, 159). I have argued for this position on different grounds (1977b, 347–48). When speaking to himself, January says "Deffie Theofraste, and herke me" (1310); the "you" who is the implicit subject of the imperatives "Deffie" and "herke" and the "me" all refer to January, not the Merchant. Chaucer uses "herke" in a similar construction in *Troilus and Criseyde*. Troilus, alone in a temple, says to himself "now herkne, for I wol nat tarie" (*T&C* IV 1029), i.e., now you [Troilus] listen to me [Troilus] for I [Troilus] will not tarry.

2. In a recent article, Van argues that "Walter's relentless testing of Griselda is an examination, by surrogate, of his own spiritual interior" (1988, 215). In this new reading, Griselda "is a symbolic extension of her husband" (219) and "a means for Walter to extend his speculation about himself" (221).

3. Pittock finds it characteristic of January "that he is capable of mouthing the truth about himself without having an inward realisation of its implications" (1967, 29).

4. See also 1624, 1626, as well as, later, 1746, 1747, 1749.

5. Paul Delany points out that January takes three kinds of wine and eight or more aphrodisiacs: "January is not just having a few drinks to give himself confidence; he is swallowing strong and probably dangerous potions in an almost maniacally compulsive way" (1967, 563–64). Rudat identifies the taking of aphrodisiacs as "a typical postlapsarian act" (1981, 114).

6. Condren argues that "January seems unable to consummate his marriage" (1985, 242). Rudat sees January described in terms of "St. Augustine's observations concerning prelapsarian and postlapsarian sexuality" (1981, 111). Holbrook discusses the wedding night (1964, 109–13); cf. Pittock (1967, 30 ff.).

7. Brewer has argued with regard to the Clerk's Tale that "The story is one of the heroism and triumph of Griselda. It is she who overcomes Walter" (1984, 217). In that light, May's triumph over January reflects the parodic diminution of the first tale by the second which, as we shall see, characterizes many Canterbury fragments.

8. Whether Damian achieved sexual climax in the pear tree or not has been discussed by Beidler (1971a), Emerson Brown (1968 and 1970a, 36), and Milton Miller (1950).

9. I discuss the more complicated restoration of Walter and January below, pp. 41–45.

10. Huppé identifies these lines as a clue to the Clerk's Tale rather than to the fragment as a whole (1964, 136).

11. Chaucer repeats the quotation from Solomon in the Merchant's Tale ("For alle thyng hath tyme, as seyn thise clerkes" [1972]) where, ironically, it refers to a conjunction of constellations that renders the time astrologically appropriate for January to sue for love.

12. Huber (1967) traces the concept of death from Chaucer's earliest work through the *Canterbury Tales*.

13. The appearance/reality theme has myriad forms in the *Canterbury Tales* as a whole as well as a particular formulation in Fragment IV, and no footnote should be obliged to describe them all. Both Schroeder (1970) and Schleusener

(1980) address the ambivalent problems of appearance and reality in the Merchant's Tale. Morrow shows how Chaucer juxtaposes actual and ideal worlds in the Clerk's Tale "in order to create value conflicts" (1968, 74), and Salter points to the confused moral ordering generated by these two worlds in the Clerk's Tale (1962, 61–62). Hardman focuses upon "the experience of the conflict between the ideal (here both the fictional and the transcendent) and the real world" (1980, 175) in both tales.

14. Harry Bailly is not alone in misconstruing. "Chaucer was expert at the business of making a poem assume a meaning unknown to the fictional narrator" (Donaldson 1958, 923). The point is particularly apt for Fragment IV. Ginsberg has argued that "the Clerk himself does not fully understand the tale he tells" (1978, 319), but that is a minority opinion. Levy justifies the Clerk in terms of his "diverse audiences" (1986, 385); Ganim blames the Clerk's flaws (1987, 121). Both Lumiansky (1955, 172) and Huppé agree that the Merchant "probably does not perceive the real point of the tale he tells. Certainly the Host does not" (1964, 162).

15. Chaucer's treatment of Damian subverts all pretensions to courtly love and is consistent with his rejection of courtly love throughout the *Canterbury Tales*. See Tatlock (1936), Schlauch (1937, 202), Mandel (1985), Holman (1951), Fichte (1973), and Stevens (1972).

16. On medieval gardens, see Robertson (1951), Crisp (1924), Kellogg (1960), Stanley Stewart (1966), Burrow (1957), Richard Hoffman (1966), Derek Pearsall (1985, 202–3), and Rosenberg (1971). Wentersdorf has written extensively on the pears (1986, 50–55).

17. Wentersdorf (1965) and Donovan (1957) argue that the history of Pluto parallels that of January; Dalby (1974) finds images of the devil and his consort in Pluto and Proserpyna who, in this view, embody earthly lusts; and Bleeth (1974) finds the scene of the gods in the garden to be a scriptural parody of Genesis.

18. Chaucer develops the theme most pointedly in Fragment VIII where he contrasts the Second Nun's authority with the Canon's Yeoman's experience. See chapter 3, p. 75.

19. The theme of obedience has been well discussed by the critics. See especially McCall (1966a), Heninger (1957), J. M. Morse (1958), and Rothman (1973).

20. Johnson carefully distinguishes between Walter's relationship with his people, which she calls the "Old Covenant," and that between Walter and Griselda, the "New Covenant" (1975, 17–20). For Walter's people, "Obedience is merely grudging acceptance rather than 'perfect liberty of service'" (19). Though Johnson does not make the connection to the Merchant's Tale, ironic parallels to these two covenants may be found in January's relationship to Placebo and Justinus.

21. Schroeder argues that "January makes everything up in his own mind and projects that image onto all he encounters" (1970, 169). The theme of fantasy is a staple of criticism on the Merchant's Tale. See, e.g., Huppé (1964, 161), Donaldson (1958, 921), and Burrow (1957).

22. The genre of the Merchant's Tale is a conundrum perhaps best solved by Sedgewick: "*The Merchant's Tale* is not a fabliau, though it incorporates one into its structure. . . . [I]t is called a fabliau because there is no other convenient name" (1948, 344). See also Arrathoon (1986). Utley (1972) identifies five genres in the Clerk's Tale. That the genre of the Clerk's Tale is an exemplum "and the example is of a woman as wise as the Stoic wise man, as faithful as the pagan

martyr, and as patient almost as Christ" has recently and convincingly been argued by Charlotte Morse (1985, 85), but see Knapp (1985) for the ways Chaucer subverts our expectations of the genre.

23. On the significance of Lombardy, see Hardman (1980), Robert Pearsall (1952), Beidler (1971b), and Paul Olson (1961). Emerson Brown notes the parallels in the opening lines of the two tales in which Lombardy becomes Pavia; he associates wealth with Walter's Lombardy and sensuality with January's Pavia (1970b, 655).

24. Of course, since no one actually likes January, the few scholars who take a positive view of him at the end qualify their approval. Donaldson allows him "occasional sympathy" (1958, 921), and Howard finds him "pathetic" (1976, 263). Bronson agrees that "January himself goes near to becoming the object of pity. And pity is sib to sympathy, not cynicism" (1961, 593). Derek Pearsall finds "a kind of warmth, a kind of humanity, albeit twisted and perverted" (1985, 202) at the end. See also David (1976, 181), Burrow (1957, 201–7), and West (1967–68, 175) who cites much the same evidence that I do. Perhaps the most enthusiastic is Condren who credits January "with the first gesture of genuine love we have seen in the entire tale" and calls the scene in the garden "one of the most hopeful moments in Chaucer" (1985, 246–47).

25. While deploring the sympathy January's behavior generates in "humanist critics," Knight rightly identifies January's treatment of Damian as "admirable" (1986, 113). Traversi unkindly understands January's goodness as limited to "infinite gullibility" (1983, 150).

26. Schleusener also believes that the reader's sympathy lies with May until the scene in the privy (1980, 241–42). Emerson Brown identifies more carefully the ambivalent response of the narrator to January and to May: "Contempt for Januarie almost leads him to sympathize with May. Contempt for May almost leads him to sympathize with Januarie" (1979a, 143). Since Brown equates the voice of the Merchant with that of Chaucer (1979b, 249), the narrator referred to as "him" may be either Chaucer or the Merchant. Knight's reading of the passage is the least sympathetic to either party. He identifies the letter as "a symbol of what people do to each other in a world in which, as Marx outlined, commodities being the fetishized bearers of value, people treat each other like commodities" (1986, 113).

27. Both Schroeder and Schleusener, on the other hand, have commented on the degree to which the garden scene ameliorates the bitterness at the end of the tale. "The interlude acts as a buffer against that ending—its good spirits break the dark tone and delay the action with a bit of witty and relieving gamesmanship" (Schroeder 1970, 178). Schleusener finds that "the Merchant's cynicism is displaced by a more generous narrative manner" (1980, 249) at the end of the poem.

28. Peter Brown has analyzed this scene and the process of January's self-deception with care (1984, 232–33). Williams shows how the "dynamic of revealing and concealing" becomes the theme of the Merchant's Tale "with extensions that include seeing and blindness, knowing and ignorance, fact and fancy. Finally it is a tale the very subject of which is fiction and truth and the ability, or inability, to distinguish between them" (1987, 39). "January cannot attain clear vision, no matter what he sees" (Lumiansky 1955, 171). Huppé argues that "Spiritual blindness is clearly more real than physical blindness" (1964, 161). See especially Howard (1976, 264), Traversi (1983, 137–41), Burlin (1977, 207–10), and Grove (1976).

29. The Clerk tells us that "The commune profit koude she redresse," and she

could pacify all "discord, rancour, [and] hevynesse" (431–32). Indeed, she even adjudicates disputes among the nobility. When Walter is absent, she pacifies the angry nobility and brings them into agreement, "So wise and rype wordes hadde she / And juggementz of so greet equitee" (438–39). Unlike May, Griselda "is an image of the harmony that should be the result of and the basis for any form of order—domestic, political, spiritual" (Johnson 1975, 20). No one has ever accused May of generating harmony. In an interesting article, Wurtele notes the echoes of the Virgin Mary in Chaucer's portrait of Griselda and then concentrates upon the Merchant's "rancorous urge to connect Mary with May" (1981, 103). In arguing that "Walter is not to be taken as a human being, but as God" (1975, 139), Stepsis has also argued for Griselda as Mary (1975, 141).

30. Only recently have critics addressed the topic of clothing and array in the Clerk's Tale. The most important of these are Ramsey (1977) and Gilmartin (1976), but both focus upon the Clerk's Tale and neither sees the way clothing works to unify the two tales in the fragment. Frese quite rightly identifies the significance of clothing in the Clerk's Tale: "the exchange of garb, old for new, is elevated from the simple episode of the folk sources to the ritual status of a religious clothing ceremony" (1973, 137). Alford (1986, 120–21) compares the Clerk's clothing with the Wife of Bath's.

31. In referring to the portraits of the Clerk and Merchant in the General Prologue, Lumiansky noted only that the Merchant lacks the Clerk's "values" (1955, 141). Less specifically, Howard noted their "pointed contrast" (1976, 258) and Alford that they are "mirror opposites"—"A more deliberate set of corresponding differences is hardly imaginable" (1986, 109). Severs contrasts the Clerk with Nicholas (1974, 147–48). It is possible, though improbable and not central to my argument, that Chaucer juxtaposed the portraits of Clerk and Merchant because at the time he composed the General Prologue he had already assigned tales to them and knew they would later form a unit joined by "as neat a link as Chaucer ever wrote" (Howard 1976, 260).

Chapter 2. Fragment VI (Group C)

BIBLIOGRAPHICAL NOTE

Middleton identifies the tales with which the Physician's Tale "shares, if not a genre, a family resemblance" (1973, 10). She includes the Franklin's Tale (see also Beidler [1969] and Lee [1987, 149]), the Prioress' Tale, the Second Nun's Tale, the Man of Law's Tale (see also Rowland [1973b, 166]), and the Clerk's Tale—but not the Pardoner's Tale. Charles Owen (1956) adds the Parson's Tale. Derek Pearsall discusses the Physician's Tale among the other religious tales (1985, 244–93) as an "*exemplum* of ruthless benevolence" (277). Most critics of the Pardoner's Tale, on the other hand, tend to link it with the Wife of Bath because of their mutually self-revelatory confessions. See especially Derek Pearsall (1985, 91–104) and Traversi (1983, 162), both of whom include a discussion of the Canon's Yeoman, an equally self-revelatory confessor, Williams (1987, 73), and Kernan (1974) who sees similarity in the aims and methods of their confessions. James Rhodes argues that "The pattern of the Wife of Bath's performance . . . resurfaces in the form and content of his [i.e., the Pardoner's] tale" (1982, 44), and Lumiansky sees a similarity between the Wife's position with regard to marriage and the Pardoner's with regard to religion (1955, 206). Bolton (1978) connects the Pardoner's Tale with the Nun's Priest's

Tale, Bixler (1986) connects it to the Second Nun's Tale, and Haines (1976) argues that Chaucer had the Parson's Tale in mind when revising the fragment.

The most important discussions of unity in this fragment are those of Cooper, who argues that "The Physician's and the Pardoner's Tales are in some respects antitypes of each other, giving exemplary portrayals of virtue and sin" and "portraying the gifts of Nature and of Fortune" (1984, 154); Traversi, who sees a connection between the two in the Pardoner's desire "to outdo the facile 'honesty'" of the Physician (1983, 168, 176–77, 193); Howard, who says that "no relationship asserts itself" (1976, 334) and yet argues that the moral of the Physician's Tale resembles the moral of the Pardoner's Tale "and if the two come back-to-back for any reason it is because of the contrast they afford" (337); and Amoils, who shows that "the two parts of the fragment complement one another thematically" (1974, 17) in terms of fruitfulness and sterility. John Gardner offers several reasons without much evidence for Chaucer's having juxtaposed these tales: both illustrate "the principle that justice in the world must come from God, since men are mentally or emotionally limited" (1977, 293); both tellers "are proud, self-loving dissemblers" (298); and "one makes bad art though his intentions are good; the other makes good art for mostly base reasons" (303). Lee, concentrating on the Physician's Tale, affirms it must be "read in conjunction with the two that precede and follow it" and that Chaucer "juxtaposed two tales of sudden death in Fragment C" (1987, 141). Dinshaw thinks it is "no coincidence" that the Pardoner follows the Physician both because of the emphasis upon the body and so that the Pardoner can explain the sordid world of the Physician's Tale (1988, 29–30). See also Haines (1976), Gerhard Joseph (1975), and the much neglected article by Trower (1978).

1. Criticism of the Pardoner's Tale has been summarized at various times in this century by Sedgewick (1940), Halverson (1970), and Rowland (1979, 140). The paucity of serious criticism on the Physician's Tale bespeaks its low valuation among scholars who tend to view it as dull, inferior, crude, and routine work. The few scholars who tend to view the Physician's Tale favorably include Bartholomew (1966), Whittock (1968), Ussery (1965 and 1972), Hanson (1972), Middleton (1973), Lee (1987), and Mandel (1977a).

2. Examining the fragment, Severs finds little systematic revision in the two tales but important revision of the link (1954, 530). Ruggiers calls the link "the fulcrum on which the two tales are balanced": if the Physician's Tale involves the gifts of nature and of fortune, the Pardoner adds the gift of grace (1967, 123). Haines argues a similar point (1972 and 1976).

3. Preston described the tellers of tales in Fragment VI as "a doctor of the body followed by a more remarkable doctor of the soul" (1969, 227). In a paper dealing with the Second Nun and the Canon's Yeoman, Rosenberg mentions in passing that the Doctor heals bodies but tells a tale about the preservation of soul, and the Pardoner, who should heal souls, tells a tale about three rioters whose souls are presumed lost (1968, 290). Amoils notes the connection in different terms: their theoretical goal is the defeat of death, each in his own way, but their actual goal is the acquisition of money (1974, 28). See Newhauser's article on "The Love of Money as Deadly Sin and Deadly Disease" (1984). In this context, Knight identifies the Pardoner as "Chaucer's most cash-obsessed pilgrim" (1986, 127) because Chaucer names coins only thirty-one times in all of his poetry, and twelve of the occurrences are in this fragment.

4. Josipovici has argued that the intent of the Pardoner's Tale is "to prove the power of words" (1965, 194), a point that Williams extends to "the Pardoner's

attack on cognition" and especially "language, icon, and Eucharist" (1987, 87–88). It is an important point well-taken and may contribute to the coherence of the fragment, but no one has yet made the same argument for the Physician's Tale where, among things, Virginius's literal conception of the language of law contributes to the martyrdom.

5. Cooper, too, sees Virginia's virtues "very precisely contrasted" with the rioters' vices and concludes that the two tales provide "one of the most striking instances" of Chaucer's juxtaposition of stories that contrast virtue and vice (1984, 155–56). See also Lee (1987, 147) and Williams (1987, 80–81). Orme calls Virginia "a model example of the well-educated aristocratic girl" (1981, 46) and compares her to the Squire. Bryan and Dempster identify Chaucer's sources for these virtues in *De virginibus* of St. Ambrose of Milan (1941, 407), to which must be added Vincent of Beauvais's *De eruditione filiorum nobilium* identified by Young (1941).

6. Amoils claims that Virginia "contrasts in every detail" (1974, 18) with the Pardoner as he is portrayed in the General Prologue, but the evidence adduced is not as convincing as that which balances Virginia against the three rioters.

7. On sermon form in the Pardoner's Tale, see Chapman (1926), Nancy Owen (1967), Luengo (1979), and Merrix (1983). Critics had long noted the irony of the Pardoner's sermon following his own desire to stop for a moment to eat and drink—the only Canterbury pilgrim to be shown doing so on the road (321–22). For an analysis of the scene as an ironic Eucharist, which leads to death in the Pardoner's Tale, see Nichols (1967), Toole (1968), Clarence Miller and Roberta Bosse (1972), and Delasanto (1973).

8. David links the Old Man's age with the Pardoner's youth (1965a, 42), and Steadman (1964) links his age with the youth of the three rioters. The psychological critics of the Pardoner's Tale tend to link the Old Man with the Pardoner. James Rhodes, for example, finds the Old Man "a surrogate for the Pardoner" and "an unconscious projection of the Pardoner's ambivalence and his dissatisfaction with life" (1982, 51–52) and the Pardoner himself as "an anal character" (53). For less extreme views, see Hamilton (1939). The precise identification of the Old Man used to be a matter of great critical concern; it is not relevant to my claims about the unity of the fragment. West summarizes the possibilities (1967–68, 182)—and adds three more!

9. Spearing cites the fourteenth-century attitudes (1965, 43–45). Approaching the scene from a modern perspective, Derek Pearsall sees the three rioters' search for death "a grotesque parody of Christ's struggle to overcome Death" (1985, 101).

10. Most modern scholars have abandoned this position. Traversi is one of the few who sees the Pardoner as "carried away, subdued to the fascination of his own eloquence" (1983, 182 and 193).

11. See Mathewson who argues that the pardoning of Claudius reflects Virginius's "readiness to acknowledge the humanity of any member of the male sex, no matter how vile" (1973, 42) and is an act of male chauvinism rather than Christian charity.

12. Understanding the confrontation between Host and Pardoner depends upon understanding the Pardoner himself, interpreting his tale, and evaluating his motive for mentioning Christ's pardon. Howard emphasizes the various ambiguities (1976, 363–71). Fritz takes the Pardoner's solicitation at the end "in deadly earnest" (1987, 350 and n. 52); Lumiansky agrees (1955, 216); and Donaldson sees that "The insult to the Host's intelligence is the first and last

failure of the Pardoner's intelligence" (1958, 929). See also Grennen (1987, 18–19), Harwood (1988, 414–19), and Chance (1988). On the other hand, Sedgewick finds it an "afterthought" (1940, 450) that is "a piece of impudent horseplay" (452); Brewer finds it "improbable but gloriously funny" (1984, 203); and Nancy Owen argues that the scene "is essentially the action of Chaucer's *fabliaux*" (1967, 247). See also Jungman (1976), Reiss (1964), Traversi (1983, 191), Josipovici (1971, 92–95), and Parsigian (1977).

13. Since "ypocras" and "galiones" were "well-known love-philtres widely purveyed by doctors," Lumiansky notes the "irony in the Host's asking God to save the aphrodisiacs sold by a man who has just completed a tale in praise of virginity" (1955, 199). By the same token, one may note the irony in the Pardoner's asking the pilgrims to buy pardons from a man who has just admitted the fraudulence of his own pardons and the supremacy of Christ's. The similarities in ironic mode and form help bind the two tales in the fragment.

14. He may have done something of this sort already with Claudius. We have no way of knowing Claudius's moral position before he meets Apius. He is defined as a "cherl" who is both "subtil" and "boold" (140–41), neither of which is a virtue in Chaucer's canon. Yet he must be threatened—ironically with beheading (145)—before he agrees to perform Apius's charade; only after agreeing, is he called the "false cherl" (164).

15. Chaucer seems to have consciously revised *cardiacle* to "cardynacle" (Severs 1954, 519).

16. Traversi (1983, 178). Traversi details the Pardoner's frauds (175) and calls him "a 'counterfeit' of the Parson" (189).

17. The passage has often been denigrated as "rather extraordinary" (F. N. Robinson 1957, 727), irrelevant (Robertson 1988, 136–37), and an "inappropriate digression" (Baugh 1963, 485). Preston is alone in reading "This shrewd aside [as] the best thing in the tale" (1969, 228). I have defended it on artistic grounds (1977a, 318–19); Cooper finds "it is less a digression than an introduction" to the Pardoner and his tale (1984, 159); Lee is more specific in arguing that it "does help establish the atmosphere of disciplined guidance that constitutes Virginia's upbringing, in contrast to that of the Pardoner's rioters" (1987, 148). Chaucer's use of digression in the opening of a story "is probably unique in thirteenth- or fourteenth-century vernacular literature" (Smallwood 1985, 437).

18. See Roache (1965) on the ownership of found treasure and Steadman (1965) on the treasure motif.

19. I count fifty-four in all: fifteen in the Physician's Tale, three in the link, eleven in the Pardoner's Prologue, and twenty-five in the Pardoner's Tale itself. Higuchi, counting words to determine "lexical cohesion," concludes that "it is the word *death* that is the integrating factor in the *Pardoner's Tale*" (1987, 167). Cooper finds death, not money, "the central theme of the tale" (1984, 158); for Traversi, the Pardoner himself is "a manifestation of death" which is also the theme of his sermon (1983, 162). See also Steimatsky (1987), Collette (1984) on the oak tree, and Hallissy (1974) on poison; and cf. Stevens and Falvey for images that "focus on organic process" and underscore the "thematic emphasis on moral decay and the quest for death" (1982, 154).

Chapter 3. Fragment VIII (Group G)

BIBLIOGRAPHICAL NOTE

The first part of this century was devoid of serious criticism either of the tales or of the fragment as a whole. Cook (1987) identifies the three basic critical approaches to the Canon's Yeoman's Tale: 1) the dramatic emphasizes the Canon and his Yeoman, 2) the scientific emphasizes alchemy, and 3) various metaphorical approaches emphasize points of comparison with the Second Nun's Tale. Although "Critics have had an easier time unifying various parts of the Canon's Yeoman's Tale with the Second Nun's Tale than in relating *prima pars* to *pars secunda*" (Harwood 1987, 342), Derek Pearsall belittles these connections (1985, 256). Nonetheless, these points of comparison, adequately summarized by Peter Brown (1983, 484–85), form the basis of all claims for unity in Fragment VIII. See also Benson (1987, 942–43, 946–48).

The four seminal articles—those of Grennen, Rosenberg, Olmert, and Peck—which revised critical thinking about the tales and the fragment were published within three years of each other. Grennen (1966) and, perhaps more importantly, Rosenberg (1968), focus primarily upon thematic parallels. Grennen points out that the two tales "show the clearest evidence of belonging together" (1966, 466) and are not "separable poetic facts" (481) because Chaucer consciously created the Second Nun's Tale "to stand against the 'confusion' of alchemy" (481) in the Canon's Yeoman's Tale: the relationship of theme and imagery contrasts alchemy with the sanctity of St. Cecilia (475). Rosenberg shows how the two tales contrast crucible (1968, 280), flames (280–82), work (282), and sight and insight (282–85) that he finds to be the governing theme linked ultimately to the doctrine of Charity and Cupidity (285–87). Olmert emphasizes the religious tone of the fragment and the thematic opposition of the two tales (1967, 71); and he notes but does not develop the "congruent, anagogical frameworks" (86) that bind the tales. Peck lists the parallels between the tales that are "too numerous to be coincidental" (1967a, 36) and argues that "The two poems enhance each other remarkably well, especially in terms of the ideas of 'entente' and translation" (34). See also Glending Olson (1982) who reviews criticism on 222–25; Derek Pearsall (1985, 254, 256, and n. 9); Paul Beekman Taylor, who argues that "The Yeoman's breath in particular, and his Prologue and Tale in general, answers directly to the Second Nun's Tale. Both stress concrete or perceptual recognition of truth, and both do so with sexual imagery" (1979, 384 and see 387); Howard, who agrees that the Canon's Yeoman's Tale "does fit nicely" with the Second Nun's Tale because of the opposition made "between aspects of good and evil" (1976, 297, and n. 94; but cf. 288 where he suggests that the tales do not have much to do with each other), sees that the Canon's Yeoman's Tale "really poses the problem of reason versus revelation" (295), but he does not see how that connects the Canon's Yeoman's Tale to the Second Nun's Tale; and Cooper, who sees the two as "a contrasting pair about the pursuit of spiritual and worldly ends, God and Mammon, and the dominant image of both tales is of sight and blindness" (1984, 188). Cooper's discussion (188–95), which largely follows Rosenberg, celebrates the interpenetration of tales in the fragment. Like the Canon's Yeoman's Tale, "the Second Nun's Tale acquires a richness of meaning from its context that does not emerge from the story taken in isolation" (188).

1. Benson summarizes the evidence for early dating of the Second Nun's

Tale (1987, 942) and late dating of the Canon's Yeoman's Tale (946). Reames has argued that Chaucer "did not even revise" the Second Nun's Tale for inclusion in the *Canterbury Tales* (1980, 55), and Peter Brown that the Canon's Yeoman's Tale is "a free-standing work which is not by Chaucer and so not part of the *Canterbury Tales*" (1983, 485)—a view later more moderately stated (488).

2. F. N. Robinson (1957, 755) credits an unpublished dissertation by Macmanus cited by Griffith (1926) that antedates W. B. Gardner's article (1947) which is most often cited by critics.

3. The phrase, of course, is Shakespeare's, not Chaucer's: *Othello* III, iii, 360.

4. Perhaps the reference is to the Canon himself. See Coffman (1944). Most critics accept the Yeoman's reason for their haste (582–92) though Harrington attributes the haste of the Canon and his Yeoman to their desire "to elude pursuers" (1968, 88) and Olmert to "the urgency which Satan must feel in his desire to overtake the pilgrims and to lure them to sin once more, before the end of their journey" (1967, 94). See also Herz (1961, 232).

5. If, as Duncan has argued, the Canon and his Yeoman "have overtaken the Canterbury pilgrims with the rather obvious intent of wrangling money from them" (1968, 638), then he fails in that endeavor as well.

6. The Yeoman's references to authority—to Arnold of the New Town, Hermes Trismegistus, the *Secreta Secretorum* attributed to Aristotle, and the story of Plato in Senior—are identified by Benson (1987, 951). Duncan (1968) discusses other alchemical authorities implicit in the Canon's Yeoman's Tale. Grennen suggests a different kind of indebtedness to authority when he argues that the Canon's Yeoman's Tale "duplicates the very structure of an alchemical treatise, a first part filled with an enormous melange of directions and ingredients, and a second part which dissolves into mystic mummery and allegory when it purports to describe the actual transmutation" (1965, 547).

7. Peck emphasizes the thematic contributions of the explication and shows how the tale itself dramatizes the meaning of Cecile's name (1967a, 23–24). Derek Pearsall reminds us that the etymology is both "edifying and 'wrong'" (1985, 252). Whether Chaucer knew it was wrong or not, he presents it as true and his audience was supposed to accept it as true. My point is that regardless of the truth or falsity of the etymology and the truth or falsity of the alchemical explanation, Chaucer has carefully balanced the interpretation with the explanation in the two tales of Fragment VIII.

8. Many critics base their understanding of the Yeoman's character upon his chaotic outpouring. For this psychological bias of earlier critics, see Coghill (1949, 175), Chute (1946, 306), and Malone (1951, 222). Speirs believes the "externalized confusion projects an original moral confusion" (1951, 198). Both Duncan (1968, 638) and John Gardner (1967, 3) remark upon the helter-skelter jumble of terms, though Duncan finds that the list is "more nearly paralleled in Geber's *Sum* than in any other treatise" (1968, 642). Brewer attributes the jumble to "the confusion of mind and matter involved in alchemy" (1984, 237). Ryan sees Chaucer using "the device of the *confessio*" (1974, 299) to reveal the character of the Canon's Yeoman; McCracken (1971), Baldwin (1962, 243), and Speirs (1951, 195) agree. Only Harrington argues that the Yeoman controls this outpouring (1968, 90–92 and n. 10) and uses "alchemical jargon as a means of impressing others" (1968, 91).

9. Reilly argues that Tiburce "received the sacrament of Confirmation" (1937, 39) after being baptized. Peck identifies the old man as an agent of the Holy Spirit and definitely not St. Paul (1967a, 27 n. 7).

10. Only Reidy attempts to generate "some sympathy" (1965, 35) for the

Canon whom he finds "a pathetic if not a tragic figure, broken through following a chimerical vision" (1965, 36). Harrington, who finds "no truly sympathetic characters" (1965, 162) in the tale, represents the majority opinion.

11. And follows her herself. Jones argues that the Second Nun's Tale is "an almost perfect example of the *de sanctis* type of sermon" (1937b, 283). To that extent, then, the Second Nun emulates St. Cecile. Eggebroten (1984) is not successful in reading the Second Nun's Tale as comic hagiography.

12. Howard argues that the Second Nun's Tale closes the theme of love and marriage in the *Canterbury Tales* and is "the last of the 'ideal' narratives" (1976, 290).

13. To this extent Cecile is "the true alchemist's stone, for she is the material of the earth transmuted into a saint and thus a citizen of the heavenly city" (Allen and Moritz 1981, 144). Indeed, what unifies the fragment is that the Second Nun's Tale and the Canon's Yeoman's Tale "are a pair . . . two stories of heavenly and earthly transformation" (ibid.). Peck discusses the theme of conversion in both tales in terms of "translation": in the Second Nun's Tale, translation implies a "change from death to life" and in the Canon's Yeoman's Tale translation was "used by alchemists as a synonym for *transmute* and *transform*" (1967a, 22). John Gardner points to the ambiguity of gold in the Canon's Yeoman's Tale—it may be associated with heaven or with "excessive love for this world" (1967, 7)—and recognizes that both tales "are ingeniously constructed on principles of alchemy, one on 'true' alchemy, the other on 'false'" (1967, 316). The theme of multiplying has been dealt with best by Grennen (twice) who sees it as the "keynote" of the Canon's Yeoman's Tale, "to be understood against the background of unity and integrity which the legend of St. Cecilia displays" (1966, 472–73; and see 1962, 226–28 *et passim*) and by Olmert who sees it both as a method of "increasing the number of damned souls" and an expression of God's grace (1967, 92). Duncan notes the term appearing in one form or another eight times in the Canon's Yeoman's Tale (1968, 635).

14. Peck connects Mary with the translator of the Second Nun's Tale (i.e., Chaucer) in an elegant pun on clothiers (1967a, 23). John Gardner discusses the clothes of the Canon and his Yeoman (1967, 11). I have found no other discussion of clothes as one of the ties that bind the Second Nun's Tale to the Canon's Yeoman's Tale. Chaucer uses clothes as a theme in Fragment IV (the Clerk's Tale and the Merchant's Tale) in a way completely different from the way he uses clothes here.

15. On the state of the Yeoman's spirit, see Herz (1961) and Ryan (1974).

16. Hamilton has shown that any medieval reader would have recognized the Canon immediately as "a Black Canon, a Canon Regular of St. Augustine" (1941, 103) and that Chaucer's pretended mystification is a dramatic device (108).

17. Hatton has developed a reading of the Miller's Tale in terms of smell and taste: "Heavenly fame is often associated in scripture with good odor and sweet taste" while "vainglory, on the other hand, gives off no odor or taste of sanctity" (1971, 73).

18. Only Paul Beekman Taylor has addressed the unity of Fragment VIII in terms of smell. He shows that "Chaucer's most explicit parody of Divine creation is carried by his images of breath, wind, and odour" (1979, 381). Therefore, "The Yeoman's breath in particular, and his Prologue and Tale in general, answers directly the Second Nun's Prologue and Tale" (384): "sight and odour are the cognitive clues to the success of Cecilia and to the failure of the Canon

and his Yeoman" (385). Peck (1967a, 35) and Preston (1969, 281) note the contrast in smell between the two tales. See also Pratt (1978).

19. Derek Pearsall is alone in suspecting that "there is less altruism in his concern for others than a vindictive desire to revenge himself vicariously on the person and the profession that he now feels have exploited him" (1985, 110). Most readers see the Yeoman's attempt to warn others through his own example an expression of his desire to atone. See, for example, Ryan (1974, 304–5).

20. Olmert observes that "the canon promises to teach the priest out of friendship; later he promises to teach his secret because of his love for the priest (1153), just as Christ teaches because of love for mankind" (1967, 77), but since Olmert's concern lies elsewhere, he does not note this particular connection with the Second Nun's Tale.

21. Traversi argues that "the urge to 'privacy' and concealment is a sign of a fundamental defect, a failure in humanizing sociability" (1983, 198). By revealing secrets, on the other hand, the Yeoman "achieves a social resolution. Within the Canterbury fellowship, or perhaps at the Martyr's shrine, he finds community" (Herz 1961, 236). With regard to the Second Nun's Tale, Reames has shown how Chaucer revised his source and "turned the saint into an isolated figure, rather than a member of a continuing community" (1980, 57). But cf. Beichner who sees only "slight changes in translating" (1974, 199).

22. Hilberry has argued that the "primary attraction [of the Canon's Yeoman's Tale] lies in the language that surrounds the practice" of alchemy (1987, 435).

Chapter 4. Fragment V (Group F)

BIBLIOGRAPHICAL NOTE

Both the Knight's Tale, perhaps because the Squire is the Knight's son, and the Merchant's Tale, perhaps because it precedes the Squire's Tale in Ellesmere, have most often been linked to the tales in Fragment V. White, following Holman (1951, 243) and Ruggiers (1965, 226–37), finds that the values of the Merchant's Tale "furnish a striking and dramatic foil" to those of the Franklin even though these values are "dramatized and explored throughout the *Canterbury Tales*" (1974, 456); or the Franklin's Tale allows the drama between January and Damian to be "played out in a less ignoble context than that provided by the Merchant" (Knight 1986, 118). The Merchant's Tale also serves as the "impetus" (Peterson 1970, 65) and "contrast" (Brewer 1984, 225) to the Squire's Tale which "banish[es] the atmosphere" (Lumiansky 1955, 176) the Merchant created and corrects the Merchant's distressing negation of *gentillesse* (Schaefer 1967; Peterson 1970, 65–66). The Franklin Tale shares with the Knight's Tale both the chivalric ideal (David 1965b, 20–24) and the "conventions of medieval romance as vehicles of a debate on moral and philosophical issues" (Mehl 1986, 171) while the Squire's values either contrast with or are similar to those of his father (Hatton 1974, 456; Derek Pearsall 1985, 139). Howard sees "posturing of the 'high style'," "various incongruities and absurdities," and a "satiric or humorous element" (1976, 265) which the Squire's Tale shares with the Knight's Tale. The Squire's Tale has also been compared to those of the Wife of Bath and Merchant (Neville 1951, 168) and Nun's Priest (Lawton 1985, chapter 5) while the Franklin's Tale has been compared to those of the Wife of Bath (David 1976, 190; Lindsay Mann 1966, 25–27), Clerk (Fyler 1987;

Morgan 1986), Physician (Beidler 1969; Morgan 1986), Prioress and Nun's Priest (Benjamin 1959, 119), Chaucer's Tale of Melibee (Silvia 1967), as well as Chaucer's Tale of Sir Thopas, the Miller's Tale, and the Pardoner's Tale (Wood 1966, 702 and 707).

Scholars have nonetheless found a variety of reasons for Chaucer's joining the Squire's Tale to the Franklin's Tale. Although Cooper sees the connections between the Franklin's Tale and those of the Knight, Wife of Bath, and Merchant, she shows the Franklin's Tale "contrasted generically and poetically" (1984, 150) with the Squire's Tale: "Fragment V is the only place in the work where two romances are juxtaposed; and they are linked by compliment" (148). More importantly, she shows how the Franklin's Tale completes the Squire's Tale: "Given the Franklin's Tale, the Squire's does not need to be finished. The narrative may be incomplete, but its themes are taken over and concluded with a profundity that the Squire's Tale itself could never have achieved" (154). Berger sees the two tales as both dramatically and dialectically connected (1966a, 88). Haller, who tends to compare the Squire with the Knight as storyteller and rhetorician, finds that the Franklin's Tale makes "the nature of the satire in [the Squire's Tale] more clear" (1965, 293–94). Burlin shows how the Franklin imitates the Squire's use of rhetoric (1967, 60); Robert Miller (1978) shows how the Franklin refines the Squire's rhetoric along Augustinian lines that lead from eloquence to wisdom. Neville sees "Nobility of heart as the source of a compassion almost quixotic" (1951, 174) coordinating the two tales of Fragment V in which the theme of freedom and the dignity of both lovers grows logically out of the Squire's Tale and anticipates the Franklin's equality between marriage partners (178). See also Hinckley (1917, 223), Huppé (1964, 163–65), Kahrl (1973, 206), Middleton (1984, 129–33), Derek Pearsall (1985, 139), and Howard (1976, 266) whose claims about the "bourgeois" Chaucer revealed in the Squire's Tale (267) bear comparison with those of David about the Franklin (1976, chapter 12, titled "The Bourgeois Sentimentalist").

1. On the ambiguity of Christianity in Breton lais and the effect of the pagan setting on our understanding of character, see the two articles by Hume (1972a and 1972b). Dimarco attributes the pagan setting of the Squire's Tale to the influence of Roger Bacon (1981, 404); Burlin attributes the pagan atmosphere of the Franklin's Tale to "ancient deities and heathenish arts of magic" (1967, 59). Gerhard Joseph is perhaps most persuasive in arguing for "an overtly Christian point of view" (1966, 29) in this otherwise thoroughly pagan tale.

2. In the Squire's Tale 48–57, 263–67, 671–72, and in the Franklin's Tale 1245–55. A basic text is Wood (1970). Brewer devotes a few pages to Astronomy (1984, 95–97) and to Astrology (1984, 97–99) and provides a brief review of their relation to fourteenth-century thought. Smyser demonstrates Chaucer's familiarity with the zodiac and argues that Chaucer "believed firmly in the possibility of astrological prediction" (1970, 361). North (1969) discusses Chaucer's command of astronomical lore and attempts to date various tales on the basis of astronomical references within the tales. See also Peavler (1971), who argues that Chaucer did not make much astrological use of the zodiac, and Evers, who shows that Chaucer uses astrology to "construct a dramatic allegory of man's pilgrimage" (1972, chapter 2).

3. Robert Miller's point, that seal and bond "in all probability refer to the magician's means of gaining the aid of demonic spirits" (1986, 236), is also possible.

4. See especially Laura Hibbard Loomis (1958) and Sherwood (1947).

Braswell views Chaucer as a scientific writer who "understood machinery in more than a cursory way" (1985, 101), but she discusses only the Franklin's Tale. See her footnote 1 for further bibliography.

5. Although Severs finds no "indication that Aurelius is aware of the dishonesty" (1966, 394) in the magic, Benjamin emphasizes the "unlawful means" of using magic to achieve his objective and concludes that Aurelius is guilty of the "same kind of moral flaw as Dorigen" (1959, 121).

6. On Canacee's ring, see Dimarco (1981); on the horse, see Braddy (1938) and Carmel Jordan (1987). Stillwell argues that Chaucer is laughing at chivalric courtesy in the strange knight's long speech on the magic gifts (1948, 183). Ian Robinson mentions that the Franklin debunks the Squire's "connection of love with wonders and marvels by introducing the illusions of the Magician" (1972, 184), but does not develop the point. See also Burger (1986, 171–72), Ruggiers (1965, 226–37), Fyler (1987, 3–5), Tatlock (1913), and, less convincingly, Bachman (1977).

7. McCall distinguishes the various responses to the gifts as romantic and fanciful on the one hand and scientific and realistic on the other (1966b, 104). Peterson (1970, 69) and Kahrl (1973, 203) comment on the Squire's "class snobbery"—his "markedly supercilious tone" and his "supercilious disdain for the honest curiosity of Cambyuskan's people."

8. Huppé sees this as "surely the most secure disguise of all, for no one would think that a husband and wife are in love!" (1964, 170). On the increasing tendency in Chaucer's day to reconcile love and marriage in a contract, see Mathew (1947). Although many have written on the topic of appearance and reality in this fragment, perhaps the most useful discussions are to be found in Brewer (1984, 231–32); Peck, who sees all the characters confused by appearance (1967b, 266); and Kearney (1969).

9. Cooper is alone in recognizing that trouthe is central to both tales in Fragment V: "Breaking of 'trouthe' destroys the apparent bliss of the falcon's love and prevents her mate from returning to her; keeping of 'trouthe' in the Franklin's Tale ensures" a happy ending (1984, 153). See also Golding (1970) and Berger (1966a). Brewer is particularly instructive on Chaucer's use of "Honour" (1973). Robert Miller points out that in the Franklin's Tale, "none of the oaths involved, in common or ecclesiastical law, are valid" (1978, 257). Both Morgan (1986, 295) and Burger (1986, 169) argue that Dorigen's promise to Aurelius expresses her love and devotion to Arveragus.

10. On the deficiencies of the Squire as storyteller, see Haller (1965), Derek Pearsall (1964 and 1985, 141–42), Mehl (1986, 163–65), Brewer (1984, 226), Peterson (1970, 66), Robert Miller (1978 and 1986) and Stillwell (1948). McCall takes the most positive modern view of the Squire's ineptitude (1966b, 103, 109). See also Orme (1981, 45, 56–57) and Fyler (1988, 10–21). Root represents the earlier, less critical view of the Squire's Tale (1922, 266–70). For the Franklin's skill or lack of it as a narrator, see Burlin (1967, 60, 67), Gaylord (1964, 332–34), Berger (1966a, 98–99; 1966b, 138), Fyler (1987), Knight (1970, 25), Derek Pearsall (1985, 148), and Harrison (1935). Kahrl compares the Franklin's and the Squire's pride in the colors of rhetoric they demonstrate (1973, 204–6).

11. Although Dunleavy discusses the derivation from Boethius of the wound and comforter motif in Chaucer (1967, 21ff.), he does not apply it to the Squire's Tale.

12. Peterson sees in the falcon "a parody of the pelican, that self-wounding bird of medieval iconography who symbolized Christ" (1970, 71). Southmayd (1981) argues that avian society parallels human society and that Chaucer's

birds represent the more bestial aspects of human nature.

13. Whether the Franklin actually interrupts the Squire or not has been argued by many scholars. See, for example, Charles Duncan (1970) and Clark (1972). The most recent scholar to address the topic is Seaman who adequately summarizes previous criticism (1986, 13 n. 1) and concludes that since the "interruptions to tales in progress in the *Canterbury Tales* contain common elements that are absent here" (14), the Franklin's address to the Squire is either "an end comment written before the Squire's Tale, in anticipation of a finished tale, or it is a comment that is meant to come after an interruption by someone else" (18).

14. Lindsay Mann provides a detailed and extended definition of *gentillesse* and concludes that "The Franklin's Tale embodies and illustrates the transformation and fusion of ideals from 'courtly' or secular to moral and religious" (1966, 15). Osgerby argues that if Chaucer had completed the Squire's Tale, the main theme would have been *gentillesse* (1959, 102). For those who take a positive view of *gentillesse* in Fragment V as a whole, see Gaylord (1964, especially 334–50), Gerhard Joseph (1966), and Silvia (1967) who sees the entire Marriage Group concerned with *gentillesse*. For less positive views of what Peterson calls "the Squire's ersatz gentillesse" (1970, 73), see Wood, who finds *gentillesse* in the Franklin's Tale "somewhat tawdry" (1966, 701) and concludes that "No one can be said to be particularly 'gentil' " (702); Lawton, who sees *gentillesse* misinterpreted (1985, 114), Haller, who sees it undercut (1965, 292); and Gray (1987).

15. Lumiansky argues that Dorigen is most *fre* (1955, 193); Neville argues for Aurelius (1951, 179); Huppé for the Clerk (1964, 174); White (1974, 461), Hatton (1974, 181), and Lindsay Mann (1966, 22) argue for Arveragus whom Peck argues strongly against (1967b, 260–61). But, as Kathryn Jacobs has argued, "Who the reader selects matters little, so long as he considers the question and, by considering, accepts the ideal on which the question rests" (1985, 134).

16. Chaucer uses chiasmus in a slightly different way to organize Fragment VII. Although Harrison claims to find "at least seventy rhetorical forms that correspond exactly to the Latin colors" (1935, 56, itemized on 57), Knight argues more convincingly that "Chaucer's knowledge of traditional rhetoric is much slighter than has been thought" (1970, 15). See also Manly (1926) and Murphy (1964).

17. Berger notes but does not develop the movement from pagan origins to Christian ethos in Fragment V (1966b, 149). Both Peck (1967b, 269) and Gerhard Joseph (1966, 29–31) provide sophisticated Christian readings of the poem that derive from the "Nowel" reference.

18. Not counting such temporally explicit words as "anon," "er that," and the like, Fragment V contains sixty-five specific temporal references. For a list of the temporal references in Fragment V, see the Appendix, pp. 191–92. McCall is the only scholar who has commented on the phenomenon: "almost every reference to time is in some serious way out of keeping with its context" (1966b, 108). Fragment VII, which contains six tales, also contains many temporal references, but they are concentrated in the first and sixth tales of the fragment. See chapter 7, pp. 161–62.

19. See Benson's note to these lines (1987, 891 [for lines 48–51] and 895). North dates it more precisely as 13 May or 14 June, 1390 [?] (1969, 260 and 262).

20. The Phebus passage in the Squire's Tale has been analyzed by Haller (1965, 287–88) as an example of the Squire's "rhetorical ability at the expense

of direct and skilful narration"; that in the Franklin's Tale by Derek Pearsall (1985, 157–58) who emphasizes the Christian undertones as does David who adds that this is "the only seasonal passage in Chaucer's poetry that celebrates winter rather than spring" (1976, 191).

21. While from the feminist/humanist perspective of the mid-twentieth century, we may applaud the Franklin's apparent liberality (an attitude supported by the Tale of Melibee), the evidence elsewhere in Chaucer's work (the Merchant's Tale, Nun's Priest's Tale, *Troilus and Criseyde*, for example) suggests that Chaucer was sufficiently a man of his age to believe that only the unwary "Do alwey so as wommen wol thee rede" (IV, 1361). Nonetheless, Brewer is surely correct in pointing out that Chaucer "is more notably orientated towards feminine interests (and indeed superiority) than any other author until Richardson" (1973, 11).

Chapter 5. Fragment III (Group D)

BIBLIOGRAPHICAL NOTE

The great influence of Kittredge's Marriage Group essay (1911–12) separated the Wife of Bath's Tale from those of the Friar and the Summoner and connected it with the tales of the Clerk, Merchant, and Franklin. The quarrel between the Friar and the Summoner together with the Squire's outlandish romance were thus seen as interruptions in the Marriage Group and discussed separately (by Derek Pearsall 1985 and Brewer 1984) or not at all (by David 1976 and Traversi 1983, for example). Brewer thinks the "Friar picks up the Wife of Bath's Tale only indirectly" (1984, 210); Szittya (1975) sees precisely defined parodic parallels of the Wife of Bath's Tale in the Friar's Tale but omits the Summoner's Tale from his discussion. Derek Pearsall sees the Friar's Tale and the Summoner's Tale as "satirical anecdotes" (1985, 217) more closely connected with the Shipman's Tale and the Reeve's Tale than with the Wife of Bath's Tale. Havely groups the Friar's and Summoner's tales with the Pardoner's Tale because the tellers are "all parasites upon the medieval church" (1976, 1). Gallacher connects the two as narrators: the Friar emphasizes the mind and the Summoner emphasizes the body (1986, 203). Baird (1969) suggests an obscene connection between the Friar's Tale and the Summoner's Prologue. For other connections between the Friar's Tale and the Summoner's Tale, see Richardson (1961) and the two essays by Baker (1962a and 1962b). For the connections between the Wife of Bath's Tale and the Clerk's Tale, see the Bibliographical Note to chapter 1, p. 196.

Nonetheless, several arguments have been put forward to justify the conjunction of the three tales in Fragment III. One emphasizes "the quality of dramatic life consistently sought by Chaucer in Fragment III" (Derek Pearsall 1985, 218); so also Lumiansky ("a context of dramatic antagonism, but also full-scale character revelation" [1955, 129]) and Charles Owen (the "most thoroughly dramatic" fragment in which each tale "expresses the personality of the teller" [1977, 168]). This view must be tempered by Robertson's sensible judgment that Alice of Bath "is not a 'character' in the modern sense at all, but an elaborate iconographic figure designed to show the manifold implications of an attitude" (1962, 330). Another argument for unity finds the Wife of Bath a "special audience toward which [the Friar and the Summoner] direct their attacks on each other" (Huppé 1964, 209), or the tales are joined "because the Wife of

Bath's is clearly, on the literal level, about magic" (Allen and Moritz 1981, 154). These are not very convincing.

More sophisticated and more convincing is the argument of Wasserman who finds in the fragment "a thematic unity which arises from a philosophical conflict . . .: the relationship between the tangible and the intangible, the concrete and the abstract" (1982, 65). In this view, "the tales told by the Friar and the Summoner may be seen as poetic amplifications of the two choices offered to the knight in the Wife's tale": the Friar adopts "the pose of a philosophical Realist" and the Summoner "adopts the pose of a Nominalist" (77). Similarly, East argues that "The D-Group . . . is a debate about debates, a disputation about academic disputations. In particular it is a debate about the two criteria used in such disputations: *experience* and *auctoritee*" (1977, 79). See also Holland (1967, 286). Cooper compares the structure of Fragment III with that of Fragment I: "Both groups start with a romance, follow it with a tale of contrasting genre that parodies the plot and ideal of the romance, and conclude with a tale that has generic, dramatic, and thematic relations with the second story" (1984, 125). Like the stories in Fragment I, the tales of Fragment III "show a steady debasement on all fronts: the courtly relationship of *trouthe* and integrity has descended through making a pact with the devil to the sordid physicality of the fart" (133). Richardson (1975) offers an equally general description of the structural parallels. See note 4 below. Nothing here contradicts the claims I shall make about the thematic and structural coherence of the fragment.

1. Richardson (1961) links the Friar's Tale with the Summoner's Tale in terms of the hunting imagery, but she does not extend the imagery to the Wife of Bath's Tale where it is also applicable (though see 1961, 20 n. 12)

2. Neuss argues that "book-making and love-making are often related" (1981, 388) in Chaucer for whom "the reading or writing of books heralds or symbolizes the act of love" (396). This point of view is clear in the Wife of Bath's Prologue though less convincing in the other tales of Fragment III. Because the friars were such "assiduous bibliophiles" and many people in the fourteenth century maintained that they *should* sell their books, the reference to books in the Summoner's Tale may allude to "a body of general antifraternal literature" (Fleming 1966, 697–98). On Chaucer and the book, see also Stearns (1942) and Josipovici (1971).

3. See the important article by Newhauser (1986) on the connection between illness and the love of money in the Middle Ages. Gallacher (1986) has also addressed the topic in reference to the Summoner's Tale.

4. Richardson has seen the identical structural patterns in the Friar's Tale and the Summoner's Tale in terms different from those I am about to show. "Structurally . . . both narratives move from (1) an initial descriptive passage which establishes the culpable nature of the protagonist, to (2) the encounter with his eventual punisher, to (3) a long, one-sided dialogue, to (4) one event, followed by (5) a second event which culminates directly and ironically from what the protagonist himself says" (1975, 230). However, she does not extend this structural analysis to include the Wife of Bath's Prologue and Tale and so does not argue for the structural coherence of the fragment. See Cooper's description of the structural similarities that Fragment III shares with Fragment I discussed in the Bibliographical Note above.

5. Self-interruption is not unique to this fragment. Like the Wife of Bath, both the Physician and the Pardoner interrupt their own tales: the Physician to

insert an apparent digression on governesses, the Pardoner to insert an apparently digressive sermon. Neither is a digression, of course, since both interruptions introduce themes important to the tales as I have argued above in chapter 2. See Daye (1968) for a discussion of this kind of narrative intrusion in the Squire's, Manciple's, Merchant's, and Nun's Priest's Tales. Dempster (1942) has shown that the numerous references to "we" and "our" in the crone's curtain speech cannot be taken to include the Wife of Bath; they mean "people" in general.

6. Orme is most eloquent in arguing that the "education of the hero is the main theme" (1981, 56) of the Wife of Bath's Tale. Indeed he traces the theme of education through the entire Marriage Group. Both Zimbardo and Brewer are more specific in identifying precisely what is learned, Zimbardo showing how the knight is led to a true understanding both of love and of the knightly code he professes (1966, 116–17), and Brewer less boldly insisting on the acceptance of female sovereignty (1984, 209). The two articles by Moore (1944 and 1949) show that Chaucer was probably the first to cast Alice of Bath in the role of the antifeminist ecclesiastic of the male persuasion preaching the "qui capit uxorem" convention. Knapp (1986) defines the generic ambiguities of the Wife of Bath's Prologue. Lenaghan, in coming to terms with the genre of the Friar's Tale, finds that "exemplum is the more useful classification" (1973, 284). Aspects of preaching in the Summoner's Tale are too obvious to mention since the Summoner delivers a full-fledged sermon on anger to a captive audience, the bedridden Thomas.

7. Hennedy relates "the old lady's cursing of the summoner to the summoner's earlier cursing of himself" (1971, 213 and see n. 2) which was motivated by his own greed. See also the article by Edward Jacobs and Robert Jungman (1985).

8. Sheila Delany draws an existential conclusion from Alice of Bath's wandering: "she reveals that her way of being is predicated in mobility—social mobility whether vertical (as ambition) or horizontal (as gregariousness and lust). She is always in motion, ready for change; stability is not her mode" (1987, 28). Fleming, writing about the antifraternalism of the Summoner's Tale, notes that the cartwheel used for dividing the fart is associated with the friar's wandering (1966, 699–700).

9. Koban finds greater significance in the knight's search which he calls "the quest for self-determination and individual purpose" (1971, 235) instead of a quest to discover what women most desire.

10. Chaucer has established the "commercial motives" (Havely 1979, 337) of the pilgrim Friar in the General Prologue. The Summoner's emphasis upon this aspect of the Friar's character in his tale reflects the interpenetration of frame and tale in Fragment III. In Knight's Marxist reading, the Friar's economic struggle with the Summoner provides "a telling socioeconomic projection of the acquisitive ideas of both Summoner and Friar" (1986, 104–5).

11. She blesses her fourth husband in a perfunctory manner at l. 501.

12. Green (1986) distinguishes between "maistrie" and "soveraynetee" to determine what the terms meant to Chaucer and his audience.

13. For the Wife of Bath's Tale as a fantasy of fulfillment, see Holland (1967, an argument which he reiterates in 1968), Steinberg (1964), Levy (1970), Traversi (1983, 119), and Palomo (1975, 312).

14. Craik quite rightly observes that "Sworn brotherhood is always regarded ironically by Chaucer, who knows well how men's plans are upset by inscruta-

ble destiny or by natural selfishness" (1964, 53). Birney, too, sees brotherhood in the Summoner's Tale as the friar's "strategem to make it easier to pry money out of this household" (1960, 215). Cooper argues that the Friar and the Summoner "use the motif of brotherhood in a way that turns its conventional associations inside out" (1984, 131). I have not been able to see Friman (1976) who seems to offer the most explicit examination of the topic.

15. The whole problem of the Wife of Bath and women's power has most recently been examined by Amsler (1987). Jewell Rhodes (1979) presents a feminist argument for the Wife as androgyne. Sturges (1983) connects the Wife of Bath with the Prioress and the Second Nun as female narrators.

16. Palomo (1975), Rowland (1973a), and most recently Wurtele (1988) have argued that Alice of Bath conspired with Jankyn to murder Alice's fourth husband. By betraying her secrets to this Alisoun who cannot keep the secret, the Wife of Bath inadvertently exposes Jankyn's deed which leads to his execution (Palomo 1975, 313) or flight (Wurtele 1988). This view, which vitiates the solidarity of the sisterhood, has not been widely followed and has been vigorously dismissed by Crane (1988).

17. This "soutiltee" "may merely mean that her mother had instructed her in such clever tactics of 'love-talk' rather than teaching her erotic magic or chemistry, yet the latter may well be hinted" (Puhvel 1986, 310).

18. On the queen's usurpation of authority, see Williams (1987, 70–71), and see Sheila Delany who identifies this act as "a gesture of class solidarity over sex solidarity" (1987, 34). For the medieval medical view that pregnancy followed from orgasm "which in turn implied a consenting will and therefore obviated rape," see Sheila Delany (35 n. 12) and especially her reference to Watts (1947). For the life and status of women around the year 1380, see Sheehan (1985). Palomo (1975, 312) discusses Alice herself as a raped woman.

Chapter 6. Fragment I (Group A)

BIBLIOGRAPHICAL NOTE

Although Kaske (1957) notes the possible relations between the Knight's Tale and the Merchant's Tale, and Middleton (1984) connects the Knight's Tale to the Squire's and Franklin's, and both Van (1971) and Stroud (1981) emphasize the poem's connections to *Troilus and Criseyde,* most discussions of unity in Fragment I concentrate on the relation between the Knight's Tale and the Miller's Tale. Norton-Smith is not convincing in arguing that the Miller's Tale is not "an intentional burlesque or parody" of the Knight's Tale (1974, 137). On the principles of contrast and contrariety that bind the Knight's Tale and the Miller's Tale, see Mehl (1986, 158–76 *passim*) and McAlindon (1986). On the principles of parallelism that bind them and all of Fragment I, see Stokoe who reads the first fragment as an "essay about quiting" (1952, 120) and Charles Owen who follows Stokoe and sees "a realistic triptych of life in the town, life in the country, and life in the city" (1954, 55).

Unseduced by the brilliance of Chaucer's juxtaposing the Miller's Tale and the Knight's Tale, some critics have argued for the integrity of the whole fragment. Howard sees "Tales of Civil Conduct" (1976, 227–47) and notes their "degenerative movement" (245); Jensen assumes the same movement and argues that "in Fragment A the focus is on males in competition" (1990, 321);

Notes

Wetherbee traces "a breakdown of social order" (8, 40–62); Knight finds unity in "the observation of social conflict" (1986, 70); Blodgett (1976) emphasizes "pryvetee"; and John Gardner finds "a cluster of poems which explore the nature of justice. . . . The whole first fragment is allegorically ordered by the old Platonic (and Aristotelian) scheme of the tripartite soul—rational, irascible, concupiscent" (1977, 228–29). Along more literary lines, Cunningham finds that "the underlying principle of order of the A Fragment as a whole" derives from dream vision (1952, 179); Fisher argues that the high, middle, and low styles of the first three tales "could almost have been designed to illustrate the distinctions set forth by John of Garland" (1973, 121); and Gerhard Joseph reads the fragment "as a paradigm of the 'game'-'ernest' opposition and the 'argument of herbergage' implicit in the *Canterbury Tales* as a whole" (1970, 84). Turner notes the mythic parallelism in the fragment, expressed in "an elaborate set of binary and triadic relations between the central characters" (1974, 292) in the first two tales (this may also be McCann's argument, 1973, which, unavailable even from the Library of Congress, I have not seen). Van Boheemen's argument for mythic structure (1979) pits Palamon and Arcite against Theseus rather than against each other. None of these have won wide following, though elements from Howard (1976), Fisher (1973), and Gerhard Joseph (1970) will appear in the argument I present below.

I have been most impressed by the arguments for unity presented by Cooper (1984, 109–20) and by Allen and Moritz (1981). The latter argue that "the tales of the first fragment are unified. They present a complex and witty interweaving of characters and ideas; they all treat the same basic love triangle; and they show a common concern for order and justice, even though each tale's action is more vulgar and disorderly than the one before" (1981, 14). Cooper sees the tales linked primarily by "equivalence" with some "inversions" (1984, 117) and recognizes the "decline in idealism from the heights of the Knight's Tale" (119). She also anticipates tangentially two of my points (about animal imagery and multiplicity of lovers).

1. The Prologue to *The Legend of Good Women*, generally dated earlier than the *Canterbury Tales*, mentions Palamon and Arcite in the F text (*LGW* 420–22). David accurately appreciates the complexity of Chaucer's art here: "Assigning the *Palamon and Arcite* to the Knight and following it with the Miller's Tale is a more creative act than any revision could have been" (1976, 78) because "The arrival of the Miller's Tale forces us to readjust the relations, proportions, and values of the Knight's Tale to the whole; the introduction of the Reeve's Tale again brings about a new order" (79–80).

2. To be sure, Chaucer's irony qualifies the religious impetus to pilgrimage by emphasizing the allure of spring. On the four constitutive elements of life, see Arthur Hoffman (1954) and Williams (1987, 27).

3. A similar relationship exists in the Second Nun's Tale, the Shipman's Tale, and less plausibly, in the Summoner's Tale, but among these tales it appears in only one tale of a multitale fragment; in none of the fragments in which these tales appear does Chaucer use or develop this particular relationship to the extent he does in Fragment I. As I indicated in the Bibliographical Note, this triadic relationship has been the subject of articles by Turner (1974) and probably McCann (1973). If, as some believe, Chaucer originally intended the Man of Law's Tale to begin the *Canterbury Tales*, it too might fit the triadic pattern (with some pushing and shoving) and include members of the older generation as well.

4. In addition to Howard (1976), John Gardner (1977, 253), and Cooper (1984), mentioned in the Bibliographical Note, scholars have traced the principle of deterioration in various ways. See especially Penninger (1964, 399–400) and her extension of the principle beyond this fragment (403). Allen and Moritz are most precise in applying the principle to the women in the fragment (1981, 132); they also apply it to a group of tales they title the moral group (178–79). O'Keefe (1973) and Hinton (1961) note the process in terms of Malyne's name. Donaldson discusses the devaluation of the romance idiom in the Miller's Tale in terms of "Chaucer's genius for devaluation" (1970b, 28). See also Robert Miller (1970–71). Orme (1981), focusing on the theme of education in the fragment, discusses the deterioration of the young men in the last three tales, and Gaylord notes that even the descriptions of the temples in the Knight's Tale mirror the principle (1974, 182).

5. Her husband discovers her in bed with the clerk and calls her "pute provee" in one of Chaucer's possible sources. See Bryan and Dempster (1941, 144–46).

6. Even though Emily represents an ideal of virginity, Chaucer shows her sufficiently like the other women in the fragment and like fabliau-women in general when she "caste a freendlich ye" (2680) upon the man who seemed to have won her. See Rumble (1964).

7. The idea of adversaries among the pilgrims, introduced in Fragment I, reappears only in Fragment III (between Wife and Pardoner, Wife and Friar, Friar and Summoner, Host and Summoner, Host and Friar), and less certainly in Fragment V (perhaps between Squire and Franklin) and Fragment VII (between Chaucer and the Host, and between the Monk and the Knight or, in some manuscripts, the Host).

8. Theseus changes his mind about the grieving women, about Acite's perpetual imprisonment, about the death-penalty for Palamon and Arcite, about the rules of the tournament, and perhaps about the relations between Athens and Thebes. "Theseus' character is a composite of opposites, and for that reason his behavior is occasionally confusing and unpredictable" (McAlindon 1986, 46).

9. Most references to Fortune, destiny, and necessity are Chaucer's addition to his source (Gaylord 1974, 176). Dorothy Bethurum Loomis has shown that "the idea of changing Boccaccio's strife of the gods to include Saturn came to Chaucer from reading . . . Bernardus Sylvestris" (1968, 150). Even so, Saturn represents a force completely congruent with the Boethian universe, "an astrological adjunct to Boethian themes of providence, destiny, and free will" (Gaylord 1974, 174). For a more recent statement of the view that the Knight's "philosophy does not account very well for the events he relates," see Rowe (1986, 181–82). Derek Pearsall's claim that the First Mover speech, which grafts Boccaccio to Boethius, "is not successful" (1985, 124) has not won wide acceptance.

10. Nicholson mentions some of these themes in an interesting article devoted to the topic of ceremony in the Knight's Tale. He is perhaps a bit excessive in claiming that "the dominant personality in the *Knight's Tale* is the public personality of the ruler, Theseus, rather than any of the passionate spirits of the romance" (1988, 193).

11. Many have written on the topic of order and chaos in the Knight's Tale, perhaps none better than Muscatine (1957). See especially Halverson for whom the idea of order is "the fundamental statement on which the poem is struc-

tured" (1960, 606) and Underwood who emphasizes contrasts as examples of a "principle of order" which "pervades every aspect of its structure" (1959, 457). McAlindon supports the point on more philosophical grounds: "the poem, being so completely impregnated by the notion of *concordia discors* (or *discordia concors*), achieves a unity which *embraces*, not one which eschews, contradiction" (1986, 54). See also Westlund (1964) and Frost (1949).

12. For the sources and traditions associated with Mercury's epic descent, see Ann Taylor who argues that "Mercury is the inversion of the fellowship and 'pitee' so regularly extolled in the *Knight's Tale*" (1976, 53).

13. See Newhauser's excellent essay (1982) on the medieval sin of curiosity. Blodgett (1976) discusses "pryvetee" in the four tales of Fragment I, though more successfully with the Knight's and the Miller's tales than with the Reeve's or Cook's. Williams's argument for "a comic and blasphemous analogy between God's mysteries and a woman's private parts" (1987, 57) is less persuasive than other portions of his argument for the connections between the Knight's Tale and the Miller's Tale (54–60).

14. In addition to Fragment I, variations of the phrase "earnest and game" appear twice in the Clerk's Tale (609, 733), once in the Merchant's Tale (1594), and once in the Manciple's Prologue (100), but it never provides the cohesion to the fragments in which those tales appear that the phrase "earnest and game" provides here. Gerhard Joseph's discussion of the topic (1970), especially as it pertains to Fragment I, is perhaps the best, but see also James Rhodes (1974).

15. Cooper (1984) and Fisher (1973) have anticipated the point I am about to make by describing the way the "vocabulary drops markedly in social and moral level" (Cooper 1984, 117) throughout the first fragment.

16. This phenomenon has been noted by both Malone (1946) and Spraycar (1980) who focus on the first eighteen lines of the poem and arrive at conclusions that differ from what follows. Both mark the beginning of the descent out of high style at l. 12.

17. Stillwell demonstrates how "would-be elegant love-diction in ironic contexts" had been "well-established in fabliau-literature long before Chaucer's time" (1955, 693). Williams's observations about the way language, speech, and fiction in the Knight's Tale become "their distorted grotesque opposites" in the Miller's Tale (1987, 60–61) are surely correct. See also Mandel (1985, 283–85) for Chaucer's debasement of courtly language in the scene between Alison and Absolon.

18. Knight denounces the Cook's Tale: "This is a new climax of churlish disgustingness in this verbal peasant revolution against decency and linguistic order" (1986, 95).

19. Allen and Moritz have noted the importance of the theme to Fragment I: "It is all, from *Knight's Tale* to *Cook's Tale*, an 'argument of herbergage.' Whatever is taken in must be dealt with—be it Theban princes or Amazonian princesses, student lodgers, cheated customers, or riotous apprentices" (1981, 131). Gerhard Joseph, earlier, had shown in greater detail that the argument of herbergage "is a controlling principle in the entire structure of Fragment I" (1970, 91) and "one of the structural principles of the frame . . . pilgrimage from London to Canterbury" (93). Frost (1949, 301) and Van (1971, 9) focus upon the ancillary theme of imprisonment especially in the Knight's Tale; Traversi extends it to the relationship between John and Alison in the Miller's Tale (1983, 71). The word "in," of course, can also mean a private home (Lumiansky 1955, 77 n. 10).

20. There are more "pages" in Fragment I than in other fragments: in addition to Arcite, Absolon, in courting Alison, "swoor he wolde been hir owene page" (3376); and the baby in the Reeve's Tale "was a propre page" (3972).

21. Food is implicit, of course, in the various feasts throughout the *Canterbury Tales* and appears to additional good effect in the Pardoner's, Summoner's, Shipman's, and Nun's Priest's Tale, and in the Tale of Sir Thopas, but in no other fragment does it appear with such consistency in all the tales which comprise that fragment. In no other fragment are food and drink elevated to the stature of a unifying theme.

22. Whether Chaucer studied or was otherwise exposed to the law at the Inns of Court or elsewhere has long been a topic of interest to his biographers. The most recent comment is that of Braswell, writing on the Shipman's Tale: "it seems safe to assume that if Chaucer did not come to public life already equipped with a legal background, he soon acquired one" (1988, 295). David notes "the legalistic language by which the bargain is sealed" (1976, 91) in the General Prologue; Traversi points at the legal language in Absalon's wooing of Alison (1983, 73). Earlier scholars were concerned with the nature of Perkyn's "papir." See Blenner-Hassett (1942), Braddy (1943), and Call (1943).

23. For general studies of Chaucer's use of music, see Robertson (1962, 121–35), Huppé and Robertson (1963, chapter 2), Higdon (1972), and Chamberlain (1967). Claire Olson (1941) discusses the music of the fourteenth century; Montgomery (1931) discusses the musical instruments on which it was played. Most of the commentary on specific tales concentrates on the music in the Miller's Tale. See especially Harwood who discusses the "acoustical code" (1981, 22–23) in the poem and the binary opposition of silence and stringed or percussive instruments (20). For David, Chaucer's use of music has sexual overtones (1976, 96), a point supported by Scott (1967), but Gellrich finds "a basic comic incongruity between spirituality and carnality" (1974, 176) in Chaucer's juxtaposition of religious musical imagery and erotic action. For discussions of specific songs and musical forms in the fragment, see Gellrich (1971), the two articles by Collins (1932 and 1933); for the Reeve's Tale, see Kaske (1959), and for the Pardoner's Tale, Boenig (1990). Williams accurately pinpoints the way Chaucer uses music: "The fact that the Miller leads the entire pilgrimage toward Canterbury playing bagpipes alerts us not only to the negative character of the player but, as well, to the potential disharmony of many of those who are following this music" (1987, 54).

24. Rowland (1964 and 1971) has written most extensively and thoroughly on Chaucer's use of animals, but see John Gardner's semi-serious caveat (1977, 380 n. 23). See also Harwood's discussion of the "zoological code" (1981, 24–26) in the Miller's Tale. Cooper traces the decline in idealism from the Knight's Tale through the fragment in terms of the animals: those in the Miller's Tale being "a world away from the lions and boars of the Knight's Tale" (1984, 112) and the animal sexuality of the Reeve's Tale being literal as well as metaphorical (119). Friedman argues that the thirteen animals in the Reeve's Tale give "a moral dimension to the fabliau" (1967, 8) because the animal comparisons ironically comment on the pretensions of the characters (18). The animal imagery (as "mere animal anarchy") acquires metaphysical dimensions when it derives from the breakdown of order in the Knight's Tale (Turner 1974, 289).

Chapter 7. Fragment VII (Group B₂)

BIBLIOGRAPHICAL NOTE

Hamel accurately sums up the predominant critical attitude which regards the fragment as fundamentally disorganized when she says "Group B$_2$ ... shows the least interplay among the pilgrims in the links, and the least coherence in the sequence and themes of the tales. . . . Perhaps as a result, there is less apparent relationship among the tales themselves, less apparent effort by successive tellers to comment on or quarrel with their predecessors' offerings" (1980, 251). What relationship exists lies primarily in "contrast, not only in genre but in theme, style, and mood" (252). F. N. Robinson finds "no principle of arrangement save that of contrast or variety" (1957, 11); Benson says it "lacks any very clear unifying theme" (1987, 910). Because of the six different genre and the many interruptions, Baum calls this fragment "The Surprise Group" (1958, 74); Knight finds these tales a "little simplistic: they tend to develop only one idea in a static context" (1986, 132); Christmas, whose concern lies primarily with the Tale of Melibee, argues that its theme, "self-control, stands in sharp contrast to the self-indulgence that underlies the tales of Fragment VII" (1969); John Gardner sees only a "series of tales on human pride" (1977, 293) which may also present "a debate on the role of position and power in this world, one view tracing them to Fortune, the other tracing them to Grace, and both views having, oddly enough, their prideful streaks" (303); Huppé argues that "Harry Bailly's efforts to provide some lively entertainment to follow up the *Shipman's Tale* provides the comic, dramatic framework for the Fragment" (1964, 230); and Allen and Moritz, after eliminating the Shipman's Tale which they number among the moral tales, find in Fragment VII "Chaucer's analysis of what happens to us when we do tell stories" (1981, 213).

There have been only a few extended attempts to point up the unity of Fragment VII. Howard, who denominates Fragment VII "The Tales of Private Conduct" (1976, 271–88), argues that while the fragment does "not appear to have thematic unity the way the tales of the 'marriage group' do" (271–72), the six tales do fall into three contrasting pairs: although the Shipman's Tale and the Prioress' Tale "have nothing in common. . . . Taken together, the two tales make a startling contrast and themselves pose a moral issue" (273); Thopas and Melibee "are a no less pointed contrast" (273); and the Monk's and Nun's Priest's Tales are "a pair in which two clergymen set out to tell moral tales using the principle of the exemplum" (273). Although "We cannot say with certainty that the group is 'about' anything" (287), the Nun's Priest's Tale gives the fragment a "retrospective structure" (288). Gaylord argues that since the stories in this fragment alternate between solace and sentence, it is about "the art of story telling" (1967, 226) and that "it comes the closest of anything we have from Chaucer to providing his literary aesthetic." He proposes calling this fragment the "Literature Group" (227). Although Howard finds this arrangement "doubtful" (272), Cooper concurs: "the series turns into a debate on literature, its methods and functions and status" (1984, 161). And although "the generic diversity is more marked than anywhere else in the work, . . . the limitations of each genre are also shown up as they are not elsewhere" (162). All of these arguments are, in point of fact, lame; there has been no successful defense of the fragment's coherence.

1. Chiasmus ("crossing") generally applies to two items but is also applicable to more than two items. A slightly more accurate term is antimetabole ("turning about") which means the repetition of elements in an inverse order and can apply, as in Fragment VII, to more than two items. See Kissin (1987, 305–6) and Sister Miriam Joseph (1947). Chaucer used chiasmus to structure the events of Fragment V, the Squire's Tale and the Franklin's Tale.

2. Traversi observes that Pertelote plays "the part of Eve in the garden" (1983, 228), but he does not draw the comparison to the similar behavior of the wife in the Shipman's Tale. Huppé titles his chapter on the Nun's Priest's Tale "The Way of Eve with Adam" (1964, 174–86). The only connection which Huppé finds between the Shipman's Tale and the Nun's Priest's Tale derives from the Shipman's Tale being "highly discreditable to the monastic profession" (223), an attitude to which the Prioress, Monk, and Nun's Priest respond with more positive presentations of monastics.

3. The most important of these temporal references contain the number "three." On "The thridde day" (75) the merchant goes up to his counting house; on the third of May (3187–90) Chauntecleer's adventures with the fox occur; the fox lives in the woods "yeres three" (3216) before meeting Chauntecleer. Further occurrences of the number three: the pilgrim in Chauntecleer's first exemplum has three dreams; there are three women in the Nun's Priest's Tale (the widow and her two daughters), three cows, three sows; and Pertelote wants Chauntecleer to avoid "a fevere terciane" (2959). With regard to the third of May, see McCall (1961) and Bolton (1967, 219); see Smith (1936) for a discussion of unlucky days in Chaucer.

4. Ironically, the monk is equally solicitous about the merchant's health. He encourages the merchant to govern his diet "Atemprely, and namely in this hete" (262, and cf. Pertelote's similar concern, 2957) and is glad to see that the merchant "in heele ar comen hom agayn" (350).

5. Both Jones (1937a) and Caldwell (1940) have written on "Taillynge Ynough." Silverman (1953) shows how this pun is the chief ironic point of the Shipman's Tale which underpins his interpretation of the poem; and Abraham argues that "The structure of the tale *is* the structure of a pun" (1977, 327).

6. On "the commercialization of the marriage relationship," see Silverman (1953, 330). Knight's thoroughly Marxist reading of the Shipman's Tale suffers from the limitations of his approach: "the whole tale appears to comprehend and realize intimately the commodity-based social relations of the capital world . . . where infidelity is normal and where sin does not exist, whether in religious or humanist terms—this is the world of fetishized commodities that Marx outlines" (1986, 133–34). Hahn identifies the medieval association of sex and money (1986, 244) and points out the merchant's "clear sublimation or substitution of one kind of activity—commercial—for another—sexual" (242) which the wife resents (243). Both Tatlock (1907, 205), and Silverman (1953, 335–36) find resemblances between the Shipman's Tale and the Merchant's Tale.

7. One further, though minor, point needs to be made about the connection between the Shipman's Tale and the Nun's Priest's Tale. The Shipman's Tale is unique among Chaucer's fabliaux in that the plot "moves swiftly to its climax, not impeded, as elsewhere in Chaucer's fabliau tales, by digressions, by citation of learned authorities, or by illustrative exempla" (Lawrence 1958, 57). To this extent, it contrasts splendidly with the Nun's Priest's Tale which, perhaps alone among Chaucer's tales, moves slowly to its climax and is constantly impeded by

digressions, by citation of learned authorities, and by illustrative exempla.

8. Brewer quite rightly observes that "Medieval tragedy does not necessarily include death, but death is traditionally seen as one of the greatest tragedies that can, and must, befall a man" (1984, 196).

9. Gaylord (1962) distinguishes between the "hard" and the "soft" ways of viewing the Prioress' Tale. More recently, scholars have tended to view the Jews as "an 'opposition,' an inhuman enemy" (Derek Pearsall 1985, 250). In this softer view, the Prioress is not anti-Semitic: "She is talking about bogeymen" because there were no Jewish communities in England from the thirteenth to the seventeenth centuries—which explains why she set the tale in Asia (Brewer 1984, 190). Mehl argues that "Neither the conventional hatred of the Jews nor the drastic punishment of the murderers is exploited beyond the necessities of the plot" (1986, 194). See also Archer (1984) and the two articles by Rex (1984 and 1986).

10. On the arming of Sir Thopas, see Linn (1936). On the fight with Sir Oliphant as a burlesque of the David and Goliath story, see Laura Hibbard Loomis (1936).

11. Both Stillwell (1944) and Scattergood (1981) have connected Chaucer's antiwar sentiments expressed in the Melibee to the distressing course of the Hundred Year's War in the reign of Richard II. Strohm extends the historical application to the allegorical by pointing out that "Prudence challenges the whole idea of the Christian warrior with her claim that the Christian is helpless without the assistance of his God" (1967, 35). Chaucer's pacifism, his burlesque of the glories of war in the Tale of Sir Thopas and his logical arguments against war in the Tale of Melibee, may have been at one time central to the *Canterbury Tales*. If the Melibee was originally assigned to the Man of Law and intended to open the *Canterbury Tales* (Carleton Brown 1937), then it might have emphasized "the theme of reconciliation with God and forgiveness of man . . . that Chaucer originally wanted to make dominant in the *Canterbury Tales*" (Charles Owen 1973, 270).

12. Rex states this point more strongly: the un-Christian sentiments of the Prioress' Tale are "refuted in Chaucer's own Tale of Melibee, in which he warns against the evil of vengeance and praises the blessing of forgiveness." Rex finds it ironic that "the Prioress condemns the 'satanic' Jews to a vengeance as exaggerated as the evil being redressed—this in the name of the Virgin" (1986, 349). See also Christmas (1969).

13. At a time when it was fashionable in criticism to find historical parallels to the figures in the *Canterbury Tales,* Hotson considered the Tale of Melibee "a political pamphlet addressed to John of Gaunt to dissuade him from entering upon what seemed to his friends a rash war" (1921, 430). He shows that the Tale of Melibee "fits, with startling exactness, many known details of John of Gaunt's case in 1385" (450). He identifies John of Gaunt with Melibee, and his own better sense or perhaps Katharine Swynford as Prudence (437). In this reading the surgeons are the clergy; the physicians, the secular arm (442); the young folk are the court party, the king's favorites (443); and the advocate, identified as "one of the old wise" and the only one to receive Prudence's approbation, is Michael de la Pole, the Lord Chancellor. Stillwell finds the Tale of Melibee directed at Richard rather than John of Gaunt. In this view, Prudence insists that older men make better counselors because "Richard was thought to rely too much upon the advice of young men" (1944, 442). Prudence demonstrates the excellence of women as counselors because "Philippa [Queen to Edward III],

Joan [of Kent, the Princess of Wales], and Anne [Richard's Queen] did in contemporary eyes fulfil the ideal requirements laid down by Dame Prudence" (444).

14. Morton Bloomfield reminded his students at Harvard that Chaucer was not joking all the time. Bloomfield was echoing the argument of George Stewart who occasionally saw "the old despair" (1929, 107) behind some of Chaucer's work. Stewart reads almost half (ten of twenty-two) of the completed Canterbury tales as "tales of holinesse," which suggests to him that Chaucer "was able to see no solution except through religion" (106).

15. So also for various different reasons Charles Owen (1973, 270), Robertson (1962, 369), and Huppé (1964, 239). Knight, reading the poem in political terms, finds that "At the core of The Canterbury Tales stands this serious and thoughtful address to the powerful on how to save their power" (1986, 139).

16. See the Bibliographical Note to this chapter. John Gardner describes the sequential order in different terms. He finds that "the opposition of points of view set up in the juxtaposed tales of the Shipman and the Prioress continues into the succeeding tales, a collection of parodies or, more precisely, pieces of intentionally unreliable art, each of which ironically qualifies those around it and complicates the theme" (1977, 307). Joselyn is more precise in defining "qualitative progressions" when she applies Burke's five aspects of form to the Nun's Priest's Tale: "The shifts Chaucer creates occur not merely according to a principle of contrast . . . but according to a principle of contrast-plus-association" (1964, 568). This more accurately describes what occurs in the sequential ordering of the tales in Fragment VII.

17. Most scholars do not note the contrastive linking of these two tales. Both Cooper (1984, 164) and Pearsall, for example, emphasize the "breathtakingly abrupt" (1985, 246) transition between the Shipman's Tale and the Prioress' Tale. On the other hand, in describing how the Prioress' imagination reshapes the Shipman's Tale, Hawkins argues that the little child "yet under the yerde" becomes the Prioress' hero; the Flemish merchants become the Jewish usurers; the monk becomes the abbott, and the merchant's wife becomes the pious widow and then the Virgin (1964, 621). Brewer argues that the Prioress' Tale "is just as much an adult folktale as the preceding comic popular tale and really just as secular, but it illustrates secular affective piety and parental love, which are just as much part of secular culture as amusement at sexual impropriety" (1984, 190).

18. In emphasizing the Prioress' spirituality to contrast with the Shipman's worldliness, I do not mean to deny her fundamental sentimentality, explicit in her portrait in the General Prologue and implicit in her tale.

19. The only other references to abbots occur in Fragment I, 167 and 3666. One is a comparison (the Monk is said to be "A manly man, to been an abbot able"); the other refers to the abbot of the cloisterer who tells Absalon that John may have gone for timber "ther oure abbot hath hym sent."

20. Hamel is typical of several scholars who find that "Sir Thopas's name associates him with the gemlike hero of the preceding tale" (1980, 254). John Gardner associates Thopas with the Prioress' image of "the miraculous pearl" (1977, 307). For other meanings and associations of "thopas," see Ross (1930), Smith (1936), and especially Conley (1978).

21. Hawkins notes some of these points of contrast, parody, and similarity in describing how the "saint's life easily shades into romance" (1964, 621–22). Hamel (1980, 254–55) emphasizes the contrasts between the two tales as well

as the "covert similarity" (252–53); she sees the Tale of Sir Thopas as a "blasphemous parody" (256, 253) of the Prioress' Tale. Knight is alone in finding a similarity between these two tales in terms of their approach: the "Prioress' Tale is a partial parody of the child-martyr story" and the Tale of Sir Thopas is "wholly a literary parody" (1986, 136). To the similarities I have noted, perhaps one should add Chamberlain's observation about music: "Although music does not control meaning in these two tales, it enriches meaning. Music is a sign of true and false innocence, of pious love and foolish eroticism" (1981, 60).

22. Lumiansky offers another reason for the sequential order of the tales of Sir Thopas and of Melibee. As the narrator, Chaucer is going to play a joke on the Host. First, Chaucer will "make plentifully and entertainingly evident the fact that Harry Bailly lacks any real literary critical ability, despite the rapidity and certainly with which he criticizes the various tales; and, second, he will jockey the Host, a hen-pecked husband, into approving a tale in which a husband profits by accepting his wife's advice" (1955, 85). Christmas (1969) argues on other grounds that Melibee is a complement to Thopas.

23. For the various ways the Nun's Priest burlesques and parodies the person, art, and philosophy of the Monk, see Hemingway (1916), Craik (1964, 74), Strange (1967, 178–79), Traversi (1983, 210), Lumiansky (1955, 115–16), and Watson (1964, 280)

24. Early in the history of criticism on the Nun's Priest's Tale, the tale was held to support the moral. More recently, the multiplicity of morals to be drawn from the Nun's Priest's Tale has generated delight in confusion. For Brody, "the tale is less about a particular moral in it than about the very existence of moral possibilities" (1979, 43). For Jill Mann, "the narrator cannot offer a guarantee that he has a moral by which he has shaped [the tale]; he can only offer St. Paul's guarantee that everything that has been written has a moral in it somewhere" (1975, 277).

25. Many scholars have noted the ways the Nun's Priest's Tale "is *The Canterbury Tales* in little" (Muscatine 1966, 111; see also 1957, 237–43) both in its "backward-looking references to previous tales" (Howard 1976, 283) and in the way it "takes up some of the deepest themes of the pilgrimage and exposes them to a subtle comic scrutiny" (Traversi 1983, 217). "There is scarcely a single genre or style or theme in the whole work that is not touched on in this tale" (Cooper 1984, 184; also Mehl 1986, 200–1). In reflecting "back on the *Canterbury Tales* as a whole . . . in terms of the theory of fiction itself" (Williams 1987, 90), the Nun's Priest's Tale becomes "a tale about how tales should work" (89). See also Charles Owen (1968, 196). For these and other reasons, at least one scholar would make the Nun's Priest the winner of the tale-telling competition (Sheps 1975, 124).

26. Some "echoes" of the Prioress' Tale in the Nun's Priest's Tale have been noted by Hawkins (1964, 622).

27. In the frame, the fiery Goodelief accuses Harry Bailly of cowardice (1905 and 1909–10). Camden's argument (1935)—that Sir Thopas's physiognomy burlesques the typical knightly hero by describing an effeminate creature who is both timid and cowardly—supports this recollection of Sir Thopas in the Nun's Priest's Tale.

28. The point has been anticipated by Matthews (1972) who finds that the Nun's Priest comically burlesques the marital debate in the Tale of Melibee.

29. Richard Hoffman cites thirty-seven references to seventeen tales. Of these a few are "merely verbal echoes or phraseological repetitions" (1969, 577 n. 48)

while some of the proverbs are "capsule summaries of themes" (567) in other tales. In noting "the large number of echoes and reminiscences of *Melibee* in others of the *Canterbury Tales*," Derek Pearsall notes that Melibee "though not itself poetry, [is] the cause of poetry in other tales: a fat dung-heap" (1985, 287–88). McGerr argues that the whole *Canterbury Tales* "embodies Augustine's ideas about the workings of memory, experience, and literature" (1985, 98).

30. Levy and Adams (1967) argue that the Nun's Priest's Tale is an allegory of the Fall and that Chauntecleer's flying up into the tree at the end symbolizes the Resurrection. Although dismissed by Pearsall (1985, 236), the argument that the Nun's Priest's Tale is a "reenactment of the Fall" has recently been argued again in different terms by Harwood (1986, 196).

Chapter 8. Conclusion

1. In this consideration I am omitting, for the most part, those from the single tale fragments: the Sultan, Alla, the knight who accuses Custance of murder, and the steward who attempts to rape her in the Man of Law's Tale; and Phebus and the "man of litel reputacioun" (IX, 199) from the Manciple's Tale. Nonetheless, they all have a place in the various categories I am about to define.

Works Cited

The single alphabetical list of works which follows is the key to the author-date reference system used in the text and notes. Therefore, date of publication immediately follows the author's name. Two items by the same author published in one year are distinguished by "a" and "b." The page numbers of articles or chapters in collections appear immediately following the editor's name. The only journal abbreviations I have used are *PLMA* for *Publications of the Modern Language Association of America* and *ELH* for *ELH: A Journal of English Literary History.*

Abraham, David H. 1977. "*Cosyn* and *Cosynage*: Pun and Structure in the *Shipman's Tale.*" *Chaucer Review* 11:319–27.

Alford, John A. 1986. "The Wife of Bath Versus the Clerk: What Their Rivalry Means." *Chaucer Review* 21:108–32.

Allen, Judson Boyce, and Theresa Anne Moritz. 1981. *A Distinction of Stories: The Medieval Unity of Chaucer's Fair Chain of Narratives for Canterbury.* Columbus: Ohio State University Press.

Amoils, E. R. 1974. "Fruitfulness and Sterility in the 'Physician's' and 'Pardoner's' Tales." *English Studies in Africa* 17:17–37.

Amsler, Mark. 1987. "The Wife of Bath and Women's Power." *Assays* 4:67–83.

Archer, John. 1984. "The Structure of Anti-Semitism in the *Prioress' Tale.*" *Chaucer Review* 19:46–54.

Arrathoon, Leigh A. 1986. " 'For Craft is Al, Whoso That Do It Kan': The Genre of *The Merchant's Tale.*" In *Chaucer and the Craft of Fiction,* edited by Leigh A. Arrathoon, 241–48. Rochester, Mich.: Solaris Press.

Atkins, J. W. H. 1943. *English Literary Criticism: The Medieval Phase.* Cambridge: Cambridge University Press.

Axelrod, Steven. 1974. "The Wife of Bath and the Clerk." *Annuale Mediævale* 15:109–24.

Bachman, W. Bryant, Jr. 1977. " 'To Maken Illusioun': The Philosophy of Magic and the Magic of Philosophy in the *Franklin's Tale.*" *Chaucer Review* 12:55–67.

Baird, Joseph L. 1969. "The Devil's 'Privetee'." *Neuphilologische Mitteilungen* 70:104–6.

Baker, Donald C. 1961. "Witchcraft in the Dispute between Chaucer's Friar and Summoner." *South Central Bulletin* 21.4:33–36.

———. 1962a. "Chaucer's Clerk and the Wife of Bath on the Subject of Gentilesse." *Studies in Philology* 59:631–40.

———. 1962b. "Exemplary Figures as Characterizing Devices in the *Friar's Tale* and the *Summoner's Tale."* *The University of Mississippi Studies in English* 3:35–41.

Baldwin, Ralph G. 1962. "The Yeoman's Canons: A Conjecture." *Journal of English and Germanic Philology* 61:232–43.

Bartholomew, Barbara. 1966. *Fortuna and Natura.* Mouton: The Hague.

Baugh, A. C., ed. 1963. *Chaucer's Major Poetry.* New York: Appleton-Century-Crofts.

———. 1951. "Fifty Years of Chaucer Scholarship." *Speculum* 26:659–72.

Baum, Paull F. 1958. *Chaucer: A Critical Appreciation.* Durham, North Carolina: Duke University Press.

Beichner, Paul E. 1974. "Confrontation, Contempt of Court, and Chaucer's Cecilia." *Chaucer Review* 8:198–204.

Beidler, Peter G. 1969. "The Pairing of the *Franklin's Tale* and the *Physician's Tale."* *Chaucer Review* 3:275–79.

———. 1971a. "The Climax in the *Merchant's Tale."* *Chaucer Review* 6:38–43.

———. 1971b. "January, Knight of Lombardy." *Neuphilologische Mitteilungen* 72:735–38.

Benjamin, Edwin B. 1959. "The Concept of Order in the 'Franklin's Tale'." *Philological Quarterly* 38:119–24.

Benson, Larry D. 1981. "The Order of *The Canterbury Tales."* *Studies in the Age of Chaucer* 3:77–120.

———, ed. 1987. *The Riverside Chaucer.* 3d ed. Oxford: Oxford University Press.

Berger, Harry F., Jr. 1966a. "The F-Fragment of the *Canterbury Tales:* Part I." *Chaucer Review* 1:88–102.

———. 1966b. "The F-Fragment of the *Canterbury Tales:* Part II." *Chaucer Review* 1:135–56.

Besserman, Lawrence. 1986. "Girdles, Belts, and Cords: A Leitmotif in Chaucer's General Prologue." *Papers on Language and Literature* 22:322–25.

Birney, Earle. 1960. "Structural Irony Within the *Summoner's Tale."* *Anglia* 78:204–18.

Bixler, Frances. 1986. "Links between Chaucer's 'Pardoner's Tale' and 'Second Nun's Tale'." *Publications of the Arkansas Philological Association* 12:1–12.

Bleeth, Kenneth A. 1974. "The Image of Paradise in the *Merchant's Tale."* In *The Learned and the Lewed: Studies in Chaucer and Medieval Literature in Honor of Bartlett Jere Whiting,* edited by Larry D. Benson, 45–60. Harvard English Studies 5. Cambridge: Harvard University Press.

Blenner-Hassett, R. 1942. " 'When He His "Papir" Soghte,' *Canterbury Tales,* A-4404." *Modern Language Notes* 57:34–35.

Blodgett, E. D. 1976. "Chaucerian *Pryvetee* and the Opposition to Time." *Speculum* 51:477–93.

Bloomfield, Morton W. 1970. "The Miller's Tale—An UnBoethian Interpretation." In *Medieval Literature and Folklore Studies: Essays in Honor of Francis Lee Utley,* edited by Jerome Mandel and Bruce A. Rosenberg, 205–11. New Brunswick, N.J.: Rutgers University Press.

Boenig, Robert. 1990. "Musical Irony in the *Pardoner's Tale."* *Chaucer Review* 24:253–58.

Bolton, W. F. 1967. "The Topic of the *Knight's Tale*." *Chaucer Review* 1:217–27.

———. 1978. "Structural Meaning in *The Pardoner's Tale* and *The Nun's Priest's Tale*." *Language and Style* 11:201–11.

Braddy, Haldeen. 1938. "Cambyuskan's Flying Horse and Charles VI's 'Cerf Volant'." *Modern Language Review* 33:41–44.

———. 1943. "Chaucerian Minutiae." *Modern Language Notes* 58:18–23.

Braswell, Mary Flowers. 1985. "The Magic of Machinery: A Context for Chaucer's *Franklin's Tale*." *Mosaic* 18:101–10.

———. 1988. "Chaucer's 'Queinte Termes of Lawe': A Legal View of the Shipman's Tale." *Chaucer Review* 22:295–304.

Brewer, Derek. 1973. "Honour in Chaucer." *Essays and Studies by Members of the English Association* 26:1–19.

———. 1984. *An Introduction to Chaucer*. London and New York: Longman.

Brody, Saul Nathaniel. 1979. "Truth and Fiction in the *Nun's Priest's Tale*." *Chaucer Review* 14:33–47.

Bronson, Bertrand H. 1961. "Afterthoughts on *The Merchant's Tale*." *Studies in Philology* 58:583–96.

Brown, Carleton. 1937. "The Man of Law's Head-Link and the Prologue of the *Canterbury Tales*." *Studies in Philology* 34:8–35.

Brown, Emerson, Jr. 1968. "The *Merchant's Tale*: Why Is May Called 'Mayus'?" *Chaucer Review* 2:273–77.

———. 1970a. "*Hortus Inconclusus*: The Significance of Priapus and Pyramus and Thisbe in the *Merchant's Tale*." *Chaucer Review* 4:31–40.

———. 1970b. "*The Merchant's Tale*: Why Was Januarie Born 'of Pavye'?" *Neuphilologische Mitteilungen* 71:654–58.

———. 1979a. "Chaucer, the Merchant, and Their Tale: Getting beyond Old Controversies, Part I." *Chaucer Review* 13:141–56.

———. 1979b. "Chaucer, the Merchant, and Their Tale: Getting beyond Old Controversies, Part II." *Chaucer Review* 13:247–62.

Brown, Peter, 1983. "Is the 'Canon's Yeoman's Tale' Apocryphal?" *English Studies* 64:481–90.

———. 1984. "An Optical Theme in *The Merchant's Tale*." *Studies in the Age of Chaucer* 1:231–43.

Bryan, W. F., and Germaine Dempster. 1941. *Sources and Analogues of Chaucer's Canterbury Tales*. Chicago: University of Chicago Press. Reprint. New York: Humanities Press, 1958.

Burger, Douglas A. 1986. "The *Cosa impossible* of *Il Filocolo* and the Impossible of *The Franklin's Tale*." In *Chaucer and the Craft of Fiction*, edited by Leigh A. Arrathoon, 165–78. Rochester, Mich.: Solaris Press.

Burlin, Robert B. 1967. "The Art of Chaucer's Franklin." *Neophilologus* 51:55–73.

———. 1977. *Chaucerian Fiction*. Princeton, N.J.: Princeton University Press.

Burrow, John. 1957. "Irony in the Merchant's Tale." *Anglia* 75:199–208.

———, ed. 1969. *Geoffrey Chaucer: A Critical Anthology*. Harmondsworth: Penguin.

Caldwell, Robert A. 1940. "Chaucer's *Taillynge Ynough*, *Canterbury Tales* B$_2$ 1624." *Modern Language Notes* 55:262–65.

Call, Reginald. 1943. "'Whan He His Papir Soghte' (Chaucer's *Cook's Tale*, A 4404)." *Modern Language Quarterly* 4:167–76.

Camden, Carroll, Jr. 1935. "The Physiognomy of Thopas." *Review of English Studies* 11:326–30.

Carruthers, Mary J. 1983. "The Lady, the Swineherd, and Chaucer's Clerk." *Chaucer Review* 17:221–34.

Chamberlain, David S. 1967. "Music in Chaucer: His Knowledge and Use of Medieval Ideas About Music (Volumes I and II)." *Dissertation Abstracts* 27:3834A. Princeton University.

———. 1981. "Musical Signs and Symbols in Chaucer: Convention and Originality." In *Signs and Symbols in Chaucer's Poetry*, edited by John P. Hermann and John J. Burke, Jr., 43–80. University: University of Alabama Press.

Chance, Jane. 1988. "'Disfigured is thy Face': Chaucer's Pardoner and the Protean Shape Shifter Fals-Semblant (A Response to Britton Harwood)." *Philological Quarterly* 67: 423–35.

Chapman, Coolidge O. 1926. "*The Pardoner's Tale*: A Medieval Sermon." *Modern Language Notes* 41:506–9.

Cherniss, Michael D. 1972. "The *Clerk's Tale* and Envoy, The Wife of Bath's Purgatory, and the *Merchant's Tale*." *Chaucer Review* 6: 235–54.

Christmas, Robert A. 1969. "Chaucer's *Tale of Melibee*: Its Tradition and Its Function in Fragment VII of the *Canterbury Tales*." *Dissertation Abstracts* 29:3093A. University of Southern California.

Chute, Marchette. 1946. *Geoffrey Chaucer of England*. New York: Dutton.

Clark, John W. 1972. "*Does* the Franklin Interrupt the Squire?" *Chaucer Review* 7:160–61.

Clawson, W. H. 1951. "The Framework of *The Canterbury Tales*." *University of Toronto Quarterly* 20:137–54.

Coffman, George R. 1944. "Canon's Yeoman's Prologue, G, ll. 563–566: Horse or Man?" *Modern Language Notes* 59:269–71.

Coghill, Neville. 1949. *The Poet Chaucer*. London.

Collette, Carolyn P. 1984. "'Ubi Peccaverant, Ibi Punirentur': The Oak Tree and the *Pardoner's Tale*." *Chaucer Review* 19:39–45.

Collins, Fletcher. 1932. "*Solas* in the Miller's Tale." *Modern Language Notes* 47:363–64.

———. 1933. "The Kinges Note: *The Miller's Tale*, Line 31." *Speculum* 8:195–97.

Condren, Edward I. 1985. "Transcendent Metaphor or Banal Reality: Three Chaucerian Dilemmas." *Papers on Language and Literature* 21:233–57.

Conley, John. 1978. "The Peculiar Name Thopas." *Studies in Philology* 73:42–61.

Cook, Robert. 1987. "The Canon's Yeoman and His Tale." *Chaucer Review* 22:28–40.

Cooper, Helen. 1984. *The Structure of the Canterbury Tales*. Athens: University of Georgia Press.

Craik, T. W. 1964. *The Comic Tales of Chaucer*. London: Methuen.

Crane, Susan. 1988. "Alison of Bath Accused of Murder: Case Dismissed." *English Language Notes* 25:10–15.

Works Cited

Crisp, Sir Frank. 1924. *Medieval Gardens*. London: John Lane.

Cunningham, J. V. 1952. "The Literary Form of the Prologue to the *Canterbury Tales*." *Modern Philology* 49:172–81.

Dalby, Marcia A. 1974. "The Devil in the Garden: Pluto and Proserpine in Chaucer's *Merchant's Tale*." *Neuphilologische Mitteilungen* 75:408–15.

David, Alfred. 1965a. "Criticism and the Old Man in Chaucer's *Pardoner's Tale*." *College English* 27:39–44.

———. 1965b. "Sentimental Comedy in *The Franklin's Tale*." *Annuale Mediævale* 6:19–27.

———. 1976. *The Strumpet Muse: Art and Morals in Chaucer's Poetry*. Bloomington: Indiana University Press.

Daye, Mary L. 1968. "The Rhetoric of Narration: A Study of Narrative Intrusion in Chaucer's Tales of the Squire, Manciple, Merchant, and Nun's Priest." *Dissertation Abstracts* 29:563A–64A.

Dean, James, 1985. "Dismantling the Canterbury Book." *PMLA* 100:746–62.

Delany, Paul. 1967. "Constantinus Africanus and Chaucer's *Merchant's Tale*." *Philological Quarterly* 46:560–66.

Delany, Sheila. 1987. "Notes on Experience, Authority, and Desire in the Wife of Bath's Recital." *Hebrew University Studies in Literature and the Arts* 15:27–35.

Delasanto, Rodney. 1973. "Sacrament and Sacrifice in the *Pardoner's Tale*." *Annuale Mediævale* 14:43–52.

Dempster, Germaine, 1942. "'Thy Gentillesse' in *Wife of Bath's Tale*, D 1159–62." *Modern Language Notes* 57:173–76.

Dimarco, Vincent. 1981. "A Note on Canacee's Magic Ring." *Anglia* 99:399–405.

Dinshaw, Carolyn. 1988. "Eunuch Hermeneutics." *ELH* 55.1:27–51.

Donaldson, E. Talbot. 1958. *Chaucer's Poetry*. New York: Ronald Press.

———. 1970a. "Idiom of Popular Poetry in the Miller's Tale." In *Speaking of Chaucer*, 13–29. New York: Norton.

———. 1970b. "The Ordering of the *Canterbury Tales*." In *Medieval Literature and Folklore Studies: Essays in Honor of Francis Lee Utley*, edited by Jerome Mandel and Bruce A. Rosenberg, 193–204. New Brunswick, N.J.: Rutgers University Press.

Donovan, Mortimer J. 1957. "The Image of Pluto and Proserpine in the *Merchant's Tale*." *Philological Quarterly* 36:49–60.

Dryden, John. 1700. "Preface to the Fables" [1700]. *Essays of John Dryden*. Edited by W. P. Ker, 1900. Reprinted. New York: Russell and Russell, 1961. Vol. II.

Duncan, Charles F., Jr. 1970. "'Straw for Youre Gentilesse': The Gentle Franklin's Interruption of the Squire." *Chaucer Review* 5:161–64.

Duncan, Edgar H. 1968. "The Literature of Alchemy and Chaucer's *Canon's Yeoman's Tale*: Framework, Theme, and Characters." *Speculum* 43:633–56.

Dunleavy, Gareth W. 1967. "The Wound and the Comforter: The Consolations of Geoffrey Chaucer." *Papers on Language and Literature* 3:14–27.

East, W. G. 1977. "By Preeve Which That Is Demonstrativ." *Chaucer Review* 12:78–82.

Eggbroten, Anne. 1984. "Laughter in the *Second Nun's Tale:* A Redefinition of the Genre." *Chaucer Review* 19:55–61.

Elbow, Peter. 1973. *Oppositions in Chaucer.* Middletown, Conn.: Wesleyan University Press.

Evers, Jim W. 1972. "Some Implications of Chaucer's Use of Astrology in the *Canterbury Tales.*" *Dissertation Abstracts International* 32:4561A. Duke University.

Faral, Edmond. 1924. *Les Arts Poétiques du XIIe et du XIIIe Siècle.* Paris: Bibliothèque de l'École des Hautes Études, vol. 238.

Fichte, Joerg O. 1973. "*The Clerk's Tale:* An Obituary to *Gentilesse.*" In *New Views on Chaucer: Essays in Generative Criticism,* edited by William C. Johnson, Jr., and Loren C. Gruber, 9–16. Denver: Society for New Language Study.

Fisher, John H. 1973. "The Three Styles of Fragment I of the *Canterbury Tales.*" *Chaucer Review* 8:119–27.

Fleming, John V. 1966. "The Antifraternalism of the *Summoner's Tale.*" *Journal of English and Germanic Philology* 65:688–700.

Frakes, Jerold C. 1987. "'Ther Nis Namoore To Seye': Closure in the *Knight's Tale.*" *Chaucer Review* 22:1–7.

Frese, Dolores Warwick. 1973. "Chaucer's *Clerk's Tale:* The Monsters and the Critics Reconsidered." *Chaucer Review* 8:133–46.

Friedman, John Block. 1967. "A Reading of Chaucer's *Reeve's Tale.*" *Chaucer Review* 2:8–19.

Friman, Anne. 1976. "Of Bretherhede: The Friendship Motif in Chaucer." *Innisfree* [Southern Louisiana University] 3:24–36.

Fritz, Donald W. 1987. "Reflections in a Golden Florin: Chaucer's Narcissistic Pardoner." *Chaucer Review* 21:338–59.

Frost, William. 1949. "An Interpretation of Chaucer's *Knight's Tale.*" *Review of English Studies* 25:289–304.

Fyler, John M. 1987. "Love and Degree in the *Franklin's Tale.*" *Chaucer Review* 21:321–37.

―――. 1988. "Domesticating the Exotic in the *Squire's Tale.*" *ELH* 55:1–26.

Gallacher, Patrick. 1986. "The *Summoner's Tale* and Medieval Attitudes Toward Sickness." *Chaucer Review* 21:200–12.

Ganim, John M. 1987. "Carnival Voices and the Envoy to the *Clerk's Tale.*" *Chaucer Review* 22:112–27.

Garbaty, Thomas J. 1973. "Satire and Regionalism: The Reeve and His Tale." *Chaucer Review* 8:1–8.

Gardner, John. 1967. "*The Canon's Yeoman's Prolouge and Tale:* An Interpretation." *Philological Quarterly* 46:1–17.

―――. 1977. *The Poetry of Chaucer.* Carbondale and Edwardsville: Southern Illinois University Press.

Gardner, W. B. 1947. "Chaucer's 'Unworthy Sone of Eve'." *Studies in English* (Texas) 26:77–83.

Gaylord, Alan T. 1962. "The Unconquered Tale of the Prioress." *Papers of the Michigan Academy of Science, Arts, and Letters* 47:613–36.

―――. 1964. "The Promises in *The Franklin's Tale.*" *ELH* 31:331–65.

——. 1967. "*Sentence* and *Solaas* in Fragment VII of the *Canterbury Tales:* Harry Bailly as Horseback Editor." *PMLA* 82:226–35.

——. 1974. "The Role of Saturn in the *Knight's Tale*." *Chaucer Review* 8:171–90.

Gellrich, Jesse M. 1971. "Nicholas' 'Kynges Noote' and 'Melodye'." *English Language Notes* 8:249–52.

——. 1974. "The Parody of Medieval Music in the *Miller's Tale*." *Journal of English and Germanic Philology* 73:176–88.

Gilmartin, Kristine. 1976. "Array as Motif in the *Clerk's Tale*." *Rice University Studies* 62:99–110. Also printed as "Array in the *Clerk's Tale*." *Chaucer Review* 13 (1979):234–46. See *Chaucer Review* 14 (1979):96 for editorial apology.

Ginsberg, Warren. 1978. "'And Speketh so Pleyn': The Clerk's Tale and Its Teller." *Criticism* 20:307–23.

Golding, Malcolm. 1970. "The Importance of Keeping 'Trouthe' in *The Franklin's Tale*." *Medium Ævum* 39:306–12.

Gray, Douglas. 1987. "Chaucer and Gentilesse." In *One Hundred Years of English Studies in Dutch Universities*, edited by G. H. V. Bunt, E. S. Kooper, J. L. Mackenzie, and D. R. M. Wilkinson, 1–27. Amsterdam: Rodopi.

Green, Donald C. 1986. "The Semantics of Power: *Maistrie* and *Soveraynetee* in *The Canterbury Tales*." *Modern Philology* 84:18–23.

Grennen, Joseph E. 1962. "The Canon's Yeoman and the Cosmic Furnace: Language and Meaning in the 'Canon's Yeoman's Tale'." *Criticism* 4:225–40.

——. 1965. "The Canon's Yeoman's Alchemical 'Mass'." *Studies in Philology* 62:546–60.

——. 1966. "St. Cecilia's 'Chemical Wedding': The Unity of the *Canterbury Tales*, Fragment VIII." *Journal of English and Germanic Philology* 65:466–81.

——. 1987. "The Pardoner, the Host, and the Depth of Chaucerian Insult." *English Language Notes* 25:18–24.

Griffith, D. D. 1926. *A Bibliography of Chaucer, 1908–1924*. Seattle: University of Washington Press.

Grove, Robin. 1976. "*The Merchant's Tale*: Seeing, Knowing, and Believing." *The Critical Review* (Melbourne, Sydney) 18:23–38.

Hahn, Thomas. 1986. "Money, Sexuality, Wordplay, and Context in the *Shipman's Tale*." In *Chaucer in the Eighties*, edited by Julian N. Wasserman and Robert J. Blanche, 235–49. Syracuse: Syracuse University Press.

Haines, R. Michael. 1972. "Fortune, Nature, and Grace in Chaucer's *Canterbury Tales*." Unpublished Dissertation. Ohio State University.

——. 1976. "Fortune, Nature, and Grace in Fragment C." *Chaucer Review* 10:220–35.

Haller, Robert S. 1965. "Chaucer's *Squire's Tale* and the Uses of Rhetoric." *Modern Philology* 62:285–95.

Hallissy, Margaret. 1974. "Poison: Imagery and Theme in Chaucer's *Canterbury Tales*." Unpublished Dissertation. Fordham University.

Halverson, John. 1960. "Aspects of Order in the Knight's Tale." *Studies in Philology* 57:606–21.

———. 1970. "Chaucer's Pardoner and the Progress of Criticism." *Chaucer Review* 4:184–202.

Hamel, Mary. 1980. "And Now for Something Completely Different: The Relationship between the *Prioress' Tale* and the *Rime of Sir Thopas*." *Chaucer Review* 14:251–59.

Hamilton, Marie P. 1939. "Death and Old Age in *The Pardoner's Tale*." *Studies in Philology* 36:571–76.

———. 1941. "The Clerical Status of Chaucer's Alchemist." *Speculum* 16:103–8.

Hanson, Thomas B. 1972. "Chaucer's Physician as Storyteller and Moralizer." *Chaucer Review* 7:132–39.

Hardman, Phillipa. 1980. "Chaucer's Tyrants of Lombardy." *Review of English Studies* 31:172–78.

Harrington, David V. 1965. "Dramatic Irony in the Canon's Yeoman's Tale." *Neuphilologische Mitteilungen* 66:160–66.

———. 1968. "The Narrator of the *Canon's Yeoman's Tale*." *Annuale Mediævale* 9:85–97.

Harrison, Benjamin S. 1935. "The Rhetorical Inconsistency of Chaucer's Franklin." *Studies in Philology* 32:55–61.

Harwood, Britton J. 1981. "The 'Nether Ye' and its Antitheses: A Structuralist Reading of 'The Miller's Tale'." *Annuale Mediævale* 21:5–30.

———. 1986. "Signs and/as Origin: Chaucer's *Nun's Priest's Tale*." *Style* 20:189–202.

———. 1987. "Chaucer and the Silence of History: Situating the Canon's Yeoman's Tale." *PMLA* 102:338–50.

———. 1988. "Chaucer's Pardoner: The Dialectics of Inside and Outside." *Philological Quarterly* 67:409–22.

Hatton, Thomas J. 1971. "Absolon, Taste, and Odor in *The Miller's Tale*." *Papers on Language and Literature* 7:72–75.

———. 1974. "Thematic Relationships between Chaucer's Squire's Portrait and Tale and the Knight's Portrait and Tale." *Studies in Medieval Culture* 4:452–58.

Havely, N. R. 1976. *Geoffrey Chaucer: The Friar's, Summoner's, and Pardoner's Tales from The Canterbury Tales*. New York: Holmes and Meier.

———. 1979. "Chaucer's Friar and Merchant." *Chaucer Review* 13:337–45.

Hawkins, Sherman. 1964. "Chaucer's Prioress and the Sacrifice of Praise." *Journal of English and Germanic Philology* 63:599–624.

Hemingway, Samuel B. 1916. "Chaucer's Monk and Nun's Priest." *Modern Language Notes* 31:479–83.

Heninger, S. K., Jr. 1957. "The Concept of Order in Chaucer's *Clerk's Tale*." *Journal of English and Germanic Philology* 56:382–95.

Hennedy, Hugh L. 1971. "The Friar's Summoner's Dilemma." *Chaucer Review* 5:213–17.

Herz, Judith Schorer. 1961. "*The Canon's Yeoman's Prologue and Tale*." *Modern Philology* 57:231–37.

Higdon, David L. 1972. "Diverse Melodies in Chaucer's 'General Prologue'." *Criticism* 14:97–108.

Works Cited

Higuchi, Masayuki. 1987. "On the Integration of the *Pardoner's Tale*." *Chaucer Review* 22:161–69.

Hilberry, Jane. 1987. "'And in Oure Madnesse Everemore We Rave': Technical Language in the *Canon's Yeoman's Tale*." *Chaucer Review* 21:435–43.

Hinckley, Henry Barrett. [1917] 1959. "The Debate on Marriage in *The Canterbury Tales*." *PMLA* 32:292–305. Reprinted in *Chaucer: Modern Essays in Criticism*, edited by Edward Wagenknecht, 216–25. New York: Oxford University Press.

Hinton, Norman. 1961. "Two Names in *The Reeve's Tale*." *Names* 9:117–19.

Hoffman, Arthur W. 1954. "Chaucer's Prologue to Pilgrimage: The Two Voices." *ELH* 21:1–16.

Hoffman, Richard L. 1966. "Ovid's Priapus in the *Merchant's Tale*." *English Language Notes* 3:169–72.

———. 1968. "The Canterbury Tales." In *Critical Approaches to Six Major English Works: Beowulf through Paradise Lost*, edited by Robert M. Lumiansky and Herschel Baker, 41–80. Philadelphia: University of Pennsylvania Press.

———. 1969. "Chaucer's Melibee and Tales of Sondry Folk." *Classica et Mediævalia* 30:552–77.

Holbrook, David. 1964. *The Quest for Love*. London: Methuen.

Holland, Norman N. 1967. "Meaning as Transformation: The Wife of Bath's Tale." *College English* 28:279–90.

———. 1968. *The Dynamics of Literary Response*, pp. 12–30. New York: Oxford University Press.

Holman, C. Hugh. 1951. "Courtly Love in the Merchant's and Franklin's Tales." *ELH* 18:241–52.

Hotson, J. L. 1921. "The Tale of *Melibeus* and John of Gaunt." *Studies in Philology* 18:429–52.

Howard, Donald R. 1976. *The Idea of the Canterbury Tales*. Berkeley: University of California Press.

Huber, Joan R. 1967. "Chaucer's Concept of Death in *The Canterbury Tales*." Unpublished Dissertation, University of Pittsburgh.

Hult, David F. 1986. "Lancelot's Two Steps: A Problem in Textual Criticism." *Speculum* 61:836–58.

Hume, Kathryn. 1972a. "The Pagan Setting of the *Franklin's Tale* and the Sources of Dorigen's Cosmology." *Studia Neophilologica* 44:289–94.

———. 1972b. "Why Chaucer Calls the *Franklin's Tale* a Breton Lai." *Philological Quarterly* 51:365–79.

Huppé, Bernard F. 1964. *A Reading of the Canterbury Tales*. Albany: State University of New York Press.

———, and D. W. Robertson, Jr. 1963. *Fruyt and Chaf*. Princeton, N.J.: Princeton University Press.

Jacobs, Edward C., and Robert E. Jungman. 1985. "His Mother's Curse: Kinship in the *Friar's Tale*." *Philological Quarterly* 64:256–59.

Jacobs, Kathryn. 1985. "The Marriage Contract of the *Franklin's Tale*: The Remaking of Society." *Chaucer Review* 20:132–43.

Jensen, Emily. 1990. "Male Competition as a Unifying Motif in Fragment A of the *Canterbury Tales*." *Chaucer Review* 24:320–28.

Johnson, Lynn Staley. 1975. "The Prince and His People: A Study of the Two Covenants in the *Clerk's Tale.*" *Chaucer Review* 10:17–29.

Jones, Claude. 1937a. "Chaucer's *Taillynge Ynough.*" *Modern Language Notes* 52:570.

———. 1937b. "The 'Second Nun's Tale,' A Medieval Sermon." *Modern Language Review* 32:283.

Jordan, Carmel. 1987. "Soviet Archeology and the Setting of the *Squire's Tale.*" *Chaucer Review* 22:128–40.

Jordan, Robert M. 1967. *Chaucer and the Shape of Creation: The Aesthetic Possibilities of Inorganic Structure.* Cambridge, Mass.: Harvard University Press.

———. 1968. "Chaucerian Narrative." In *Companion to Chaucer Studies.* Edited by Beryl Rowland, 85–102. Toronto: Oxford University Press.

Joselyn, Sister M., OSB. 1964. "Aspects of Form in *The Nun's Priest's Tale.*" *College English* 25:566–71.

Joseph, Gerhard. 1966. "The *Franklin's Tale:* Chaucer's Theodicy." *Chaucer Review* 1:20–32.

———. 1970. "Chaucerian 'Game'—'Ernest' and the 'Argument of Herbergage' in *The Canterbury Tales.*" *Chaucer Review* 5:83–96.

———. 1975. "The Gifts of Nature, Fortune, and Grace in the *Physician's, Pardoner's,* and *Parson's Tales.*" *Chaucer Review* 9:220–35.

Joseph, Sister Miriam, C.S.C. 1947. *Rhetoric in Shakespeare's Time.* New York: Harcourt, Brace, and World.

Josipovici, Gabriel. 1965. "Fiction and Game in *The Canterbury Tales.*" *Critical Quarterly* 2:185–97.

———. 1971. *The World and the Book.* London: Macmillan. 2d ed. 1979.

Jungman, Robert E. 1976. "The Pardoner's Quarrel with the Host." *Philological Quarterly* 55:279–81.

Kahrl, Stanley J. 1973. "Chaucer's *Squire's Tale* and the Decline of Chivalry." *Chaucer Review* 7:194–209.

Kane, George. 1984a. *Chaucer.* Oxford: Oxford University Press.

———. 1984b. "John M. Manly (1865–1940) and Edith Rickert (1871–1938)." In *Editing Chaucer: The Great Tradition,* edited by Paul G. Ruggiers, 207–29. Oklahoma: Pilgrim Books.

Kaske, Robert E. 1957. "The Knight's Interruption of the Monk's Tale." *ELH* 24:249–68.

———. 1959. "An Aube in the 'Reeve's Tale'." *ELH* 26:295–310.

Kean, P. M. 1982. *Chaucer and the Making of English Poetry.* London: Routledge and Kegan Paul. 1972. Shortened ed. 1982.

Kearney, A. M. 1969. "Truth and Illusion in *The Franklin's Tale.*" *Essays in Criticism* 19:245–53.

Kellogg, Alfred. 1960. "Susannah and the *Merchant's Tale.*" *Speculum* 35:275–79.

Kernan, Anne. 1974. "The Archwife and the Eunuch." *ELH* 41:1–25.

Kissin, Ana. 1987. "Figures of Causality and Order in Sidney's *Arcadia:* Gradatio as Symbolic Form." Unpublished Master's Thesis. Tel Aviv University.

Kittredge, George Lyman. 1911–12. "Chaucer's Discussion of Marriage." *Mod-*

ern *Philology* 9:435–67. Reprinted in *Chaucer: Modern Essays in Criticism,* edited by Edward Wagenknecht, 188–215. New York: Oxford University Press.

———. 1915. *Chaucer and His Poetry.* Cambridge, Mass.: Harvard University Press.

Knapp, Peggy Ann. 1985. "Knowing the Tropes: Literary Exegesis and Chaucer's Clerk." *Criticism* 27:331–45.

———. 1986. "Alisoun Weaves a Text" *Philological Quarterly* 65:387–401.

Knight, Stephen. 1970. "Rhetoric and Poetry in the *Franklin's Tale.*" *Chaucer Review* 4:14–30.

———. 1986. *Geoffrey Chaucer.* Oxford: Blackwell.

Koch, J., ed. 1925. *Canterburyerzählungen.* Translated by Wilhelm Hertzberg (1866). Berlin: H. Stubenrauch.

Koban, Charles. 1971. "Hearing Chaucer Out: The Art of Persuasion in the *Wife of Bath's Tale.*" *Chaucer Review* 5:225–39.

Lawler, Justus George. 1979. *Celestial Pantomime: Poetic Structures of Transcendence.* New Haven: Yale University Press.

Lawrence, William W. 1958. "Chaucer's *Shipman's Tale.*" *Speculum* 33:57–68.

Lawton, David. 1985. *Chaucer's Narrators.* Cambridge: Brewer.

Lee, Brian S. 1987. "The Position and Purpose of the *Physician's Tale.*" *Chaucer Review* 22:141–60.

Lenaghan, R. T. 1973. "The Irony of the *Friar's Tale.*" *Chaucer Review* 7:281–94.

Levy, Bernard S. 1970. "The Wife of Bath's Queynte Fantasye." *Chaucer Review* 4:106–22.

———. 1977. "*Gentilesse* in Chaucer's *Clerk's* and *Merchant's Tales.*" *Chaucer Review* 11:306–18.

———. 1986. "The Meanings of *The Clerk's Tale.*" In *Chaucer and the Craft of Fiction,* edited by Leigh A. Arrathoon, 385–409. Rochester, Mich.: Solaris Press.

———, and George P. Adams, 1967. "Chauntecleer's Paradise Lost and Regained." *Medieval Studies* 29:178–92.

Leyerle, John. 1976. "Thematic Interlace in *The Canterbury Tales.*" *Essays and Studies* 29:107–21.

Linn, Irving. 1936. "The Arming of Sir Thopas." *Modern Language Notes* 51:300–11.

Longsworth, Robert. 1974. "Chaucer's Clerk as Teacher." In *The Learned and the Lewed: Studies in Chaucer and Medieval Literature in Honor of Bartlett Jere Whiting,* edited by Larry D. Benson, 61–66. Harvard English Studies 5. Cambridge: Harvard University Press.

Loomis, Dorothy B. 1968. "Saturn in Chaucer's *Knight's Tale.* In *Chaucer und Seine Zeit.* Edited by Arno Esch. Tübingen: Max Niemeyer.

Loomis, Laura Hibbard. 1936. "Sir Thopas and David and Goliath." *Modern Language Notes* 51:311–13.

———. 1958. "Secular Dramatics in the Royal Palace, Paris, 1378, 1389, and Chaucer's 'Tregetours'." *Speculum* 33:242–55.

Luengo, A. 1979. "Audience and Exempla in the *Pardoner's Prologue and Tale.*" *Chaucer Review* 11:1–10.

Lumiansky, Robert M. 1955. *Of Sondry Folk: The Dramatic Principle in the Canterbury Tales*. Austin: University of Texas Press.

McAlindon, T. 1986. "Cosmology, Contrariety and the Knight's Tale." *Medium Ævum* 55:41–57.

McCall, John P. 1961. "Chaucer's May 3." *Modern Language Notes* 76:201–5.

———. 1966a. "The Clerk's Tale and the Theme of Obedience." *Modern Language Quarterly* 27:260–69.

———. 1966b. "The Squire in Wonderland." *Chaucer Review* 1:103–9.

McCann, Garth A. 1973. "Chaucer's First Three Tales: Unity in Trinity." *Bulletin of the Rocky Mountain Modern Language Association* (now the *Rocky Mountain Review of Language and Literature*) 27:10–16.

McCracken, Samuel. 1971. "Confessional Prologue and the Topography of the Canon's Yeoman." *Modern Philology* 68: 289–91.

McGerr, Rosemarie Potz. 1985. "Retraction and Memory: Retrospective Structure in the *Canterbury Tales*." *Comparative Literature* 37:97–113.

Malone, Kemp. 1946. "Style and Structure in the Prologue to the *Canterbury Tales*." *ELH* 13:38–45.

———. 1951. *Chapters on Chaucer*. Baltimore.

Mandel, Jerome. 1976. "'Boy' as Devil in Chaucer." *Papers on Language and Literature* 11:407–11.

———. 1977a. "Governance in the *Physician's Tale*." *Chaucer Review* 10:316–25.

———. 1977b. "Other Voices in the *Canterbury Tales*. *Criticism* 19:338–49.

———. 1985. "Courtly Love in the *Canterbury Tales*." *Chaucer Review* 19:277–89.

———. 1988. "The Unity of Fragment IV (Group E): The *Clerk's Tale* and the *Merchant's Tale*." *Hebrew University Studies in Literature and the Arts* 16:27–50.

Manly, J. M. 1926. "Chaucer and the Rhetoricians." *Proceedings of the British Academy* 12:95–113.

Mann, Jill. 1975. "The *Speculum Stultorum* and the *Nun's Priest's Tale*." *Chaucer Review* 9:262–82.

Mann, Lindsay A. 1966. "'Gentilesse' and the *Franklin's Tale*." *Studies in Philology* 63:10–29.

Markman, Alan. 1966. "The Concern of Chaucer's Poetry." *Annuale Mediævale* 7:90–103.

Mathew, Gervase. 1947. "Marriage and *Amour Courtois* in Late Fourteenth Century England." In *Essays Presented to Charles Williams*, 128–35. Oxford: Oxford University Press.

Mathewson, Jeanne T. 1973. "For Love and Not for Hate: The Value of Virginity in Chaucer's *Physician's Tale*." *Annuale Mediævale* 14:35–42.

Matthews, Lloyd J. 1972. "The Latent Comic Dimensions of Geoffrey Chaucer's *Tale of Melibee*." *Dissertation Abstracts International* 32:4572A. University of Virginia.

Mehl, Dieter. 1986. *Geoffrey Chaucer: An Introduction to His Narrative Poetry*. Cambridge: Cambridge University Press.

Merrix, Robert P. 1983. "Sermon Structure in the *Pardoner's Tale*." *Chaucer Review* 17:235–49.

Middleton, Anne. 1973. "The *Physician's Tale* and Love's Martyrs: 'Ensamples Mo Than Ten' as a Method in the *Canterbury Tales*." *Chaucer Review* 8:9–31.

———. 1984. "War by Other Means: Marriage and Chivalry in Chaucer." *Studies in the Age of Chaucer* 1:119–33.

Miller, Clarence H., and Roberta Bux Bosse. 1972. "Chaucer's Pardoner and the Mass." *Chaucer Review* 6:171–84.

Miller, Milton. 1950. "The Heir in the *Merchant's Tale*." *Philological Quarterly* 29:437–40.

Miller, Robert P. 1970–71. "The Miller's Tale as Complaint." *Chaucer Review* 5:147–60.

———. 1978. "Augustinian Wisdom and Eloquence in the F-Fragment of the *Canterbury Tales*." *Mediævalia* 4:245–75.

———. 1986. "Chaucer's Rhetorical Rendition of Mind: The Squire's Tale." In *Chaucer and the Craft of Fiction*, edited by Leigh A. Arrathoon, 219–40. Rochester, Mich.: Solaris Press.

Minnis, A. J. 1985. Review of Helen Cooper. *The Structure of the Canterbury Tales*. *Essays in Criticism* 35:265–69.

Montgomery, Franz. 1931. "The Musical Instruments in 'The Canterbury Tales'." *Musical Quarterly* 17:439–48.

Moore, Arthur K. 1944. "Alysoun's Other Tonne." *Modern Language Notes* 49:481–83.

———. 1949. "The Pardoner's Interruption of the *Wife of Bath's Prologue*." *Modern Language Quarterly* 10:49–57.

Morgan, Gerald. 1986. "Boccaccio's *Filocolo* and the Moral Argument of the *Franklin's Tale*." *Chaucer Review* 20:285–306.

Morrow, Patrick. 1968. "The Ambivalence of Truth: Chaucer's 'Clerkes Tale'." *Bucknell Review* 16:74–90.

Morse, Charlotte. 1985. "The Exemplary Griselda." *Studies in the Age of Chaucer* 7:51–86.

Morse, J. M. 1958. "The Philosophy of the Clerk of Oxenford." *Modern Language Quarterly* 19:3–20.

Murphy, J. J. 1964. "A New Look at Chaucer and the Rhetoricians." *Review of English Studies* NS 15:1–20.

Muscatine, Charles. 1957. *Chaucer and the French Tradition*. Berkeley: University of California Press.

———. 1966. "*The Canterbury Tales*: Style of the Man and Style of the Work." In *Chaucer and Chaucerians*, edited by D. S. Brewer, 88–113. London: Nelson.

Mustanoja, Tauno F. 1968. "Chaucer's Prosody." In *Companion to Chaucer Studies*, edited by Beryl Rowland, 58–84. Toronto: Oxford University Press.

Neuss, Paula. 1981. "Images of Writing and the Book in Chaucer's Poetry." *Review of English Studies* 32 [128]: 385–97.

Neville, Marie. 1951. "The Function of the *Squire's Tale* in the Canterbury Scheme." *Journal of English and Germanic Philology* 50:167–79.

Newhauser, Richard. 1982. "Towards a History of Human Curiosity: A Prolegomenon to its Medieval Phase." *Deutsche Vierteljahrs Schrift für Literaturwissenschaft und Geistesgeschichte* 56:559–75.

———. 1986. "The Love of Money as Deadly Sin and Deadly Disease." In *Zusammenhänge, Einflüsse, Wirkungen, Kongressacten zum Ersten Symposium des Mediävistenverbandes in Tübingen, 1984,* edited by Joerg O. Fichte, Karl Heinz Göller, and Bernhard Schimmelpfennig, 315–26. Berlin and New York: Walter de Gruyter.

Nichols, Robert E., Jr. 1967. "The Pardoner's Ale and Cake." *PMLA* 82:498–504.

Nicholson, R. H. 1988. "Theseus's 'Ordinaunce': Justice and Ceremony in the *Knight's Tale*." *Chaucer Review* 22:192–213.

North, J. D. 1969. "Kalenderes Enlumyned Ben They: Some Astronomical Themes in Chaucer." *Review of English Studies* NS 20:129–54, 257–83, 418–44.

Norton-Smith, John. 1974. *Geoffrey Chaucer.* London: Routledge and Kegan Paul.

O'Keefe, Timothy J. 1973. "Meanings of 'Malyne' in *The Reeve's Tale.*" *American Notes and Queries* 12:5–7.

Olmert, K. Michael. 1967. "*The Canon's Yeoman's Tale:* An Interpretation." *Annuale Mediævale* 8:70–94.

Olson, Claire C. 1941. "Chaucer and the Music of the Fourteenth Century." *Speculum* 16:64–91.

Olson, Glending. 1982. "Chaucer, Dante, and the Structure of Fragment VIII (G) of the *Canterbury Tales.*" *Chaucer Review* 16:222–36.

Olson, Paul. 1961. "The Merchant's Lombard Knight." *Texas Studies in Literature and Language* 3:259–63.

Orme, Nicholas. 1981. "Chaucer and Education." *Chaucer Review* 16:38–59.

Osgerby, J. R. 1959. "Chaucer's Squire's Tale." *Use of English* (London) 11:102–7.

Owen, Charles A., Jr. 1954. "Chaucer's *Canterbury Tales:* Aesthetic Design in Stories of the First Day." *English Studies* 35:49–56.

———. 1956. "The Relationship between the *Physician's Tale* and the *Parson's Tale.*" *Modern Language Notes* 71:84–87.

———. 1968. "The Design of the Canterbury Tales." In *Companion to Chaucer Studies,* edited by Beryl Rowland, 192–207. Toronto: Oxford University Press.

———. 1973. "*The Tale of Melibee.*" *Chaucer Review* 7:267–80.

———. 1977. *Pilgrimage and Storytelling in the Canterbury Tales: The Dialectic of "Ernest" and "Game."* Norman: University of Oklahoma Press.

———. 1982. "The Alternative Reading of *The Canterbury Tales:* Chaucer's Text and the Early Manuscripts." *PMLA* 92:237–50.

Owen, Nancy H. 1967. "The Pardoner's Introduction, Prologue, and Tale: Sermon and *Fabliau.*" *Journal of English and Germanic Philology* 66:541–49.

Palomo, Dolores. 1975. "The Fate of the Wife of Bath's 'Bad Husbands'." *Chaucer Review* 9:303–19.

Parsigian, Elsie K. 1977. "A Note on the Conclusion of *The Pardoner's Tale.*" *Rackham Literary Studies* (University of Michigan) 6:51–54.

Patch, Howard Rollin. 1939. *On Rereading Chaucer.* Cambridge: Harvard University Press.

Patterson, Lee W. 1978. "The 'Parson's Tale' and the Quitting of the 'Canterbury Tales'." *Traditio* 34:331–80.

Payne, Robert O. 1968. "Chaucer and the Art of Rhetoric." In *Companion to Chaucer Studies,* edited by Beryl Rowland, 38–57. Toronto: Oxford University Press.

Pearsall, Derek. 1964. "The Squire as Story-Teller." *University of Toronto Quarterly* 34:82–92.

———. 1985. *The Canterbury Tales.* London: Allen and Unwin.

Pearsall, Robert B. 1952. "Chaucer's 'Panik' (*Clerk's Tale,* 590)." *Modern Language Notes* 67:529–31.

Peavler, James M. 1971. "Chaucer's 'Natural' Astronomy." *Dissertation Abstracts International* 32:3264A–65A. University of Missouri—Columbia.

Peck, Russell A. 1967a. "The Ideas of 'Entente' and Translation in Chaucer's *Second Nun's Tale.*" *Annuale Mediævale* 8:17–37.

———. 1967b. "Sovereignty and the Two Worlds of the *Franklin's Tale.*" *Chaucer Review* 1:253–71.

Penninger, F. Elaine. 1964. "Chaucer's *Knight's Tale* and the Theme of Appearance and Reality in *The Canterbury Tales.*" *South Atlantic Quarterly* 43:398–405.

Peterson, Joyce E. 1970. "The Finished Fragment: A Reassessment of *The Squire's Tale.*" *Chaucer Review* 5:62–74.

Pittock, Malcolm. 1967. "The Merchant's Tale." *Essays in Criticism* (Oxford) 17:26–40.

Pratt, Robert A. 1978. "Albertus Magnus and the Problem of Sound and Odor in the Summoner's Tale." *Philological Quarterly* 57:267–68.

Preston, Raymond. 1952. *Chaucer.* London: Sheed and Ward. Reprint. Greenwood, 1969.

Puhvel, Martin. 1986. "The Wife of Bath's 'Remedies of Love'." *Chaucer Review* 20:307–12.

Ramsey, Roger. 1977. "Clothing Makes a Queen in *The Clerk's Tale.*" *Journal of Narrative Technique* 7:104–15.

Reames, Sherry L. 1980. "The Cecilia Legend as Chaucer Inherited It and Retold It: The Disappearance of an Augustinian Ideal." *Speculum* 55:38–57.

Reidy, John. 1965. "Chaucer's Canon and the Unity of *The Canon's Yeoman's Tale.*" *PMLA* 80:31–37.

Reilly, Cyril A. 1937. "Chaucer's Second Nun's Tale: Tiburce's Visit to Pope Urban." *Modern Language Notes* 69:37–39.

Reiss, Edmund. 1964. "The Final Irony of the *Pardoner's Tale.*" *College English* 25:260–66.

Rex, Richard. 1984. "Chaucer and the Jews." *Modern Language Quarterly* 45:107–22.

———. 1986. "Wild Horses, Justice, and Charity in the Prioress' Tale." *Papers on Language and Literature* 22:339–51.

Rhodes, James F. 1974. "Pilgrimage: Chaucer's Ernest Game." *Dissertation Abstracts International* 35:1669A. Fordham University.

———. 1982. "Motivation in Chaucer's *Pardoner's Tale*: Winner Take Nothing." *Chaucer Review* 17:40–61.

Rhodes, Jewell Parker. 1979. "Female Stereotypes in Medieval Literature: Androgyne and the Wife of Bath." *Journal of Women's Studies in Literature* 1:348–52.

Richardson, Janette. 1961. "Hunter and Prey: Functional Imagery in Chaucer's *Friar's Tale*." *English Miscellany (Rome)* 12:9–20.

———. 1975. "Friar and Summoner, The Art of Balance." *Chaucer Review* 9:227–36.

Roache, Joel. 1965. "Treasure Trove in the *Pardoner's Tale*." *Journal of English and Germanic Philology* 64:1–6.

Robertson, D. W., Jr. 1951. "The Doctrine of Charity in Medieval Literary Gardens: A Topical Approach through Symbolism and Allegory." *Speculum* 26:24–49.

———. 1962. *A Preface to Chaucer*. Princeton: Princeton University Press.

———. 1988. "The Physician's Comic Tale." *Chaucer Review* 23:129–39.

Robinson, F. N. 1957. *The Works of Geoffrey Chaucer*. 2d ed. Boston: Houghton Mifflin.

Robinson, Ian. 1972. *Chaucer and the English Tradition*. Cambridge: Cambridge University Press.

Root, R. K. 1922. *The Poetry of Chaucer*. 2d ed. Boston.

Rosenborg, Bruce A. 1968. "The Contrary Tales of the Second Nun and the Canon's Yeoman." *Chaucer Review* 2:278–91.

———. 1971. "The 'Cherry-Tree Carol' and the *Merchant's Tale*." *Chaucer Review* 5:264–76.

Ross, Woodburn O. 1930. "A Possible Significance of the Name *Thopas*." *Modern Language Notes* 45:172–74.

Rothman, Irving N. 1973. "Humility and Obedience in the *Clerk's Tale*, with the Envoy Considered as an Ironic Affirmation." *Papers on Language and Literature* 9:115–27.

Rowe, Elizabeth Ashman. 1986. "Structure and Pattern in Chaucer's *Knight's Tale*." *Florilegium* 8:169–86.

Rowland, Beryl. 1964. "Aspects of Chaucer's Use of Animals." *Archiv für das Studium der Neueren Sprachen und Literaturen* 201:110–14.

———. 1968. "Chaucer's Imagery." In *Companion to Chaucer Studies*, edited by Beryl Rowland, 103–22. Toronto: Oxford University Press.

———. 1970–71. "The Play of the *Miller's Tale*: A Game Within a Game." *Chaucer Review* 5:140–46.

———. 1971. *Blind Beasts: Chaucer's Animal World*. Kent: Kent State University Press.

———. 1973a. "On the Timely Death of the Wife of Bath's Fourth Husband." *Archiv für das Studium der Neueren Sprachen und Literaturen* 209:273–82.

———. 1973b. "The Physician's 'Historial Thyng Notable' and the Man of Law." *ELH* 40:165–78.

———. 1974. "Chaucer's Blasphemous Churl: A New Interpretation of the *Miller's Tale*. In *Chaucer and Middle English Studies in Honour of Rossell Hope Robbins*, edited by Beryl Rowland, 43–55. London: Allen and Unwin.

———. 1979. "Chaucer's Idea of the Pardoner." *Chaucer Review* 14:140–54.

Rudat, Wolfgang E. H. 1981. "Chaucer's Spring of Comedy: The *Merchant's Tale* and Other 'Games' with Augustinian Theology." *Annual Mediævale* 21:111–20.

Ruggiers, Paul G. 1965. *The Art of the Canterbury Tales*. Madison: University of Wisconsin Press.

Rumble, T. C. 1964. "Chaucer's *Knight's Tale*, 2680–83." *Philological Quarterly* 43:130–33.

Ryan, Lawrence V. 1974. "The Canon's Yeoman's Desperate Confession." *Chaucer Review* 8:297–310.

Salter, Elizabeth. 1962. *Chaucer: The Knight's Tale and The Clerk's Tale*. Woodbury, N.Y.: Barron.

Scattergood, V. J. 1981. "Chaucer and the French War: *Sir Thopas* and *Melibee*." In *Court and Poet*, edited by Glyn S. Burgess, 287–96. Liverpool: Francis Cairns.

Schaefer, Willene. 1967. "The Evolution of a Concept: *Gentilesse* in Chaucer's Poetry." *Dissertation Abstracts* 27:3850A–51A. Louisiana State University.

Schlauch, Margaret. 1937. "Chaucer's *Merchant's Tale* and Courtly Love." *ELH* 4:201–12.

Schleusener, Jay. 1980. "The Conduct of the *Merchant's Tale*." *Chaucer Review* 14:237–50.

Schroeder, Mary C. 1970. "Fantasy in *The Merchant's Tale*." *Criticism*. 12:167–79.

Scott, Kathleen L. 1967. "Sow-and-Bagpipe Imagery in the Miller's Portrait." *Review of English Studies* 18:287–90.

Seaman, David M. 1986. "'The Wordes of the Frankelyen to the Squier': An Interruption?" *English Language Notes* 24:12–18.

Sedgewick, G. G. 1940. "The Progress of Chaucer's Pardoner, 1880–1940." *Modern Language Quarterly* 1:431–58.

———. 1948. "The Structure of *The Merchant's Tale*." *University of Toronto Quarterly* 17:337–45.

Severs, J. Burke. 1954. "Author's Revision in Block C of the *Canterbury Tales*." *Speculum* 29:512–30.

———. 1966. "Appropriateness of Character to Plot in the *Franklin's Tale*." In *Studies in Language and Literature in Honor of Margaret Schlauch*, edited by Mieczyslaw Brahmer, Stanislaw Helsztynski, and Julian Krzyzanowski, 385–96. Warsaw: Panstwowe Wydawnictwo Naukowe.

———. 1974. "Chaucer's Clerks." In *Chaucer and Medieval English Studies in Honour of Rossell Hope Robbins*, edited by Beryl Rowland, 140–52. London: Allen and Unwin.

Sheehan, Michael M. 1985. "The Wife of Bath and Her Four Sisters: Reflections on a Woman's Life in the Age of Chaucer." *Mediævalia et Humanistica* 13:23–42.

Sheps, Walter. 1975. "'Up roos oure Hoost, and was oure aller cok': Harry Bailly's Tale-Telling Competition." *Chaucer Review* 10:113–28.

Sherwood, Miriam. 1947. "Magic and Mechanics in Medieval Fiction." *Studies in Philology* 44:567–92.

Silverman, Albert H. 1953. "Sex and Money in Chaucer's *Shipman's Tale*." *Philological Quarterly* 32:329–36.

Silvia, D. S. 1967. "Geoffrey Chaucer on the Subject of Men, Women, Marriage, and *Gentilesse*." *Revue des Langues Vivantes* (Bruxelles) 33:228–36.

Slaughter, E. E. 1950. "Clerk Jankyn's Motive." *Modern Language Notes* 65:530–34.

Smallwood, T. M. 1985. "Chaucer's Distinctive Digressions." *Studies in Philology* 82:437–49.

Smith, Roland M. 1936. "Two Chaucer Notes." *Modern Language Notes* 51:314–17.

Smyser, Hamilton M. 1970. "A View of Chaucer's Astronomy." *Speculum* 45:359–73.

Southmayd, David Edward. 1981. "Chaucer and the Medieval Conventions of Bird Imagery." *Dissertation Abstracts International* 41:3596A. McGill University.

Spearing, A. C., ed. 1965. *The Pardoner's Prologue and Tale*. Cambridge: Cambridge University Press.

Speirs, John. 1951. *Chaucer the Maker*. London: Faber and Faber.

Spraycar, Rudy S. 1980. "The Prologue to the 'General Prologue': Chaucer's Statement about Nature in the Opening Lines of the *Canterbury Tales*." *Neuphilologische Mitteilungen* 81:142–49.

Steadman, John. 1964. "Old Age and *Contemptus Mundi* in the *Pardoner's Tale*." *Medium Ævum* 33:121–30.

———. 1965. "Chaucer's Pardoner and the *Thesaurus Meritorium*." *English Language Notes* 41:4–7.

Stearns, Marshall W. 1942. "Chaucer Mentions a Book." *Modern Language Notes* 57:28–31.

Steimatsky, Noa. 1987. "The Name of the Corpse: A Reading of *The Pardoner's Tale*." *Hebrew University Studies in Literature and the Arts* 15:36–43.

Steinberg, Aaron. 1964. "The *Wife of Bath's Tale* and Her Fantasy of Fulfillment." *College English* 26:187–91.

Stepsis, Robert. 1975. "*Potentia Absoluta* and the *Clerk's Tale*." *Chaucer Review* 10:129–46.

Stevens, Martin. 1972. "'And Venus Laugheth': An Interpretation of the *Merchant's Tale*." *Chaucer Review* 7:118–31.

———, and Kathleen Falvey. 1982. "Substance, Accident, and Transformations: A Reading of the *Pardoner's Tale*." *Chaucer Review* 17:142–58.

Stewart, George R., Jr. 1929. "The Moral Chaucer." *Essays in Criticism* (University of California Publications in English) 1:89–109.

Stewart, Stanley. 1966. *The Enclosed Garden*. Madison: University of Wisconsin Press.

Stillwell, Gardiner. 1944. "The Political Meaning of Chaucer's *Tale of Melibee*." *Speculum* 19:433–44.

———. 1948. "Chaucer in Tartary." *Review of English Studies* (Original Series) 24:177–88.

———. 1955. "The Language of Love in Chaucer's Miller's and Reeve's Tales and in the Old French Fabliaux." *Journal of English and Germanic Philology* 54:693–99.

Works Cited

Stokoe, William C., Jr. 1952. "Structure and Intention in the First Fragment of the Canterbury Tales." University of Toronto Quarterly 21:120–27.

Strange, William C. 1967. "The Monk's Tale: A Generous View." Chaucer Review 1:167–80.

Strohm, Paul. 1967. "The Allegory of the Tale of Melibee." Chaucer Review 2:32–42.

Stroud, Theodore A. 1981. "Chaucer's Structural Balancing of Troilus and 'Knight's Tale'." Annuale Mediævale 21:31–45.

Sturges, Robert S. 1983. "The Canterbury Tales' Women Narrators: Three Traditions of Female Authority." Modern Language Studies 13:41–51.

Szittya, Penn R. 1975. "The Green Yeoman as Loathly Lady: The Friar's Parody of the Wife of Bath's Tale." PMLA 90:386–94.

Tatlock, J.S.P. 1907. The Development and Chronology of Chaucer's Works. [London:] Chaucer Society.

———. 1913. "Astrology and Magic in Chaucer's Franklin's Tale." In Anniversary Papers by Colleagues and Pupils of George Lyman Kittredge, 339–50. Boston: Ginn.

———. 1936. "Chaucer's Merchant's Tale." Modern Philology 33:367–81.

Taylor, Ann M. 1976. "Epic Descent in the Knight's Tale." Classical Folia 30:40–56.

Taylor, Paul Beekman. 1979. "The Canon's Yeoman's Breath: Emanations of a Metaphor." English Studies 60:380–88.

Toole, William B., III. 1968. "Chaucer's Christian Irony: The Relationship of Character and Action in the Pardoner's Tale." Chaucer Review 3:37–43.

Traversi, Derek. 1983. The Canterbury Tales: A Reading. London: Bodley Head.

Trower, Katherine B. 1978. "Spiritual Sickness in the Physician's and the Pardoner's Tales: Thematic Unity in Fragment VI of the Canterbury Tales." American Benedictine Review 29:67–86.

Turner, Frederick. 1974. "A Structuralist Analysis of the Knight's Tale." Chaucer Review 8:279–96.

Underwood, Dale. 1959. "The First of The Canterbury Tales." ELH 26:455–69.

Ussery, Huling E. 1965. "The Appropriateness of the Physician's Tale to Its Teller." Papers of the Michigan Academy of Science, Arts, and Letters 50:545–56.

———. 1972. Chaucer's Physician: Medicine and Literature in Fourteenth-Century England. Tulane Studies in English 19. New Orleans: Tulane University Press.

Utley, Francis Lee. 1972. "Five Genres in the Clerk's Tale." Chaucer Review 6:198–228.

Van, Thomas A. 1971. "Imprisoning and Ensnarement in Troilus and The Knight's Tale." Papers on Language and Literature 7:3–12.

———. 1988. "Walter at the Stake: A Reading of Chaucer's Clerk's Tale." Chaucer Review 22:214–24.

van Boheemen, Christel. 1979. "Chaucer's Knight's Tale and the Structure of Myth." Dutch Quarterly Review of Anglo-American Letters 9:176–90.

Wasserman, Julian N. 1982. "The Ideal and the Actual: The Philosophical Unity of Canterbury Tales, MS Group III." Allegorica 7:65–99.

Watson, Charles S. 1964. "The Relationship of *The Monk's Tale* and *The Nun's Priest's Tale*." *Studies in Short Fiction* 1:277–88.

Watts, P. R. 1947. "The Strange Case of Geoffrey Chaucer and Cecily Chaumpaigne." *The Law Quarterly Review* 63:491–515.

Wentersdorf, Karl P. 1965. "Theme and Structure in *The Merchant's Tale*: The Function of the Pluto Episode." *PMLA* 80:522–27.

———. 1986. "Imagery, Structure, and Theme in Chaucer's *Merchant's Tale*." *Chaucer and the Craft of Fiction*, edited by Leigh A. Arrathoon, 35–62. Rochester, Mich.: Solaris Press.

West, Michael D. 1967–68. "Dramatic Time, Setting, and Motivation in Chaucer." *Chaucer Review* 2:172–87.

Westlund, Joseph. 1964. "The *Knight's Tale* as an Impetus for Pilgrimage." *Philological Quarterly* 43:526–37.

Wetherbee, Winthrop. 1989. *Geoffrey Chaucer The Canterbury Tales*. Cambridge: Cambridge University Press.

White, Gertrude M. 1974. "*The Franklin's Tale*: Chaucer or the Critics." *PMLA* 89:454–62.

Whittock, Trevor. 1968. *A Reading of the Canterbury Tales*. Cambridge: Cambridge University Press.

Williams, David. 1987. *The Canterbury Tales: A Literary Pilgrimage*. Boston: Twayne.

Woo, Constance, and William Matthews. 1970. "The Spiritual Purpose of the *Canterbury Tales*." *Comitatus* 1:85–109.

Wood, Chauncey, 1966. "Of Time and Tide in the *Franklin's Tale*." *Philological Quarterly* 45:688–711.

———. 1970. *Chaucer and the Country of the Stars: Poetic Uses of Astrological Imagery*. Princeton, N.J.: Princeton University Press.

Wurtele, Douglas J. 1981. "The Blasphemy of Chaucer's Merchant." *Annuale Mediævale* 21:91–110.

———. 1988. "Chaucer's Wife of Bath and the Problem of the Fifth Husband." *Chaucer Review* 23:117–28.

Young, Karl. 1941. "The Maidenly Virtues of Chaucer's Virginia." *Speculum* 16:340–49.

Zacher, Christian. 1976. *Curiosity and Pilgrimage: The Literature of Discovery in Fourteenth-Century England*. Baltimore: Johns Hopkins University Press.

Zimbardo, Rose A. 1966. "Unity and Duality in *The Wife of Bath's Prologue and Tale*." *Tennessee Studies in Literature* 11:11–18.

Index

The main entries of this index list all pertinent persons, tales, and topics in the book. Among these are themes listed individually followed by the fragments and tales in which they appear and the characters and pilgrims to whom they apply. In addition, significant themes of individual tales follow the subentry "themes in" in the specific tale; they are identified parenthetically after the page references. A more comprehensive list of themes in the *Canterbury Tales* as a whole appears under the main entry "Theme." References to extended discussions of structure follow the main entry "Structure," where subentries are arranged by fragment, and, more specifically, in the individual tale under the subentry "structure of." In general, the arrangement of subentries is from larger to smaller entity: references to the *Canterbury Tales* precede those to the fragments; fragments precede the alphabetical listing of specific persons, tales, or topics. The names of pilgrims remain capitalized, as in the text; the names of potentially confusing characters who appear in the tales are lowercase or, when necessary, identified parenthetically by the tale in which they appear. The following abbreviations appear in the index where they are alphabetized according to the expanded form of the reference.

ClkT	The Clerk's Tale	MT	The Miller's Tale
CookT	The Cook's Tale	NPT	The Nun's Priest's Tale
CT	*The Canterbury Tales*	PardT	The Pardoner's Tale
CYP	The Prologue to the Canon's Yeoman's Tale	ParsT	The Parson's Tale
		PhyT	The Physician's Tale
CYT	The Canon's Yeoman's Tale	PriorT	The Prioress' Tale
		RT	The Reeve's Tale
Frag	Fragment	2NP	The Prologue to the Second Nun's Tale
FrankT	The Franklin's Tale		
FrT	The Friar's Tale	2NT	The Second Nun's Tale
GP	The General Prologue	ShipT	The Shipman's Tale
KT	The Knight's Tale	Sir T	Chaucer's Tale of Sir Thopas
LGW	*Legend of Good Women*		
MancP	The Manciple's Prologue	SqT	The Squire's Tale
MancT	The Manciple's Tale	SumT	The Summoner's Tale
Mel	Chaucer's Tale of Melibee	T&C	*Troilus and Creseyde*
MerchT	The Merchant's Tale	WBP	The Prologue to the Wife of Bath's Tale
MLT	The Man of Law's Tale		
MnkT	The Monk's Tale	WBT	The Wife of Bath's Tale

Abbots, 173, 222 n.19
Acquisitiveness: in Fragg III, 120–23; in Frag VI (PhysT-PardT), 53, 68; in ShipT, 163–64. See also Gold
Alison: and genre, 45; portrait of, 132, 154
Almache: compared to the canon, 89
Amor/Amor Dei: in Frag IV (ClkT-MerchT), 33; in Frag V (SqT-FrankT), 104; in Frag VII, 181
Amplificatio: FT as, 212; in PhysT, 64–65 (and cf. CYT, 77); SumT as, 212
Anger: in Frag III, 115–17, 118, 124, 125; of Cook, 143; of Friar, 107; of Harry Bailly, 61; of Pardoner, 62; of Pertelote, 179–80; of Prudence, 179–80; of Reeve, 143; of Summoner, 107; of Theseus, 137; of Wife of Bath, 115
Animals: in Frag I, 154–56, 218 n.24; in FrankT, 99; in FrT, 111; in KT, 139; in MerchT, 29; in NPT, 179; in PhysT, 55; in RT, 153; in 2NT, 81; in Sir T, 174, 179; in SqT, 104. See also Bird(s)
Antimetabole, 186, 220 n.1
Aphrodisiacs, 29, 197 n.5, 203 n.13
Appearance/Reality: in Frag IV (ClkT-MerchT), 34–37, 197 n.13; of magicians at feasts in Frag V (SqT-FrankT), 94–95; in CYT 77, 83; in FrankT, 96, 209 n.8; in SqT, 97, 209 n.8; of wounds, 99. See also Deception; Fraud; Illusion
Array: in Frag IV (ClkT-MerchT), 187; in Frag VIII (2NT-CYT), 82–83, 91; of Canon, 75, 82–83, 90; of Canon's Yeoman, 81, 83; in CYT, 46, 84, 206 n.14; of Clerk, 48; in ClkT, 30, 46–48, 200 n.30; in CookT, 146; in FrankT, 96; in FrT, 121; in MerchT, 26–27, 30, 46–48; in NPT, 178, 179; in 2NT, 46, 75, 82, 206 n.14; in ShipT, 46, 178; in Sir T, 179; in SumT, 122
Ars poetica, 14–15
Arveragus, 95, 188
Assay: of Fortune in Mel, 176; by Merchant, 40; in ShipT, 177; by Walter, 40. See also Test

Astrology: in Frag V (SqT-FrankT), 94–95; in MT, 141–42
Audience: of Chaucer, 43, 57, 143, 144; of CT, 147, 171; of CYT, 71, 86; of Mel, 171; and narrators in Frag III, 113; of NPT, 177–78; of PardT, 53, 59, 62; of PhysT, 64–65; of 2NT, 75, 79, 85–86, 86–87; of WBP, 114; of WBT, 112
Authority/Experience: in Frag I, 137; in Frag III, 212; in Frag IV (ClkT-MerchT) 25, 37–41; and Canon's Yeoman, 76, 80, 205 n.6; in CYT, 75, 205 n.6; in Mel, 180; in MerchT, 25, 189; in NPT, 180; in 2NT, 75; in SqT, 100; and Wife of Bath, 113; in WBT, 114–15
Avarice. See Acquisitiveness; Gold

Bed: in Frag III, 108–9
Beryn, Tale of, 13
Bird(s): Absolon compared to, 152; Arcite compared to, 152, 155; in FrankT, 105; in GP, 129, 181; Harry Bailly as, 155–56; and human nature, 209 n.12; and interpenetration of frame and tale, 155–56; and Jesus, 209 n.12; in KT, 152, 153; and appropriate language, 98; in MT, 154; Monk compared to, 157, 177; music of, 151; and Nun's Priest, 157, 177; in NPT, 163, 179; Pertelote compared to merchant's wife (in ShipT), 162; and Pilgrims, 155–56; and priest (in CYT), 79; in RT, 153, 155; in ShipT, 162, 163; Sir Thopas compared to, 166; and Squire, 155; in SqT, 97, 98, 100, 101–2, 104; and Summoner, 155. See also Animals
Blindness: and alchemy, 80; of Almache, 78–79, 85, 88, 89; in CYT, 73, 79, 89; of Dorigen, 94–95; of January, 27, 29, 32, 42, 44–45; in KT, 154; in 2NT, 73, 85; of summoner, 121; of Walter, 36, 42
Book(s): in Frag III, 108, 212 n.2; of Clerk, 151; in MnkT, 177; in NPT, 178; in 2NT, 82; in WBP, 114, 115, 125, 126
Brotherhood: in CT, 19; in Frag III, 125–27, 213 n.14; in FrT, 122; in GP,

Index

135; in KT, 136; in PardT, 56; in PhysT, 56–57; of Pilgrims, 57; in PriorT, 173; in ShipT, 173. See also Contract

Bruges, 175

Canon (in CYT): compared to Almache, 89; compared to Cecile, 89–90; as teacher, 86

Canon: clothes of, 82–83; compared to Cecile, 89–90; compared to Pardoner, 80; and Pilgrims, 83; compared to Physician, 80

Canon's Yeoman: and Canon, 90; character of, 76, 81, 200; clothes of 83; conversion of, 81; as example to avoid, 76, 79–80, 86, 207 n.19; and Harry Bailly, 62; compared to Pardoner, 53; and Pilgrims, 86, 183; as teacher, 86

Canon's Yeoman's Tale: in Frag VIII, chapter 3, 71–91; Bibliographical Note, 204–5; characters in, 88–91; conversion in, 77–78, 80–82, 91, 206 n.13; explanation of alchemy, 76–77; and FrT, 72; invocation, 74–76; final preaching, 79–80; and 2NT, 27, 184–85; structural diagram, 74; structure of, 73–80, 91, 184–85; and SumT, 72; themes in, 46, 82–83, 91 (clothes), 83–85, 91, 206 n.18 (smell), 85–87 (teachers), 87–89 (secrecy)

Canterbury Tales: character in, 19–20; as collection of fragments, 17; married men in, 188–90; principles of organization in, 13–14, 17, 18–19, 20–21, 193 nn. 1, 2, 3, and 4, 194 n.11; themes in, 19, 195 n.13; unity of, 16–17, 128–29, 193 n.3, 194 n.9

Cecile: array of, 82; compared to Canon, 89–90; compared to canon, 89–90; and genre, 45; compared to Pardoner, 80; compared to Physician, 80; as teacher, 85; test of, 27

Chance. See Fortune

Character(s): in CT, 19–20, 187–90, 195 n.14; distribution of, in Frag I, 130–32; and pagan setting, 208 n.1; parallel in Frag IV (ClkT-MerchT), 41–49; parallel in Frag V (SqT-FrankT), 105–6; parallel in Frag VIII (2NT-CYT), 88–91

Chaucer, Geoffrey: as artist, 14, 17, 18, 20, 50, 101, 138, 143, 182–83, 183–84, 194 n.8; and audience(s), 49, 143, 147, 171; use of birds, 155; Harry Bailly and, 166; historical sense, 93; January and, 41–45; and language, 16, 98, 144, 147, 190, 208 n.4; pacifism of, 166, 221 n.11; as Pilgrim, 117; and remedy for misfortune, 170–71, 222 n.14; and themes in CT, 19, 30–31, 62, 111; Walter and, 41–45; and women, 211 n.21

Chaunticleer: and fox, 90; compared to other married men in CT, 188–89; compared to merchant (in ShipT), 19–20

Chiasmus: antimetabole as, 186, 220 n.1; and structure of Frag V (SqT-FrankT), 100–102; and structure of Frag VII, 160–71, 172, 175

Clerk: and authority/experience, 37–38; character of, 28, 32, 33–34, 35, 37–38, 48–49; compared to Grieselda, 38; Harry Bailly and, 33–34, 62; compared to Merchant, 48–49; and music, 151; and theme of death, 32–33

Clerk's Tale: in Frag IV, chapter 1, 23–49; Bibliographical Note, 196–97; character in, 41–49; councils in, 24–26; feasts in, 27; and FrankT, 207; genre of, 33–34, 35, 39, 41, 42, 198 n.22; and KT, 196; marriage agreement in, 26–27; and PhysT, 200; restoration scenes in, 29–30; and 2NT, 72; structural diagram, 24; structure of, 23–30; tests in, 27–29; themes in, 31–32 (time), 32–34 (death), 34–37 (appearance/reality), 37–41 (authority/experience); and WBT, 196, 211

Clocks: in CT, 162

Clothes, Clothing. See Array

Commons: and array, 47; faith destroyed in Frag VIII (2NT-CYT), 89; fear of death, 35; fickle, 23, 43; January's attitude toward, 25; language of, 173; in MT, 130, 136; in PriorT, 179; in SqT, 96; concern for time, 32; Walter and, 25, 26, 38, 43

Conclusion, Double: in Frag III, 113–15

Confrontation Scene: in Frag VI (PhysT-PardT), 57–58; in 2NT, 85, 90

Conspiracy: in Frag VI (PhysT-PardT), 56–57

Contract (Tretee, Tretys): in Frag I, 148–49; in Frag III, 125–27; in ClkT, 27, 38; with Devil, 212; in FrankT, 209 n.8; in GP, 37; in MerchT, 26. See also Brotherhood

Conversion: in Frag VIII (2NT-CYT), 77–78, 80–82, 87, 88, 91, 187, 206 n.13; alchemical, 86; of Claudius, 64; and clothes, 46; of Pilgrims into birds, 156; by smell, 84

Cook: Harry Bailly and, 135, 138, 148, 165–66

Cook's Tale: in Frag I, chapter 6, 128–50, Bibliographical Note, 214–15; contract in, 149; language of, 145, 217 n.18; lodging in, 146; meat and drink in, 147–48; music in, 153; structural diagram, 131; structure of, 129–45

Council(s): in Frag IV (ClkT-MerchT), 24–26, 34, 41; in KT, 133; in Mel, 167–70; in Sir T, 166, 167, 169

Counselor(s): in ClkT, 25; in CookT, 142; Justinus as, 25, 37, 40; in Mel (surgeons, physicians, false friends and flatterers, lawyers, young folk, the old wise, and Prudence), 166, 167–70; Placebo as, 25, 37, 40; in Sir T, 166; women as, 176–77, 179–80, 180, 188–89, 221 n.13

Crucifixion: in PardT, 54, 58–59, 69–70; in PhysT, 58–59; in NPT, 181

Custance: and genre, 45

Dance: in Frag V (SqT-FrankT), 93–94, 98; in KT, 152; in PardT, 53; in PhysT, 53, 67, 93; in RT, 153; and WB, 93; in WBT, 127

Dante, 73, 113

Damian: as courtly lover, 189; at marriage feast, 27; lust of, 23; May and, 28–29, 30; sexual climax of, 197 n.8; sickness of, 34, 36, 44

Death: in Frag IV (ClkT-MerchT), 25, 30, 32–34; in Frag VII, 177; in FrankT, 98, 101, 102, 104; and gold, 58, 201 n.3; of Jews, 168; by knives, 69; in KT, 138, 140; and language, 98–99; in MnkT, 164–65, 165; in NPT, 178; attitude of Pardoner to, 50–51; in PardT, 50, 54–55, 55–56, 57, 58–59, 69, 201 n.3, 202 n.7, 203 n.19; attitude of Physician to, 50–51; in PhysT, 50, 54–55, 55, 57, 58, 58–59, 190; in PriorT, 164–65, 178; in 2NT, 78, 79; and time, 33–34; and tragedy, 221 n.8; women threatened with, 99. See also Tree

Debate. See Discussion

Decay: in Frag I, 129–45 (as principle of unity), 132–35 (of beloved, quality of love, and marriage), 135–37 (of adversaries), 137–38 (of older generation), 139–43 (of order), 142–43 (of earnest and game), 143–45 (of language), 146 (of lodging), 149–50, 153–54 (and music), 185–86, 214–15, 216 n.4 (of women); in Frag III, 212; inverted in Frag V (SqT-FrankT), 101; in CYT, 80; in GP, 132; of Harry Bailly, 138; of Pilgrims, 135, 156; in 2NT, 80; in Sir T, 174–75

Deception: in Frag I, 130, 141; in Frag III, 107; in CYT, 73, 78, 89; in CookT, 140, 141; and dance, 93; in FrT, 127; in KT, 138, 141; in Mel, 176–77; in MT, 136, 137, 141; in NPT, 163, 177; in RT, 137, 141; in ShipT, 163; in SumT, 127; and women, 127. See also Appearance/Reality; Fraud; Illusion

Degeneration, as organizing principle. See Decay

Deterioration, as organizing principle. See Decay

Devil: in Frag VI (PhysT-PardT), 56; in CYT, 73, 77, 84; in FT, 90, 107–8, 109, 111, 113, 116–17, 119, 120, 121, 122, 123–24; and magicians, 208 n.3; in MT, 56, 89; in PardT, 53–54, 56; in PhysT, 56, 64; in PriorT,

56, 89, 164; in 2NT, 73, 75, 85–86; in SumT, 109; and troth, 125–26; in WBT, 109

Dice: in CookT, 140; in PardT, 53, 59

Discussion (Debate): in Frag III, 212; in Frag VI (PhysT-PardT), 58; in Frag VIII (2NT-CYT), 78; in Mel, 169; in MT, 140; in NPT, 170, 178; in WBP, 116; in WBT, 108

Dorigen: character of, 93–94, 95; compared to falcon, 105; deceived by Nature, 104; and God, 96, 104; test of, 27

Dryden, John, 14, 182, 188, 190

Earnest and Game: in CT, 217 n.14; in Frag I, 143, 148, 215; Canon's Yeoman and, 86; in CYT, 75; Chaucer and, 143; in ClkT, 31, 33; in FrankT, 97, 102; in GP, 129–30, 132; gentils and, 62; Harry Bailly and, 143, 156; Harry Bailly and Pardoner, 60–62, 65–66, 202 n.12; Harry Bailly and Physician, 60–62; in KT, 142; in MerchT, 33; in MT, 142–43, 143; Pardoner and, 61; in PardT, 65; in RT, 143; in 2 NT, 75

Eucharist, 68, 201 n.4, 202 n.7

Experience. *See* Authority/Experience

Feast: in ClkT, 27, 31; in FrankT, 27, 101; in KT, 27, 152; and magicians, 94–95; in MerchT, 27, 28, 30; in MLT, 27; in PhysT, 53; in ShipT, 172–73, 178; in SqT, 96, 101, 103, 105. *See also* Food

Food: in Frag I, 143, 147–48, 218 n.21; in NPT, 161; Pardoner and, 202 n.7; in PardT, 53, 54, 56, 68–69; in RT, 142; in ShipT, 161; in SumT, 114, 119, 120. *See also* Feast

Fortune: in CT, 19; in Frag I, 139–40; in Frag VII, 164–65, 170–71; in GP, 129–30, 135; in KT, 137, 138, 216 n.9; in Mel, 176, 176–77; in MnkT, 169–70, 177; in NPT, 163–64, 170, 177; in PardT, 50; in RT, 133; in ShipT, 163–64

Frame and Tale (the interpenetration of frame and tale): in CT, 31, 145, 188; in Frag I, 135–36, 143, 144, 145–47, 149–50, 151 (music), 153; in Frag III, 109, 111, 113–15, 115, 118, 124, 213 n.10; in Frag IV (ClkT-MerchT), 31, 32, 49; in Frag VI (PhysT-PardT), 56, 57, 59; in Frag VII, 177; and birds, 155–56; in FrankT, 105; in Mel, 171

Franklin, 97, 150

Franklin's Tale: in Frag V, chapter 4, 92–106; Bibliographical Note, 207–8; characters in, 95, 105–6; and ClkT, 207; genre of, 208, 208 n.1; and KT, 207, 214; and Mel, 208; and MerchT, 196, 207; and NPT, 208; and PardT, 208; and PhysT, 194 n.12, 200, 208; and PriorT, 208; and Sir T, 208; and SqT, 95–96; structural diagram, 101–2; structure of, 101–6; themes in, 31 (marriage), 94–95 (astrology), 95–96 (marvel/magic), 96–97 (illusion), 97–98, 209 n.9 (troth), 98–99 (death and wounds), 99–100, 210 n.14 (gentillesse), 191–92 (time); and WBT 207, 211

Fraud: in Frag VIII (2NT-CYT), 82–83, 83, 90, 187; in Frag V (SqT-FrankT), 92, 95–96; and governors, 67; Harry Bailly and, 65; Pardoner and, 52, 59, 65–66; in PardT, 60–62, 65; in PhysT, 52, 63–65. *See also* Appearance/Reality; Deception; Illusion

Friar, 113–14, 151, 213 n.10

Friar's Tale: in Frag III, chapter 5, 107–27; Bibliographical Note, 211–12; and CYT, 72; double conclusion of, 113–15; end of anger in, 115–17; genre of, 112–13, 211, 212, 213 n.6; interruptions in, 111–12; and PardT, 211; and RT, 211; and ShipT, 211; structural diagram, 110; structure of, 109–18, 185; themes in, 118–19 (wandering), 120–23 (acquisitiveness), 123–25 (mastery-control), 125–27 (contract)

Game. *See* Earnest and Game

Gamelin, Tale of, 13

Garden: in Frag III, 118; in FrankT, 84, 96, 97, 100; in KT, 84, 152, 161; in

MerchT, 28, 30, 37, 43, 44–45, 47, 84; in NPT, 161, 220 n.2; in ShipT, 84, 161; in SqT, 84, 102–3

Gaudi, Antoni, 186

General Prologue: in Frag I, chapter 6, 128–56; Bibliographical Note, 214–15; as introduction, 128–29; Pilgrims in, 135; structure, 129–45; themes in, 145, 147 (lodging), 147–48 (meat and drink), 148 (contract), 150 (weapons), 151 (music), 155 (animal imagery)

Genre: and portrayal of women, 45

Gentillesse: in Frag V (SqT-FrankT), 99–100, 106, 187, 200 n.14, 210 n.14; in ClkT, 196; in KT, 134; in MerchT, 196; in WBT, 108, 196

Gentil(s): in Frag VI (PhysT-PardT), 18, 62; in Chaucer's audience, 147; in ClkT, 38; Franklin's son and, 99; Friar addresses, 114; in KT, 136; birds in SqT as, 100; in WBT, 116, 122

God: in CYT, 73, 75, 80; ClkT, 35, 39, 43; in FrankT, 93, 94, 96, 104; in GP, 129, 130; Harry Bailly and, 61, 172; and KT, 93, 134, 136, 139, 140, 141–42, 152; in Mel, 60, 169, 171; in MT, 149; in MnkT, 165; in PardT, 69; in PhysT, 52–53, 54, 57, 60, 64, 66, 67, 93; Pilgrims and, 39; in PriorT, 164–65, 174, 178; as remedy for misfortune, 164, 167, 176; in 2NT, 73, 75, 78, 80, 84; in Sir T, 174; in WBT, 115, 116

Gold (Money, Treasure, Silver, Property, Wealth): acquisitiveness in Frag III, 120–23; in Frag VIII (2NT-CYT), 80–81; Canon and, 75, 81, 205 n.5; in CYT, 72–73, 76, 78, 79, 80, 83, 84, 86, 88, 90, 206 n.13; Clerk and, 49; in CookT, 133, 154; and death, 201 n.3; in FrankT, 97; in FrT, 112, 113, 116, 121; in MT, 137; Merchant and, 48–49; in MerchT, 26–27; Pardoner and, 50; in PardT, 50, 54, 58, 68, 203 n.18; Physician and, 50; in Prior T, 172; in RT, 134–35; in 2NT, 72–73, 82; in ShipT, 163–64, 168, 172, 188; in SumT, 113, 117, 121–22, 122, 124. See also Acquisitiveness

Goodelief, 176, 223 n.27

Governance: in Frag VI (PhysT-PardT), 54–55, 66–70; in ClkT, 38, 39, 43; in CookT, 137–38; in FrankT, 97–98, 101, 105; of Friar by Summoner, 124; Harry Bailly and, 37, 115, 135, 138, 148; in KT, 138, 140, 154, 188; in Mel, 170, 180; in MnkT, 169–70; in NPT, 178; in PardT, 69; in PhysT, 52–53, 55, 60, 63, 64, 69; in PriorT, 165; in ShipT, 163; in SqT, 96, 101, 105; of Summoner by Friar, 124; WB and, 111 (by Friar), 115, 119, 120, 122, 124–25; in WBT, 115, 120–21, 126, 127. See also Mastery/Control

Greed. See Acquisitiveness; Gold

Griselda: and appearance/reality, 36; attitude of commons to, 26; audience response to, 49; compared to Emily, 46; compared to May, 29, 45–48, 199 n.29; compared to January, 44–45; and God, 32, 39; as January's ideal, 25, 28; and obedience, 23; restoration of, 30, 32, 46–47; test of, 28; triumph over time, 32

Harry Bailly: and appearance/reality, 35, 198 n.14; and authority/experience, 37, 138 (deterioration of authority); as bird, 155–56; compared to other married men in CT, 188–89; Canon's Yeoman and, 62, 87; Chaucer and, 166; Clerk and, 31, 33, 35, 37–38, 62, 157; Cook and, 135, 138, 148, 165–66; and earnest and game, 18, 65–66, 129–30, 132, 143, 156, 219; Friar and, 112; Franklin and, 97, 99; and fraud, 65; Goodelief and, 176, 223 n.27; and governance, 135, 138, 148; language of, 61, 172; in MLT, 162; and Mel, 157; Miller and, 135, 138, 149; Merchant and, 39; Monk and, 62, 157, 165–66, 177; Nun's Priest and, 62, 157; Pardoner and, 60–62; Physician and, 60–62; Prioress and, 172; Reeve and, 138; Shipman and, 172; in Sir T, 112, 117; Summoner and, 112; and women, 176–77

Haste: of Canon, 74, 83; in ClkT, 32; of January, 28, 32; in PardT, 56; in

PhysT, 65; in PriorT, 173; in ShipT, 173; in Sir T, 179

Illusion: in Frag V (SqT-FrankT), 96–97, 99, 100, 106. See also Appearance/Reality; Deception; Fraud

Impulse for Action: in Frag VI (PhysT-PardT), 55–56

Incarnation, 181; in 2NT, 75, 82

Interpretation and Explanation: in Frag VIII (2NT-CYT), 76–77

Interruption(s): in Frag III, 54, 111–12, 123, 124, 212 n.5; in Frag VI (PhysT-PardT), 54–55, 62, 212 n.5; by devil in FrT, 116; in MancP, 117; in Mel, 170 (of counselor by young folk); of Miller by Reeve, 117–18; of Monk by Harry Bailly, 157; of Monk by Knight, 117, 157; of Sir T by Harry Bailly, 117; of SqT by Franklin, 117

Introductory Material: in Frag III, 111; GP as, 128–29

Invocation: in CYT, 74–76; in 2NT, 74–76

Janicula, 26, 38, 190

January: audience response to, 42–45, 49; and commons, 25; compared to Griselda, 34, 44–45; compared to Walter, 19, 25–30, 41–45; compared to Wife of Bath, 40; in council, 24–26, 28, 42; and marriage, 23, 24, 28–29, 30, 197 n.1; May and, 28–29; patience of, 44–45, 46; restoration of, 44–45; sexual consummation of, 29, 197 n.6; sickness of, 34; and time, 32; and women, 40. See also Aphrodisiacs; Blindness; Justinus; Placebo

Jerusalem, 118, 139, 165

Jews: in Mel, 168, 221 n.12; in MnkT, 165; in PriorT, 56, 178, 179, 221 n.9, 222 n.17; in Sir T, 175

Justinus: and appearance/reality, 37; as counselor, 25, 37, 40; January and, 26, 29, 42, 46, 198; and women, 40

Knight, 62, 150, 157

Knight's Tale: in Frag I, chapter 6, 128–56; Bibliographical Note, 214–15; animal imagery in, 154; and ClkT, 196; and FrankT, 207, 214; genre of, 144; language of, 144, 217 n.17; lovers in, 188, 189; marriage feast in, 27; and MerchT, 214; and MT, 180; and SqT, 207, 214; structural diagram, 131; structure, 129–45; themes in, 145–46 (lodging), 147–48 (meat and drink), 149 (contract), 149–50 (weapons), 151–52 (music); and T&C, 214

Language: in Frag I, 143–45 (decay), 154–56 (animal imagery), 215; in Frag III, 112 (interruptions); in Frag V (SqT-FrankT), 98–99; in Frag VI (PhysT-PardT), 55–56, 57; alchemical, 80, 91, 207 n.22; of Canon, 74; of Chaucer, 14, 16, 147, 190; of Clerk, 48–49; in ClkT, 38; in CookT, 145, 217 n.18; in FrankT, 94, 98, 98–99; in FrT, 121; of Harry Bailly, 31, 35, 61; in KT, 144, 154, 217 n.17; legal, 201 n.4, 218 n.22; in MT, 136, 144, 217 n.17; nature of, 15–16; in NPT, 179; of Pardoner, 52; in PardT, 201 n.4; in PhysT, 63, 64–65, 201 n.4; in RT, 133, 138, 144–45; scientific, 208 n.4; in 2NT, 75; in ShipT, 164, 173–74; in Sir T, 166; in SqT, 98

Lodging: in Frag I, 145–47, 217 n.19; in RT, 142; in ShipT, 145; in SqT, 145

Magic/Marvel: in Frag III, 108; in Frag V (SqT-FrankT), 94, 95–96; in CYT, 73; in 2NT, 73; in WBT, 116, 211–12. See also Appearance/Reality; Illusion; Miracle

Malyne, 45

Manciple, 149

Manciple's Tale, 13, 21, 31; and MerchT, 196; and ParsT, 195 n.15

Man of Law, 148–49, 221 n.11

Man of Law's Tale, 13, 21, 190; and Frag I, 215 n.3; and PhysT, 200; and 2NT, 72; themes in, 27 (feast, test), 118 (wandering)

Marriage Agreement: in ClkT, 26–27, 40, 43; decay of, in Frag I, 143; in FrankT, 26, 96–97, 102; and gold,

134–35; in KT, 133; in MerchT, 26–27, 44, 47; in ShipT, 220n.6; in WBT, 26, 116, 126

Mary: compared to Canon, 74–75; as *hortus conclusus*, 37; in PriorT, 164–65, 172–74, 174–75, 221n.12, 222n.17; in 2NT, 71, 75, 86–87, 172; in Sir T, 174

Mass, 172–73

Mastery/Control: in Frag III, 123–25. See also Governance

May: audience response to, 44; compared to Emily, 46; compared to Griselda, 23, 29, 45–48, 199n.29; test of, 29

Meat and Drink: in Frag I, 147–48. See also Feast; Food

Melibee, 60, 166, 188–89

Melibee, Chaucer's Tale of: in Frag VII, chapter 7, 157–81; Bibliographical Note, 219; central to Frag VII, 158–59; council in 167–70; form of, 160; Fortune in, 176; and FrankT, 208; genre of, 166; historical parallels to, 221n.13, 222n.15; Man of Law as narrator of, 211n.11; and MnkT, 169–70, 176–77; and NPT, 170; and PardT, 180; and PriorT, 167, 168; recapitulates Frag VII, 180, 223n.29; remedy for misfortune, 171; and ShipT, 167–68; and Sir T, 165–71, 175–76; and SumT, 180

Merchant (ShipT): compared to Chaunticleer, 19–20; compared to other married men in CT, 188

Merchant: character of, 36, 48, 49; compared to Clerk, 48–49; compared to other married men in CT, 188; compared to Walter, 39–40; Harry Bailly and, 39; and women, 28, 39–40

Merchant's Tale: in Frag IV, chapter 1, 23–49; Bibliographical Note, 196–97; characters in, 41–49; and ClkT, 196; councils in, 24–26; and FrankT, 196, 207; genre of, 41, 42, 43–44, 198n.22; and KT, 214; and MancT, 196; marriage agreement in, 26–27; and MT, 196; and ParsT, 196; and RT, 196; restoration scene in, 29–30; and ShipT, 220n.7; and SqT, 207; structural diagram, 24; structure of, 23–30; tests in, 27–29; themes in, 31–32 (time), 32–34 (death), 34–37 (appearance/reality), 37–41 (authority/experience); and WBT, 196, 211

Miller: breaks contract, 149; Harry Bailly and, 135, 138, 149; and music, 151; Reeve and, 135; weapons of, 150

Miller's Tale: in Frag I, chapter 6, 128–56; Bibliographical Note, 214–15; animal imagery in, 154; courtly love in, 189; earnest and game in, 143; genre of, 130; and KT, 180; language of, 144, 217n.17; and MerchT, 196; structural diagram, 131; structure of, 129–45; themes in, 146 (lodging), 147–48 (meat and drink), 149 (contract), 150 (weapons), 152–53 (music)

Miracle: in FrankT, 96–97; in PriorT, 165, 173, 175; in 2NT, 78, 89. See also Appearance/Reality; Illusion; Magic/Marvel

Money. See Gold

Monk (ShipT): compared to other lovers in CT, 189

Monk: as bird, 177; compared to Sir Thopas, 177; Harry Bailly and, 62, 165–66, 177; and law, 148; and music, 151

Monk's Tale: in Frag VII, chapter 7, 157–81; Bibliographical Note, 219; Fortune in 177; interrupted, 112; and Mel, 169–70, 176–77; and NPT, 177–80; poetic form, 160; and PriorT, 164–65; 177; recapitulates Frag VII, 176–77; and ShipT, 177

Music: in CT, 195n.13; in Frag I, 151–54, 218n.23; in GP, 129; in Mel, 170; in MT, 128; in NPT, 162, 178; in PardT, 53; in PriorT, 164–65, 178, 222n.21; in ShipT, 162; in Sir T, 222n.21

Mutability: in Frag IV (ClkT-MerchT), 23

Narrator(s): of Frag VI (PhysT-PardT), 49, 60–62; of Frag VIII (2NT-CYT), 49; Canon's Yeoman as, 75, 76, 79, 83, 86, 205n.8; of CYT, 87; character of, in CT, 195n.14; Chaucer as, 72,

Index

144, 166, 175–76, 223 n.22; in ClkT, 24; Franklin as, 94, 98, 106, 208, 209 n.10; of FrankT, 92; Friar as, 113, 118, 124, 211; of GP, 144; Merchant as, 198 n.14; of MerchT, 24; Pardoner as, 67; Second Nun as, 75, 79, 85–86; of 2NT, 71, 87; Shipman as, 158; of ShipT, 157; Squire as, 98, 100, 106, 208, 209 nn. 7 and 10, 210 n.20; Summoner as, 113, 118, 124, 211; Wife of Bath as, 107, 112, 113

Nature: compared to Pardoner, 52–53; in FrankT, 95, 104; in GP, 129; in PhysT, 50, 52–53, 57, 63, 64, 66; in SqT, 101

Nun's Priest: as bird, 177; and Harry Bailly, 62

Nun's Priest's Tale: in Frag VII, chapter 7, 157–81; Bibliographical Note, 219; deception in, 177; Fortune in, 177; and FrankT, 208; genre of, 179; and Mel, 170, 178–79; and MnkT, 177–80; and PardT, 200–201; and PriorT, 178–79; recapitulates Frag VII, 177–78, 223 n.25; and ShipT, 160–64, 220 n.2; and Sir T, 178–79

Old Man (PardT): identity of, 90, 202 n.8; and Pardoner, 202 n.8; and Three Rioters, 69; and Virginia, 69; and Virginius, 57–58

Old Man (2NT): clothes compared to those of Canon, 82; identity of, 205 n.9; as teacher, 78, 85

Page: as motif in Frag I, 218 n.20
Pardon, 59–60 (PhysT, PardT, Mel)
Pardoner: character of, 50, 52, 53, 65–66, 67–68, 202 n.12; compared to Canon, 80; compared to Canon's Yeoman, 53; compared to Cecile, 80; compared to Nature, 52–53; compared to Old Man (PardT), 202 n.8; compared to Virginia, 202 n.6; and music, 151; and Pilgrims, 59, 60–62, 65; and Wife of Bath, 53, 112; and women, 68
Pardoner's Tale: in Frag VI, chapter 2, 50–69; Bibliographical Note, 200–201; confrontation scene in, 57–58; conspiracy in, 56–57; death in, 58–59, 69; and FrankT, 208; and FrT, 211; genre of, 113; impulse for action in, 55–56; interruptions in, 54–55; locus of, 118; and Mel, 180; and NPT, 200–201; pardon in, 59–60; portraits in, 53–54; and 2NT, 201; structural diagram, 51–52; structure of, 18, 51–62; and SumT, 211; themes in, 63–66 (fraud), 66–70 (governance); and WBT, 200

Parson: and law, 149; and music, 151
Parson's Tale, 13, 21; and Frag VI, 201; and MancT, 195 n.15; and MerchT, 196; and PhysT, 200; as sermon, 158
People. See Commons
Petrarch, 32–33, 37
Phebus: in SqT, 93, 94, 103–4 (in March and December compared)
Physical: in Frag I, 132–35, 139, 148, 151; in Frag VI (PhysT-PardT), 50; in Frag VII, 172–74, 181; in Frag VIII (2NT-CYT), 85, 91; in CYT, 73, 75, 77–78, 79, 80–82; in FrankT, 99; in FrT, 123–24; in GP, 129, 143; in MerchT, 25, 28–29, 33, 48; in MT, 154; Pardoner and, 68; in ShipT, 167; in SqT, 101; in SumT, 121–22; and portrayal of women, 45–46

Physician: character of, 50; compared to Canon, 80; compared to Cecile, 80

Physician's Tale: in Frag VI, chapter 2, 50–69; Bibliographical Note, 200–201; and ClkT, 200; confrontation scene in, 57–58; conspiracy in, 56–57; death in, 58–59, 190; and FrankT, 194 n.12, 200, 208; genre of, 200; impulse for action in, 55–56; interruptions in, 54–55; and MLT, 200; and ParsT, 200; pardon in, 59–60; portraits in, 53–54; and PriorT, 200; and 2NT, 200; structural diagram, 51–52; structure of, 18, 51–62; themes in, 63–66 (fraud), 66–70 (governance)

Pilgrims: in CT, 60, 145, 181, 182; in Frag III, 109 (penetrate characters); as adversaries, 135, 216 n.7; and audience, 112, 147; as birds, 155–56; Canon and, 74, 81, 83, 87; Canon's Yeoman and, 86; Friar and, 113–14; in NPT, 178

Placebo: appearance/reality and, 37; authority/experience and, 40; as counselor, 25, 26, 37, 40; January and, 28, 42
Plowman, 149
Pluto and Proserpyna, 24, 29, 32, 37, 40–41, 198 n.17
Portraits: in Frag VI (PhysT-PardT), 53–54, 55; of Alison, 132, 154; of Aurelius, 105; of Cambyuskan, 92; of Canon's Yeoman, 76; of Cecile, 76; of Emily, 132; of Friar, 111; of friar, 111; as introductory material, 111; of Jews, 165; in KT, 144, 150; of Merchant, 49; of Pilgrims, 129, 132; of Prioress, 222 n.18; of Squire, 105; of Summoner, 111, 114; of summoner, 111; of Theseus, 137, 216 n.8; of Three Rioters, 54; of Virginia, 55, 65; of Wife of Bath, 111, 115, 118–19
Preacher(s): in Frag III, 113–15; Cecile as, 78–79, 81; friar as, 108, 119; Pardoner as, 50, 52, 54–55, 59, 68; Reeve as, 138; in WBP, 119; in WBT, 108. *See also* Preaching; Sermon; Teacher(s)
Preaching: in CYT, 79–80; Clerk and, 33–34; in Mel, 170; in 2NT, 79–80. *See also* Preacher(s); Sermon; Teacher(s)
Priest (CYT): compared to Valerian, 88–89
Prioress: and music, 151; portrait of, 222 n.18
Prioress' Tale: in Frag VII, chapter 7, 157–81; Bibliographical Note, 219; and FrankT, 208; genre of, 222 nn. 17 and 21; haste in, 173; and Mel, 167, 168; money in, 172; and MnkT, 164–65, 177; and PhysT, 200; poetic form, 160; and ShipT, 172–74, 222 n.17; and Sir T, 174–75, 222 n.20
Privitee. *See* Secrecy
Procession: in Frag I, 139; in Frag IV (ClkT-MerchT), 24, 29; in FrT, 121; in KT, 151–52; in PardT, 55; in RT, 153; in WBP, 119
Property. *See* Gold
Proserpyna. *See* Pluto and Proserpyna

Redemption: in FrankT, 104
Reeve: Harry Bailly and, 138; Miller and, 135; weapons of, 150
Reeve's Tale, in Frag I, chapter 6, 128–56; Bibliographical Note, 214–15; animal imagery in, 154–55; earnest and game in, 143; and FrT, 211; language of, 144–45; lovers in, 189; and MerchT, 196; structural diagram, 131; structure of, 129–45; and SumT, 211; Symkyn compared to other married men in CT, 188; themes in, 146 (lodging), 147–48 (meat and drink), 149 (contract), 150–51 (weapons), 153 (music)
Remedy to Misfortune: in Frag VII, 159, 180; in Mel, 164, 166–67, 167, 169, 170, 175–76, 176; in MnkT, 164, 176; in NPT, 163–64; in PriorT, 164, 165; in ShipT, 163–64; in Sir T, 164, 166–67, 175
Restoration: scene in ClkT, 29–30; scene in FrankT, 29; of Griselda, 32, 39, 43, 46–47; of January, 44–45; scene in MLT, 29; scene in MerchT, 29–30; of Walter, 43
Resurrection: in PardT, 202 n.9; in NPT, 224 n.30
Riddle: in Frag III, 107, 123; in KT, 134; in SumT, 114, 122, 124, 125; in WBT, 113, 119, 120

Second Nun: as teacher, 85, 86
Second Nun's Tale: in Frag VIII, chapter 3, 71–91; Bibliographical Note, 204–5; and Frag I, 215 n.3; and CYT, 27, 184–85; characters in, 88–91; and ClkT, 72; feast in, 27; genre of, 75, 206 n.11; interpretation of St. Cecile, 76–77; invocation in, 74–76; and MLT, 72; and PardT, 201; and PhysT, 200; final preaching in, 79–80; structural diagram, 74; structure of, 73–80, 91, 184–85; themes in, 46, 82–83, 91 (array), 77–78, 80–82, 91, 206 n.13 (conversion), 87–88 (secrecy), 83–85, 91, 206 n.18 (smell), 85–87 (teachers); Valerian compared to other young married men in CT, 188; and WBT, 72

Index

Secrecy (Privitee, Secrets): in Frag I, 217n.13; in Frag VII, 174; in Frag VIII (2NT-CYT), 75, 87–88, 187; in CYT, 76, 79, 81, 86; in FrT, 123; in husbands, 162; in KT, 141; in MT, 141–42, 148; in PriorT, 173; in RT, 142; in 2NT, 90; in ShipT, 173; in WBP, 126–27

Secrets. See Secrecy

Senex Amans: January as, 42, 44–45, 189; John as, 189

Sermon: in NPT, 170; of Pardoner, 54, 68; ParsT as, 158; in SumT, 117, 213n.6. See also Preacher(s); Preaching; Teacher(s)

Shipman: weapons of, 150

Shipman's Tale: in Frag VII, chapter 7, 157–81; Bibliographical Note, 219; and Frag I, 215n.3; and FrT, 211; genre of, 168, 220n.7; haste in, 173; and MerchT, 220n.7; money in, 172; monk in, compared to other lovers in CT, 189; and MnkT, 177; and NPT, 160–64, 220n.2; and PriorT, 172–74, 222n.17; and Sir T, 175; and SumT, 211; WB as narrator of, 107, 157

Sickness: of Damian, 34, 36, 44; and diet, 162, 220n.4; in FrT, 109; of January, 34; in ShipT, 163; in SumT, 108–9, 117, 124; of Virginia, 63; as concern of women, 162

Sight: in Frag VIII (2NT-CYT), 73, 88–89, 90; in FrankT, 88, 95, 96; in KT, 134; in MerchT, 34; in PardT, 68; as impetus for action in PhysT, 55, 64; in 2NT, 77, 88

Sir Thopas: character of, 166, 167; compared to bird, 166; compared to other courtly lovers in CT, 189

Sir Thopas, Chaucer's Tale of: in Frag VII, chapter 7, 157–81; Bibliographical Note, 219; council in, 169; poetic form, 160; genre of, 113, 166, 179, 222n.21; haste in, 179; and FrankT, 208; and Mel, 165–71, 175–76; and PriorT, 174–75, 222n.20; and ShipT, 175; wandering in, 118

Sisterhood: in Frag III, 125–27

Smell: in Frag I, 84; in Frag VIII (2NT-CYT), 83–85, 91, 187, 206n.18; in MancP, 83–84; in MT, 84, 206n.17; in 2NT, 81; in SumT, 108

Solomon, 31, 40, 124, 146

Soul: in Frag I, 139, 151; in Frag VIII (2NT-CYT), 87; in FrT, 116; in Mel, 171; in PardT, 68, 201n.3; PhysT, 50, 201n.3; in PriorT, 173; in 2NT, 74, 75, 79; in SumT, 108, 124

Sovereignty. See Governance

Spiritual: in Frag I, 132–35, 139, 148, 151; in Frag VI (PhysT-PardT), 50; in Frag VII, 172–74, 181; in Frag VIII (2NT-CYT), 85, 91; in CYT, 82; in ClkT, 25, 28, 33, 48; in FrankT, 101; in GP, 129, 143, 155; Pardoner and, 68; in 2NT, 73, 75, 77–78, 79, 80–82; in SumT, 121–22; and portrayal of women, 45

Spiritual Vision. See Sight

Squire: compared to Virginia, 202n.5; and music, 151; weapons of, 150

Squire's Tale: in Frag V, chapter 4, 92–106; Bibliographical Note, 207–8; characters compared to those in Frank T, 95–96; parallel characters in, 105–6; response of characters in, 95; genre of, 208, 211; interrupted by Franklin, 112; and KT, 207, 214; and MerchT, 207; structural diagram, 101–2; structure of, 101–6; tercelet compared to other unmarried lovers in CT, 189; themes in, 94–95 (astrology, marvel/magic), 96–97 (illusion), 97–98, 209n.9 (troth), 98–99 (death and wounds), 99–100, 210n.14 (gentillesse); time in, 191–92; and WBT, 207

Structure: of CT, 14, 17–19, 184–87; of Frag I, 18–19, 129–45, 185–86; of Frag III, 109–18, 185; of Frag IV (ClkT-MerchT), 23–30; of Frag V (SqT-FrankT), 101–6; of Frag VI (PhysT-PardT), 18–19, 51–62; of Frag VII, chiasmic order, 160–71, 186; of Frag VII, sequential order, 172–80, 186, 222n.16, 223n.22; of Frag VIII (2NT-CYT), 73–80, 91, 184–85; grammatical and aesthetic, 15–16

Summoner: character of, 114, 148–49; and music, 151 (cf. 153)

Summoner's Tale: in Frag III, chapter 5, 107–27; Bibliographical Note, 211–12; end of anger in, 115–17; and CYT, 72; double conclusion of, 113–15; genre of, 112, 112–13, 211, 212, 213 n.6; interruptions in, 111–12; introductory material in, 111; and Mel, 180; and PardT, 211; and RT, 211; and ShipT, 211; structural diagram, 110; structure of, 109–18, 185; themes in, 118–19 (wandering), 120–23 (acquisitiveness), 123–25 (mastery/control), 125–27 (contract)

Teacher(s): in Frag III, 113–15; in Frag VIII (2NT-CYT), 85–87; Clerk as, 33–34; in FrT, 113; in Mel, 171; in MnkT, 177; in NPT, 177; in 2NT, 78; Wife of Bath as, 114; as WBT, 114. See also Preacher(s); Preaching; Sermon

Test: in Frag IV (ClkT-MerchT), 27–29; in Frag VIII (2NT-CYT), 78. See also Assay

Themes: in CT, 19, 187, 195 n.13; in Frag I, 145–56; in Frag III, 118–27; in Frag V (SqT-FrankT), 94–100; in Frag VI (PhysT-PardT), 62–70; in Frag VII, 181; in Frag VIII (2NT-CYT), 80–88. See also the following themes and major motifs: Acquisitiveness; Anger; Animals; Appearance/Reality; Array; Assay; Astrology; Authority/Experience; Bed; Bird; Blindness; Book; Brotherhood; Contract; Conversion; Dance; Death; Decay; Deception; Earnest and Game; Feast; Food; Fortune; Fraud; Gentillesse; Gold; Governance; Haste; Illusion; Lodging; Marvel/Magic; Mastery/Control; Meat and Drink; Miracle; Music; Physical; Preachers; Procession; Remedy to Misfortune; Riddle; Secrecy; Sermon; Sickness; Sight; Smell; Spiritual; Teachers; Tests; Time; Troth; Wandering

Theseus: character of, 137, 149, 216 n.8; compared to other married men in CT, 188; compared to Saturn, 138; deceived, 141; and governance, 140; and KT, 216 n.10; limits of power, 146; marriage feast of, 27

Three Rioters: compared to Virginia, 53–54; as exempla, 68; Pardoner and, 68

Time: in Frag IV (ClkT-MerchT), 31–32, 33–34, 187; in Frag V (SqT-FrankT), 94, 103–4, 104–5, 191–92, 208 n.2; in Frag VIII (2NT-CYT), 89; authority/experience and, 38; Chaucer and, 101–4, 162; clocks, 162; in FrankT, 92, 191–92; in GP, 144; Harry Bailly and, 138, 162; the number "3" and, 220 n.3; in NPT, 161–62; in RT, 140; in ShipT, 161–62; in SqT, 191–92

Tradesmen: weapons of, 150

Treasure. See Gold

Tree: in Frag VI (PhysT-PardT), 69–70; in MerchT, 28, 30, 34, 45; in NPT, 181, 224 n.30; in PardT, 58, 68–69; 203 n.19; in PhysT, 60; in SqT, 99

Tretee, Tretys. See Contract

Troilus and Creseyde, 13, 15, 184; and KT, 214

Troth: in Frag III, 212; in Frag V (SqT-FrankT), 97–98, 105, 209 n.9; in FrT, 125; in GP, 135; in WBT, 125, 126

Valerian: compared to priest (CYT), 88–89

Vinsauf, Geoffrey de, 15

Virginia: compared to the Pardoner, 202 n.6; compared to the Squire, 202 n.5; compared to the Three Rioters, 53–54; death of, 58–59; and fraud, 63; and genre, 45; and God, 54, 67; and governance, 63, 67; and old man (PardT), 57–58, 69

Virginius: as governor, 66; and old man (PardT), 57–58; pardons Claudius, 60, 202 n.11; and Virginia, 60, 189–90

Walter: blindness of, 36, 42; compared to other young married men in CT, 188; compared to January, 19, 25–30, 41–45; compared to the Merchant, 39–40; in council, 24–26, 38; and God, 39, 43; Griselda and, 28, 197 n.1; and marriage, 23, 24,

Index

25, 38; restoration of, 42–43; and time, 31–32
Wandering: in Frag III, 118–19, 120; Chaunticleer and, 162; in ShipT, 162
Wealth. *See* Gold
Weapons: in Frag I, 149–51; in Frag VI (PhysT-PardT), 69; in FrankT, 99; in MT, 136, 141, 143; in PardT, 59; in Sir T, 221 n.10
Weeping: in Frag I, 128
Wife (ShipT): and genre, 45
Wife of Bath: acquisitiveness of, 120; character of, 115, 118–19, 124–25, 211, 213 n.8, 214 n.16; and governance, 122; and old crone (WBT), 124; Pardoner and, 53, 112; as teacher, 114; and women, 214 n.15
Wife of Bath's Prologue: authority/experience in, 37; and the end of anger, 115–17; double conclusion of, 113–15; genre of, 213 n.6; interruptions in, 111–12; introductory material, 111; structural diagram, 110; structure of, 109–19, 185; themes in, 118–19 (wandering), 120–23 (acquisitiveness), 123–25 (mastery/control), 125–27 (contract)
Wife of Bath's Tale: in Frag III, chapter 5, 107–27; Bibliographical Note, 211–12; and the end of anger, 115–17; and ClkT, 196, 211; double conclusion of, 113–15; and FrankT, 207, 211; genre of, 112–13, 212; interruptions in, 111–12; introductory material, 111; Jankyn compared to other young married men in CT, 188; and magic, 211–12; and marriage feast, 27; and MerchT, 196, 211; and PardT, 200; and 2NT, 72; and SqT, 207; structural diagram, 110; structure of, 109–18, 185; themes in, 118–19 (wandering), 120–23 (acquisitveness), 123–25 (mastery/control), 125–27 (contract)
Women: in CT, 19, 72, 162, 188; in Frag I, 132–35, 216 n.4; in Frag III, 107–8; in Frag IV (ClkT-MerchT), 29, 41–42; in Frag V (SqT-FrankT), 99, 105–6; in Frag VII, 173; in ClkT, 25, 35, 39, 40–41; counsel of, 176; as counselors, 176–77, 179–80, 180, 188–89, 221 n.13; distaff and, 150; Emily and, 216 n.6; genre and, 45, 216 n.6; in FrT, 121; as Love's Physician, 162, 167; attitude of Merchant to, 28, 39–40; in MerchT, 25, 40; in NPT, 162, 178, 179; Pardoner and, 68; in PriorT, 174; in RT, 136; in ShipT, 162, 188; in Sir T, 179; sisterhood of, 126–27; Wife of Bath and, 112, 114, 214 n.15; in WBP, 120, 126, 127; in WBT, 113, 116, 120–21, 127, 214 n.18
Wounds: in Frag V (SqT-FrankT), 98–99

Yeoman: weapons of, 150